the library of
Rabbi Karen Companez

The Passover
Anthology

PHILIP GOODMAN

The Passover Anthology

The Jewish Publication Society

Philadelphia • Jerusalem

5753 / 1993

Copyright © 1961 by
THE JEWISH PUBLICATION SOCIETY OF AMERICA
First paperback printing, 1993
Introduction © 1993 by The Jewish Publication Society
All rights reserved   Manufactured in the United States
Designed by Elaine Lustig

Library of Congress Catalog Card Information

The Passover Anthology. Philip Goodman, comp.
   1961, 1993.
Cloth, ISBN 0–8276–0019–4   Paper, ISBN 0–8276–0410–6
1. Passover.   I. Goodman, Philip, 1911–
BM695.P3G6   296.437   61–11706

מוקדש
לנכדתי הצברה
נחמה לאה
בת אברהם חיים ושרה מינדל

PREFACE

During the course of the years I compiled this book, I have profited from the advice and guidance of many scholars and librarians, and owe them a sincere debt of gratitude. I would also like to single out for special thanks those of my collaborators who have made original contributions to this volume.

Mrs. Rachel Wischnitzer, the distinguished historian and critic of Jewish art, has written the interesting study of Passover in art to be found in this volume. Mrs. Judith K. Eisenstein, who has contributed significant works in the field of Jewish music, has written the illuminating chapter on Passover music and included in it a number of musical illustrations.

I am grateful to the following persons who have been kind enough to offer various helpful suggestions: the late Rabbi Joseph L. Baron, Milwaukee, Wisconsin; Leah M. Jaffa, executive secretary, National Jewish Music Council; Bernard Postal, director, Bureau of Public Information, National Jewish Welfare Board; Dr. Cecil Roth, Oxford, England; and Dr. Zalmen Slesinger, American Association for Jewish Education.

Abraham Berger, chief, Jewish Division, New York Public Library, and Dr. I. Edward Kiev, librarian, Hebrew Union College-Jewish Institute of Religion, New York, have made available the resources of their libraries.

I am especially indebted to the following good friends who have read all or parts of the manuscript and have given me the benefit of their critical judgment: Dr. Mortimer J. Cohen, rabbi, Congregation Beth Sholom, Philadelphia; Solomon Feffer, instructor, Jewish Theological Seminary of America; Dr. Sidney B. Hoenig, director, Adult Education, Yeshiva University; and Dr. A. Alan Steinbach, president, Jewish Book Council of America. Joan Green of The Jewish Publication Society of America prudently prepared the manuscript for press. Dr. Solomon Grayzel, editor, The Jewish Publication Society of America, has been a tower of strength in every phase of the editing of this anthology.

My daughter, Judith, on whom I tested much of the contents of this volume, freely gave of her frank and often judicious criticism. Last, but far from least, I am most thankful to my wife, Hanna, for her infinite patience and unstinted cooperation.

Philip Goodman

New York, N.Y.
Tishri 18, 5721 [1960]

viii

INTRODUCTION

The festival of Passover commemorates the Jewish people's redemption from slavery and its exodus from Egypt. It also celebrates the spring wheat and barley harvest in Israel. Its Hebrew name, *Pesakh*, derives from the biblical episode of the Tenth Plague, when God "passed over"—*pasakh*—the homes of the Israelites, only slaying the first-born of Egypt (Exod. 12:27). Because of its historical and agricultural associations, Passover has two additional names: *hag ha-aviv* (Holiday of Spring) and *z'man heruteinu* (Season of Our Liberation), which share in common the symbolism of hope and rebirth. It is also called *hag ha-matzot* (Holiday of Unleavened Bread) in recognition of the principal symbolic food of this festival. Passover is one of three pilgrimage festivals (with Shavuot and Sukkot) during which Jews in ancient times gathered together in Jerusalem.

Passover takes place in the month of Nisan, which is called by the Torah "the first of the months of the year" (Exod. 12:2) because it marks both the anniversary of Jewish nationhood and the beginning of the agricultural year. (Rosh Hashanah is the liturgical New Year.) Besides the special prayers recited in synagogue during this eight-day holiday (seven days in Israel and among Reform and Reconstructionist Jews), Passover is celebrated in Jewish homes with an evening Seder—an elaborate festival meal filled with many rituals, symbolic foods, songs, discussion, and prayers. A special book called the *haggadah* provides the "script" for the ceremony. It is traditional for the Seder leader to wear a white garment called a *kittel*. It is also traditional at this meal to extend hospitality to those in need.

Among the special foods central to the Seder ceremony are *matzah* (unleavened bread), symbolic of freedom and slavery as well as humility; *maror* (bitter herbs), symbolic of the bitterness of Egyptian slavery; *ḥaroset* (a paste of fruits, nuts, and wine), symbolic of the mortar made by the Hebrew slaves; the *afikoman* (a broken piece of matzah that serves as the final course), symbolic of incomplete redemption; and four cups of wine, symbolizing God's four redemptive acts during the Exodus. The paschal sacrifice, no longer performed (except by the Samaritans in Israel), is represented symbolically by a roasted shankbone.

Perhaps more than any other Jewish holiday, Passover requires considerable expenditures of time, energy, and material resources. Because all foods that contain *ḥametz* (leaven) are forbidden during the entire holiday, preparations for Passover involve thorough housecleaning, elaborate kitchen arrangements, and the purchase of special foods. Yet despite—or perhaps because of—its considerable demands, the Seder continues to be the principal home ritual of the Jewish festival calendar, serving as a unifying link among Jewish families as well as a symbol of continuity with past and future generations. It symbolizes the constant cycles of Jewish and universal history: from winter to spring, from slavery to freedom, from death to life. It also embodies the ideals of spiritual and political freedom, redemption, and resistance so central to Jewish tradition.

The twenty-four sections of *The Passover Anthology*,

which are divided into five "books," provide valuable resource materials for teachers, rabbis, parents, students, and newcomers to Judaism. Book One—*Passover in History*—gives the reader a comprehensive view of the historical evolution of this holiday. The twelve essays in the section, "Passover in Many Lands," attest to the remarkable diversity typical of the observance of this holiday. All who read the essays in Book One that deal with the evolution of the *haggadah* will find themselves on a kind of "archeological dig," uncovering the contributions of generations of Jews to this remarkable text, which to this day continues to evolve. "Passover and the Last Supper" and "Passover and the Ritual Murder Libel" address the problematic connections of this holiday with the development of Christianity, which has derived so much of its symbolism and narrative tradition from this festival.

Book Two—*Passover in Literature, Art, and Music*—provides the reader with a comprehensive framework for observing the holiday. Four sections—"Passover in the Bible," "Passover in Postbiblical Writings," "Passover in Talmud and Midrash," and "Passover in Medieval Jewish Literature"—present traditional texts for study and historical background. The next section, "Passover in Jewish Law," along with the anthology's fifth and final "book"—*Commemoration of Passover*—explains the complex preparations and observances traditionally performed on this holiday. Five additional sections in Book Two—which include essays by Franz Rosenzweig, Winston Churchill, Ahad Ha'Am, and Andre Neher; short stories by Sholom Aleichem, Martin Buber, and S. Y. Agnon; poems by Judah Halevi, Hayyim Nahman Bialik, and A. M. Klein; a study of Passover music by Judith Eisenstein; and a study of Passover art by Rachel Wischnitzer—provide ample material for the reader's intellectual and aesthetic appreciation of this holiday.

Book Three—*Passover for Young People*—offers many stories and poems that will delight children, parents, and teachers. Among the authors included are perennial favorites like Sadie Rose Weilerstein, Deborah Pessin, and I. L. Peretz. In addition, Book Four—*Passover Rejoicing*—offers many programs, games, arts, crafts, dances, and recipes to engage children—and their families—in the holiday festivities. Many of these activities can be adapted for home or classroom use. Readers of all ages will enjoy "Passover Curiosities" and "Passover Folklore," which present some of the customs, wit, and wisdom unique to this festival.

From its inception, Passover has been regarded as a festival of redemption. Originally, of course, this redemption referred to the Israelites' liberation from slavery in Egypt. In subsequent centuries, especially during periods of persecution, Jews came to connect this past redemption with a future one, when the Messiah would come to usher in the end to all human suffering.

The Passover Seder is filled with symbols of redemption, both past and future. One such symbol is the *afikoman*, derived from a Greek word meaning either "aftermeal songs and entertainment" or "dessert." The *afikoman* is "created" when the leader of the Seder breaks the middle of three matzahs at the beginning of the Seder and hides the larger half. This piece of matzah must be eaten by all guests in order for the Seder to conclude.

The middle matzah represents the Levites, descendants of the priestly tribe that once served in the Holy Temple in Jerusalem. The *afikoman*'s disappearance from the Seder table reminds us of the Levites' exile from the destroyed Temple; its reappearance foretells their return to divine service. In addition, because the *afikoman* is created by being broken and its retrieval is needed to complete the festival meal, it is also a symbol of messianic *tikkun*, the repair of our broken world. In retrieving the *afikoman* and returning it to the table, the children, whom the tradition regards as "messiahs of humankind," symbolically redeem not only the exiled Levites, but also the Jewish people and, indeed, the whole world.

Another very important symbol of redemption at the Seder is the prophet Elijah. In Jewish folklore, Elijah serves as the guardian angel of newborn children. Tradition also assigns him the task of upholding *brit ha-dorot*, the covenant between the generations. In the Messianic Age, "he shall reconcile parents with their children and children with their parents, so that, when I come, I do not strike the whole earth with utter destruction" (Mal. 3:24). At the Passover Seder, a full cup of wine, called Elijah's Cup, is set out on the table but not drunk, in expectation that the prophet will arrive to announce the dawn of the Messianic Age.

Each Passover, we are reminded that once we were all slaves and that God has redeemed us from bondage. But we are also reminded that we are not yet fully redeemed as long as other human beings remain enslaved. Each year we are commanded to teach our children the same para-doxical lesson: *"Dayenu*—It is enough!" Not only have we been redeemed from slavery but we have been given so much more—the Sabbath, the Torah, the Land of Israel. But we also proclaim to ourselves and our children: *"L'shanah ha-ba'ah*—Next year we shall be redeemed!"; we are not yet satisfied with the way things are. We have not yet arrived at our final destination: the world has yet to be redeemed.

For that destination to be reached, we will need not only Elijah but the next generation, our children, to con-tinue to search for the broken half of the matzah. Only then can we fully conclude the telling of the story and bring Elijah home.

Ellen Frankel

Philadelphia
1993/5753

CONTENTS

CONTENTS

CONTENTS

CONTENTS

LIST OF ILLUSTRATIONS

Photo by Frank J. Darmstaedter. Courtesy of The Jewish Museum, New York.

Book Openings

BOOK ONE

Passover in History

*Every person in every generation
must regard himself as having been
personally freed from Egypt.*

Pesahim 10.5

THE ORIGINS OF PASSOVER

I

The Bondage and Exodus of Israel[1]

HARRY M. ORLINSKY

The second important epoch in the career of ancient Israel began with the descent of a group of Hebrews into Egypt sometime around the late seventeenth or early sixteenth century B.C.E. By the time their descendants had found their way back to Canaan, several centuries later, they were on the verge of nationhood. The Egyptian experience was a decisive factor in the development of Israel as a people. Here the Hebrew families grew in number, and their conception of God and His covenant with them was extended to cover the entire Hebrew folk. Here also they continued to oppose state autocracy, in contrast to the spineless submission of the Egyptian people at large. The ancient custom of deifying kings, nowhere more elaborately developed than in Egypt, left them fundamentally untouched. In this great episode, the heroic figure of Moses stands out in epic grandeur.

EISODUS: EGYPT AND THE HYKSOS

Whenever a drought and famine desolated the region of Palestine, it was common for whole tribes to pick up their belongings and seek refuge in Egypt. There the periodic overflow of the Nile gave life to the land, as it does today, and helped to regulate the agriculture of the country. The Egyptians learned early to dig channels for the seasonal flood and to irrigate the grain-producing land. Migration into Egypt was therefore an ancient expedient.

In Palestine, on the other hand, the rains did not always come when needed. A late thirteenth-century Egyptian document, for example, tells how the semi-nomadic inhabitants of Edom, south of Palestine, left their homes in time of drought to come to Egypt "to keep themselves alive and to keep their cattle alive." It was famine, too, as the Bible says, which compelled Abraham and Isaac in an earlier period to go south ⟨Gen. 12 and 26⟩, and the same reason is given for Jacob's sending his sons to Egypt, where grain could still be procured even in a time of general drought (Gen. 42 ff.). As a result of this mission, the entire family finally settled there.

At the same time, this Eisodus—a "going into," as distinguished from the Exodus, a "going out of"—may also have been encouraged by certain ethnic disturbances which for a period disrupted Egyptian suzerainty in Canaan and reduced the sovereignty of the Egyptian homeland as well. Following upon the increasing disintegration of the Egyptian state, a mixed group of Asiatics, apparently mostly Semites, known generally as Hyksos (literally, "rulers of foreign countries"), appeared in the north and swarmed down through Syria and Palestine. By about 1720 B.C.E. they had crossed the land bridge into Africa and conquered much of Egypt, a domination that was not to be completely broken until about 1550.

Between the Hyksos and the Hebrews there appear to be a number of points of contact. It is known, for instance, that a certain Hyksos chieftain in Egypt bore the name Jacob-el, or perhaps Jacob-har, which means "May El, or Har [the mountain god], Give Protection." Another Hyksos leader was called Jacob-baal, "May Baal Protect." The verbal element, Jacob, which means "protect," is identical with the name of the Hebrew patriarch

4

Jacob who settled in Egypt. Again, the historical kernel which resides in the dramatic story of the career of Joseph in Egypt, of the coming to power of a Hebrew in the Egyptian court, could well have derived from the period of the Hyksos, when Semites, and in all probability Habiru* among them, were prominent among the new rulers of Egypt. For it was not Egyptian habit to nourish the ambitions of strangers in their midst. Furthermore, it would seem to be more than a mere coincidence that the Hebrews, according to the Bible, settled in Goshen in the Delta, the very area which the Hyksos built up around their new capital, Avaris, the later Tanis.

In this connection it is also interesting to note that Josephus, the Jewish historian of the first century C.E., quotes the Egyptian historian Manetho (about 275 B.C.E.), to the effect that a large number of Hyksos made their way from Avaris to Canaan and there built Jerusalem. These Hyksos, according to Manetho, were "not fewer in number than 240,000,"[2] a figure which recalls the biblical statement (Nu. 1.46) that 603,550 Hebrew males, exclusive of Levites, women, and children, participated in the Exodus from Egypt.

All these facts suggest that the Hebrews and the Hyksos may have been on terms of considerable intimacy; so that the entry of the Hebrews into Egypt would have been facilitated by the presence of Hyksos in positions of power, and the bondage accounted for by the enslavement of foreign elements after the fall of the Hyksos invaders. If this hypothesis be accepted, it provides evidence that the biblical version of the Hebrew sojourn in Egypt (Gen. 39-50, Ex. 1 ff.) derives from the same period as the events which it describes. For the Egyptians themselves, humiliated by their conquest at the hands of the Hyksos, avoided and suppressed any reference to the events of the

---

* Habiru, or Hapiru (or Apiru), was a name by which Eastern documents referred to various unsettled groups of people. They were chiefly Semitic, and have been associated with the biblical Hebrews.

period, and it would have been well-nigh impossible for anyone to learn the historical details very much later.

THE SOJOURN

The Bible itself elaborates only on the final period of the bondage in Egypt. But what was there to say? After the Egyptians had overthrown the Hyksos, they enslaved those foreigners who had not fled, thus reversing the status of the non-Egyptians in the land as the Bible records: *And a new king arose in Egypt who did not know Joseph . . . And they* [the Egyptians] *set taskmasters over them* [the Hebrews] *to afflict them with forced labor. And they built for Pharaoh store-cities, Pithom and Rameses* (Ex. 1.8-11).

Under the Hyksos domination, Egyptian culture had sunk so low that the period has been described as "The Great Humiliation." But the successful war of liberation against the Hyksos led to an Egyptian revival on such a grand scale that the period of the New Kingdom which followed, especially during the Eighteenth and Nineteenth Dynasties (about 1550-1150), has been called the Golden Age and was the subject of a recent book which bore the suggestive title, *When Egypt Ruled the East.*[3] The development of literature, art, and building, the inculcation of individual physical prowess in sport and in battle, the marked extension of the influence of women in the royal court and in upper-class circles generally—all of these manifested a new cosmopolitanism, and even secularism, brought on by imperial expansion abroad and urbanization at home.

There was much in the Egyptian environment that the Hebrews could emulate. But the kind of life which they and others led in the Egyptian slave camp did not encourage cultural apprenticeship. "Slave troops on a government building project," as one authority puts it, "have no opportunity for discussion with priests and scribes. Their simple desert souls would see and shrink from some of the abominations of the effete civilization and long to

6

escape dreary enslavement rather than admire the cultural triumph of the land of bondage."[4]

MOSES, LEADER OF THE EXODUS

It was probably sometime in the thirteenth century that a group of Hebrews and others united under the leadership of Moses, of the tribe of Levi, to escape from Egypt. This tribe was foremost in organizing those state slaves who were willing to chance the break for freedom. Several outstanding Levites bore Egyptian names—for example, Moses, Miriam, Hophni, Phinehas, Merari, Puti-el, and perhaps Aaron. This alone indicates a considerable period of residence in Egypt, also a surprising degree of resistance and determination to be free, despite a long period of slavery.

The Bible makes it amply clear that many non-Hebrew elements, "the mixed multitude" of Exodus (12.38) and Numbers (11.4), accompanied Moses and the Hebrews out of Egypt. The Egyptian sources, in turn, provide a very clear background for this circumstance. Tens of thousands of workers, natives of many countries and members of different ethnic groups, labored for the Egyptian state. Already in the fifteenth century, as a result of the military conquests of Amenophis II in Syria and Palestine, large numbers of Semitic and non-Semitic captives of war, including 3,600 Apiru (Habiru), were brought to Egypt as state slaves. The military campaigns of other Egyptian kings, from the fourteenth to the twelfth centuries, produced similar results. The great building projects of Rameses II (about 1301-1234), at such places as Pithom and Rameses, employed these "mixed multitudes," many of whom were eager to escape from slavery.

Scholars have long been troubled by the fact that Egyptian records make no mention of Moses and the Exodus, and some have expressed the belief that a document or two may yet turn up with reference to them. Yet the modern student of ancient Egyptian history should share

7

neither this worry nor this optimism. First, when the Egyptians lost a battle, they customarily either recorded it as a victory or else passed over it in silence. Thus the prolonged Hyksos rule was not mentioned in contemporaneous Egyptian sources until the Hyksos were expelled, and even the victory over them was apparently not officially recorded. And second, the scope of the Exodus and the significance of it for the Egyptian government were so meager as not to merit any documentary mention.

Israel in Egypt: The Historical Problems[5]

JOSEPH H. HERTZ

WHO WAS THE PHARAOH OF THE OPPRESSION?

There are several candidates for the infamous title of "Pharaoh of the Oppression," under whom the bondage of the Israelites ended in a systematic attempt at their extermination. The majority of scholars identify him with the splendor-loving and tyrannical Rameses II, whose dates are variously given as 1300-1234 B.C.E. (Petrie) and 1347-1280 (Mahler). "He was a vain and boastful character who wished to dazzle posterity by covering the land with constructions whereon his name was engraved thousands of times, and who prided himself in his inscriptions upon great conquests which he never made" (Naville). The Exodus itself is held to have taken place under his son, Merneptah, with whom the decline of Egypt began. Merneptah (or Menephtah) was an obstinate and vain despot. He too had the habit of claiming as his own the achievements of others. He was "one of the most unconscionable usurpers (and defacers) of the monuments of his predecessors, including those of his own

8

father, who had set him the example . . . due to a somewhat insane desire to perpetuate his own memory."[6]

Some scholars, however, date the oppression and the Exodus in the century preceding Rameses II, and connect it with the religious revolution of Amenophis IV, or Ikhnaton (1383-1365). This extraordinary personality abolished the multitudinous deities of the Egyptian Pantheon, and devoted himself exclusively to the worship of the sun. These scholars hold that there was some relation between the faith of the Israelites and the solar monotheism of Ikhnaton, and that Israelite influence was partly responsible for this assault on the gross idolatry of Egypt. Ikhnaton was hated by the people as the "heretic king," and his innovations were abandoned by his son-in-law Tut-an-khamen who succeeded him, eventually to be altogether uprooted by Haremrab, the last pharaoh of the Eighteenth Dynasty. When the native religion was restored—these scholars maintain—the Israelites suffered persecution and degradation; and the oppression formed part of the extirpation of Ikhnaton's heresy.

Other egyptologists go back still another century to Thotmes III (1503-1449), and declare him to have been the Pharaoh of the Oppression. They connect the oppression and the departure of the Israelites from Egypt with the movements of the Habiru people in the Amarna age and believe that the recently discovered inscriptions on the Sinai Peninsula likewise favor this theory.

One of the main reasons which induce both these groups of scholars to dissent from the general view that Rameses II was the Pharaoh of the Oppression, is the fact that the name "Israel" is alleged to occur on an inscription of Merneptah. That inscription (discovered in 1896) is a song of triumph of Merneptah, describing in grandiloquent language his victories in Canaan; and, among other conquests, he boasts that "Canaan is seized with every evil; Ashkelon is carried away; Gezer is taken; Yenoam is annihilated; Ysiraal is desolated, its seed is not." From the phrase, "Ysiraal is desolated," these scholars deduce

9

that the Israelites must in those days have been in possession of Canaan, and that therefore the Exodus must have
taken place long before the time of Merneptah. However,
it is not at all certain that the words, "Ysiraal is desolated," refer to Israel. Thus, Professor Kennett takes the
phrase as analogous with that concerning Ashkelon and
Gezer, and therefore merely stating that Merneptah had
devastated the district of Jezreel. And if "Ysiraal" *does*
mean Israel, then it refers to the settlements in Palestine
by Israelites from Egypt before the Exodus (Jampel).
From various notices in I Chronicles we see that during
the generations preceding the oppression, the Israelites
did not remain confined to Goshen or even to Egypt
proper, but spread into the southern Palestinian territory,
then under Egyptian control, and that they even engaged
in skirmishes with the Philistines. When the bulk of the
nation had left Egypt and was wandering in the wilderness, these Israelite settlers had thrown off their Egyptian
allegiance. And it is these settlements which Merneptah
boasts of having devastated during his Canaanite cam-
paign. There is, therefore, no cogent reason for dissenting
from the current view that the Pharaoh of the Oppression
was Rameses II, with his son Merneptah as the Pharaoh
of the Exodus.

THE "INCONVENIENCE" OF BIBLICAL TRADITIONS

Little need be said in regard to the extreme and baseless
skepticism, recently revived in Soviet anti-religious circles,
that the Israelites never were in Egypt; and that, in consequence, there could not have been either an oppression
or an Exodus.

There is one conclusive answer to the doubts as to the
historicity of the Exodus and other crucial events in scriptural history; and that is, what has aptly been called the
"inconvenience" of biblical traditions. One or two examples will both explain this argument and make clear its
unanswerable force. The first example is taken from the
story of Abraham. For centuries, the Hebrew tribes

waged a life-and-death struggle with the native population for the possession of ancient Palestine. But instead of the Hebrews claiming that they too were natives of Canaan, or that they were the true aborigines of its soil, Bible tradition concerning the beginnings of the Hebrew people is emphatic that its ancestors were *not* born in Canaan, but were nomads, immigrant shepherds, and had their origin in Ur of the Chaldees. Now, even the skeptical historian is forced to admit that such a tradition must be based on strict history, as no people would invent such an "inconvenient" tradition in regard to a matter of vital importance like its right and title to its national homeland. To take another example. The record in Genesis that Isaac and Jacob married Aramean wives must be based on *fact*, and could not have arisen, as some Bible critics maintain, in the days of Monarchy. For throughout the days of the Monarchy, Aram was the hereditary enemy of Israel, and was guilty of the most hideous barbarities in its continued attempts to annihilate Israel. It is clear that here too the tradition that the "Mothers" of the Israelite people were Aramean women, was an "inconvenient" one—and cannot therefore be an invention of later legend (Cornill, Jirku).

All this applies with immeasurably greater force in regard to the historicity of the oppression in Egypt. Compared with the Egyptian bondage and the deliverance therefrom, everything else in Bible history is of secondary importance. The memory of that bondage and deliverance is woven into the message of legislator, historian, psalmist, prophet and priest; and a large portion of Jewish life both in the biblical and the post-biblical ages is but a reminder of the Exodus from Egypt, an echo of that divine event which meant the birth of Israel as a nation. Now, it is unthinkable that any nation, unless forced to do so by the overwhelming compulsion of unforgettable fact, would of its own account have wantonly affixed to its forefathers the stain and dishonor of slavery in a foreign country. No people has ever yet invented a *dis-*

graceful past for itself. The invention by a later age of a story so humiliating to national self-respect would be still more astounding in the case of Israel, when we consider that after the days of Merneptah the decline of Egypt began, and the invented national bondage would have been to a weak and waning power. If, therefore, Israel's sojourn and bondage in Egypt were merely a fiction, such fiction would be quite inexplicable—in fact, a psychological miracle. Even a radical student of this question like Professor Peet sums up his conclusions as follows: "That Israel was in Egypt under one form or another no historian could possibly doubt; a legend of such tenacity representing the early fortunes of a people under so unfavorable an aspect, could not have arisen save as a reflection of real occurrences."

PASSOVER AND THE LAST SUPPER[1]

II

SOLOMON ZEITLIN

According to the synoptic gospels Jesus was arrested on the night that the paschal lamb was sacrificed. In the Gospel according to Mark the disciples asked Jesus, *Where wilt thou that we go and prepare that thou mayest eat the passover?* (Mark 14.12). The gospel further says, *Jesus took bread, and blessed, and brake it, and gave to them, and said, Take, eat: this is my body. And he took the cup, and when he had given thanks, he gave it to them: and they all drank of it. And he said unto them, This is my blood of the new testament, which is shed for many. . . . And when they had sung an hymn, they went out into the mount of Olives (ibid., 22-26).*

The same account is given by the Gospel according to Matthew (26.17-30). The Gospel according to Luke relates that on the day of the unleavened bread when the paschal lamb was to be killed, Jesus sent Peter and John to prepare a place to eat it. This gospel adds, *And when the hour was come, he sat down, and the twelve apostles with him. And he said unto them, With desire I have desired to eat this passover with you before I suffer: For I say unto you, I will not any more eat thereof, until it be fulfilled in the kingdom of God. . . . And he took bread, and gave thanks, and brake it, and gave unto them, say-*

13

ing, This is my body which is given for you: this do in remembrance of me. Likewise also the cup after supper, saying, This cup is the new testament in my blood, which is shed for you (Luke 22.14-20).

The description of the Last Supper given in the gospels is undoubtedly a record of the Seder of the first night of Passover. The bread which Jesus ate was unleavened bread, and the wine that used by the Jews on the first night of Passover. The hymn sung by Jesus and the apostles after the meal was the *Hallel*, which is still sung by the Jews on that night.

Mark and Matthew make no mention that Jesus ate the paschal lamb. Luke relates that Jesus said to his apostles, *With desire I have desired to eat this passover with you.* The reason that Mark, Matthew and Luke did not mention that Jesus ate the paschal lamb was that they held that Jesus himself was the paschal lamb that was to be sacrificed to redeem men. As Justin Martyr said, "And the blood of the pascha, sprinkled on each man's doorposts and lintel, delivered those who were saved in Egypt, when the first-born of the Egyptians were destroyed. For the pascha was Christ who was afterwards sacrificed. . . . And as the blood of the Passover saved us who were in Egypt, so also the blood of Christ will deliver from death those who have believed."[2]

According to the Gospel of John the Last Supper was an ordinary meal, since Jesus was crucified on the eve of Passover. Hence the meal which Jesus ate with his disciples on the preceding night could not have been the Passover meal. The Last Supper, according to John, was on Thursday night, the 13th of the month, and Jesus was arrested and crucified the following morning, Friday the 14th, a day before Passover.[3]

Paul, in his letter to I Corinthians, says that Jesus on the last night took bread, *And when he had given thanks, he brake it, and said, Take, eat: this is my body, which is broken for you: this do in remembrance of me. After the same manner also he took the cup, when he had supped,*

*saying, This cup is the new testament in my blood: this do
ye, as oft as ye drink it, in remembrance* . . . (I Cor.
11.24-25).

In the early days of Christianity the followers of Jesus
gave thanks *(eucharistia)* over the bread and the cup in
the sacrament mystery. The Eucharist was called by the
Church Fathers *sacramenta altaris*[4] and was applied to
the sacrament of the Blood and Body of Jesus. Cyprian
explained *eucharistia* by the following words: *id est sanctum Domini corpus.*[5]

The term *eucharistia* never occurs in the Septuagint. It
appears a few times in the apocryphal literature[6] and has
the connotation of thanks. Philo used the term *eucharistia*
in a wider sense. In one place he connects the term
eucharistia with hymns, prayers and sacrifices.[7] In another
place he associates it with the offering of thanks to God
for the creation of the universe.[8] The term *eucharistia* as
used by Philo carries more of a spiritual idea than ordinary thanks and had great influence on early Christianity.[9]

The pagans, not knowing about the mystery (sacrament) of the Eucharist, accused the Christians of devouring the flesh of infants and using their blood in the sacraments. This monstrous libel was transferred later by the
Christians to the Jews—charging that they used human
blood in their paschal meal. Thousands upon thousands of
Jews were tortured and put to death as the result of this
false accusation. It is true that from time to time some
popes issued *bulla* in which they refuted such libels and
said that the Jews were prohibited by their religion from
using the blood of animals.

The early Christians celebrated the resurrection of
Jesus and called it pascha.[10] It was observed at the same
time that the Jews observed Passover. Epiphanius said,
"So long at least as the first fifteen bishops of Jerusalem
(those of Jewish descent) continued, the pascha was celebrated everywhere by all (Christians), or by a great majority of them, according to the lunar computation and
method of the Jews."[11]

15

The bishop sent out epistles, called paschal epistles,[12] to notify the Christians when pascha (Easter) would fall. At the Council of Nicea, 325 C.E., the Christians were prohibited from celebrating pascha at the time the Jews were celebrating Passover. The emperor Constantine, who presided over the Council, said, "Let us have nothing in common with the detestable Jewish crowd." However, down to our time, the date of pascha (Easter) has depended on the vernal Equinox and has not become a fixed date in the Church. It is usually celebrated approximately about the same time the Jews observe Passover, but in exceptional cases on the Sunday after the festival of Purim, as is the case in the year 1948.

Not only was pascha (Easter) celebrated at the same time as Passover among the Jews but its origin is very much interwoven with Passover. Even the institution of the Eucharist is really based on the Jewish custom, during the Second Commonwealth, of giving thanks to God on the first night of Passover for their redemption, over unleavened bread and a cup of wine. The writings of Philo were a further stimulus to the institution of the Eucharist.

PASSOVER AND THE RITUAL MURDER LIBEL

Like flame the lyrics flower
In every heart that hears;
I've spoken with all my power,
The pain of a thousand years.[1]

SOLOMON GRAYZEL

The Rabbi of Bacharach,* Heinrich Heine's unfinished novelette, opens with the preparations for a Seder. As the festivities are about to begin, two strangers enter the rabbi's house and claim that they have no other place to observe the holiday. They take their place among the family and guests. Before long, the rabbi discovers that these men have hidden the body of a murdered child under the table. He realizes that a cry will soon be raised and that he and the other Jews will have to face the frightful accusation of ritual murder.

It is one of the saddest aspects of Jewish experience that on the very evening when the Jew is supposed to re-call the joys of freedom, he has frequently been made to feel the bitterest sorrows of exile. It is no less strange that a people so restricted in their choice of food should have been accused of eating human flesh and drinking human blood. Yet the charge has been made hundreds of

---

* A portion of this novelette appears in this book; see below, p. 202.

times, in lands and periods which we consider fairly civilized. That this libel was cast upon the Jews at all, that it was so widely credited, and that it became connected with Passover, are facts which insistently call for explanation.

Ultimately much that is tragic in human relationships goes back to a weakness in human nature, namely, that man suspects and mistrusts the unknown. Any group that is little known and ill understood is, for that very reason, feared. The same accusation of consuming a human sacrifice was levelled by the pagans against the early Christians. The *agape,* the shared love-feast which those Christians used to celebrate, at which much was said about the redeeming powers of the sacrificed man-god Jesus, gave countenance to the charge among the frightened and ignorant pagans. Later, Christian sects accused one another of similar crimes.[2]

Even earlier a charge of this nature had been made against the Jews. During the Maccabean struggle against hellenization, the unscrupulous Antiochus, king of Syria, sought to justify his attempt to uproot Judaism by spreading a fantastic tale. The Jews claimed that their worship was absolutely pure. In reality, Antiochus' propagandists said, the Jews were accustomed to kidnap a Greek man, hide him in their mysterious Temple which none was permitted to enter, and later sacrifice him to their God and eat of his entrails.[3] These charges were not, however, intended to horrify the pagans of that day, since a ritual of human sacrifice was still known among the Greeks and Romans. The charges were meant merely to discredit Jewish assertions of religious superiority. In any event, none but the extreme enemies of the Jews believed or repeated this nonsense.

No such accusation was, in fact, made against the Jews all through the first eleven centuries of Christianity.[4] Everyone knew, of course, that the Jews denied the claims of Christianity and that they rejected Jesus as the Messiah. For this they were made to suffer indignities and persecutions. But they were not accused of murder for

18

religious reasons. Then, the crusading movement created a climate of hostility against them. They began to be considered plotters against the Church and dangerous antagonists of Christianity. From that it was but an easy step to justifying these accusations by giving substance to the fears which the Jews aroused.

Suddenly, in the year 1144, the charge of religiously-motivated murder appeared in Norwich, England. It was on the second day of Passover that the boy William was said to have disappeared, and a number of Jews were soon accused of having caused his death. A convert from Judaism was not slow in coming forward to assert that the murder was part of a Jewish conspiracy, since the Jews performed the sacrifice of a Christian every year at about the time of the original Crucifixion. It appears that this first charge against the Jews resulted in no Jewish victims, evidently the falsity of the accusation was too obvious.[5]

The entire story was of a nature to have a wide appeal. Within the next few decades it cropped up in various parts of England and France, and later in Germany and countries farther east. There are those who say that it could not have been altogether accidental that the abbeys and churches where these presumed martyrs were buried gained considerably from the pilgrimages of which they became the goal. Certainly stories of miracles connected with such graves were spread far and wide by wandering monks and preachers. One recalls Chaucer's "Prioress' Tale." It was one of hundreds such "examples," involving not only the Blood Accusation but also the desecration of the Host and other blasphemies, used to illustrate Christian piety and the murderous intent of its enemies.

Another result of these tales was the suffering of the accused Jews. Few Christians waited for investigations and trials. It became customary to throw the Jewish communal leaders into prison, to extort confessions by means of the cruelest tortures, and to execute those arrested and expel the rest, if any were still left to be expelled.

Passover did not, at first, play any more significant role in the accusation than other parts of the year. The convert mentioned above was a generation or so ahead of his time in making the connection. The early charges were usually merely blood accusations. It was quite in conformity with the mental outlook of the Middle Ages to believe in the magical curative powers of blood, especially of blood mingled with, or redeemed by, the blood of Jesus. The idea was widespread that Jews suffered from peculiar diseases which did not attack other men, or that they emitted a pungent odor not characteristic of Christians. Baptized, the Jews lost these peculiarities. But, since they obstinately refused to be baptized, they could cure themselves by the application or the intake of the blood, the heart or the liver of a simple, sinless Christian, a male child by preference.[6]

It was inevitable, however, that the charge should before long assume a more ritualistic aspect. After all, the primary difference between Jew and Christian was the former's rejection of Jesus whom, as everyone was taught from childhood, they had wilfully crucified. Besides, as time went on and the Jews' defenselessness became more apparent, their property became their greatest source of danger. A religious excuse was an excellent cloak for whatever robbery might be planned against them. By the middle of the thirteenth century, the accusation became one of ritual murder, and began to be connected with Passover.

The new situation appears clearly in the declarations on the subject made by various popes. For a century after the appearance of the accusation no mention of it is to be found in papal pronouncements about the Jews. Officially the Church took no notice of the new type of martyr venerated in various parts of Europe. But by the middle of the thirteenth century, the attacks had become so frequent and their motivation so obvious that, when Jews brought the matter to the attention of the highest authority in the Church, defense could not be denied them.

On May 28, 1247, Pope Innocent IV wrote to the Archbishop of Vienne, in France, pointing out that various noblemen as well as the Bishop of Trois Chateaux had perpetrated against the Jews of Valrias cruelties of a most inhuman kind. The body of a little girl had been found in a ditch. At once the Jews were accused and tortured beyond endurance. It was, the pope said, merely an excuse to rob them of their property, for there had been no proof and no witnesses of any crime. The pope ordered the freeing of the imprisoned and the restitution of their property; but for the dead and the broken in body this came, of course, too late.[7]

A few days later, the same pope wrote in a similar vein to the clergy of the German provinces where like events had occurred. He said that the Jews had tearfully complained about ecclesiastics and members of the German nobility who, in order to rob them of their property, devised all sorts of schemes to accuse them. They charged that in the observance of Passover the Jews shared the heart of a murdered child. The pope ordered that this kind of accusation must not be made again, since the charge was clearly false and Jews were warned in the Bible not even to touch a dead body.[8] A similar refutation of the charge was appended to the regular Bull of Protection which this and later popes used to issue to the Jews.[9] In all such cases the popes said, or clearly implied, that the Christians themselves were the kidnappers and the murderers and had the sole object of robbing the Jews, or of taking over the property of those killed.

It is obvious that these repeated warnings and orders of the popes had little effect. The charge spread like wildfire during the second half of the thirteenth century in Germany, when imperial authority was non-existent or not feared, and served as an excuse for massacres and expulsions in later centuries as well. It cannot be said that the clergy, high or low, exerted themselves to pass the papal refutation along to the populace, though, to be sure, the charge was never openly raised in Rome itself. In the course of time, the accusation developed new facets. Pope Martin V, in 1422, not only accused Christian preachers of fomenting hatred of the Jews, but also spoke with horror of the libel that Jews mixed blood with the dough of the Passover *matzah*.[10] These preachers of the fifteenth century, nevertheless, continued to harp on the subject. They desperateley needed an enemy of Christianity to point to, in order to draw attention away from those conditions within the Church that were bringing Europe closer to the Reformation.

More than a century later, in 1540, Pope Paul III repeated and amplified Pope Martin's statement. "Blinded with avarice," this pope said, the enemies of the Jews assert that they "murder infants and drink their blood . . . thus trying to stir up against them the minds of simple Christians."[11]

A number of these cases were subjected to close investigation by Church authorities who invariably found the accusation to have been false or unproved. In several instances religious worship of these presumed martyrs' graves was forbidden by Rome. But local ecclesiastics disregarded such prohibition and encouraged the populace to believe in miracles performed at such graves. Eventually, of course, sometimes centuries after their death, some of these children were canonized: the Church dared not cast doubt on the accumulated stories of miracles.

In 1758, almost on the eve of the French Revolution, the Polish Jews found themselves so afflicted with the constant repetition of this charge that they sent a deputation to the Pope in Rome. Benedict XIV appointed Cardinal Lorenzo Ganganelli to look into the matter and report. A year later the report was submitted to Pope Clement XIII, Benedict's successor. The entire situation was here reviewed and the falsity of the charges once more made clear.[12] A decade later, Cardinal Ganganelli himself became pope (Clement XIV). Nevertheless, the accusation continued to be raised. Almost every year saw

22

its revival somewhere, especially in eastern Europe, to cast a cloud over and mar the observance of the Passover feast.

Even in the nineteenth century, despite the triumphs of liberalism, the charge was raised whenever economic and political ambitions needed the support or the cloak of religious prejudice. In 1840, in the so-called Damascus Affair, "enlightened" French politicians stooped to uphold the accusation in order to curry favor with the populace and thus gain political influence in the Near East.[13] Toward the end of the century it was revived in a number of notorious trials in Bohemia and Hungary, where it served as a tool in the nationalist struggle against German domination.[14] Czarist Russia showed that it could also play the game in order to bolster its tottering power. The trial of Mendel Beilis in 1912, with its scandalous accusation of an obviously innocent man, was an attempt to deflect popular attention from the government's tyranny and corruption. In all these cases the luridly described ritual murders were connected with Passover and the use of blood in the preparation of *matzah*.[15] It is not surprising that Nazi Germany made the libel part of its propaganda.[16]

A number of churches in central and southeastern Europe continue to this day to ship pictures and wax statues of Jews in the process of performing the ritual murder act, even to slaughtering the child and greedily collecting its blood. Thousands of pious pilgrims flock to these churches, drawn by well advertised miracles. A useful lie is not easily abandoned. As recently as 1952 a bishop in Austria refused the petition of the Austrian League for Human Rights to have the false story removed from a church in his jurisdiction. He is reported by the press to have made the astonishing statement that "the Jews had not yet proved that they never did such things."[17] There is clearly no difference in attitude between the modern bishop and the people of Norwich in 1144.

23

A well-known Jewish legend tells of the Golem, the powerful automaton, created by Rabbi Judah-Loew of Prague about the middle of the seventeenth century. Its main purpose, the legend said, was to guard the Jewish community against the constant threat of attack resulting from the repeated charges of ritual murder. Eventually Rabbi Judah-Loew destroyed the Golem: not the answer even to greed fortified by bigotry and ending in falsehood and murder. It is closer to Jewish tradition to hope that the ideal of physical and spiritual freedom, as symbolized by Passover, will in time prevail.

Passover in Temple Days[1]

SOLOMON IBN VERGA

(Extract from a letter written by Versovius to King
Alfonso the Pious, who copied it from a written report
sent by Marcus, Consul of Jerusalem, to Rome during
the Second Temple.)

The Pesach sacrifice, a part of which I witnessed, and
the entire ceremony, I was told, take place in the following manner. When the beginning of the month which they
call Nisan approached, by the command of the king and
the judges, swift messengers visited every one in the
vicinity of Jerusalem who owned flocks of sheep and
herds of cattle, and ordered him to hasten to Jerusalem
with them, in order that the pilgrims should have sufficient animals for sacrifices and food; for the people were
then very numerous, and whoever did not present himself
at the appointed time, his possessions were confiscated for
the benefit of the Temple. Consequently all owners of
flocks and droves came hastily on, and brought them to a
creek near Jerusalem, and washed and cleaned them of all
dirt. This they did in pursuance of that which Solomon

25

had said: *A flock of well-selected sheep, which are come up from the washing* (Song of Songs 4.2).

When they arrived at the mountains which surround Jerusalem, the multitude was so great that the grass was not seen any longer, as everything was turned white, by reason of the white color of the wool. When the tenth day approached—as on the fourteenth day of the month the sacrifice was brought—every one went out to buy his paschal lamb. And the Jews made an ordinance, that when going forth on that mission, nobody should say to his neighbor, "Step aside," or "Let me pass," even if the one behind was King Solomon or David. When I remarked to the priests that this was not seemly nor polite, they made answer that it was so ordered, to show that there is no rank before the eyes of God, not even at the time of preparing to serve Him, more especially at the service itself; at that time all were equal in receiving His goodness.

When the fourteenth day of the month arrived, they went to the highest tower of the Temple, which the Hebrews called Lul, and whose stairway was made like those in our church towers, and held three silver trumpets in their hands, with which they blew. After the blowing, they proclaimed the following: "People of the Lord, in the name of Him who rests in the great and holy house, listen! The time for slaughtering the paschal lamb has arrived." As the people heard the proclamation, they donned their holiday attire; for since midday it was holiday for the Jews, being the time for sacrifice. At the entrance of the great hall stood twelve Levites on the outside with silver staves in their hands, and twelve within with gold staves in their hands. The duties of those on the outside were to prevent quarrels, to direct and to warn the incoming people not to injure one another in their great haste and not to press forward in the crowd— for it happened previously on one of the feasts of Pesach that an old man, together with his sacrifice, was crushed in consequence of the great rush. Those on the inside were to preserve order among the outgoing people, that they should not crush each other. They were also to close the gates of the hall when they saw that it was already full to its capacity.

When they reached the slaughtering place, rows of priests stood with gold and silver bowls in their hands: one row had all gold bowls and another row had all silver bowls. This was done to display the glory and splendor of the place. Every priest who stood at the head of the row received a bowl full of the sprinkling blood. He passed it to his neighbor, and he to his, until the altar was reached; and the priest who stood next to the altar returned the bowl empty, and it went back in the same manner, so that every priest received a full bowl and returned an empty one. And there occurred no manner of disturbance, as they were so used to the service that the bowls seemed to fly back and forth, as arrows in the hand of a hero. For thirty days previously they had practiced that service and, therefore, were aware of where there was the chance of a mistake or a mishap. There were also two tall pillars, on which stood two priests with silver trumpets in their hands, who blew when each division began the sacrifice (the paschal lamb was slaughtered in three divisions) in order to signal to the priests, who stood on their eminence, to begin *Hallel* amid jubilee and thanksgiving, accompanied by all their musical instruments; on that day, namely, they brought forward all the instruments. The sacrificer also prayed the *Hallel*. If the sacrifice was not ended, *Hallel* was repeated.

After the sacrifice, they went into the halls, where the walls were full of iron hooks and forks. The sacrifices were hung upon them and skinned. There were also many bundles of sticks; for when there were no more empty hooks, they put a stick upon the shoulders of two of their number, hung the sacrifice upon it, skinned it, and put the particular portion upon the altar, and went away rejoicing, as one who went to the war and returned victorious. The one who did not bring the paschal lamb at the appointed time was eternally disgraced.

During the service the priests were dressed in scarlet,

that the blood which might accidentally be spilled on them should not be noticed. The garment was short, reaching only to the ankle. The priests stood barefoot, and the sleeves reached only the arms, so they should not be disturbed during the service. On their heads they had a cap, around which was tied a three-ell-long band; but the high priest, as they told me, had a band which he could tie around his cap forty times. His was white. The ovens in which they roasted the paschal lambs were in front of their doors, in order, as they told me, to perform their religious ceremonies and to display their festival joys in public. After the roast, they ate amid jubilee songs and thanksgiving, so that their voices were heard from afar. No gate of Jerusalem was closed during Passover night, because of those who were constantly coming and going who were considerable in number. The Jews also told me that on the Feast of Pesach the number of those present was double of that which went out of Egypt, for they wished to acquaint the king with their number.

The Samaritan Passover[2]

THEODOR H. GASTER

There is one part of the world in which the ancient paschal sacrifice is still performed as in biblical times. At Nablus, site of the ancient city of Shechem in Palestine, lives the fast-dwindling community of the Samaritans. Reduced to no more than two hundred souls, the Samaritans claim that they are the surviving remnant of the House of Israel, the descendants of men who were never carried into captivity but remained always on their ancestral soil. They reject every part of the Bible except the Five Books of Moses, and they claim that the appointed place of God is not Zion (as the Jews maintain) but Mount Gerizim, at the foot of which they reside. Here, according to their tradition, the patriarchs are buried and it was here too that Abraham prepared to sacrifice his only son Isaac.

The Samaritans live under the governance of a high priest and in strict conformity with the Mosaic Law. They believe, however, that in consequence of sin and transgression, they are at present passing through a period of divine displeasure, marked by the withdrawal of God's presence and the suspension of the sacrificial system. The only sacrifice which they still offer is that of the Passover. The rite is performed on the slopes of Mount Gerizim, the entire community repairing thither and spending the week under canvas.

The following account of the ceremony is translated from a voluminous work on Samaritan beliefs and practices compiled, toward the end of the nineteenth century, by the then high priest, Jacob ben Aaron (1840-1918). The work, which is entitled "The Guide" *(Dalil)* and which still exists only in manuscript form, is drawn from older sources, and is therefore obviously more reliable and authoritative than the many journalistic descriptions with which curious tourists and ill-informed spectators have flooded the popular prints during recent years.

"When the fourteenth day of the first (lunar) month approaches, they all get ready and foregather at the Chosen Place, at the spot selected on the soil of the Mountain for the performance of the sacrifice. Men and women alike foregather, and each pitches his tent with great rejoicing and gladness of heart. On the fourteenth day itself, they remove all yeast from their places, and wash all the vessels. They also wash their clothes and change their garments. They refrain from all leaven and ban it from their midst. On that day, they eat no bread whatsoever, be it leavened or unleavened, in accordance with a tradition passed down from antiquity concerning the observance of this institution. The tradition is based

29

on the commandment of Exodus 23.18: *Thou shalt not sacrifice over leaven the blood of My sacrifice.* The Samaritans, then, are forbidden to keep possession of anything fermenting into yeast on the fourteenth day of the month.

"If, in any given year, the day of the paschal sacrifice—that is, the fifteenth day of the month—falls on a Sabbath, the ceremony has to take place on the Friday, after sunset. The leaven has therefore to be removed during the course of the day itself, so that the consumption of the paschal meal shall be free of contamination therefrom, i.e., so that there shall not be in their stomachs any matter which is fermenting into leaven.

"At the beginning of the tenth hour, the high priest goes to the place where they have the oven, accompanied by the elders of the community and the slaughterers, and together they light the fire in it. The oven is dug out in the ground, after the manner of a well, and is lined with stones, put together without mortar. It is three cubits deep from the ground-surface, but its length and width depend on the number of sheep to be sacrificed. One of the elders stands by until the flame catches and the stones glow. At half past the tenth hour the altar itself is lighted. On it they lay wood for the burning of the fat. In the middle they place copper vessels to boil water for the removal of the fleece from the sacrificial sheep . . . the sheep itself being destined later to have its flesh torn in pieces by human hands. The fire is kept burning under three vessels.

"Half an hour before sunset, the members of the community present themselves amid great rejoicing and pomp. Those of the elders who are advanced in years dress in beautiful clothes, entirely white. Then they all foregather in a large cluster beside the altar on which the sacrifice is to be offered, standing in rows on its south side; the priest especially appointed for the task stands in front of them. Lads and young children come too, all clad in linen coats and linen breeches and wearing linen girdles

and linen caps. All stand around the altar, those who are
to do the slaughtering taking up a position at the very
edge of it. Each of these holds in his hand a sharp, flawless
knife. Then the priest proceeds to inspect the lambs
which they have prepared for the sacrifice, removing
those in which a blemish is detected. Thereafter, the lads
take them and round them up, and place them in front of
the altar, themselves standing all round them. Some
twenty minutes or a quarter of an hour before sunset, the
priest begins to intone hymns appropriate to the praise of
God, and he seeks divine pardon for sin, and acceptance
of the offering. All this is recited in the holy tongue,
Hebrew.

"The priest next begins a short prayer for the slaughtering. Thereafter he continues in Hebrew: *For I call on
the name of the Lord; ascribe ye greatness unto our God,
The Rock,—His work is perfect, for all His ways are
justice; a God of faithfulness and without perversity,
righteous and upright is he* (Deut. 32.3-4). 'Blessed be
our God forever, and blessed be His name forever!' Then
he reads a portion of that section of the Law in which the
Lord has commanded Israel to offer the paschal sacrifice
(Ex. 12). When he reaches the words: *and all the congregation of the community of Israel shall slaughter it at
twilight,* the slaughterers proceed to slay the sheep
quickly, in accordance with the prescribed regulations,
sprinkling its blood on the altar round about, and all saying in a loud voice: 'They proclaim and say, There is no
God but one!' This they repeat three times. Then they
add: *The Lord, a God gracious, and merciful, long-suffer-
ing and abundant in loving-kindness and truth* (Ex. 34.6).

"The slaughtering takes place at twilight. The rules by
which eventide is determined among the Samaritans are as
follows: The first stage is from the moment when the sun
grows red until the moment it begins visibly to set. The
second is from the moment it begins visibly to set until it is
altogether obscured. This lasts about an hour and a half.
Real twilight is the space of two minutes after the actual

going-down of the sun. This is the moment when the paschal sacrifice is slaughtered.

"When the slaughtering is finished, the people exchange greetings. First, they kiss the hand of the high priest and of all the men of his family, and later pass to the other members of the congregation, starting with the eldest and ending with the youngest. The men who stand around the altar then proceed to pluck the hair from the sacrificial victims, loading the animals upon the shoulders of the serving-lads, and removing the stomach, dung, fat, kidneys, and midriff, which they place above the wood on the altar, sprinkling the whole with salt and washing them clean of all impurity. Then they cut deep gashes into the lamb and remove the ischiatic nerve, concerning which it is said in the Torah: *Therefore the children of Israel eat not the ischiatic nerve unto this day* (Gen. 32.33). They also drain off the blood, applying liberal applications of salt. No bone is allowed to be broken, in accordance with the commandment of Exodus 12.46. The whole body of the lamb is placed on wooden spits, head downward. While all this is being done, part of the bystanders recite from the Torah, beginning at Exodus 12.1 and ending at the conclusion of Chapter 15. They accompany the reading with hymns and praises, and add also several other verses from the Torah in which mention is made of the paschal sacrifice. Meanwhile, the priest takes unleavened bread, together with bitter herbs, and gives to each to eat.

"When they have finished preparing the lambs, they take them and lower them by the spits into the midst of the oven, which faces the altar on its eastern side. Over the top of the oven they place a wooden trellis, covering it with greenstuff and applying to the top of it a paste of mud, which they plaster firmly over it to prevent the smell from coming through. All the while, they sing and intone hymns to God. The flesh is then left in the oven for three hours, during which they recite the evening prayer handed down from remote antiquity. The fire is left burning on the altar until no fragment of the fat or legs is left. It is *a pleasant savor unto the Lord!*

"When night has fallen and the evening prayer has been concluded, they come and remove the sacrificial meat from the oven. At that juncture, they have their loins girded, sandals on their feet, and staves in their hands, as ordained in Exodus 12.11. Each lamb is then taken apart, and when all have been thus dismembered, the congregation begins to recite hymns to a pleasing tune. These are composed in Aramaic and are the work of ancient sages. After this, the priest recites the words: 'Blessed art Thou, O Lord, our God. There is no God but one, and His is the greatness. May our festive season be happy through God's grace!' Then they sit down to eat of the paschal sacrifice, doing so in haste. Each family eats separately, men and women apart. With the meat they partake of wafers of unleavened bread, together with bitter herbs.

"None of the meat is removed from the place where they happen to be encamped. When they have finished eating of the sacrifice, they gather all the remnants and burn them on the altar.

"That same night, when dawn breaks, they rise up and recite the morning prayer. This continues until two hours after sunrise. When it is over, each man returns to his tent in joy and in gladness of heart.

"Such then is the institution of the paschal offering among the Samaritans. It should be added that if there be any internal blemish in the lamb, or if it be maimed or scarred, it is removed to a place apart. It is not eaten nor merely thrown away, but burnt separately. It may not be given to a Gentile to eat. It should also be observed that during the time in which the sacrifice is being prepared, no Gentile may come into contact with a Samaritan, nor may anyone eat of the sacrifice or even approach it if he be in a state of ritual uncleanness.

"Whatever is found next morning lying over on the ground is gathered up and burnt on the altar."

33

The Marranos Observe Passover[3]

HAYYIM SCHAUSS

At the end of the European Middle Ages there was evolved a notable method of observing Pesach among the marranos, the secret Jews of Spain and Portugal. These marranos were entirely separated from Jews and from Jewish life. They had no Jewish books, and the only book on which they could draw for rules of Jewish life was the Latin Bible of the Catholic Church. Basing their ideas about Jews and Judaism on this one book, their conception of Jewish life became an entirely false one. They tried to live, not as the Jews of their day did, but as the Jews of the time of the Kings and the Prophets. They knew nothing of the development of Pesach through the ages; they practiced the Pesach described in the Bible.

The question arises: How did these marranos, who had no Jewish calendars and no contacts with other Jews, know when to observe the various Jewish festivals? Actually, they did not; they reckoned the Jewish holidays by the calendar in general use, applying the Jewish days to the secular month. Thus they observed Yom Kippur on the tenth day after the New Moon of September and Pesach at the full moon of March. When the spies of the Inquisition discovered these observances, the marranos of Spain advanced the dates of the festivals, observing Yom Kippur on the eleventh day following the New Moon of September and celebrating the Seder (the ceremony of Pesach night) on a Pesach eve that came sixteen days after the appearance of the New Moon of March, instead of fourteen days.

On this sixteenth day they would bake their *matzot*; on the two preceding days which, according to their curious

34

Jewish-secular calendar, were really Pesach, they ate neither bread nor *matzot*. There was no ceremony of the burning of the *hametz*. Instead they burned a piece of dough prepared for the baking of the *matzot*. In the evening they observed a secret Seder in their homes, eating an entire roast sheep, all the participants wearing their traveling shoes and bearing staves in their hands, exactly as described in the Bible. There were even marranos, those of Mexico, who followed the old biblical injunction to smear the blood of the sheep on their doorposts.

One noteworthy custom grew up among these marranos: the custom of beating the waters of a stream with willow branches, which they interpreted as a reminder of the separating of the waters of the Red Sea. It is interesting to note that to this very day the Jews of Morocco make their way to a stream on the last day of Pesach and there recite prayers and blessings. It is possible that this was an old Spanish Jewish custom and that the marranos took it over and added to it the ceremony of the willow branches which rightly belongs to Sukkot. That holiday they could not observe at all, since one of the requirements of the festival is to sit in booths in the open.

The Pesach of the marranos is not entirely a thing of the past. There are, to this very day, marranos in Portugal who still observe Pesach in the manner just described.

*The Passover as Observed by the Falashas** [4]

JACQUES FAITLOVITCH

The Falashas [Jews of Ethiopia] observe Passover for seven days, and during this time they eat only unleavened bread and do not drink any fermented drinks. Several days before the feast, the homes are carefully cleaned, all

* Ethiopian Jews call themselves *Beta Yisrael*, a term that has replaced *Falashas*.

35

articles of clothing are properly washed, and all vessels and utensils thoroughly scoured and cleaned. Three days before Passover, they stop eating leavened bread and take nothing but dried peas and beans; and on the eve of Passover, they abstain from all food until after the sacrifice of the paschal lamb. On this day, a little before the setting of the sun, all assemble in the court of the synagogue and, in the name of the entire community, the sacrificer offers the paschal lamb upon the altar. The ceremony is observed with great pomp; the ritual prescribed in the Bible for this sacrifice is followed punctiliously, and after the sacrifice is slaughtered and roasted, the meat is eaten with unleavened bread by the priestly assistants. It is in this manner that the festival is inaugurated. On the following days they assemble in the *Mesgid* (the place of prayer) at fixed hours, observing a special ritual and reciting various prayers and biblical texts having reference to the Exodus of the Israelites from Egypt.

Passover in the Caucasus[5]

ZVI KASDAI

Towards evening, the Caucasian Jews put on what they call "liberty-clothes" having wide, loose sleeves. Into their belts they stick a short spear or dagger, and some even put their pistols there and then go to the synagogue to chant and pray. On this night they chant, together with their *hakham* (learned man), the *Hallel* Psalms, word for word.

Upon returning home, they find their homes illuminated with many candles in honor of the festival. The old women wrap themselves in their shawls; but the young women and girls are dressed mostly in linen dresses, and put roses and other kinds of flowers in their braids. They hastily get together all the food they have prepared—such as roasted geese, stuffed turkeys, *matzot*, bitter herbs and a bowl of *haroset*—and carry it to the house of the *hakham*. It is the custom with the Caucasian Jews to have many families gather in the house of a learned man, or in the house of any man who knows enough Hebrew to explain the Haggadah in the Tatar's language. Then they sit down, in accordance with their custom, upon the ground and the learned man translates and explains the Haggadah to them.

It is a very impressive scene; the sturdy men sit dressed in their liberty-clothes, with a belt on their loins and a short spear at their sides. They sit in rows in the formation of soldiers resting after active battle. Between the rows there are spread costly carpets on which stand very attractive candlesticks.

All year the women are kept confined in their rooms, and are never seen with uncovered faces in public. But on the night of Passover, they come to the Seder with their faces uncovered, adorned with golden earrings and costly rings of sapphires and diamonds; around their necks they have gold and silver beads strung on a blue thread, and on their loins they wear belts made of silver chains. The young women and the girls have roses and fragrant flowers in their braids. On this night they fear neither an evil-eye nor evil spirits, because it is a night watched over by God himself.

When the learned man reads the parts of the Haggadah that speak of the future deliverance from exile, they all raise their hands heavenward and say the following with great devotion and deep sadness: "May it be the will of God that the Messiah, the son of David, come and bring Redemption to all the people in exile, as the Lord our God has redeemed our ancestors in time of old." All the women thereupon respond: "Amen, may this be God's will."

37

While reading the paragraph beginning with: "Every person in every generation must regard himself . . . ," the learned man rises, wraps up a piece of *matzah* in an old kerchief, puts it on his shoulder, walks four paces, shows it to everybody, and explains to them in their language that in this fashion did our ancestors go out of Egypt. At the same time he makes rapid motions with his body to indicate that the Israelites left Egypt in haste.

In the meantime, the young fellows go into a separate room, select one out of their midst whom they dress in torn clothes, put a sack on his shoulders, give him a thick stick in his hand and send him outside. After a short interval, a loud knocking on the door is heard. Someone is asking for permission to enter and participate in the Seder service. All those assembled inquire: "Who are you, and what may your wish be?"

"I am a Jew and I desire to celebrate with you the Passover, the festival of our freedom," answers the voice from behind the door.

"How can we believe that you are a Jew?"

"I wear a *tallit-katan* (a ritual garment for prayer) with fringes attached thereto."

"This is not sufficient proof; give us some other sign."

"Then my *peot* (temple-locks) will prove what I say."

"Even this is not sufficient proof; it is not yet the real proof."

"Just let me in, and you will then see that I am telling you the truth," pleads the voice from behind the door. And at the same time he becomes angry and excited and begins knocking with his heavy stick on the door. Thereupon the assembly asks further:

"If you really are a Jew, why do you arrive so late? Do you not know that today is a festival in Israel, and that everybody must stay home?"

"You see, I have just come from Jerusalem, the Holy City; it is a very long distance from here, and the roads are full of danger at every pace and step. Our enemies lie

38

in wait for us, and are always in our way. These enemies stand between you and me like an impassable iron wall, so that I was unable to come to you before the festival."

Thereupon the stranger breaks out in loud weeping and wailing and the assembly sits quietly as if absorbed in deep meditation; a deadly silence prevails in the whole house, but from time to time it is broken by a deep heavy sigh.

Everybody's eyes are now riveted on the door, when, at a given sign from the learned man, somebody opens it. Immediately the young man enters and walks directly to the center of the room; he has a sword at his side stuck in a leather belt; he has a heavy stick in his hand and a sack on his shoulders. On his feet, he wears sandals with their points bent upward and his clothes are all covered with dust. Suddenly a feeling of joy and happiness seizes upon all the assembly. With joyous laughter they surround the stranger, and from all sides attack him with questions such as these:

"How fares it in Jerusalem, the Holy City?"

"How fare our brethren there, in the Holy City, who are always in the presence of the Almighty?"

"When, oh when, will the Redeemer come to redeem us?"

"Do you bring us a message of our liberation and Redemption?"

And the newcomer gives them hearty greetings from Jerusalem, the sages, the towns and villages, the fields and forests, and from the holy graves. He informs them in the name of the wise men from the Holy City that there are signs pointing out that the Redeemer will soon come and destroy the iron wall that separates them from the Holy City. Those assembled listen very attentively to every word and syllable uttered by the messenger; and when the messenger is through speaking, they all raise their hands heavenward, and with a deep, long, heart-breaking sigh they loudly say several times: "Amen, may this be his will, may this be his will!"

*Springtime in Swislowitz** [6]

SHMARYA LEVIN

Passover was coming, the greatest and most splendid of the festivals. New clothes for everybody, everything brand new, from head to foot. So there were visits to Hershel the tailor, who spent one half of his time working and the other half running down his rival, Yenkel the tailor. There were visits to Isar the shoemaker, Isar with the red nose whom everybody in the town, from the president of the *Shul* to the water-carrier, feared because of his fiery advocacy of the cause of absolute justice. First were the necessary visits—for measurement. Then came the unnecessary visits—at least, so they were regarded by Hershel and Isar. But how was it possible for Hershel to sew pockets in my suit, or for Isar to put a stiff strip of raw leather in my shoes, to make them creak with newness when I put them on, unless I was present to watch? My visits to Hershel took place in the daytime, and to Isar I went in the evening. I had a friend in Isar's best apprentice, a certain Shaikin who taught me how to twist a waxed shoemaker's thread, and even let me hammer a few nails into the sole of a shoe. But he would not permit me to handle the awl which made the holes for the nails. And when I hammered straight, and the nail did not bend or break, I was a happy boy: I knew a trade already! But Shaikin exploited my friendship. He made me bring him a pound of sugar and a quart of whiskey. Not in payment

* From *Childhood in Exile,* by Shmarya Levin, trans. by Maurice Samuel, copyright, 1929, by Harcourt, Brace & World, Inc.; renewed, 1957, by Maurice Samuel. Reprinted by permission of the publishers.

40

Mural painting. Tomb of Rekhmere

1. Asiatic Captives Making Bricks in an Egyptian Brickyard

Wall painting. Synagogue of Dura-Europos

2. Passage of the Israelites Through the Red Sea

Wall painting. Synagogue of Dura-Europos

3. Discovery of the Infant Moses

4. Ancient Haggadah Manuscript

The Cairo Genizah

5. The Rabbis at B'ne B'rak

Haggadah, British Museum

for these privileges, but because he needed them, he told me, to make the leather strip without which the new shoes would not creak. And how could I wear a pair of new shoes if they did not creak?

Last, but certainly not least, there was the *matzot* bakery. There were really several bakeries for *matzot*, but the most distinguished belonged to Mottye Kailes. His product was delicate, thin as paper and neatly holed in lines, as if with the best machine. I used to go from one bakery to the other and watch them punch the holes in the *matzot*. I had pull with Mottye Kailes, for we had our own *matzot* made there; and the chief "holer" was a Talmud student who ate Fridays and Saturdays in our house. Cherneh the widow was the chief dough-kneader at Mottye Kailes' bakery, and she instructed me in all the details of the work—the pouring out of the dough in equal quantities and the flattening of it into *matzah* cakes. My greatest joy was when the Talmud student let me take the holer in my hand, roll it across the dough, and produce the line of neat punctures . . .

The evening draws close, and the last sunlight is spilled on the town of Swislowitz. Every Jewish home shines that evening, renewed and purified, and on every table the biggest and richest and whitest cloth is spread. The children are dressed in new clothes, and even the street has been swept, and the entrance to the house covered with clean, yellow sand. Along those quiet streets, with their trees in first blossom, we go, young and old, to the synagogue. There is contentment in the air, peace and the feeling of plenty. For at what other season of the year can every Jewish family in Swislowitz boast that it is provided with food for every bit of eight days ahead— the duration of the festival? The poorest household, haunted by hunger fifty-one weeks in the year, is stocked up till the last day of Passover: such is the Law. And when else, in the course of the year, can they lay aside their pitiful cares and rejoice in the festival and in the spring? What wonder that Passover is the most beloved

41

of the festivals? On the eve of that day the poorest man in Swislowitz could repeat with generous sincerity the prayer which opens the home ceremonies, "Let every man that is hungry enter and eat, let every man that is thirsty enter and drink." It is forbidden for any one to be hungry. And the sages of the town argued, knowingly, "Could God have chosen a lovelier festival than Passover on which to liberate the Jews from Egypt?"

We have returned from the *Shul.* We are at home. Nothing, in the memories of my childhood years, shines so clearly and so lovingly as this evening of the Passover. The luminous shadows of it have been cast forever across my life, and the magic does not decrease with the years. For on that evening the house was a palace, my father was a king, and all of us were members of a royal family— queen and princes and princesses. Even the poorest guest that sat at table with us was an ambassador. My joy was too full to be contained; it spilled over, and poured itself through the room and over the people in it. I wanted the older people to tell me wonderful stories, and I wanted to tell others in return. I was full of the glorious Exodus from the land of Egypt, and I lived, in my own way, through all the acts of that greatest of world-dramas.

The table had been stretched for that evening, filled in with extra boards to accommodate the guests. At the head my father sat, leaning upon cushions at his right hand—a symbol of his freedom, majesty, and rule. My mother sat by his side. After them, in places of honor, were the guests, and then the members of the family. Countless beakers and glasses of wine sparkled on the table, and they were flanked by glowing carafes. My father conducted the Seder ceremonies with royal dignity, without haste, without impatience. My younger brother being still too young to ask the Four Questions, that part of the ceremony fell to me. But I was almost ashamed to take so simple a part, for I understood nearly the whole of the ritual. And I repeated the four questions in Hebrew, with their Yiddish translations, like one who obeys a command.

After the questions came the reading of the answers. Great was my glee when we reached the counting of the plagues which were inflicted on the Egyptians: greater still was it when we repeated the complicated calculations of certain sages who proved by a logic of their own that the Egyptians were smitten not with ten, but with every bit of two hundred and fifty plagues. Serves them right, I thought: that'll teach them to leave the Jews alone.

There is a certain tradition attached to the Seder ceremony, the stealing of the *afikoman* (a specially dedicated *matzah*) from under the cushion of the father. Of course it must be stolen between the time it is tucked away, near the beginning of the service, and the end, when it is drawn out to be divided and eaten. My brother wanted to aid me in the theft, on condition that we divided the reward which must be paid by the father. But an excellent idea came to me. I went up to my father and asked him what reward he would give me if I did *not* steal the *afikoman*. The idea pleased him mightily, and he promised me more than I would have expected in payment for a successful theft. I got my reward and remained honest into the bargain. Not only did I make no attempt to steal the *afikoman*, but I even watched my brothers to prevent them from stealing it.

In the center of the table stood a beaker of wine which is set apart for Elijah the Prophet. None may drink from it but he, when he appears invisibly at the right moment. And I watched it closely for a sign of diminution in its brimming contents. Of course none of us doubted that Elijah appeared that evening in every Jewish home. But we also knew that it was quite impossible for him to drink up those thousands and thousands of beakers of wine set apart for him. A tiny drop he *might* have taken from every cup, and I watched, fascinated, for the slight shrinkage. When the moment came we stood up, my father flung open the door and repeated the tremendous words, "Pour forth Thy wrath on the nations that know Thee not . . ." I held my breath and looked and

43

listened. Oh, I knew well that Elijah would not enter like a common mortal, grossly visible and audible! But I waited for a shadow, a ghost of a sound, a whisper of footsteps. The invocation ended, the door was closed, and I could not tell. Had I heard something? Had I felt something pass? I looked back at the table, and scrutinized the beaker of the prophet. But again my own intensity had defeated me, and I could not remember exactly where the wine had stood before. Perhaps the lips of the prophet had touched the wine, invisibly, faintly. And all that evening I wondered, and wondering, slipped into a half sleep, till my father woke me up and bade me sing with everyone else the last of the songs of that evening, *"Had Gadya, Had Gadya,* a little kid, a little kid, which my father bought for two *zuzzim, Had Gadya, Had Gadya."*

We children were not the only ones who believed that Elijah the Prophet was going to appear, and that he was compelled, by elementary considerations of courtesy, at least to touch the wineglass with his lips: for millions of Jews had prepared it for him, and millions of Jews had shown their faith in him. There were adults, bearded Jews, who expected his momentary appearance, who would not have been at all surprised if the stern Tishbite had suddenly swept in through the open door. Far from regarding it as supernatural, they would have said that even a prophet should not let himself be asked too often. And after all, it would not have put the prophet much out of the way. Saints less illustrious than he had achieved the magic "conquest of distance," and could fly over hundreds of miles in the twinkling of an eye. There were faithful believers who were bitterly disappointed when, year after year, Elijah the Prophet failed to put in an appearance when the door was thrown open on the Passover night.

There was only one man in our town, the most illiterate among the Jews of Swislowitz—none other than Asher Pakess, keeper of the free lodging-house, and public water-carrier—who had been honored by a glimpse of the prophet, and that not only once, but fully twice. He was a man of extreme simplicity; that is, he had carried over into his manhood the naïveté of his childhood, and understood all things literally. And he was as honest as a child; his mind did not bend to the right or the left by the breadth of a hair. No one ever had to watch Asher Pakess: and in this he differed greatly from Palahei the peasant woman, another water-carrier, who could not be trusted in the kitchen if a wooden spoon were lying around. Asher Pakess could be trusted alone in the kitchen with a fistful of gold coins on the table. Often enough, householders, not having change, would run up a debt with Asher Pakess, to as much as four and five buckets of water. And then they would give him a ten-kopek piece and trust him for the change. And Asher Pakess could not rest until he had returned the last kopek.

To this same Asher Pakess the privilege was granted of looking twice on Elijah the Prophet in person. During the Passover, the free lodging-house was empty, for even the beggars found some sort of home during that festival. So Asher and his wife remained there alone, and the two of them went through the ritual. Asher's wife, somewhat more intelligent than he, knew all the details of the ceremony. She knew, therefore, that among the beakers on the table the largest and handsomest was set for Elijah the Prophet. She also knew that when that passage, "Pour forth Thy wrath," was reached, the door had to be opened wide. Right enough, when the moment came, Pakicha flung open the door—and a goat entered at once. Neither Asher nor his wife thought of driving the goat out. They knew who the goat was. This was Elijah the Prophet himself, in one of those disguises that are spoken of in the folk stories. The goat, finding this friendly welcome, advanced to the center of the room, leaped with its two forefeet on the table, mouthed one of the *matzot* as if saying a prayer over it, and upset the beaker of Elijah the Prophet.

And at this point Asher Pakess could not contain him-

45

self. "Rabbi, Prophet," he exclaimed breathlessly. "Don't be angry, please. Eat as much as you like. Drink as much as you like. But oh, please, don't break anything."

On the second evening of the Passover, when the same ceremony is repeated in detail, a second visitor appeared at this point. A man, dressed in a long white gown, his face covered by his hat, appeared at the door, entered and strode up to the table. Asher was much more terrified by this visitor than by the goat. He cried out in his terror. But the visitor only lifted the cup of the prophet, drained it, and disappeared. Among the Jews of Swislowitz it was known that the visitor had been Israel, the son of Joseph Bear, the cantor. But Asher Pakess was convinced that none other than Elijah the Prophet had appeared again, in another disguise, to empty the beaker of wine.

These two stories were very popular in Swislowitz, and Asher was always ready to repeat them on request, to the vast amusement of his auditors. He told them simply, straightforwardly, as a child recounts something. But there were some who did not laugh. They asked themselves: Who knew who the goat was? Who knew who the visitor in the gown was—despite the claim of Israel, son of Joseph Bear? And above all, who knew who Asher Pakess the simpleton was? Had it not often turned out that the woodchopper was no woodchopper, the water-carrier no water-carrier? And what of the Thirty-six Hidden Saints, the modest, silent spirits who haunt the earth in humble guise, and whose merits keep the world going? Who could tell when he had met, under the guise of some pious, honest simpleton, one of these?

In between the first two high festival days of Passover, and the last two days, are four days of half festival. It is still Passover. All leavened things are forbidden. But you may work—you may carry on. And during the full festival days at the beginning and the end, we lived a happy life. Nothing to do after synagogue services but to visit and be received in style. Cakes, cookies, ginger candies, special delicacies made of *matzah* flour and filled with the baked paring of beets and carrots . . . And then chicken necks and chicken guts, roasted and stuffed, and jams and fruits of all kinds. And on top of all these they gave us wine and mead to sip—as much as we wanted. And we could drink a great deal of it, for it was a home-made raisin wine on which it was difficult to get drunk.

The traditional game for the Passover is with nuts—little Brazil nuts and big walnuts. With the walnuts the game was difficult. Five or six of them were placed in a row; the challenger stood at a distance of twenty paces and tried to hit them with a small steel pellet. The girls played at Pots and Pans. Among the boys the favorite game was Odds and Evens. All you had to do was guess whether your opponent held an odd or an even number of nuts in his hand. But there were sharks and swindlers among us, too. Jakey, the son of Reuben the bathman, introduced us once to a new game. He took up a fistful of nuts and held his hand over the table. Any one who wanted to gamble with him had to place one nut on the table for the privilege of guessing odd, two nuts on the table for guessing even. And then the nuts would be counted. If Jakey won, he kept the one or the two nuts. If he lost, his opponent would get the entire fistful. It looked like a marvelous and attractive gamble. We played with Jakey and lost. We played again and lost. We played with him all day, and all the next day, and Jakey never lost a fistful of nuts. We were stripped of our hoard, with never a single pause in the process.

I was amazed and baffled. How could a man be so lucky, never lose once to an opponent, always hold even when his opponent said odd, odd when he said even? I complained to my father. My father heard the description of the game carefully, then smiled and said, "Stupid! Don't you see that Jakey always puts an odd number of nuts in his hand? When you guess odd, and pay one nut for guessing, he adds the nut to the odd number and that makes it even. When you guess even and pay two nuts for guessing, he adds the two nuts to the odd number in his hand, and that leaves it odd."

Burning with rage, I ran out to my playmates and

explained the swindle to all of them. We did not speak to Jakey for nearly a year.

On the afternoon of the eighth day of Passover they gave us *matzot* doubled and bent—a symbol of the fact that Passover was closing. And with it was closing also my first *heder* year. I was still a child, but with something of the adult. I already knew much about our people and the lore of our people. I understood something of the meaning of that dark word *Galut,* exile, which recurs so frequently in our talk, and I also understood why the Jews pray so often for the coming of the Messiah. The child in me was still happy, carefree, merry—but now and again a sigh escaped from my lips—a sigh which I could not account for and could not explain.

Matzah-Baking in an East-European Town[1]

SOMA MORGENSTERN

The sons of the scribe were ten years old when, for the first time, they came to know the twin daughters of the baker and spent a whole day in the same room with them. This took place in the week preceding the paschal feast in the great bakery in the house of the baker. According to an ancient custom the pious people of the city assembled there annually in order to make their contribution to the baking of the *matzot* for the poor and needy. Young, and old, poor and rich—they were all there. Whoever had the will to lend a hand was welcome to share in this benevolent work. The largest baking room of the most important bakery in the town could scarcely hold these voluntary bakers.

The baking of the *matzot* is an equally pious and merry

48

task. All the children of the town wanted to help. The fun in baking *matzot* which the children enjoyed came from the great and obvious haste which the adults use. This haste is necessary in the baking of *matzot*, in order to eliminate any possibility of the contamination of the unleavened by leaven. Haste in this occupation is, moreover, a pious gesture by which the bakers are reminded of the great and holy haste of our ancestors when they baked in preparation of their hasty departure from Egyptian bondage and their swift entry into freedom.

Now whenever haste is necessary, work must be largely divided. Hence, from time immemorial we observe in the baking of *matzot* a significant as well as useful division of labor. We discriminate between those who pour the dough and those who knead it, those who cut it into cakes and those who smooth it, those who keep the oven hot and those who shove the cakes into the oven, not to speak of the carriers and the expert bakers.

The finest and the merriest task, so apt to delight the heart of children, is that of using the little cog wheels. In order to prevent the *matzot* from rising in the heat of the oven and to keep them flat, one passes from time to time small, handy cog wheels over the smooth squares or circles of dough. This is more play than work, and so a game for children.

Though it is a game, it must be learned. The sons of the Torah scribe found this out soon enough, the first time they tried to handle the little cog wheels. Scarcely had they taken their place at the proper tables and made their first, awkward attempts, when the two daughters of the baker came up and quizzically surveyed what the boys had done. With the self-importance of little girls they began at once to instruct the embarrassed newcomers. One of the little girls, swift of gesture and arch of glance, said to Jochanan, "That's not the way to do it!" And she took the little cog wheel out of his hand; with swift fingers she rolled it over the soft surface of the dough and in an instant had completed the pointed lines of a perfect piece

49

of *matzah*. The other girl did the same thing for Nehemiah. This second girl was gentle of eye and slow of gesture and her admonition was mild and considerate: "You'll do better this way."

To be thus publicly instructed by little girls seemed to the young scholars at first a derogation from their dignity. But since they did want to learn, they obeyed with what grace they could, and when the two girls left the twins alone, they secretly wished that their little teachers might come back and stay longer.

In the course of the day this wish of theirs was repeatedly fulfilled. The girls came and went and came again and for the greater part of the day remained at the table of the twins. But the sons of the scribe on this day learned from the daughters of the baker not only how to pass the little cog wheels swiftly and accurately over the *matzot*. They learned in addition how attractive and merry are the songs which are sung at the baking of the paschal bread.

Bakers are pertinacious singers, especially the younger journeymen. And particularly tireless are young Jewish bakers. By day and night they baked. By day and night there was singing in the house of the baker. His children had heard the songs of the young bakers, and what they had learned in the course of the years they displayed during the baking of the paschal bread.

To the children of the Torah scribe, who had been brought up according to the entire sternness of the Law, singing was no profane pastime. They sang while they studied; they sang while they prayed. To them singing was study or prayer. The children of the baker sang songs of quite a different fashion, gay or sad little songs, which refresh the heart like the fragrance of fresh baked *matzot*. Moreover, the little girls sang in harmony, a thing which the sons of the scribe had never heard. And the way in which the two voices blended with each other enchanted the Talmud students beyond measure.

They were most enchanted by a song which the sisters

sang mockingly to the two brothers. The little song had three stanzas. The first went as follows:

> Good people who have time today,
> Active and true and pure,
> Come hither all to bake the bread,
> The *matzot* of the poor.

The gentler of the two girls sang this stanza alone. Her sister undertook the second:

> Hands that are small and delicate,
> Whom all but books bring irk,
> Once in the month of Nisan try
> This rough and useful work.

In the third stanza the voices of the two girls blended:

> Sensitive children, knead the dough
> With hands the whitest seen,
> Aye, knead the dough, with prayer glow,
> Good and pure and clean.

The boys were so pleased with this song and its gay sweet tune that they learned it on the spot and sang it repeatedly with the sisters. The patterning of the *matzot* was not so much fun any more, especially since the work of the children was not taken quite seriously. Even as the children used a special table, so the *matzot* prepared by them were baked in a separate oven and, so soon as they were done, eaten by the children too.

Passover in a Union Camp[8]
A Reminiscence of the Civil War

JOSEPH A. JOEL

The approaching Feast of Passover reminds me of an incident which transpired in 1862, and which as an index

of the times, no doubt, will prove interesting to a number
of your readers. In the commencement of the war of 1861,
I enlisted from Cleveland, Ohio, in the Union cause, to
sustain intact the Government of the United States, and
became attached to the 23d Regiment, one of the first sent
from the "Buckeye State." Our destination was West
Virginia, a portion of the wildest and most mountainous
region of that State, well adapted for the guerillas who
infested that part and caused such trouble to our pickets
all through the war. After an arduous march of several
hundred miles through Clarksburgh, Weston, Sommer-
ville and several other places of less note, which have
become famous during the war, we encountered on the
10th of September, 1861, at Carnifax Ferry, the forces
under the rebel Gen. Floyd. After this, we were ordered
to take up our position at the foot of Sewell Mountain,
and we remained there until we marched to the village of
Fayette, to take it and to establish there our Winter
quarters, having again routed Gen. Floyd and his forces.
While lying there, our camp duties were not of an arduous
character, and being apprised of the approaching Feast
of Passover, twenty of my comrades and co-religionists
belonging to the Regiment united in a request to our
commanding officer for relief from duty, in order that we
might keep the holidays, which he readily acceded to. The
first point was gained, and, as the Paymaster had lately
visited the Regiment, he had left us plenty of greenbacks.
Our next business was to find some suitable person to
proceed to Cincinnati, Ohio, to buy us *matzos*. Our sutler,
being a co-religionist and going home to that city, readily
undertook to send them. We were anxiously awaiting to
receive our מצות and about the middle of the morning of
ערב פסח a supply train arrived in camp, and to our delight
seven barrels of *matzos*. On opening them, we were
surprised and pleased to find that our thoughtful sutler
had enclosed two Hagodahs and prayer books. We were
now able to keep the סדר nights, if we could only obtain
the other requisites for that occasion. We held a consulta-

52

tion and decided to send parties to forage in the country, while a party stayed to build a log hut for the services. About the middle of the afternoon the foragers arrived, having been quite successful. We obtained two kegs of cider, a lamb, several chickens and some eggs. Horseradish or parsley we could not obtain, but in lieu we found a weed, whose bitterness, I apprehend, exceeded anything our forefathers "enjoyed." We were still in a great quandary; we were like the man who drew the elephant in the lottery. We had the lamb, but did not know what part was to represent it at the table; but Yankee ingenuity prevailed, and it was decided to cook the whole and put it on the table; then we could dine off it, and be sure we had the right part. The necessaries for the *choroutzes* we could not obtain, so we got a brick which, rather hard to digest, reminded us, by looking at it, for what purpose it was intended.

At dark we had all prepared, and were ready to commence the service. There being no *Chasan* present, I was selected to read the services, which I commenced by asking the blessing of the Almighty on the food before us, and to preserve our lives from danger. The ceremonies were passing off very nicely, until we arrived at the part where the bitter herb was to be taken. We all had a large portion of the herb ready to eat at the moment I said the blessing; each ate his portion, when horrors! what a scene ensued in our little congregation it is impossible for my pen to describe. The herb was very bitter and very fiery like cayenne pepper, and excited our thirst to such a degree that we forgot the law authorizing us to drink only four cups, and the consequence was we drank up all the cider. Those that drank the more freely became excited, and one thought he was Moses, another Aaron, and one had the audacity to call himself a pharaoh. The consequence was a skirmish, with nobody hurt—only Moses, Aaron and Pharaoh had to be carried to the camp, and there left in the arms of Morpheus. This slight incident did not take away our appetite and, after doing justice to our lamb,

53

chickens and eggs, we resumed the second portion of the service without anything occurring worthy of note.

There, in the wild woods of West Virginia, away from home and friends, we consecrated and offered up to the ever-loving God of Israel our prayers and sacrifice. I doubt whether the spirits of our forefathers, had they been looking down on us, standing there with our arms by our side ready for an attack, faithful to our God and our cause, would have imagined themselves amongst mortals enacting this commemoration of the scene that transpired in Egypt.

Since then a number of my comrades have fallen in battle in defending the flag they volunteered to protect with their lives. I have myself received a number of wounds all but mortal, but there is no occasion in my life that gives me more pleasure and satisfaction than when I remember the celebration of Passover of 1862.

The Last Passover in the Warsaw Ghetto*•

WLADYSLAW PAWLAK

The people in the dugout were not sure whether it was day or night. Only the entry of a handful of men was their signal that the sun had set over the fighting ghetto. The newcomers were five men. Abram Rosze was their leader, the man in charge of the entire group hiding in this bunker. He was called "Commander." He was 28 and the oldest of them. And he had a gun. Not heeding the tense faces of those inside, he proceeded to give orders.

* A fictional account based upon real characters and opinions they expressed a few days before the uprising in the Warsaw Ghetto actually took place.

He was assigning posts to those who had to remain on duty. Two men were to stand guard above ground, one at the entrance to the passage leading to the cellars above their heads. The rest could go to sleep.

The questions which had tortured them all along now came in a downpour. For this was April 19, 1943, the first day in the defense of the ghetto. The men gave their answers reluctantly, haphazardly. What could they reply to that stereotyped question: "What's new?" which reflected all their hopes and fears? What should they tell them? That the Germans were using their powerful tanks, armored cars, flamethrowers and machine guns? That against this fiendish might they—a handful of desperate men—fought? Their voices lowered to half whispers were tense, making more noise than ordinary speech. Bluntly Rosze broke the spell, speaking up in his normal voice:

"There is no doubt what our situation is like. The Germans began the attack at dawn. The gunfire was violent, but our losses were light. They tried to block the sewers, but our men managed to blow up the obstructions. The passage to the other side is still clear. The Germans withdrew before nightfall. They are sure to return tomorrow."

The whole group listened with bated breath, trying to draw courage from his words. They needed it badly. They wanted to believe that the Germans would leave them alone and let them some way survive in their caves, that they would one day see the sun again, and breathe once more the air of outdoors.

They were taking apart Rosze's words, weighing their chances of survival, and reaching the same tragic conclusions over and over again. Gradually they subsided into silence and the solitude of their own thoughts.

Again Rosze's voice aroused them from their torpor.

"Distribute the food. There is no point in despairing. We knew what would be the outcome, and we know what our line of action must be. Light two more candles, take

55

out the biscuits and let us have some sugared water. No cooking."

Two women brought along a basketful of dried bread, a bag of sugar and jugs with water. As they were distributing the rations, a voice spoke out from one of the corners:

"Do you know what day this is?"

The answers came half mockingly, half annoyed at such an irrelevant question.

"Monday." "The 19th of April."

The questioner was not deterred.

"No, no, I don't mean that. But do you know that today is a holiday?"

"What, is he crazy?" "A fine sort of a holiday this is!" "We're dying and he blabbers about holidays." And so the comments ran on.

Szmul Gelber, a homely fellow and one of the oldest in the group, rose from his bunk. His usually calm and friendly eyes were shining. He seemed very tall as he towered above them.

"And I am telling you, today is a great holiday. It is Passover, the Seder night."

All the tenseness of his words could not pierce the wall of stubborn indifference. Some tried to calm him with casual remarks:

"A holiday? So what?" "This is no time for celebrating." "If it makes you happy, why don't you conduct Seder for yourself?" "Passover without *matzot!* What kind of Passover is that?"

Gelber seemed to grow even more in stature. The indifference of those present spurred him on. He seized a piece of black bread, dry as shavings and hard as wood, and called out:

"Verily, I say unto you, this is the bread of affliction, such as our forefathers never knew in the land of Egypt."

A deep silence fell over them all of a sudden. Gelber shrank into himself again and sitting down on an improvised bench sighed mournfully:

"I haven't got a Haggadah, and I don't remember the

56

words. I've never been for religion in all my life, but I am longing for the old traditions of our own."

Now they begged him to conduct the Seder by heart, just as he remembered it, and they would help him in every way they could. Gelber protested:

"There are no *matzot,* no bitter herbs, no lamb's bone. There are none of these things that symbolize the clay of Egypt. How am I to conduct the Seder for you?"

Abram Rosze, the commander, who had silently followed the conversation, cut the knot with these words:

"We need no bitter herbs. Sufficient bitterness and humiliation have been our lot. Are we not slaves? Are we not orphans who have been forsaken? We need no wine, let us drink water."

And another added:

"We need no *matzot.* As Gelber said, this bread tastes more bitter than the *matzot* of Egypt. He has begun, let him proceed."

Gelber looked upon the piece of bread in his hand, he looked upon the cup of water at his feet and intoned in a sad voice:

"Let all who are hungry come in and eat. Let all who are needy come to our Passover feast."

The irony of this traditional formula was felt like a sting by these men and women who were seeking refuge in this underground hideout so as to prolong their lives by a few days. To feed . . . to feast . . . Those were fine words, tokens of an age-old tradition of hospitality which today had become meaningless in the world that they had to face.

Chaim Sztork interrupted the silence.

"I am the youngest. It behooves me to ask the questions:

"Why is this night different from all other nights?

"On all other nights we may eat either leavened or unleavened bread, but on Passover night only unleavened bread . . . *And why do we have neither leavened nor unleavened bread this night?*

"On all other nights we may eat any kind of herbs, but

on this night only bitter herbs . . . *And why do we have neither sweet nor bitter herbs this night?*

"On all other nights we do not dip even once, but on this night twice . . . *And why is it all the same to us this night?*

"On all other nights we eat either sitting or leaning, but on this night we all lean . . . *And why do we neither sit nor lean this night?"*

Led on by the familiar rhythm, Gelber replied:

"Because we were slaves unto Pharaoh in Egypt . . ." and he continued the biblical tale of the Egyptian bondage, how they were beaten and harassed, and how they built the two cities for the Pharaoh. And he told them how Moses came to them, how he killed the surveyor and cursed the people of Egypt . . .

They listened in silence, but when he came to enumerate the plagues, they repeated in a chorus:

"Blood, Frogs, Lice, Beasts, Blight, Boils, Hail, Locust, Darkness, Slaying of the First-Born."

As they proceeded, their voices became more and more vengeful, and they spoke the words in anger. No one was thinking of the ancient past in the valley of the Nile. The oppressor they faced was a hundredfold worse. He was alive and powerful, and only a few walls and the dusk of spring night separated him from them.

When they had finished with the plagues, Gelber resumed the tale. He came to the words:

"And the Lord has freed us from the bondage of Egypt."

"It's a lie!" interrupted Chaim Szter. "It's a lie, I'm telling you. God has never freed us from bondage, for it followed us wherever we go. We were slaves by the rivers of Babylon; Spain was one big prison; and so were the ghettos of the Middle Ages."

One great cry of despair rose from their lips.

"Woe unto us, we are slaves, and as slaves do we die."

"Quiet!" The commander spoke, and his words had the power of shots. "Fools! He was right who said that

58

today we celebrate a holiday. Passover is a holiday of freedom. Don't you see that we are free? No longer do we listen to orders. They tell us: Come out of your hiding—and we refuse to come out. They lure us with promises, and we answer with gunfire. We have thrown off the bands which they made us wear for our humiliation, and we turned them into banners. Today is the day of freedom, and that freedom is within us.

"Do not seek it in a restful and comfortable life, but rather seek it within your own hearts and souls. Do not think of victory and glory, of homes and riches. Remember that thousands of our dear ones died before us, and that we too must perish. We will go down in defeat but we will die as free men and women. Let us be proud and honor our dead."

"*El male rahamim*—God of mercy, that art enthroned on high," rang out the words of the prayer for the deceased. The voice of the commander sounded firm and clear among all the others. ". . . accept the souls of the millions who have perished and the souls of us who must perish tomorrow." And when the sacramental "Amen" had died away, they added these words:

"For the day of our defeat will be the day of our glory."

G.I. Passover in World War II[10]

"Tonight you are eating unleavened bread just as your forebears ate unleavened bread because the Exodus came so quickly the dough had no time to rise." The speaker was Lieutenant General Mark W. Clark, Commander of the U.S. Fifth Army, addressing thousands of Jewish

59

men and women of his command, and their guests of other faiths, who had gathered for a Seder on the hard-fought road to Rome.

The general's words were not of antiquity but of the present. "There was a time of unleavened bread in this war," he said. "The time when it looked as though we might not have time to rise—time to raise an army and equip it, time to stop the onrush of a Germany that was already risen. But the bread has begun to rise. It started at Alamein. It was rising higher when the Fifth Army invaded Italy. It is reaching the top of the pan and soon the time will come when it will spread out and into a finished product."

That note of optimism, of buoyant hope, which found its inspiration in the symbol of an historic deliverance was sounded on lands and seas throughout the globe, wherever men and women of the American fighting forces were sitting down to Seder. Sergeant Barney Ross of the Marines had voiced it, too, when he came back, invalided after Guadalcanal. In a radio broadcast on Passover eve, he had declared:

"There is going to be a Seder tonight for the Jewish boys in Guadalcanal. A couple of months ago it didn't look that way. Shells were exploding all around me then. Waves of bombing planes were coming over and I hid in a foxhole that had been getting a little deeper every day since I dug it.

"I couldn't have imagined that in a few months I'd be standing here before a microphone, talking about Passover, or that Guadalcanal would be completely in American hands with Jewish men among our troops there holding Seder out in the open air to celebrate both our victory on Guadalcanal and the victory of the children of Israel who fought for freedom against Pharaoh."

At an advanced base on New Guinea, six hundred men had gathered for Seder, prepared in an army's mobile cooker, served in the Red Cross hut. Somewhere on the mainland, the supply officer had promised the fantastic

60

luxury of chicken, and a special detail of men had been selected to go fishing for the Seder meal.

In covering his command, which involved traveling 10,000 miles by air, thousands by water and jeep, Chaplain Eleazar A. Levi had come down with malaria and tropical fever. But he had persuaded the medical officer to permit him to remain and conduct the Seder. He organized seven Seders on New Guinea, one in a cocoa-nut grove within sight and sound of the Japanese lines.

To all the officers and men celebrating the historic deliverance of their people, the commanding officer of the base had issued this inspiring message:

"The ideals of personal freedom suggested by the story of the Exodus are part of the American tradition. It should be of particular significance to you that this year you are observing this festival under the circumstances in which we now find ourselves.

"The struggle in which we are engaged is the struggle to deliver all mankind from the slavery of a new and more dangerous pharaoh than that of ancient Egypt.

"We shall have many hardships and heartbreaks before victory is won, but win we will; and with our hands and hearts strengthened by faith in God, we shall restore to the people of the earth the God-given freedom set forth in the Bible in the account of the deliverance of your ancestors from that other pharaoh."

A gigantic task of world-wide organization, begun months before by the National Jewish Welfare Board, had been fulfilled. Tons of *matzot*, tens of thousands of Haggadahs, some printed by the army itself when actual requirements fell short of estimated needs, had reached their destinations in India, China, Burma, Iraq, Alaska, Newfoundland, Greenland, Hawaii, Australia, Great Britain, North Africa, at battle stations, naval bases around the globe, on convoys and battleships at sea. In North Africa, Chaplain Earl Stone, advancing with the liberating Allied armies across Tunisia, paused at every town, as it was freed from the Axis, to arrange with the local rabbi and leading Jews for community Seders for Jewish soldiers, leaving *matzot* and other Passover supplies. Army flour was issued to Jewish bakers, who prepared the unleavened bread in the ancient kilns and manner of their forefathers.

On the Gold Coast of Middle Africa, a Christian chaplain of much energy and sincere devotion arranged three Sedarim for 275 Jewish men. Fearful lest his Passover supplies might not arrive in time, he had ordered supplies from Egypt before the JWB shipment arrived.

Chaplain David Rubin, in Iran, had a "hunch" that 'his supplies could not reach the Middle East in time. He wired the American Consulate in Jerusalem and verified his fears—no transportation had been available. Whatever Passover supplies the men in this widely scattered area were to have would need to be produced on the spot. He asked the army for its help. Flour was issued. The field bakery and its staff were turned over to him. Some necessary tools were available. Others were specially made by ordnance. New pans, new utensils were procured, all baking of bread halted. Army bakers kneaded and rolled and hemstitched, until a plentiful supply of *matzot* for the area was assured. Then, traveling by plane and jeep and ferry, the chaplain commenced his reconnaissance tour. At every airfield and camp, he hunted up cooperative military personnel and civilians, made arrangements for Seder services, drew flour from quartermasters' supplies, taught army cooks to bake unleavened bread. At one encampment where the bakery could not be used, he found an old field oven of brick and mud, fired it with a blowtorch and supervised detachments of Allied and American soldiers who volunteered to bake "the bread of affliction."

Chaplain Rubin extended his search to find supplies of wine. The warehouses of the British NAAFI yielded four cases of Palestinian sherry. He divided it, quotas for each encampment, supplies for a small group of men at a lonely gulf port, at a hot, dusty military resort in the foothills further north. He returned to his own station to direct the task of bringing five hundred dishes on the heads of native porters over six miles of rocky, rutted roads into camp. The men had declined to eat *knaidlach* from their mess kits and their Seder feast was eaten from brand-new dishes rented from native bazaars.

"You will understand," the chaplain wrote afterwards, "how unbelievably like home everything was and what an effort it was to beg, borrow and buy the materials to make this the grandest Seder I have ever had the pleasure of conducting. All of this would not have been possible without the coordination and cooperation of the soldiers. In all there were six Seders in this command that were carefully supervised and arranged. There may have been several others, to which supplies were sent via the chaplains. Wherever we knew of Allied troops of the Jewish faith, we invited them to be our guests . . . This was the first Passover away from home and in a foreign land. We did the best we could and were happy in so doing. All of us closed the Seder with the hope and the prayer to be home for Seder next year with our families and our friends, in our blessed land, with a victory that will bring peace and healing to stricken peoples everywhere and justice and security to us and all humanity."

No such primitive demands of supplies and contacts affected the plans for observance of the holiday in the Carribean and Hawaiian theaters of the war. There the problem was the staggering one of organization for hospitality on a mass scale. In the Canal Zone, 2,000 servicemen and women were guests at JWB Sedarim on the Atlantic and Pacific sides. Seders were held in the USO Club, a Scottish Rite Temple, the Balboa Union Church, the Panama City Congregation and in a hotel. The bakers and cooks school at Corozal was for three days used exclusively for Passover preparations. New utensils and silverware were provided by the army. In the Hawaiian area, the Army Transport Service delivered two and a half tons of *matzot*, and other Passover products, 100 gallons of wine, 7,000 Haggadahs for 12 Seders held within this theater of war. Supplies were flown to Midway and other distant islands. In the British Isles, more than a dozen community Seders were held and hundreds of homes opened to soldier guests.

In the heart of Australia, three Jewish local residents were guests of the Jewish soldiers at their Seder. Said one of these civilians: "This is the first Seder I have attended in thirty years. Until now I had been worried about the continuity of our people. With only three of us within hundreds of miles, and with stories of the virtual wiping out of Jewry in central Europe, I had begun to believe that perhaps our stock was dying out. Suddenly, I see several hundred young vigorous American Jews and now I know that our people are still carrying on. This splendid sight warms my heart, for it is a token that, come what may to you or me, our people will go on forever."

Passover Letters from the Desert[11]

MOSHE MOSENSON

A Palestinian Jew in the British Army

March 13, 1942

You write that you wish that I could come to the Seder. My little girl! My comrades and I will celebrate the Passover very far from our country this year. The Passover holiday is the holiday of spring and of liberation. And we are all working for another liberation, both the soldiers here and you and the other comrades at home. It is difficult for us to celebrate the spring here. The desert does not have a springtime. There is only bitter cold or blazing heat and always the same dust storms and the

same barren desolation. The spring that we love so much
never comes here at all. When we, too, speak of the
spring here, we mean the day of the great attack when—
we hope and pray—the enemy will be beaten and liberation will be achieved.

But write me how the Seder is at home.

Here, too, in our unit, we are preparing for the Seder.
It will be different from your Seder at home. I will write
you about our Seder and you write me about yours at
home, right away.

March 15, 1942

I visited some of the marvelous relics here, the tombs
of the kings of Egypt. During the winter, tourists from
all over the world visit here, but now, during the war, this
stream of visitors has ceased. This is a whole city built
over ruins, an ancient Egyptian city. There is great wealth
and treasure buried here. It's amazing to see the walls of
the caves covered with drawings in a very cultivated style,
with colors that are still fresh today and that you could
swear had been mixed only a decade instead of four
thousand years ago. The bodies of these kings have also
been preserved for thousands of years. This is an entire
city of tombs in which whole dynasties are buried. In one
of the tombs lies the Minister of Agriculture for Egypt,
and on the walls are pictures representing the processes of
agriculture and the functions of the Egyptian farmer, all
in brilliant and lively colors.

When you walk about among these enormous relics of
remote history, you feel like a dwarf against the background of this lofty past. But even when you are most
impressed by the brilliant art that flourished thousands of
years ago, you cannot forbear asking: Where are they
all today? Where are their heirs and the bearers of their
tradition and their art? Sunk into oblivion. But we, a small
tribe, oppressed and enslaved by them, we who were
slaves here, creatures without culture, without art, without science or architecture—we fled from this and were

65

purified by forty years of wandering and we built our civilization and then were exiled and scattered, martyred in every country, slaughtered, burned and plundered—and we are still alive. Today, after four thousand years, I, the great-great grandson of those very slaves, walk among their ruins, visit their tombs and admire the wealth and the culture that reigned here and that have been petrified by death.

March 26, 1942

This is my second Seder away from home and I feel very sad about it. When I picture to myself how our dining room looks on a holiday evening—with all the light shining in the eyes of the comrades—I am overcome by homesickness. It seems to me that this year there is a deeper yearning in this festival of freedom. For actually we, too, are at a point in history where we must fight for freedom, the freedom of our people and the freedom of man. If I were at home this year, I would suggest that we renew an old folk-tradition on the Seder night, the tradition of Elijah's cup. We should set aside a whole table in the dining room, set the same as the other tables, but with no one sitting at it. This would be the table for all the thousands and tens of thousands of people whose personal and national freedom has been crushed by the Nazis, while our very existence depends on their liberation and their joining us.

On the eve of the festival of freedom we, in the camp that is fighting for freedom, can have no rest because of the thought that we, too, are not pure; for the air is not clean of oppression and slavery in our own camp, for whose victory we fight. Nevertheless, we believe that the freedom of the individual and the nation will be the cornerstones of the post-war world.

Festival of Spring in an Israeli Kibbutz[12]

SYBIL ROGOW LANGER

"Is the day done?" questions the reaper,
And the people answer, "Yea, yea."

It is the hour before sundown, and the central courtyard is filling up fast with the men, women and children of the kibbutz and their guests from the nearby cities. Men greet each other; the women, in their gaily embroidered blouses, smile and murmur; the children wear a look of excited expectation, and some of the younger set need restraining. To one side stands a stone arch around which have been twined glowing masses of orange gladioli, burnt-umber poppies, and what appear to be big fat roses, each as wide as a cake.

It is the eve of Passover, and the ceremonies—time-honored and time-ripened, yet infused with new meanings—are about to begin. As in all other kibbutzim of Israel, the Passover here, in this farming community of 600 souls inhabiting the northern gateway to the fertile Jezreel Valley, will be celebrated in unique fashion, with individual color and beauty. For Passover is, in origin, a festival of the spring and of the soil, and these people are farmers, whose life is the soil.

Soon the company of celebrants forms itself into a procession behind an appointed leader, and the people march, singing, beneath the arch of flowers, out to one of the fields, where barley is ripening, and where the *Omer* ceremony is to take place. Some of the men carry farm implements and thick sticks of resinous wood. Here and there a couple walk arm in arm. More than ever, Israel's sky looks like an inverted bowl.

67

Gathering at the side of a slight hill overlooking a natural platform of flat ground, the singers halt. Within eye-catching distance rises the Carmel range and, more westerly, the bareness of Gilboa, that David cursed; shortly, it may be possible to glimpse the lights of Haifa, twenty miles north.

Now the leader steps forward and in a ringing voice begins a catechism of prayer and hope. Or a hymn to earth is chanted: strophe, antistrophe; leader, people, leader, people.

A few of the men go into the barley field with their scythes. Some women follow them, bind the cut barley into sheaves, and carry it, for stacking, to a cart made elegant for the occasion by festoons of fresh flowers.

Then dancing follows—in peasant costume, and participated in with extra enthusiasm by the older children. Besides the traditional *horas* and folk-dances, there are also slower, more sophisticated dances, ballet style, which seem to have been prepared in advance for the festivity.

Suddenly, a young girl, not more than sixteen, dressed in a simple white blouse and white, full skirt, steps forward. She wears no lipstick. Her wide-apart eyes tilt upward and her smooth cheeks are flushed. She wears her hair in two calm, silken braids as thick as her own wrist, falling to her waist. When she dances, as someone plays a flute, the braids mark their own melodic patterns upon the air. Her dance tells of Miriam, the sister of Moses, dancing her dance of triumph on the banks of the Red Sea. At its conclusion she sinks to the ground, her gestures all grace, and her skirt billows down slowly after her.

By this time, the swift Palestinian night has fallen. The stars are very blue, very steady. The black is velvet. The men light their torches and, by starlight and firelight, the procession sings itself back to the central courtyard, where all disperse to make ready for the Seder.

The Seder takes place in the large main dining room of the kibbutz. At the individual tables, arranged in holiday fashion, beakers of flowers have been set—wine for the soul in Israel. Again, the room itself will have been especially decorated—perhaps with a frieze of ancient Judean coins (a cup of wine, a bunch of grapes, a lamb), executed with loving exactitude by the kibbutz artist.

The barley which has been cut in the fields is brought into the dining room, heaped in stacks in the center, a symbolic offering. The choir sings (mature voices, grave voices, fresh young voices) old and new songs, both much loved; while some of the youngsters sit squirmily in their seats, as if trying to hide their impatience for dinner—a dinner justly awaited for its excellence and the presence of unusual quantities of meat or chicken.

Everyone, of course, has his or her own Haggadah, but unlike the custom of the Diaspora, reading is done in turn, each reader standing up in his own place. Readings are interspersed with songs, and some parts of the Haggadah are sung to melodies invented by the *populus loci* and fixed by repetition.

There are two or three courses more than the usual kibbutz fare, and the watchword for tonight is "gusto."

By about eleven o'clock, the formal part of the festivity is over. Very likely, someone with a strong sense of rhythm and a guitar will set off another cycle of singing and dancing. The older people join in some of the dance groups, but for the most part just watch with happy faces; the young wear themselves out. And this continues till, at about 4 a.m., the general "good-nights" give way to general silence.

The emergence into freedom, which the Passover traditionally recalls, has also a special meaning and poignancy here in this newly independent land, many of whose citizens have been only recently liberated from fear and from dread. This release, like the release of nature in the springtime, the kibbutz celebrates in song, in dance, and in the joy of the heart.

THE DEVELOPMENT OF THE PASSOVER HAGGADAH

The Haggadah, the book that presents the order of the home service for the first two evenings of Passover,[1] occupies a unique place in Jewish liturgy. It is an anthology of readings from the Bible, appropriate talmudic and midrashic selections and legends, prayers and blessings, hymns and songs. All these are interwoven with the ritual for the Seder—the order of the service.

Product of many hands, the Haggadah has had a long development. The antiquity of the Haggadah, having its origin in the Bible, has been well established. Certain portions antedate the period of the Maccabees. Its present character was largely formed by about 200 C.E., for it is described in some detail in the Mishnah, compiled by Rabbi Judah the Patriarch at that time. It was further embellished, however, during the course of succeeding centuries.

The spirit pervading the Haggadah is one of longing for redemption and freedom, a belief in the survival of the Jewish people and an unyielding confidence in divine salvation. It was, therefore, natural for this work to capture the hearts of the Jewish people in all generations and to give them a sense of pride in Jewish destiny and broad perspectives on the precious values of freedom and liberty for all mankind.

Endeared to Jews, the Haggadah has appeared in innumerable editions—printed, illuminated, illustrated—some without commentaries and one with as many as 238 commentaries. More than a score of translations of the Haggadah have been made and it has been adapted in various ways to serve different needs and interests.

THE PURPOSE OF THE HAGGADAH

The purpose of the Haggadah,[2] or "The Narrative," is generally attributed to the biblical injunction: *And thou shalt tell* (ve-higadta) *thy son on that day, saying: It is because of that which the Lord did for me when I came forth out of Egypt* (Ex. 13.8). This passage sets forth the obligation to narrate the account of the Exodus; this took place originally at the family feast of the paschal lamb. A close examination of the Pentateuchal laws concerning the paschal lamb substantiates this explanation, according to Professor Solomon Zeitlin. The lamb, slaughtered on the fourteenth day of Nisan, was eaten by each household (*ibid.*, 12.3-4,21). From this, Dr. Zeitlin deduces that there was a family gathering which lasted all night (*ibid.*, 22) and that the people spent the time relating the history of the Exodus.[3] Notwithstanding the cessation of sacrifices following the destruction of the Temple, the festive meal continued to be held. Now the *Zeroa* on the Seder plate—a bone with roasted meat attached to it —serves as a reminder of the paschal lamb.

The responsibility of parents to tell their children about the miraculous deliverance from Egyptian bondage is emphasized in four different passages of the Bible.[4] This recurring biblical command undoubtedly accounts for the redaction of the Haggadah and its widespread popularity. The fourfold repetition of the injunction, the rabbis explained, was to serve the needs of different types of children; hence, the Four Sons concept was developed and included.

The Haggadah incorporates various pedagogic devices to stimulate children to attend to its content and message. Thus Jewish children and parents have always had a common share in this literary heritage bequeathed from generation to generation. But the Haggadah is not merely a juvenile masterpiece. According to Maimonides, the reading of the Haggadah is reckoned as one of the positive commandments of the Torah that are incumbent upon all Jews:

"It is a positive commandment of the Law to narrate the miracles and wonders that happened to our ancestors in Egypt on the night of the fifteenth of Nisan, as it is said: *Remember this day, in which ye came out from Egypt* (Ex. 13.3)."[5]

THE REDACTION OF THE HAGGADAH

The oldest portions of the Haggadah are Psalms 113 and 114. One authority has claimed that they were sung by the Levites in the pre-Ptolemaic Passover rites observed when Palestine was still under the rule of Persia. They were known as the "Egyptian *Hallel*," as the latter psalm deals with the Exodus and the former serves as an introduction. Later, this name was applied to the entire *Hallel*. In the Haggadah, the "Passover *Hallel*," Psalms 113-118, is divided into two parts: the first part, consisting of two psalms, is said before the meal, and the remainder of the *Hallel* is recited following the Grace after the Meal.[6]

A further analysis of the Haggadah reveals that substantial portions may have originated in the pre-Maccabean period, possibly as early as the third century B.C.E. These selections include the first introductory statement: "We were Pharaoh's slaves in Egypt . . ."; the second or alternative opening: "In the beginning our ancestors were idolators . . ."; the Midrash on Deuteronomy 26.5-8: "Go forth and learn . . .," which is the sum and substance of the reply to the Four Questions; and the hymn *Dayyenu:* "It would have been sufficient for us . . ."

The first introduction is believed to have been composed in the third century B.C.E., reflecting the reaction in Palestine to the sovereignty of Egypt which prevailed at that time. The second introduction, intended to stress

מְגִיד הַמְּבִיאֵל הֲדָבָרִים
אֲשֶׁר לֹא יֶעֱרוֹך
הַמַּמְלָכָה אֲשֶׁר בַּשֵּׁם

Darmstadt Haggadah

6. The Rabbis at B'ne B'rak and the Four Sons

Haggadah, British Museum

7. Carrying the Symbolic Foods

Nuremberg Haggadah

8. The Wicked Son

Haggadah, British Museum

9. Washing the Passover Vessels in the Mikvah

Haggadah, British Museum

10. The Exodus and the Crossing

the antiquity of Israel and its origin in Mesopotamia rather than in Egypt, as might be deduced from the first introduction, is attributed to the high priest Jason, 175-172 B.C.E.[7] It is also claimed that he was the author of the *Dayyenu*.[8]

Particularly interesting from the historical and theological viewpoints is the midrashic commentary on Deuteronomy 26.5-8, likewise attributed to the pre-mishnaic period, which begins thus:

> Go forth and learn what Laban, the Aramean, plotted against our father, Jacob. While Pharaoh decreed death for the male children only, Laban planned to uproot us all. As it is said: "An Aramean sought my father's death . . ."

According to Professor Louis Finkelstein, the statement that Laban—symbolic of the Syrian king—was more cruel than Pharaoh was included as a gesture to pacify the Egyptians because the Ptolemies then ruled Palestine. Yet the Midrash also implies a protest against emigration to Egypt and a plea to Egyptian Jewry to avoid assimilation:

> *And he* [my father] *went down into Egypt:* he was compelled to do so by the Divine decree . . .
> *And there he became a nation:* this teaches that the Israelites were a distinctive people there.

The historical setting of the above selections helps date this Midrash. Further evidence is found in the controversial theological views of the Midrash including the denial that angels participated in the Exodus and that God visibly appeared:

> *And the Lord brought us forth from Egypt.* Not by the hands of an angel, nor by the hands of a fiery seraph, nor by the hands of a messenger; but the Holy One, blessed be He, Himself . . .
> *And with great awe:* this is the visible manifestation of the Divine Presence . . .

73

Such theological views were "opposed by the main body of the Pharisees, viz., the plebeians, though they received some support from the patrician minority of the Order. It is inconceivable that, after the organization of the Pharisaic Order, either doctrine could have been included in a tract intended for universal use on the Passover night. Their inclusion [in the Midrash] indicates that it originated before the rise of the Pharisaic Order, and therefore before the Maccabean period. The subjects of angels and the appearance of God in visible form were already controversial issues, however; and the compiler was trying to use the Passover celebration to foist his opinions on the people."[9]

By the time the Mishnah was compiled in the second century C.E., the contents of the Haggadah including the ritual for the eve of Passover were largely formulated as we know and read them today. The "Questions" to be asked by the son, a passage which is still a highlight of the ceremonial, is found in the Mishnah; it includes the following: "On all other nights we eat meat roasted, stewed, or cooked; why on this night only roast?"[10] This substantiates that the "Questions," although only three, were already in use during the period of the Second Temple when the paschal lamb was sacrificed as an offering and roasted and eaten at the home celebrations.[11] After the destruction of the Temple, the question concerning leaning—an outmoded custom—was substituted for the one about the roast offering. The question about bitter herbs was also a later addition.[12]

The Mishnah also contains Rabban Gamaliel's formula: "Whosoever has not said [the verses concerning] these three things on Passover has not fulfilled his obligation. And these are they: Pesach, *matzah* (unleavened bread) and *maror* (bitter herbs) . . ."[13] These passages are a direct though partial response to the Four Questions.[14]

The pivotal passage of the Haggadah—"Every person in every generation must regard himself as having been

74

personally freed from Egypt . . ."—is based on the Mishnah.[15] The *Kiddush* and the order of the four cups is likewise found in this source.[16]

The Mishnah also prescribes the benediction on redemption and the benediction on song, which follow the first and second parts of the *Hallel*, respectively.

Additions to the Haggadah relating to Israel's bondage in Egypt were made by the early Amoraim in the third century, for the Mishnah states that one is obligated to begin the narration by recalling the degradation of the Israelites when they were slaves and to conclude with the glory that they achieved.[17] Thus, the two alternate introductions—"We were slaves of Pharaoh in Egypt . . ." and "In the beginning our ancestors were idolators . . ." —both commence with recalling the shame of our forebears.[18] At different times one or the other introduction was used. When the Haggadah was redacted both were included.

Further midrashic interpretations were added during the period of the Gaonim (6th to 11th century). One of these is that of the four types of son, found in the Jerusalem Talmud[19] and the *Mekhilta de-Rabbi Ishmael,*[20] who raise different questions.[21] The sons are to be instructed by the father in accordance with their ability to understand.[22] The questions are actually rooted in the Pentateuch—the wise son: *What mean the testimonies, and the statutes, and the ordinances . . . ?* (Deut. 6.20); the wicked son: *What mean ye by this service?* (Ex. 12.26); the simple son: *What is this?* (*ibid.*, 13.14); and the one who does not know how to ask: *And thou shalt tell thy son . . .* (*ibid.*, 13.8).

The story of the five rabbis of the second century C.E. —Eliezer, Joshua, Eleazer ben Azariah, Akiba and Tarfon—who spent the entire night in B'ne B'rak recounting the Exodus from Egypt is not found elsewhere in rabbinic literature.[23]

A number of other selections became part of the Haggadah in later generations. *Pour out Thy wrath . . .,*[24]

a group of biblical verses protesting against cruel out-
rages and invoking retribution on heathens, was introduced during the Middle Ages when the Jews were
subjected to false accusations and dire persecutions, particularly during the Passover season.[25]

The portions previously mentioned, with different variations, comprised the Haggadah that was common to all
Jews. Most of the selections were formulated during
the period of the Tannaim. These formed the basis for the
Haggadah included by Rav Amram Gaon, *ca.* 850, in the
Siddur, the daily prayer book, which he edited. The prayer
book of Rav Saadia Gaon (10th century) presents the
earliest complete text of the Haggadah, although its beginning varies from the current one. The version in
Mahzor Vitry (11th century) is more nearly the same as
that in vogue today. The *Mishneh Torah* of Maimonides
(1135-1204) contains the text of the Haggadah which
is essentially the same as in present use. Incomplete versions of the Haggadah have been found in the Cairo
Genizah.

The earliest individual manuscripts of the Haggadah
probably did not appear before the twelfth century. None
of these included the poems that were later appended.

An adaptation of a poem, "The Passover Seder is
Complete," by Joseph Tob Elam, was added in the
eleventh century. With the publicaton of the Haggadah
as a separate volume, German and Polish Jews added a
number of hymns, the first four being coincidentally
alphabetical acrostics. "And so it came to pass in the
middle of the night . . . ," a poem by Rav Jannai, the early
Palestinian, which is also included in the Ashkenazi liturgy
for the Sabbath before Passover, enumerates historical
events that, according to the Midrash,[26] occurred on the
night of Passover. Another hymn, by Eleazar Kalir, uses
as a refrain the phrase: "And ye shall say: *It is the sacrifice of the Lord's Passover"* (Ex. 12.27). The author of
"It is proper to praise Him" *(Ki Lo Na'eh)* is unknown.
"Mighty is He" *(Addir Hu)* already appears in the

Darmstadt Haggadah of the fourteenth century. There are also two so-called "nursery songs"—*Ehad Mi Yode'a* (Who Knows One?) and *Had Gadya* (An Only Kid). The former is a counting rhyme while the latter has been interpreted as a ballad of divine retribution with the "only kid" as a symbol of Israel. "Who knows One" and "An Only Kid" first appeared in print in a Haggadah published in 1590 in Prague by the family of Gershom Cohen.[27]

THE PRINTED HAGGADAH

Undoubtedly more different printed editions of the Haggadah have been published than any other Jewish book. At the beginning of this century, Samuel Wiener recorded 909 Haggadahs.[28] These editions include a total of 370 different commentaries and translations in thirteen languages. Wiener was well aware that his bibliography was only a partial listing and urged others to fill in the gaps. However, it was not until three decades later that other bibliographers began to add hundreds of editions to the original record.[29] The library of the Jewish Theological Seminary of America alone has a collection of 2,000 different editions.[30] The bibliographer Abraham Yaari has listed 2,713 editions of the Haggadah, printed in 170 places.[31]

The *editio princeps* was printed in Guadalajara, Spain, about 1482. The next edition made its appearance four years later in Soncino, Italy.

The earliest extant Haggadah with a commentary, that of Don Isaac Abarbanel, was published in Constantinople in 1505.

Three leaves in the library of the Jewish Theological Seminary of America have been identified as having been part of the first illustrated printed Haggadah that may have appeared in Spain or Portugal before the expulsions from those countries in 1492 or 1496, respectively, or in Constantinople about 1515. In 1526, Gershom Cohen of Prague issued a printed illustrated Haggadah that is still completely extant and which has served as a model for many others that were to follow.[32]

The first American edition of the Haggadah was published by S. H. Jackson in New York in 1837. It includes an English translation by David Levi that appeared originally in London in 1794.[33]

COMMENTARIES

Over the years many commentators have interpreted and embellished the Haggadah. Many a dialectic discussion and homiletic discourse has been devoted to elucidating the various passages of the text. In 1892, a Haggadah with 115 commentaries was published in Vilna. A fourth revised edition of this work appeared in 1907 and, perhaps to compete with it, the same year there was printed in Podgorze, a Haggadah "with 238 commentaries," which were by and large fragmentary. Yaari records works by 437 commentators.

Commentaries on the text have been written by such noted scholars as Amram Gaon (9th century), Rashi (1040-1105), David ben Joseph Abudarham (14th century), Isaac ben Judah Abarbanel (15th and 16th centuries), the Maharal of Prague (16th century), Jacob Zevi Emden and Elijah Gaon of Wilna (18th century). More recent editions of the Haggadah present significant commentaries written or compiled by J. D. Eisenstein (New York, 1920), Cecil Roth (London, 1934), Daniel Goldschmidt (Tel Aviv, 1947, and Jerusalem, 1960) and Menahem M. Kasher (Jerusalem, 1955).

TRANSLATIONS

Moses Isserles (1520-1572) advocated the practice of making the Haggadah available in the vernacular so that women and children could understand it and mentioned that this was done in England.[34] Until today there have been published 258 editions of the Haggadah with English translations. A Latin translation appeared as early as 1512 in Frankfort-on-the-Main. Yaari states that this work was "intended for Christian theologians interested in Jewish customs." In 1609, Ladino, Italian and Judeo-German translations were published in Venice. A bilingual Haggadah in Hebrew and in Marathi translation was published in Bombay in 1846 for the use of the Bene Israel of India. The Haggadah has been made available in more than twenty languages including Afrikaans, Arabic, Danish, Dutch, Hungarian, Persian, Polish and Spanish.

HAGGADAH VARIATIONS

While the basic portions of the Haggadah are identical and common to all Jewish communities, a number of variations do occur. Different editions with minor textual changes, some omissions and some additions are used by Ashkenazi, Sephardi, Yemenite, North African and other Jews. Each community naturally holds fast to the text, melodies, and differences in customs inherited from its ancestors.

Reform Judaism produced several editions of the Haggadah in keeping with Reform principles. The earliest was that of Leopold Stein (Frankfort-on-the-Main, 1841). David Einhorn included a Haggadah with a German translation in his prayer book, *Olat Tamid* (1858). An English Haggadah entitled *Easter Eve* [sic] was prepared by H. M. Bien (Cincinnati, 1886). The first edition of the *Union Prayer Book* (Chicago, 1892) contained a Haggadah edited by I. S. Moses. In 1907, the Central Conference of American Rabbis published *The Union Haggadah;* it was revised and re-issued in 1923. This last edition, widely used by Reform Jews, omits certain selections, adds others and makes textual emendations to suit its ideology, although most of the symbolism is retained.[35] The Foreword to the 1907 edition states that "the effort has been made to embody the quaint form and the traditional sentiment of the Haggadah, as far as this is consonant with the spirit of the present time."[36] Radical departures from the traditional text are evi-

dent in *The New Haggadah for the Pesah Seder,* edited
by Mordecai M. Kaplan, Eugene Kohn and Ira Eisenstein for the Jewish Reconstructionist Foundation.[37] A
considerable number of deletions have been counterbal-
anced by the addition of new English readings and legends
about Moses in Hebrew and English. The editors state:
"We have retained the traditional framework, with its
archaic charm, but we have filled it with the living, com-
pelling content of present-day idealism and aspirations.
. . . We have steadily kept in mind the needs of the young
American Jew . . ."

Numerous Haggadahs have been supplemented with
special readings and songs. A noteworthy addition is the
"Seder Ritual of Remembrance" for the six million Jews
who perished at the hands of the Nazis and for the heroes
of the ghetto uprisings, prepared by Rufus Learsi, which
has been widely disseminated as a leaflet and in the Jewish
press.[38] Approved by many rabbis, the brief ritual, me-
morializing the European Jewish martyrs, including those
who perished in the Warsaw Ghetto uprising which began
on the first day of Passover, has been incorporated in the
Passover service in many homes.[39] A variation of Learsi's
text is included in a recently published Haggadah.[40]

Current Jewish history is the cause of certain textual
emendations that have been proposed in the State of
Israel. The prologue to the Haggadah, an invitation to
the needy and a prayer for redemption, reads:

> Behold the bread of poverty which our fore-
> fathers ate in the land of Egypt. Let all who hunger
> enter and eat; let all who are needy come and cele-
> brate Passover. This year we are here; next year
> may we be in the Land of Israel. This year we are
> slaves; next year may we be free men.

The question has been raised in Israel about the appropriateness of expressing hope to be "next year . . . in the
Land of Israel." Rabbi Menahem M. Kasher, in the

Haggadah which he edited, proposed the following change, based on a Genizah manuscript:

> This year we are here; next year may we be in Jerusalem. Yesterday we were slaves and today we are free men.[41]

Years ago in Palestine the closing prayer, "Next year may we be in Jerusalem," was emended to read: "Next year may we be in Jerusalem rebuilt."

Rabbi Kasher in his edition of the Haggadah has also added the drinking of a fifth cup of wine in honor of the establishment of the State of Israel. The four cups of wine are said to symbolize the four biblical expressions for the redemption of the children of Israel from slavery in Egypt: *I am the Lord* and I will bring you out *from under the burdens of the Egyptians,* and I will deliver you *from their bondage,* and I will redeem you *with an outstretched arm, and with great judgments;* and I will take you *to Me for a people* . . . (Ex. 6.6-7). From the next verse, *And I will bring you in unto the land* . . . ,[42] Rabbi Kasher deduces that an additional cup of wine should be used to mark the ingathering of the exiles in the new State. This practice, recently introduced in an American Haggadah,[43] has been followed by Yemenite Jews, although for a different reason.[44]

MILITARY HAGGADAHS

A new Haggadah appeared in Israel to meet the need for a version that would be acceptable at the communal Sedarim in military camps by soldiers of different communities. One of the significant functions of the Israeli army is to serve as a melting-pot for the new immigrants from many lands and many cultural backgrounds. To achieve this aim during the observance of Passover, Chief Chaplain Shlomoh Goren edited a Haggadah that represents a fusion of the accepted texts of Ashkenazi, Sephardi, Yemenite and other Jewries. This eclectic text is based upon a careful examination of early, authoritative sources.[45]

To serve the needs of Jewish personnel in the armed forces of the United States, the National Jewish Welfare Board has, since World War I, published several Haggadahs, of which hundreds of thousands of copies have been distributed. These included different English translations by Mrs. Philip Cowen, David and Tamar de Sola Pool and Albert S. Goldstein. The Foreword to the latest edition states:

> It is to the Jewish men and women of the Armed Forces of the United States that this American version of the ancient story of liberation is gratefully dedicated.
>
> May this Haggadah fortify their faith in freedom and their endurance in the continuing struggle for liberty, even as it warms their hearts with sweet memories of loved ones and of home.[46]

In an emergency situation, a limited edition of 1,250 copies of a Haggadah was "prepared for use of Jewish Personnel of the Army and Navy of the United States in French North Africa during the Passover of the year 5703" (Casablanca, 1943). There is also a "Service Edition for Australian Sailors, Soldiers and Airmen" (Melbourne, 1943).

Individual Jewish chaplains have edited, abbreviated or otherwise compiled Haggadahs that were printed in their military camps and naval stations, both within the U.S.A. and abroad.[47]

A special and distinctive Haggadah, arranged and illustrated by Y. D. Sheinson, was issued for the Seder services conducted by Chaplain Abraham J. Klausner in the Deutsches Theatre Restaurant, Munich, Germany, on April 15-16, 1946. The Hebrew and Yiddish text recalls not only the ancient bondage to Pharaoh in Egypt but also the slavery to Hitler in Germany. The introduction, in English, states:

And the khaki-clad sons of Israel commanded by Lieutenant General Truscott gathered together, as was the custom in Israel, to celebrate the Passover festival. They came from the Ninth Division in the West and the First Division in the East. They came from . . . the UNRRA and the American Joint Distribution Committee, all of them came to the city of Munich, there to relate as of old the miracle of freedom. They spoke of Pharaoh and the Egyptian bondage. They spoke of slave labor and the torture cities of Pithom and Rameses . . . But in their hearts they felt very close to all that which was narrated. Pharaoh and Egypt gave way to Hitler and Germany. Pithom and Rameses faded beneath fresh memories of Buchenwald and Dachau . . . Just beyond the sounds of the Seder, in the wreckage of the city, the former slave sat in company with his tantalizing memories and celebrated his first Passover since the liberation . . .

THE KIBBUTZ "HAGGADAH"

In the past two score years, hundreds of "Haggadahs" for Passover were written and published by the kibbutzim, the workers' cooperative settlements in Israel, in an effort to formulate a modern Haggadah that would express the strivings and yearnings of the pioneers and yet not be religiously oriented. While these editions are parodies based on the traditional Haggadah, they are most serious both in form and content.[48]

In early years, each kibbutz created its own version. All prayers and benedictions were meticulously deleted, care being taken to omit any selection that might be construed to have a religious connotation. Such a Haggadah may include verses from the Book of Exodus, poems and songs of Yehudah Halevi, Hayyim Nahman Bialik and S. Shalom, comments on current events, and parodies on the Four Sons, *Dayyenu* and other traditional passages, highlighting life in the commune.[49] Some of the material

83

is undoubtedly irrelevant to the traditions and spirit of the festival of Passover. In recent years, many a kibbutz Haggadah has been revised to incorporate more of the traditional elements, including the mention of the Deity. This reversion is perhaps symptomatic of the readier acceptance of "Jewish consciousness" on the part of the socialist laboring class in Israel.[50]

A typical specimen of a parody in a kibbutz Haggadah is translated herewith:

> The law of the kibbutz was intended for Four Sons: one is wise and loyal, one is wicked and pessimistic, one is simple, and one is not even able to ask a question.
>
> What does the wise son say? "What are these obligations and duties which our kibbutz places upon us?" You will explain to him the laws of our movement: "Go forth to the road and stand watch. Do not be satisfied with opinions!"
>
> What does the wicked son say? "What is this drudgery of yours?" Since he has removed himself from the group, he has denied a basic principle and sought the illusions of the crumbling city. You should set his teeth on edge and answer him thus: "It is because *we* have been redeemed for a life of co-operativeness and equality; but *he* has not been redeemed."
>
> What does the simple son say? "What is this?" And you shall say to him: "Come and see with your own eyes, and you shall recognize our life and you will come to dwell in our camp."
>
> And as for the one who is not even able to ask, you must open [his mouth] for him, as it is said: "And you shall tell your comrade, and you shall narrate to him all the events that happened to us from the time of our return . . . until today.[51]

For many long centuries Jews in all climes and in all

conditions have recited the Haggadah every year as a reaffirmation of the Jew's historic sense of community, of his link with the Jewish people throughout the world, of his hope in the ultimate Redemption of mankind and of his faith in God.

Every person in every generation must regard himself as having been personally freed from Egypt. . . . It was not only our fathers that the Holy One, blessed be He, redeemed, but ourselves also did He redeem along with them (Haggadah).

THE BAKING OF MATZOT

VI

THE FIRST UNLEAVENED BREAD

Matzah, unleavened bread, was first baked to serve un-expected visitors, as it could be prepared hastily; because of the hot climate of the East, food could not be stored, lest it deteriorate. This practice was in vogue as far back as the days of Abraham. When the three men came to Abraham at the terebinths of Mamre, he instructed Sarah: *Make ready quickly three measures of fine meal, knead it, and make cakes* (Gen. 18.6). A specific refer-ence to *matzot* is found in the Bible shortly thereafter. When the angels visited Lot in Sodom, he offered them hospitality . . . *and he made them a feast, and did bake unleavened bread, and they did eat (ibid.,* 19.3). Another instance is that of the woman of En-Dor who, when Saul visited her, *had a fatted calf in the house; and she made haste, and killed it; and she took flour, and kneaded it, and did bake unleavened bread thereof* (I Sam. 28.24).

MATZOT WITH FIGURES

In the days of the Talmud some *matzot* were made with designs on them. This is revealed in a lengthy discussion by rabbis of the time. Even though the use of *matzot* decorated with figures was not encouraged for compliance

86

with the law of eating unleavened bread, the sages said that if one does eat them he acquits himself of his duty.

Boethus ben Zonin raised the question: "Why is it not permitted to prepare figured cakes on Passover?" The rabbis answered: "Because the woman in preparing them tarries over her work (to illustrate the *matzot,* and does not put them quickly into the oven) and in the meantime the dough becomes leavened." Boethus was not satisfied with this reply and he rejoined: "Perhaps she could form the dough in a mold or plate, thus impressing the figures on the cake quickly, without loss of time?" To this proposal they replied: "In that event, it would be said that all figured cakes are prohibited and only those made by Boethus are permitted." The opposition of the rabbis was based on the ground that no discrimination can be shown in favor of any particular stamping as most of the bakers did not have a ready-made figured plate.

Rabbi Elazar bar Zadok related that one Passover he went with his father to the house of Rabban Gamaliel and there they served *matzot* with perforations that represented figures. When he called his father's attention to the admonition of the sages not to make figured cakes on Passover, Zadok replied: "This prohibition does not apply to every householder who bakes for himself as one does not expect that he will beautify them to such an extent that he will delay and allow the dough to become leavened. This was said about bakers who sell their products and therefore they are careful about their appearance and spend time on the design."

There were other rabbis who maintained that figured *matzot* of bakers are not forbidden as they are expert and have the necessary molds.[1]

Maimonides agreed with the latter and permitted bakers to make unleavened bread with illustrations but prohibited householders from doing so even if they had a mold, lest others do so without a mold.[2]

The figures used to ornament the *matzot* were likenesses of doves, fishes and other forms, according to

Rabbi Isaac ibn Gayyat.[3] Other artistic perforations were evidently also in usage, such as animals and flowers, but all of these were later prohibited except such designs as could be made with a comblike implement and with perforated holes.[4] The use of a mold or plate was likewise forbidden as the dough enters into it and becomes leaven.[5]

Later on, perforations were made with a sharp-toothed wheel, called a *redel*, attached to a handle. The purpose of using the *redel* was to prevent the dough from rising during the baking, rather than to beautify the *matzot*.

In some communities there was a custom of inscribing the three *matzot* used at the Seder with "Cohen," "Levi" and "Israel," the names by which each was called, to be able to differentiate among them. Others marked each of them with one of the first three letters of the Hebrew alphabet.

In a number of illustrated Haggadahs there are pictures of *matzot* with various designs. A Haggadah manuscript in the Michaelis Collection at Oxford has an illustration of a *matzah* with a design of chains, symbolizing the Egyptian bondage.[6]

In the Middle Ages *matzot* were an inch thick, or about the thickness of a finger.[7] Later on, they were made much thinner.

Until the past century *matzot* were usually round. This is undoubtedly due to the biblical term *uggot matzot* (Ex. 12.39) which has a double meaning: cakes of unleavened bread and circles of unleavened bread. Many are still scrupulous to use the round *matzot*.[8] With the advent of machine-made *matzot*, the shape became square.

HAND-BAKED MATZOT

Until the middle of the nineteenth century all *matzot* were baked by hand according to detailed specifications which provided that: the kneading of the dough be continuous to prevent leavening from setting in; the dough be guarded from sudden heat until it is placed in the oven; no particles of the dough be left on the kneading table as they might become leaven and thus make the rest of the dough unfit for use; during the kneading all kernels of wheat not crushed during the milling must be sifted out. To assure that all these precautions were taken, the work was entrusted to adults only.

In many Jewish communities each householder had *matzot* baked in the local bakery on a day set aside for him and he supervised the entire operation so that he might share in the *mitzvah*. He and members of his family appeared before dawn at the bakery so that they might participate from the start to the finish.

Extra help was still needed to handle the seasonal demand and employment was thus provided for many unskilled persons—the aged, women and children—who were engaged by the bakers as helpers. Many a poor Jew earned the wherewithal to observe Passover by working in the *matzah* bakery. Special tasks were assigned to each employee, many of whom became expert in their particular functions. In the mishnaic period, evidently three women sufficed for the process: one to knead, another to roll the dough, and a third to bake.[9] In the course of later generations, a bureaucracy of functionaries developed. The *Mehl-Mester* measured the amount of flour required by the kneader. The *Vasser-Gisser* poured the cold water into the dough as the kneader required. The expert kneader may have had a number of assistants who continued the kneading of the batter, rolling the water out of the dough and thinning it into cakes. Then the *Redler* took over and with his cog wheel he made the perforations. He, in turn, passed the batter to the *Derlanger,* who bore it on a rolling pin to the *Shiber*. The latter, usually an expert at his task, was responsible for placing the dough in the oven. When the *matzah* was baked, he removed it from the oven and handed it over to the *Treger,* who proudly carried the finished product to the place where it was stored or packed.

It was the custom to start the fire for the baking of the *matzot* with the willows and the *lulab* used on Sukkot for, having been used for one *mitzvah*, they should be used for another.[10]

Matzot were usually baked during the thirty days preceding Passover. However, the *matzot mitzvah* were made on the afternoon of the eve of Passover, which was the time of sacrificing the paschal lamb.[11] Many Hasidim still wait until the day before Passover to bake their *matzot*. Dressed in their festive clothing, they gather at noon at the bakery and each one is assigned a task. The work proceeds enthusiastically with the singing of *Hallel*, and often concludes with a *Le-Hayyim*. Water for the batter is drawn from wells on the previous evening and is kept overnight in a cool place. The water-drawing is accompanied by joyous singing and lively dancing.[12]

Many Hasidim are involved in the preparations for *matzah*-baking during the summer months when they go into the fields and granaries to oversee the reapers and make certain that no rain or moisture will dampen the wheat. Packed in new sacks, the wheat is brought to the mill. Some use millstones which make a coarse flour, while other Hasidim employ an electric mill which produces a fine flour.[13]

In Jerusalem many of the hasidic groups operate their own bakeries for hand-made *matzot* for Passover. In New York City there are at least six bakeries where about 75,000 pounds of *matzot* are made by hand.[14]

THE DEBATE ON MACHINE-MADE MATZOT

In about 1857 the first *matzah*-baking machine was invented in Austria, beginning a heated controversy which raged for half a century. Dr. Solomon B. Freehof has given us a full account of this dispute which he calls "one of the most acrimonious discussions in the history of the responsa literature." However, this should not be surprising as this was, indeed, a radical innovation for the fulfilment of a duty whose execution had long ago been elaborately defined to the minutest detail.

The newly invented machine kneaded the dough and

rolled it through two metal rollers from which it came out thin, perforated and round. It was then placed in an oven. As the corners of the dough, cut to make the *matzot* round, were re-used, it was feared that the time elapsing until these pieces of dough were used again might allow them to become leavened. A later machine was developed which produced square *matzot* so that there would be no leftovers. Other subsequent improvements in the machinery speeded up the entire process of production, leading to a general acceptance of the modern method. Meanwhile, many distinguished rabbis raised their voices in protest against the new machine, while others, equally respected, permitted its use.

Solomon Kluger of Brody, in a letter to Rabbi Hayyim Nathan and Rabbi Leibush Horowitz of Cracow, Galicia, where the machine was already in use, prohibited the eating of the machine-made *matzot*, especially for the *matzot mitzvah*. This letter and similar pronouncements by other rabbis were published under the title: *Moda'ah le-Bet Yisrael* ("Announcement to the House of Israel," Breslau, 1859). In rebuttal, Rabbi Joseph Saul Nathanson published a pamphlet: *Bittul Moda'ah* ("Annulment of the Announcement," Lemberg, 1859).

One of Kluger's most telling arguments was that the opportunity given to the poor to earn money for their Passover needs by working in *matzah* bakeries would be denied to them, as the use of machinery required fewer manual workers. He and his adherents also argued that *matzah shemurah,* particularly, must be made with the intention of fulfilling the precept which requires the understanding of a mature adult. They also claimed that there was a suspicion that the pieces of dough left in the wheels of the machine, which were difficult to clean, would become leavened.

In the forefront of the rabbis who permitted the use of machinery was Joseph Saul Nathanson of Lemberg. They refuted the arguments of the opposition seriatim. If concern need be expressed about the displacement of

91

the hand-bakers, the same solicitude should be shown to scribes whose replacement by the printing press had been universally accepted. They also held that these *matzot* are baked with the intent to comply with the law, as it is necessary for an adult to start the machine. They had no fear that dough would be left in the machines as they are cleaned well and often. Furthermore, they contended that the machine speeds the process and is more efficient than the men and women who worked in the bakery day and night. The views of Nathanson and those who sided with him have been accepted by most Jews.[15]

COMMUNAL BAKERIES

In the eighteenth and nineteenth centuries, and most likely even earlier, the baking of *matzah* was very often a communal responsibility handled by the local *kehillah*[16] or a congregation. In London, at the end of the eighteenth century, when prices skyrocketed as a result of the war with France, the congregations joined in a united effort to obtain flour for Passover by arranging to have "all the wheat ground at the same mill under joint supervision, thus considerably reducing overhead costs." This responsibility finally devolved on the Great Synagogue of London.[17] Nearly a century later, in 1877, the United Synagogue and the Spanish and Portuguese Synagogue organized the "Conjoint Flour Committee" for the purpose of controlling the supply of flour to bakers, maintaining standards of *kashrut* and supervising the distribution of free *matzot* to the poor, to hospital patients and to prison inmates. A tax is levied on the flour which is applied towards the cost of the *matzot* distributed without charge.[18]

Another type of communal bakery is reported by Daniel Persky. At the beginning of the present century in Minsk, White Russia, on the day following Purim, a "Zionist *matzah* factory" was opened, one of many bakeries in the city. This business was established by the local Zionist leaders to raise funds for the Jewish National

Fund which received the entire profit. Rabbis of the Mizrachi Organization served as *kashrut* supervisors. All of the employees were volunteers who willingly donated their services to share in this holy work. Before Purim hundreds of boys and girls enrolled as volunteers, but only those who came early were engaged as the bakery could not employ all of them. Working in devotion and harmony, the voices of the young people rang out in Hebrew songs of Zion as they baked the bread of affliction.[19]

It was not uncommon to have a *matzah* bakery located within the precincts of a synagogue, either in the cellar or its courtyard. In describing a medieval synagogue in Carpentras, France, Marvin Lowenthal wrote:

"A low vaulted cellar, entered from the courtyard south of the main structure and lighted dimly by its doorway, houses two complete *matzah* bakeries—both equipped with ovens pierced deep in the walls, long-handled wooden shovels still resting on their racks over-head, pronged markers to stamp a design in the cakes, and huge stone kneading-blocks.[20] The bakeries existed as early as 1625, and perhaps long before. One of the kneading-blocks, naturally, bears the name of its donor: 'Gad of Digne—a gift—1652.' The courtyard provides a well, near at hand so no time should be lost and leavening set in before the cakes were done. The bakeries have long been out of use; and decay, neglect, and that ineluctable quality which permeates a human tool, be it book, palace or *matzah* shovel, once it is discarded and for generations undisturbed, lend their touching appeal. In a thousand towns of Europe similar bakeries have rotted into nothingness, leaving of the shouting bustle, the meticulous ritual, and the mingled fear and joy that once marked their use, no trace save Egyptian darkness."[21]

MATZAH-BAKING IN OLD NEW YORK

Congregation Shearith Israel played the leading role in Jewish communal life in New York during the seventeenth and eighteenth centuries, and exercised a monopoly on various aspects of religious observance. *Matzot* for Passover were obtainable only through the congregation. Each year the officers would estimate the amount of *matzot* required both for sale to families and for free distribution to the poor as well as to the congregation's officials.

Congregation Shearith Israel usually had its own *matzah*-baking oven, which was turned over to a Christian baker with the proviso that the baking of unleavened bread would be under the constant supervision of the *shammash*.[22] In some years, it was the duty of the *shammash* to have the *matzot* baked in his own house.[23]

In 1819, a committee of the congregation recommended that the baking of *matzot* "be done by Mr. Hunter in his new patent bakery under the supervision of two or more persons to be appointed and paid by Trustees; at a cost of $8.50 a hundred pounds, which is $2.50 less than the cost of the baking the preceding year by the old process."[24] This "patent" bakery "apparently consisted of an iron stove instead of the more usual brick oven" and was considered more in accordance with Jewish law, as objections had been raised to the old ovens which used shingle boards that may not have been completely free from leaven.

Before the middle of the nineteenth century Shearith Israel's monopoly in providing unleavened bread was broken. Other congregations developed and made their own arrangements with different Jewish and non-Jewish bakeries. Hyman B. Grinstein wrote: "In the mid-forties many bakers found it profitable to solicit *matzot* patronage of the several synagogues. As a rule, they permitted the synagogue to send one or two of its own men to supervise the baking. In exchange for the patronage of the congregation, the bakers donated a certain number of pounds of *matzot* for distribution among the poor. In 1846, the newly-formed Temple Emanu-El, when approached by a baker who sought its patronage, refused to give him preference over any other, claiming that this

94

was a matter for the individual members to decide. Emanu-El's action was the herald of a new day."[25]

BAROMETER OF JEWISH LIFE

The quantity of *matzot* baked and consumed may well be a true barometer of the vitality of Jewish life throughout the world. The increase in the distribution of unleavened bread in particular countries usually reflects the increase of immigration, population growth and a greater interest in Jewish observances. On the other hand, a decrease in the amount of *matzot* baked may signify immigration restrictions, lessening of population growth and a weakening of participation in traditional Jewish life.

In the middle of the nineteenth century, the growth of the Jewish community of Cincinnati was measured by the statistics of *matzah* production. In 1824, when Bene Israel Congregation was founded, 100 pounds sufficed to meet the Passover requirements of the Jews in the Ohio Valley. Twenty-five years later, 20,000 pounds of *matzot* were baked.[26]

In New York City, an estimate of the Jewish population in 1859 was made on the basis of the *matzah* production. Approximately 274,000 pounds were consumed that year. Figuring an average of five pounds per person, it was estimated that at least 40,000 Jews resided then in New York.[27] It was reported that in 1904, in New York City, 10,000 barrels of flour were used in making about 1,700,000 pounds of unleavened bread which were produced by fifteen bakeries, including one that made it by hand and another that specialized in *matzah shemurah*.[28] Again taking the same average of five pounds per person, the estimate of the Jewish population might be said to be 340,000, although the *American Jewish Year Book* of 1904 estimates the Jewish population of New York State to be 600,000.[29] Whether *matzah* consumption is more or less reliable than other methods of estimating Jewish population must be left to demographers to determine.

BOOK TWO

Passover in Literature, Art and Music

Thus saith the Lord, the God of Israel: Let My people go . . .
Exodus 5.1

ISRAEL IN EGYPTIAN BONDAGE

Joseph died, and all his brethren, and all that generation. And the children of Israel were fruitful, and increased abundantly, and multiplied, and waxed exceeding mighty; and the land was filled with them.

Now there arose a new king over Egypt, who knew not Joseph. And he said unto his people, "Behold, the people of the children of Israel are too many and too mighty for us; come, let us deal wisely with them, lest they multiply, and it come to pass that when there befalleth us any war, they also join themselves unto our enemies and fight against us, and get them up out of the land." Therefore they did set over them taskmasters to afflict them with their burdens. And they built for Pharaoh store-cities, Pithom and Rameses. But the more they afflicted them, the more they multiplied and the more they spread abroad. And they were adread because of the children of Israel. And the Egyptians made the children of Israel to serve with rigor. And they made their lives bitter with hard service, in mortar and in brick, and in all manner of service in the field; in all their service, wherein they made them serve with rigor.

And Pharaoh charged all his people, saying: "Every

99

son that is born ye shall cast into the river, and every daughter ye shall save alive" (Ex. 1.6-14,22).

And there went a man of the house of Levi, and took to wife a daughter of Levi. And the woman conceived, and bore a son; and when she saw him that he was a goodly child, she hid him three months. And when she could not longer hide him, she took for him an ark of bulrushes, and daubed it with slime and with pitch; and she put the child therein, and laid it in the flags by the river's brink. And his sister stood afar off, to know what would be done to him. And the daughter of Pharaoh came down to bathe in the river, and her maidens walked along by the river-side; and she saw the ark among the flags, and sent her handmaid to fetch it. And she opened it, and saw it, even the child; and behold a boy that wept. And she had compassion on him, and said: "This is one of the Hebrews' children." Then said his sister to Pharaoh's daughter: "Shall I go and call thee a nurse of the Hebrew women, that she may nurse the child for thee?" And Pharaoh's daughter said to her: "Go." And the maiden went and called the child's mother. And Pharaoh's daughter said unto her: "Take this child away, and nurse it for me, and I will give thee thy wages." And the woman took the child, and nursed it. And the child grew, and she brought him unto Pharaoh's daughter, and he became her son. And she called his name Moses, and said: "Because I drew him out of the water."

And it came to pass in those days, when Moses was grown up, that he went out unto his brethren and looked on their burdens; and he saw an Egyptian smiting a Hebrew, one of his brethren. And he looked this way and that way, and when he saw that there was no man, he smote the Egyptian, and hid him in the sand. And he went out the second day and, behold, two men of the Hebrews were striving together; and he said to him that did the wrong: "Wherefore smitest thou thy fellow?" And he said: "Who made thee a ruler and a judge over us? thinkest thou to kill me, as thou didst kill the Egyptian?"

100

And Moses feared, and said: "Surely the thing is known." Now when Pharaoh heard this thing, he sought to slay Moses. But Moses fled from the face of Pharaoh, and dwelt in the land of Midian (*ibid.*, 2.1-15).

MOSES AND THE BURNING BUSH

Now Moses was keeping the flock of Jethro his father-in-law, the priest of Midian; and he led the flock to the farthest end of the wilderness, and came to the mountain of God, unto Horeb. And the angel of the Lord appeared unto him in a flame of fire out of the midst of a bush; and he looked and, behold, the bush burned with fire, and the bush was not consumed. And Moses said: "I will turn aside now, and see this great sight, why the bush is not burnt." And when the Lord saw that he turned aside to see, God called unto him out of the midst of the bush, and said: "Moses, Moses." And he said: "Here am I." And He said: "Draw not nigh hither; put off thy shoes from off thy feet, for the place whereon thou standest is holy ground." Moreover He said: "I am the God of thy father, the God of Abraham, the God of Isaac, and the God of Jacob." And Moses hid his face; for he was afraid to look upon God. And the Lord said: "I have surely seen the affliction of My people that are in Egypt, and have heard their cry by reason of their taskmasters; for I know their pains; and I am come down to deliver them out of the hand of the Egyptians, and to bring them up out of that land unto a good land and a large, unto a land flowing with milk and honey; unto the place of the Canaanite, and the Hittite, and the Amorite, and the Perizzite, and the Hivite, and the Jebusite. And now, behold, the cry of the children of Israel is come unto Me; moreover I have seen the oppression, wherewith the Egyptians oppress them. Come now therefore, and I will send thee unto Pharaoh, that thou mayest bring forth My people the children of Israel out of Egypt." And Moses said unto God: "Who am I, that I should go unto Pharaoh and that I should bring forth the children of Israel out

101

of Egypt?" And he said: "Certainly I will be with thee; and this shall be the token unto thee, that I have sent thee; when thou hast brought forth the people out of Egypt, ye shall serve God upon this mountain." And Moses said unto God: "Behold, when I come unto the children of Israel, and shall say unto them: The God of your fathers hath sent me unto you; and they shall say to me: What is His name? what shall I say unto them?" And God said unto Moses: "I AM THAT I AM"; and He said: "Thus shalt thou say unto the children of Israel: I AM hath sent me unto you." And they shall hearken to thy voice. And thou shalt come, thou and the elders of Israel, unto the king of Egypt, and ye shall say unto him: the Lord, the God of the Hebrews hath met with us. And now let us go, we pray thee, three days' journey into the wilderness, that we may sacrifice to the Lord our God. And I know that the king of Egypt will not give you leave to go, except by a mighty hand. And I will put forth My hand and smite Egypt with all My wonders which I will do in the midst thereof. And after that he will let you go" *(ibid.,* 3.1-14, 18-20).

And Moses answered and said: "But, behold, they will not believe me, nor hearken unto my voice; for they will say: The lord hath not appeared unto thee." And the Lord said unto him: "What is that in thy hand?" And he said: "A rod." And He said: "Cast it on the ground." And he cast it on the ground, and it became a serpent; and Moses fled from before it. And the Lord said unto Moses: "Put forth thy hand, and take it by the tail"—and he put forth his hand, and laid hold of it, and it became a rod in his hand—"that they may believe that the Lord, the God of their fathers, the God of Abraham, the God of Isaac, and the God of Jacob, hath appeared unto thee." And the Lord said furthermore unto him: "Put now thy hand into thy bosom." And he put his hand into his bosom; and when he took it out, behold, his hand was leprous, as white as snow. And He said: "Put thy hand back into thy bosom." And he put his hand back into his

102

bosom, and when he took it out of his bosom, behold, it was turned again as his other flesh. "And it shall come to pass, if they will not believe thee, neither hearken to the voice of the first sign, that they will believe the voice of the latter sign. And it shall come to pass, if they will not believe even these two signs, neither hearken unto thy voice, that thou shalt take of the water of the river, and pour it upon the dry land; and the water which thou takest out of the river shall become blood upon the dry land." And Moses said unto the Lord: "Oh Lord, I am not a man of words, neither heretofore, nor since Thou hast spoken unto Thy servant; for I am slow of speech, and of a slow tongue." And the Lord said unto him: "Who hath made man's mouth? or who maketh a man dumb, or deaf, or seeing, or blind? is it not I the Lord?" And the anger of the Lord was kindled against Moses, and He said: "Is there not Aaron thy brother the Levite? I know that he can speak well. And also, behold, he cometh forth to meet thee; and when he seeth thee, he will be glad in his heart. And thou shalt speak unto him, and put the words in his mouth; and I will be with thy mouth, and with his mouth, and will teach you what ye shall do. And he shall be thy spokesman unto the people; and it shall come to pass, that he shall be to thee a mouth, and thou shalt be to him in God's stead. And thou shalt take in thy hand this rod, wherewith thou shalt do the signs."

And Moses went and returned to Jethro his father-in-law, and said unto him: "Let me go, I pray thee, and return unto my brethren that are in Egypt, and see whether they be yet alive." And Jethro said to Moses: "Go in peace." And the Lord said unto Moses in Midian: "Go, return into Egypt; for all the men are dead that sought thy life." And Moses took his wife and his sons, and set them upon an ass, and he returned to the land of Egypt; and Moses took the rod of God in his hand.

And the Lord said to Aaron: "Go into the wilderness to meet Moses." And he went, and met him in the moun-

tain of God, and kissed him. And Moses told Aaron all
the words of the Lord wherewith He had sent him, and
all the signs wherewith He had charged him. And Moses
and Aaron went and gathered together all the elders of
the children of Israel. And Aaron spoke all the words
which the Lord had spoken unto Moses, and did the signs
in the sight of the people. And the people believed; and
when they heard that the Lord had remembered the children of Israel, and that He had seen their affliction, then
they bowed their heads and worshipped (*ibid.*, 4.1-11,
14-20,27-31).

MOSES AND AARON BEFORE PHARAOH

And afterward Moses and Aaron came, and said unto
Pharaoh: "Thus saith the Lord, the God of Israel: Let
My people go, that they may hold a feast unto Me in the
wilderness." And Pharaoh said: "Who is the Lord, that
I should hearken unto His voice to let Israel go? I know
not the Lord, and moreover I will not let Israel go." And
they said: "The God of the Hebrews hath met with us.
Let us go, we pray thee, three days' journey into the
wilderness, and sacrifice unto the Lord our God, lest He
fall upon us with pestilence, or with the sword." And the
king of Egypt said unto them: "Wherefore do ye, Moses
and Aaron, cause the people to break loose from their
work? get you unto your burdens." And Pharaoh said:
"Behold, the people of the land are now many, and will
ye make them rest from their burdens?" And the same
day Pharaoh commanded the taskmasters of the people
and their officers, saying? "Ye shall no more give the
people straw to make brick as heretofore. Let them go
and gather straw for themselves. And the tale of the
bricks, which they did make heretofore, ye shall lay
upon them; ye shall not diminish aught thereof; for they
are idle; therefore they cry, saying: Let us go and sacrifice to our God. Let heavier work be laid upon the men,
that they may labor therein; and let them not regard
lying words." And the taskmasters of the people went

out, and their officers, and they spoke to the people, saying: "Thus saith Pharaoh: I will not give you straw." So the people were scattered abroad throughout all the land of Egypt to gather stubble for straw. And the taskmasters were urgent, saying: "Fulfil your work, your daily task, as when there was straw."

Then the officers of the children of Israel came and cried unto Pharaoh, saying: "Wherefore dealest thou thus with thy servants? There is no straw given unto thy servants, and they say to us: Make bricks; and, behold, thy servants are beaten, but the fault is in thine own people." But he said: "Ye are idle, ye are idle; therefore ye say: Let us go and sacrifice to the Lord. Go therefore now and work; for there shall no straw be given you; yet shall ye deliver the tale of bricks."

And Moses returned unto the Lord, and said: "Lord, wherefore hast Thou dealt ill with this people? why is it that Thou hast sent me? For since I came to Pharaoh to speak in Thy name, he hath dealt ill with this people; neither hast Thou delivered Thy people at all" (*ibid.*, 5.1-10,12-13,15-18,22-23).

And the Lord said unto Moses: "Now shalt thou see what I will do to Pharaoh; for by a strong hand shall he let them go, and by a strong hand shall he drive them out of his land."

GOD'S REASSURANCE TO MOSES

And God spoke unto Moses, and said unto him: "I am the Lord, and I appeared unto Abraham, unto Isaac, and unto Jacob, as God Almighty, but by My name Adonai I made Me not known to them. And I have also established My covenant with them, to give them the land of Canaan, the land of their sojournings, wherein they sojourned. And moreover I have heard the groaning of the children of Israel, whom the Egyptians keep in bondage; and I have remembered My covenant. Wherefore say unto the children of Israel: I am the Lord, and I will bring you out from under the burdens of the Egyptians, and I will

105

deliver you from their bondage, and I will redeem you with an outstretched arm and with great judgments; and I will take you to Me for a people, and I will be to you a God; and ye shall know that I am the Lord your God who brought you out from under the burdens of the Egyptians. And I will bring you in unto the land, concerning which I lifted up My hand to give it to Abraham, to Isaac, and to Jacob; and I will give it you for a heritage: I am the Lord" (*ibid.*, 6.1-8).

THE PLAGUES

And the Lord spoke unto Moses and unto Aaron, saying: "When Pharaoh shall speak unto you, saying: Show a wonder for you; then thou shalt say unto Aaron: Take thy rod, and cast it down before Pharaoh, that it become a serpent." And Moses and Aaron went in unto Pharaoh, and they did so, as the Lord had commanded; and Aaron cast down his rod before Pharaoh and before his servants, and it became a serpent. Then Pharaoh also called for the wise men and the sorcerers; and they also, the magicians of Egypt, did in like manner with their secret arts. For they cast down every man his rod, and they became serpents; but Aaron's rod swallowed up their rods. And Pharaoh's heart was hardened, and he hearkened not unto them, as the Lord had spoken.

And the Lord said unto Moses: "Pharaoh's heart is stubborn; he refuseth to let the people go. Get thee unto Pharaoh in the morning; lo, he goeth out unto the water; and thou shalt stand by the river's brink to meet him, and the rod which was turned to a serpent shalt thou take in thy hand. And thou shalt say unto him: The Lord, the God of the Hebrews, hath sent me unto thee, saying: Let My people go, that they may serve Me in the wilderness; and, behold, hitherto thou hast not hearkened; thus saith the Lord: In this thou shalt know that I am the Lord— behold, I will smite with the rod that is in my hand upon the waters which are in the river, and they shall be turned to blood."

106

And the Lord said unto Moses: "Say unto Aaron: Take thy rod, and stretch out thy hand over the waters of Egypt, over their rivers, over their streams, and over their pools, and over all their ponds of water, that they may become blood; and there shall be blood throughout all the land of Egypt, both in vessels of wood and in vessels of stone." And Moses and Aaron did so, as the Lord commanded; and he lifted up the rod and smote the waters that were in the river, in the sight of Pharaoh and in the sight of his servants; and all the waters that were in the river were turned to blood. And the magicians of Egypt did in like manner with their secret arts; and Pharaoh's heart was hardened, and he hearkened not unto them; as the Lord had spoken *(ibid., 7.8-17, 19-20, 22)*.

And Aaron stretched out his hand over the waters of Egypt; and the frogs came up, and covered the land of Egypt.

Aaron stretched out his hand with his rod and smote the dust of the earth, and there were gnats upon man and upon beast; all the dust of the earth became gnats throughout all the land of Egypt.

There came grievous swarms of flies into the house of Pharaoh and into his servants' houses; and in all the land of Egypt the land was ruined by reason of the swarms of flies.

And Pharaoh called for Moses and for Aaron and said: "Go ye, sacrifice to your God in the land." And Moses said: "It is not meet so to do; for we shall sacrifice the abomination of the Egyptians to the Lord our God; lo, if we sacrifice the abomination of the Egyptians before their eyes, will they not stone us? We will go three days' journey into the wilderness, and sacrifice to the Lord our God, as He shall command us." And Pharaoh said: "I will let you go that ye may sacrifice to the Lord your God in the wilderness; only ye shall not go very far away; entreat for me." And Moses said: "Behold, I go out from thee and I will entreat the Lord that the swarms of flies may depart from Pharaoh, from his servants, and from his people, tomorrow; only let not Pharaoh deal deceitfully any more in not letting the people go to sacrifice to the Lord." And Moses went out from Pharaoh, and entreated the Lord. And the Lord did according to the word of Moses; and He removed the swarms of flies from Pharaoh, from his servants, and from his people; there remained not one. And Pharaoh hardened his heart this time also and he did not let the people go (*ibid.*, 8.2,13,20-28).

All the cattle of Egypt died; but of the cattle of the children of Israel died not one.

And they took soot of the furnace and stood before Pharaoh, and Moses threw it up heavenward; and it became a boil breaking forth with blains upon man and upon beast. And the magicians could not stand before Moses because of the boils, for the boils were upon the magicians and upon all the Egyptians.

And Moses stretched forth his rod towards heaven; and the Lord sent thunder and hail, and fire ran down unto the earth, and the Lord caused to hail upon the land of Egypt.

And Pharaoh sent, and called for Moses and Aaron, and said unto them: "I have sinned this time; the Lord is righteous, and I and my people are wicked."

And Moses went out of the city from Pharaoh, and spread forth his hand unto the Lord; and the thunders and hail ceased, and the rain was not poured upon the earth. And when Pharaoh saw that the rain and the hail and the thunders were ceased, he sinned yet more, and hardened his heart, he and his servants (*ibid.*, 9.6,10-11, 23,27,33-34).

And Moses stretched forth his rod over the land of Egypt, and the Lord brought an east wind upon the land all that day and all the night; and when it was morning, the east wind brought the locusts. And the locusts went up over all the land of Egypt, and rested in all the borders of Egypt; very grievous were they; before them there were no such locusts as they, neither after them shall be such.

And Moses stretched forth his hand toward heaven; and there was a thick darkness in all the land of Egypt three days; they saw not one another, neither rose any from his place for three days; but all the children of Israel had light in their dwellings (*ibid.*, 10.13-14,22-23).

And the Lord said unto Moses: "Yet one plague more will I bring upon Pharaoh, and upon Egypt; afterwards he will let you go hence; when he shall let you go, he shall surely thrust you out hence altogether."

And Moses said: "Thus saith the Lord: About midnight will I go out into the midst of Egypt; and all the first-born in the land of Egypt shall die, from the first-born of Pharaoh that sitteth upon his throne, even unto the first-born of the maid-servant that is behind the mill; and all the first-born of cattle. And there shall be a great cry throughout all the land of Egypt, such as there hath been none like it, nor shall be like it any more. But against any of the children of Israel shall not a dog whet his tongue, against man or beast; that ye may know how that the Lord doth put a difference between the Egyptians and Israel. And all these thy servants shall come down unto me, and bow down unto me, saying: Get thee out and all the people that follow thee; and after that I will go out." And he went out from Pharaoh in hot anger.

And the Lord said unto Moses: "Pharaoh will not hearken unto you; that My wonders may be multiplied in the land of Egypt." And Moses and Aaron did all these wonders before Pharaoh; and the Lord hardened Pharaoh's heart, and he did not let the children of Israel go out of his land (*ibid.*, 11.1,4-10).

THE PASSOVER

And the Lord spoke unto Moses and Aaron in the land of Egypt, saying: "This month shall be unto you the beginning of months; it shall be the first month of the year to you. Speak ye unto all the congregation of Israel, saying:

In the tenth day of this month they shall take to them every man a lamb, according to their fathers' houses, a lamb for a household. And ye shall keep it unto the four-teenth day of the same month, and the whole assembly of the congregation of Israel shall kill it at dusk. And they shall take of the blood and put it on the two side-posts and on the lintel, upon the houses wherein they shall eat it. And they shall eat the flesh in that night, roast with fire, and unleavened bread; with bitter herbs they shall eat it.

And thus shall ye eat it: with your loins girded, your shoes on your feet, and your staff in your hand; and ye shall eat in haste—it is the Lord's passover. For I will go through the land of Egypt in that night, and will smite all the first-born in the land of Egypt, both man and beast; and against all the gods of Egypt I will execute judgments: I am the Lord. And the blood shall be to you for a token upon the houses where ye are; and when I see the blood, I will pass over you, and there shall no plague be upon you to destroy you, when I smite the land of Egypt. And this day shall be unto you for a memorial, and ye shall keep it a feast to the Lord; throughout your generations ye shall keep it a feast by an ordinance for ever. Seven days shall ye eat unleavened bread; howbeit the first day ye shall put away leaven out of your houses; for whosoever eateth leavened bread from the first day until the seventh day, that soul shall be cut off from Israel. And in the first day there shall be to you a holy convocation and in the seventh day a holy convocation; no manner of work shall be done in them, save that which every man must eat; that only may be done by you. And ye shall observe the feast of unleavened bread; for in this selfsame day have I brought your hosts out of the land of Egypt; therefore shall ye observe this day throughout your generations by an ordinance forever. In the first month, on the fourteenth day of the month at even, ye shall eat unleavened bread, until the one and twentieth day of the month at even. Seven days shall there be no leaven found in your houses; for whosoever eateth that which is leavened, that soul shall be cut off from the congregation of Israel, whether he be a sojourner, or one that is born in the land. Ye shall eat nothing leavened; in all your habitations shall ye eat unleavened bread."

Then Moses called for all the elders of Israel, and said unto them: "Draw out and take you lambs according to your families, and kill the passover lamb. And ye shall take a bunch of hyssop, and dip it in the blood that is in the basin, and strike the lintel and the two side-posts with the blood that is in the basin; and none of you shall go out of the door of his house until the morning. For the Lord will pass through to smite the Egyptians; and when He seeth the blood upon the lintel, and on the two side-posts, the Lord will pass over the door and will not suffer the destroyer to come in unto your houses to smite you. And ye shall observe this thing for an ordinance to thee and to thy sons for ever. And it shall come to pass, when ye be come to the land which the Lord will give you, according as He hath promised, that ye shall keep this service. And it shall come to pass, when your children shall say unto you: What mean ye by this service? that ye shall say: It is the sacrifice of the Lord's passover, for that He passed over the houses of the children of Israel in Egypt when He smote the Egyptians and delivered our houses." And the people bowed the head and worshipped. And the children of Israel went and did so; as the Lord had commanded Moses and Aaron, so did they.

And it came to pass at midnight, that the Lord smote all the first-born in the land of Egypt, from the first-born of Pharaoh that sat on his throne unto the first-born of the captive that was in the dungeon, and all the first-born of cattle. And Pharaoh rose up in the night, he, and all his servants, and all the Egyptians; and there was a great cry in Egypt; for there was not a house where there was not one dead. And he called for Moses and Aaron by night and said: "Rise up, get you forth from among my people, both ye and the children of Israel; and go, serve the Lord, as ye have said. Take both your flocks and your herds, as ye have said, and be gone; and bless me also." And the Egyptians were urgent upon the people, to send them out of the land in haste; for they said: "We are all dead men." And the people took their dough before it was leavened, their kneading troughs being bound up in their clothes upon their shoulders. And the children of Israel did according to the word of Moses.

THE EXODUS

And the children of Israel journeyed from Rameses to Succoth, about six hundred thousand men on foot, beside children. And a mixed multitude went up also with them, and flocks, and herds, even very much cattle. And they baked unleavened cakes of the dough which they brought forth out of Egypt, for it was not leavened; because they were thrust out of Egypt and could not tarry, neither had they prepared for themselves any victual. Now the time that the children of Israel dwelt in Egypt was four hundred and thirty years. And it came to pass at the end of four hundred and thirty years, even the selfsame day it came to pass, that all the host of the Lord went out from the land of Egypt. It was a night of watching unto the Lord for bringing them out from the land of Egypt; this same night is a night of watching unto the Lord for all the children of Israel throughout their generations (*ibid.*, 12.1-3,6-8,11-35,37-42).

And Moses said unto the people: "Remember this day in which ye came out from Egypt, out of the house of bondage; for by strength of hand the Lord brought you out from this place; there shall no leavened bread be eaten. This day ye go forth in the month Abib. And it shall be when the Lord shall bring thee into the land of the Canaanite and the Hittite and the Amorite and the Hivite and the Jebusite, which He swore unto thy fathers to give thee, a land flowing with milk and honey, that thou shalt keep this service in this month. Seven days thou shalt eat unleavened bread, and in the seventh day shall be a feast to the Lord. Unleavened bread shall be eaten throughout the seven days; and there shall no leavened bread be seen with thee, neither shall there be leaven seen with thee, in all thy borders. And thou shalt tell thy son in that day, saying: It is because of that which the Lord did for me when I came forth out of Egypt. And it shall be for a sign unto thee upon thy hand, and for a memorial between thine eyes, that the law of the Lord may be in thy mouth; for with a strong hand hath the Lord brought thee out of Egypt. Thou shalt therefore keep this ordinance in its season from year to year.

THE PURSUIT TO THE SEA

And it came to pass, when Pharaoh had let the people go, that God led them not by the way of the land of the Philistines, although that was near; for God said: "Lest peradventure the people repent when they see war and they return to Egypt." But God led the people about, by the way of the wilderness by the Red Sea; and the children of Israel went up armed out of the land of Egypt. And Moses took the bones of Joseph with him; for he had straitly sworn the children of Israel, saying: "God will surely remember you; and ye shall carry up my bones away hence with you." And they took their journey from Succoth, and encamped in Etham, in the edge of the wilderness. And the Lord went before them by day in a pillar of cloud to lead them the way, and by night in a pillar of fire to give them light, that they might go by day and by night: the pillar of cloud by day and the pillar of fire by night departed not from before the people (*ibid.*, 13.3-10, 17-22).

And it was told the king of Egypt that the people were fled; and the heart of Pharaoh and of his servants was turned towards the people, and they said: "What is this we have done, that we have let Israel go from serving us?" And he made ready his chariots, and took his people with him. And he took six hundred chosen chariots, and all the chariots of Egypt, and captains over all of them. And the

113

Lord hardened the heart of Pharaoh king of Egypt, and he pursued after the children of Israel; for the children of Israel went out with a high hand.

And when Pharaoh drew nigh, the children of Israel lifted up their eyes and, behold, the Egyptians were marching after them, and they were sore afraid; and the children of Israel cried out unto the Lord. And they said unto Moses: "Because there were no graves in Egypt, hast thou taken us away to die in the wilderness? wherefore hast thou dealt thus with us, to bring us forth out of Egypt? Is not this the word that we spoke unto thee in Egypt, saying: Let us alone, that we may serve the Egyptians? For it were better for us to serve the Egyptians, than that we should die in the wilderness." And Moses said unto the people: "Fear ye not, stand still, and see the salvation of the Lord, which He will work for you today; for whereas ye have seen the Egyptians today, ye shall see them again no more for ever. The Lord will fight for you, and ye shall hold your peace."

And the Lord said unto Moses: "Wherefore criest thou unto Me? speak unto the children of Israel that they go forward. And lift thou up thy rod and stretch out thy hand over the sea, and divide it; and the children of Israel shall go into the midst of the sea on dry ground."

And the angel of God, who went before the camp of Israel, removed and went behind them; and the pillar of cloud removed from before them and stood behind them; and it came between the camp of Egypt and the camp of Israel; and there was the cloud and the darkness here, yet gave it light by night there; and the one came not near the other all the night. And Moses stretched out his hand over the sea and the Lord caused the sea to go back by a strong east wind all the night and made the sea dry land, and the waters were divided. And the children of Israel went into the midst of the sea upon the dry ground and the waters were a wall unto them on their right hand and on their left. And the Egyptians pursued and went in

114

after them into the midst of the sea, all Pharaoh's horses, his chariots and his horsemen. And it came to pass in the morning watch that the Lord looked forth upon the host of the Egyptians through the pillar of fire and of cloud, and discomfited the host of the Egyptians. And He took off their chariot wheels and made them to drive heavily; so that the Egyptians said: "Let us flee from the face of Israel; for the Lord fighteth for them against the Egyptians."

And the Lord said unto Moses: "Stretch out thy hand over the sea that the waters may come back upon the Egyptians, upon their chariots and upon their horsemen." And Moses stretched forth his hand over the sea and the sea returned to its strength when the morning appeared; and the Egyptians fled against it, and the Lord overthrew the Egyptians in the midst of the sea. And the waters returned, and covered the chariots and the horsemen, even all the host of Pharaoh that went in after them into the sea; there remained not so much as one of them. But the children of Israel walked upon dry land in the midst of the sea, and the waters were a wall unto them on their right hand and on their left. Thus the Lord saved Israel that day out of the hand of the Egyptians, and Israel saw the Egyptians dead upon the seashore. And Israel saw the great work which the Lord did upon the Egyptians, and the people feared the Lord; and they believed in the Lord, and in His servant Moses (*ibid.*, 14.5-8, 10-16,19-31).

THE SONG OF MOSES

Then sang Moses and the children of Israel this song unto the Lord, and spoke, saying:

I will sing unto the Lord, for He is highly exalted;
The horse and his rider hath He thrown into the sea.
The Lord is my strength and song,
And He is become my salvation;
This is my God, and I will glorify Him;

My father's God, and I will exalt Him.
The Lord is a man of war,
The Lord is His name.
Pharaoh's chariots and his host hath He cast into the
  sea,
And his chosen captains are sunk in the Red Sea.
The deeps cover them—
They went down into the depths like a stone.
Thy right hand, O Lord, glorious in power,
Thy right hand, O Lord, dasheth in pieces the enemy.
And in the greatness of Thine excellency Thou over-
  throwest them that rise up against Thee;
Thou sendest forth Thy wrath, it consumeth them as
  stubble.
And with the blast of Thy nostrils the waters were
  piled up—
The flood stood upright as a heap;
The deeps were congealed in the heart of the sea.
The enemy said:
"I will pursue, I will overtake, I will divide the spoil;
My lust shall be satisfied upon them;
I will draw my sword, my hand shall destroy them."
Thou didst blow with Thy wind, the sea covered them;
They sank as lead in the mighty waters.
Who is like unto Thee, O Lord, among the mighty?
Who is like unto Thee, glorious in holiness,
Fearful in praises, doing wonders?
Thou stretchedst out Thy right hand—
The earth swallowed them.
Thou in Thy love hast led the people that Thou hast
  redeemed;
Thou hast guided them in Thy strength to Thy holy
  habitation.
The people have heard, they tremble;
Pangs have taken hold on the inhabitants of Philistia.
Then were the chiefs of Edom affrighted;
The mighty men of Moab, trembling taketh hold upon
  them;

All the inhabitants of Canaan are melted away.
Terror and dread falleth upon them;
By the greatness of Thine arm they are as still as a
stone;
Till Thy people pass over, O Lord,
Till the people pass over that Thou hast gotten.
Thou bringest them in, and plantest them in the moun-
tain of Thine inheritance,
The place, O Lord, which Thou hast made for Thee
to dwell in,
The sanctuary, O Lord, which Thy hands have
established.
The Lord shall reign for ever and ever.

And Miriam the prophetess, the sister of Aaron, took
a timbrel in her hand, and all the women went out after
her with timbrels and with dances. And Miriam sang
unto them:
Sing ye to the Lord, for He is highly exalted:
The horse and his rider hath He thrown into the sea
(*ibid.*, 15.1-18,20-21).

THE OBSERVANCE OF PASSOVER

Three times thou shalt keep a feast unto Me in the year.
The feast of unleavened bread shalt thou keep; seven
days thou shalt eat unleavened bread, as I commanded
thee, at the time appointed in the month Abib—for in it
thou camest out from Egypt; and none shall appear before
Me empty; and the feast of harvest, the first-fruits of thy
labors, which thou sowest in the field; and the feast of
ingathering, at the end of the year, when thou gatherest
in thy labors out of the field. Three times in the year all
thy males shall appear before the Lord God (*ibid.*,
23.14-17).
These are the appointed seasons of the Lord, even holy
convocations, which ye shall proclaim in their appointed
season. In the first month, on the fourteenth day of the
month at dusk, is the Lord's passover. And on the fif-

teenth day of the same month is the feast of unleavened bread unto the Lord; seven days ye shall eat unleavened bread. In the first day ye shall have a holy convocation; ye shall do no manner of servile work. And ye shall bring an offering made by fire unto the Lord seven days; in the seventh day is a holy convocation; ye shall do no manner of servile work (Lev. 23.4-8).

The feast of unleavened bread shalt thou keep. Seven days thou shalt eat unleavened bread, as I commanded thee, at the time appointed in the month Abib, for in the month Abib thou camest out from Egypt. All that openeth the womb is Mine; and of all thy cattle thou shalt sanctify the males, the firstlings of ox and sheep. And the firstling of an ass thou shalt redeem with a lamb; and if thou wilt not redeem it, then thou shalt break its neck. All the first-born of thy sons thou shalt redeem. And none shall appear before Me empty. Six days thou shalt work, but on the seventh day thou shalt rest; in plowing time and in harvest thou shalt rest. And thou shalt observe the feast of weeks, even of the first-fruits of wheat harvest, and the feast of ingathering at the turn of the year. Three times in the year shall all thy males appear before the Lord God, the God of Israel. For I will cast out nations before thee, and enlarge thy borders; neither shall any man covet thy land, when thou goest up to appear before the Lord thy God three times in the year. Thou shalt not offer the blood of My sacrifice with leavened bread; neither shall the sacrifice of the feast of the passover be left unto the morning (Ex. 34.18-25).

Observe the month of Abib, and keep the passover unto the Lord thy God; for in the month of Abib the Lord thy God brought thee forth out of Egypt by night. And thou shalt sacrifice the passover-offering unto the Lord thy God, of the flock and the herd, in the place which the Lord shall choose to cause His name to dwell there. Thou shalt eat no leavened bread with it; seven days shalt thou eat unleavened bread therewith, even the bread of affliction; for in haste didst thou come forth out of the land of Egypt; that thou mayest remember the day when thou comest forth out of the land of Egypt all the days of thy life. And there shall be no leaven seen with thee in all thy borders seven days; neither shall any of the flesh, which thou sacrificest the first day at even, remain all night until the morning. Thou mayest not sacrifice the passover-offering within any of thy gates, which the Lord thy God giveth thee; but at the place which the Lord thy God shall choose to cause His name to dwell in, there thou shalt sacrifice the passover-offering at even, at the going down of the sun, at the season that thou camest forth out of Egypt. And thou shalt roast and eat it in the place which the Lord thy God shall choose; and thou shalt turn in the morning, and go unto thy tents. Six days thou shalt eat unleavened bread; and on the seventh day shall be a solemn assembly to the Lord thy God, thou shalt do no work therein (Deut. 16.1-8).

When thy son asketh thee in time to come, saying: "What mean the testimonies, and the statutes, and the ordinances, which the Lord our God hath commanded you?" then thou shalt say unto thy son: "We were Pharaoh's bondmen in Egypt; and the Lord brought us out of Egypt with a mighty hand. And the Lord showed signs and wonders, great and sore, upon Egypt, upon Pharaoh, and upon all his house, before our eyes. And He brought us out from thence, that He might bring us in, to give us the land which He swore unto our fathers" *(ibid.,* 6.20-23).

THE FIRST ANNIVERSARY

And the Lord spoke unto Moses in the wilderness of Sinai, in the first month of the second year after they were come out of the land of Egypt, saying: "Let the children of Israel keep the passover in its appointed season. In the fourteenth day of this month, at dusk, ye shall keep it in its appointed season; according to all of the statutes of it, and according to all the ordinances thereof, shall ye keep it." And Moses spoke unto the children of Israel, that

119

they should keep the passover. And they kept the passover in the first month, on the fourteenth day of the
month, at dusk, in the wilderness of Sinai; according to
all that the Lord commanded Moses, so did the children
of Israel (Nu. 9.1-5).

IN THE DAYS OF JOSHUA

And the Lord said unto Joshua: "This day have I rolled
away the reproach of Egypt from off you." Wherefore
the name of that place was called Gilgal, unto this day.

And the children of Israel encamped in Gilgal; and they
kept the passover on the fourteenth day of the month at
even in the plains of Jericho. And they did eat of the
produce of the land on the morrow after the passover,
unleavened cakes and parched corn, in the selfsame day
(Josh. 5.9-11).

WHEN KING SOLOMON RULED

Then Solomon offered burnt-offerings unto the Lord on
the altar of the Lord, which he had built before the porch,
even as the duty of every day required, offering according
to the commandment of Moses, on the sabbaths, and on
the new moons, and on the appointed seasons, three times
in the year, even in the feast of unleavened bread, and in
the feast of weeks, and in the feast of tabernacles (II
Chron. 8.12-13).

IN THE REIGN OF KING JOSIAH

And Josiah kept a passover unto the Lord in Jerusalem;
and they killed the passover lamb on the fourteenth day
of the first month. And he set the priests in their charges,
and encouraged them to the service of the house of the
Lord.

So all the service of the Lord was prepared the same
day, to keep the passover, and to offer burnt-offerings
upon the altar of the Lord, according to the commandment of king Josiah. And the children of Israel that were
present kept the passover at that time, and the feast of

unleavened bread seven days. And there was no passover like to that kept in Israel from the days of Samuel the prophet; neither did any of the kings of Israel keep such a passover as Josiah kept, and the priests, and the Levites, and all Judah and Israel that were present, and the inhabitants of Jerusalem. In the eighteenth year of the reign of Josiah was this passover kept *(ibid.,* 35.1-2, 16-19).

IN THE TIMES OF EZEKIEL

In the first month, in the fourteenth day of the month, ye shall have the passover; a feast of seven days; unleavened bread shall be eaten. And upon that day shall the prince prepare for himself and for all the people of the land a bullock for a sin-offering. And the seven days of the feast he shall prepare a burnt-offering to the Lord, seven bullocks and seven rams without blemish daily the seven days; and a he-goat daily for a sin-offering. And he shall prepare a meal-offering, an ephah for a bullock, and an ephah for a ram, and a hin of oil to an ephah (Ezek. 45.21-24).

PASSOVER OF THE RETURNED EXILES

And the children of the captivity kept the passover upon the fourteenth day of the first month. For the priests and the Levites had purified themselves together; all of them were pure; and they killed the passover lamb for all the children of the captivity, and for their brethren the priests, and for themselves. And the children of Israel, that were come back out of the captivity, and all such as had separated themselves unto them from the filthiness of the nations of the land, to seek the Lord, the God of Israel, did eat and kept the feast of unleavened bread seven days with joy; for the Lord had made them joyful, and had turned the heart of the king of Assyria unto them, to strengthen their hands in the work of the house of God, the God of Israel (Ez. 6.19-22).

121

THE SECOND PASSOVER

And the Lord spoke unto Moses, saying: "Speak unto the children of Israel, saying: If any man of you or of your generations shall be unclean by reason of a dead body, or be in a journey afar off, yet he shall keep the passover unto the Lord; in the second month on the fourteenth day at dusk they shall keep it; they shall eat it with unleavened bread and bitter herbs; they shall leave none of it unto the morning, nor break a bone thereof; according to all the statute of the passover they shall keep it (Nu. 9.9-12).

THE SECOND PASSOVER IN THE DAYS OF KING HEZEKIAH

And Hezekiah sent to all Israel and Judah, and wrote letters also to Ephraim and Manasseh, that they should come to the house of the Lord at Jerusalem, to keep the passover unto the Lord, the God of Israel. For the king had taken counsel, and his princes, and all the congregation in Jerusalem, to keep the passover in the second month. For they could not keep it at that time, because the priests had not sanctified themselves in sufficient number, neither had the people gathered themselves together to Jerusalem. And the thing was right in the eyes of the king and of all the congregation. So they established a decree to make proclamation throughout all Israel, from Beer-Sheba even to Dan, that they should come to keep the passover unto the Lord, the God of Israel, at Jerusalem; for they had not kept it in great numbers according as it is written.

And there assembled at Jerusalem much people to keep the feast of unleavened bread in the second month, a very great congregation. And they arose and took away the altars that were in Jerusalem, and all the altars for incense took they away, and cast them into the brook Kidron. Then they killed the passover lamb on the fourteenth day of the second month: and the priests and the

122

Levites were ashamed, and sanctified themselves, and brought burnt-offerings into the house of the Lord. And they stood in their place after their order, according to the law of Moses the man of God; the priests dashed the blood, which they received of the hand of the Levites. For there were many in the congregation that had not sanctified themselves; therefore the Levites had the charge of killing the passover lambs for every one that was not clean, to sanctify them unto the Lord. For a multitude of the people, even many of Ephraim and Manasseh, Issachar and Zebulun, had not cleansed themselves, yet did they eat the passover otherwise than it is written. For Hezekiah had prayed for them, saying: "The good Lord pardon every one that setteth his heart to seek God, the Lord, the God of his fathers, though [he be] not [cleansed] according to the purification that pertaineth to holy things." And the Lord hearkened to Hezekiah, and healed the people. And the children of Israel that were present at Jerusalem kept the feast of unleavened bread seven days with great gladness; and the Levites and the priests praised the Lord day by day, singing with loud instruments unto the Lord. And Hezekiah spoke encouragingly unto all the Levites that were well skilled in the service of the Lord. So they did eat throughout the feast for the seven days, offering sacrifices of peace-offerings, and giving thanks to the Lord, the God of their fathers.

And the whole congregation took counsel to keep other seven days; and they kept other seven days with gladness. For Hezekiah king of Judah did give to the congregation for offerings a thousand bullocks and seven thousand sheep; and the princes gave to the congregation a thousand bullocks and ten thousand sheep; and priests sanctified themselves in great numbers. And all the congregation of Judah, with the priests and the Levites, and all the congregation that came out of Israel, and the strangers that came out of the land of Israel, and that dwelt in Judah, rejoiced. So there was great joy in Jerusalem; for since the time of Solomon the son of David king of Israel there was not the like in Jerusalem. Then the priests, the Levites, arose and blessed the people; and their voice was heard [of the Lord], and their prayer came up to His holy habitation, even unto heaven (II Chron. 30.1-5,13-27).

Introductory Note

During the period following the Babylonian capture of
Jerusalem, a number of Jews emigrated to Egypt and
established a Jewish colony there. Some of them, settling
near the Egyptian border, served as frontier guards.
Among the Aramaic papyri discovered at Elephantine,
Egypt, in 1905, there is a remarkable letter containing
a rescript of the Persian king Darius II, who then reigned
over Egypt, addressed to the Jewish garrison in 419
B.C.E., which directs his Jewish frontier guards to observe the Passover. It would seem that the Egyptians
were objecting to the Passover commemoration in their
land but that the Persian administration sided with the
Jews.[1]

Jews in the Diaspora for a period of more than half a
millennium, about 330 B.C.E. to about 200 C.E., developed significant literary creations in the Greek language.
Many of these hellenistic Jewish works reveal interesting
aspects of the origin of Passover and the traditions of its
observance that had developed. Foremost among these
writings is the Septuagint, a Greek translation of the
Hebrew Bible made by Jews in Alexandria, which includes

a number of additional or "hidden books" known as the Apocrypha. One of these works, *The Wisdom of Solomon,* is an example of philosophical or didactic writing. The selection from this book quoted below attempts to demonstrate the appropriateness of the plague of darkness inflicted on the Egyptians.

Drama was likewise represented in hellenistic Jewish literature, as is evidenced by *The Exodus from Egypt,* by Ezekiel (Ezekielos) of Alexandria, the first Jewish dramatist, who lived in the second century B.C.E.

Philo of Alexandria (about 20 B.C.E. to about 50 C.E.) whose original thinking has left an indelible impression on the religious philosophy of western Europe, did not exert much influence in Jewish life. He is noted both for his literal and historical acceptance of the Bible and for his allegorical interpretations. The excerpts below demonstrate Philo's use of Jewish Law to expound ethical ideals.

Flavius Josephus (about 38 C.E. to about 100 C.E.), the controversial Jewish historian, in his *Against Apion* describes the antisemitism that existed in Egypt and, in *Jewish Antiquities,* the Exodus and the origin of the feast of unleavened bread. In the latter work, he gives his interpretation of the prayer of Moses at the Red Sea. In *The Jewish War,* Josephus narrates the Passover observance at the time of the fall of the Second Temple.

Hananiah to Jedoniah, Head of the Jewish Community of Elephantine[2]

To my Brethren, Jedoniah and his colleagues the Jewish garrison, your brother Hananiah. The welfare of my brethren may the gods seek.

Now this year, the fifth year of King Darius [Darius

II, King of Persia, 424-404 B.C.E.], word was sent from the King to Arsames [Persian governor of Egypt] saying: In the month of Tybi let there be a Passover for the Jewish garrison. Now do you accordingly count fourteen days of the month Nisan and keep the Passover, and from the fifteenth day to the twenty-first day of Nisan [shall be] seven days of unleavened bread. Be clean and take heed. Do not work on the fifteenth day and on the twenty-first day. Also drink no beer, and anything at all in which there is leaven do not eat from the fifteenth day from sunset till the twenty-first day of Nisan, seven days; let it not be seen among you; do not bring [it] into your dwelling, but seal [it] up during those days. Let this be done as Darius the King commanded.

[Address] To my brethren, Jedoniah and his colleagues the Jewish garrison, your brother Hananiah.

The Plague of Darkness[3]

For when lawless men thought they were oppressing a
    holy nation
They lay shut up under their roofs, exiled from the eternal
    providence,
Prisoners of darkness and captives of the long night . . .
And the delusions of magic art were prostrate,
And their boasted wisdom suffered a contemptuous
    rebuke,
For those who claimed to drive away fears and troubles
    from sick souls
Were sick themselves with ridiculous fear . . .
For they were all bound with one chain of darkness.
Whether there was a whistling wind,
Or a melodious sound of birds in spreading branches,

127

Or the regular noise of rushing water,
Or a harsh crashing of rocks thrown down,
Or the unseen running of bounding animals,
Or the sound of the most savage wild beasts roaring,
Or an echo thrown back from a hollow in the mountains,
It paralyzed them with terror.
For the whole world was bathed in bright light,
And occupied in unhindered work;
Only over them was spread a heavy night,
A picture of the darkness that was to receive them . . .
    But your holy ones enjoyed a very great light;
And the others, hearing their voices but not seeing their
    forms,
Thought them happy, because they had not suffered,
But they were thankful because the others, though they
    had before been wronged, did not hurt them,
And prayed to be separated from them.
Therefore you provided a blazing pillar
As guide on their unknown journey,
And an unharmful sun for their honorable exile.
For they deserved to be deprived of light and imprisoned
    in darkness
Who had kept your sons shut up,
Through whom the imperishable light of the Law was to
    be given to the world *(The Wisdom of Solomon*
    17.2,7-8,17-21,18.1-4).

The Exodus from Egypt[4]

EZEKIELOS OF ALEXANDRIA

MOSES

Methought upon Mount Sinai's brow I saw
A mighty throne that reached to heaven's high vault,

128

Whereon there sat a man of noblest mien
Wearing a royal crown; whose left hand held
A mighty scepter; and his right to me
Made sign, and I stood forth before the throne.
He gave me then the scepter and the crown,
And bade me sit upon the royal throne,
From which himself removed. Thence I looked forth
Upon the earth's wide circle, and beneath
The earth itself, and high above the heaven.
Then at my feet, behold! a thousand stars
Began to fall, and I their number told,
As they passed by me like an armed host:
And I in terror started up from sleep.

REUEL

This sign from God bodes good to thee, my friend.
Would I might live to see thy lot fulfilled!
A mighty throne shalt thou set up, and be
Thyself the leader and the judge of men!
And as o'er all the peopled earth thine eye
Looked forth, and underneath the earth, and high
Above God's heaven; so shall thy mind survey
All things in time, past, present, and to come.

MOSES

Ha! See! What sign is this from yonder bush?
A marvel such as no man might believe,
A sudden mighty fire flames round the bush,
And yet its growth remains all green and fresh,
What then? I will go forward, and behold
This wondrous sign, that passes man's belief.

GOD

Stay, Moses, faithful servant, draw not nigh,
Ere thou hast loosed thy shoes from off thy feet:
The place thou standest on is holy ground;
And from this bush God's word shines forth for thee.
Fear not, My son, but hearken to My words.

129

Of mortal birth, thou canst not see My face;
Yet mayest thou hear the words I came to speak.
Thy fathers' God, the God of Abraham,
Of Isaac, and of Jacob, I am God.
I do remember all My gifts to them,
And come to save My people Israel;
For I have seen their sorrows and their toils.
Go, then, and signify thou in My name,
First to the Hebrews gathered by themselves,
Then to the king of Egypt, this My will,
That thou lead forth My people from the land.

MOSES

I am not eloquent, O Lord, but slow
Of speech my tongue, and weak my stammering voice
To utter words of mine before the king.

GOD

Thy brother, Aaron, I will send with speed.
First tell thou him all I have told to thee;
And he before the king, and thou with Me
Alone shalt speak, he what he hears from thee.

Say, what is that thou holdest in thine hand?

MOSES

A rod, wherewith to smite beasts or men.

GOD

Cast it upon the ground, and flee in haste;
For a fierce serpent will affright thine eye.

MOSES

Lo, there I cast it. Save me, gracious Lord!
How huge, how fierce! In pity spare Thou me.
I shudder at the sight, in every limb.

130

GOD

Fear not: stretch forth thy hand, and seize the tail.
Again 'twill be a rod. Now thrust thy hand
Into thy bosom; take it out again.
See, at My word, 'tis leprous, white as snow.
Now thrust it in again; 'tis as before.

With this thy rod thou shalt work all these plagues.
The river first shall flow all red with blood,
And every spring, and stream, and stagnant pool.
Then frogs and lice shall swarm o'er all the land.
Next, ashes from the furnace sprinkled 'round,
In ulcers sore shall burst on man and beast,
And swarms of flies shall come, and sore afflict
The bodies of the Egyptians. After that,
On those hard hearts the pestilence and death
Shall fall. And heaven's wrath let loose on high
Shall pour down fire and hail and deadly storm
On man, and beast, and all the fruits of earth.
Then shall be darkness over all the land
For three whole days, and locusts shall devour
All food, all fruits, and every blade of grass.
Moreover, I will slay each first-born child,
And crush this evil nation's wanton pride.
Yet none of these My plagues shall touch the king,
Until he sees his first-born son lie dead;
Then will he send you forth in fear and haste.
This also speak to all the Hebrew race:
This month shall be the first month of your year,
Wherein I bring you to that other land,
As to the fathers of your race I sware.
Also command the people, in this month,
At evening ere the moon's full orb appear,
To sacrifice the Passover to God,
And strike the side-posts of the door with blood;
So shall My messenger of death pass by.

But the flesh eat ye roast with fire at night.
Then will the king drive forth your gathered host
In haste; but ere ye go, I will give grace
To this My people in the Egyptians' eyes,
So that each woman from her neighbor's store
All needful vessels freely shall receive,
Silver and gold, and raiment meet for man,
To make requital for their evil deeds.
And when ye shall have reached your promised land,
Take heed that, from the morn whereon ye fled
From Egypt and marched onward seven whole days,
From that same morn so many days each year
Ye eat unleavened bread, and serve your God,
Offering the first-born of all living things,
All males that open first the mother's womb.

And when the tenth day of this month is come,
Let every Hebrew for his household choose
Unblemished lambs and calves, and keep them up
Until the fourteenth day; and then at eve
Offer the solemn sacrifice; and eat
The flesh and inward parts all roast with fire.
Thus shall ye eat, with your loins girt up,
And shoes upon your feet, a staff withal
Held ready in your hand; for in great haste
The king will bid them drive you from his land.
Let each man's eating for the lamb make count;
And when the victim has been duly slain,
Take a full bunch of hyssop in your hand,
Dipped in the sacred blood, and therewith strike
The posts and upper lintel of the door;
That death may pass o'er every Hebrew's house.
Keep ever thus this feast unto the Lord,
Eating for seven days unleavened bread,
And in your houses let no leaven be found,
For ye shall be delivered, and the Lord

Shall lead you forth from Egypt in this month,
Henceforth to be the first month of your year.

MESSENGER

For when King Pharaoh from his house set forth
With all this crowd of countless men-at-arms,
With horsemen, and with four-horsed chariots,
In serried ranks in front and on each flank,
The embattled host was dreadful to behold.
The center footmen held in phalanx deep
With spaces for the chariots to drive through.
And on the right wing and the left were set
The best of all the Egyptian chivalry.
The numbers of our army which I asked,
Were thousand thousands of brave well-armed men.
The Hebrews, when o'ertaken by our host,
Lay some in groups hard by the Red Sea shore
Worn out with toil, and others with their wives
To feed their tender infants were intent;
Cumbered with flocks and herds and household goods.
The men themselves with hands not armed for fight,
At sight of us, set up a doleful cry,
And all, with hands uplift to heaven, invoked
Their father's God. Great was their multitude;
But on our side all jubilant our camp.
Behind them close we pitched, where by the sea
There lies a city, Baal-zephon hight.
And as the sun was nearing his western couch,
We waited, longing for the fight at dawn,
Trusting our mighty host and deadly arms,
But now the signs of heaven's own wrath began,
A dread and wondrous sight. For suddenly
A pillar of cloud rose high above the earth
Midway between the Hebrew camp and ours;
And then their leader Moses took his rod
Of power divine, which late on Egypt wrought
So many baneful signs and prodigies.

133

Therewith he struck the waves, and the deep sea
Was cleft asunder; and with eager steps
Their host rushed swiftly o'er that briny path.
We then upon their track without delay
Trod the same path, and marching forward, met
The darkness of the night, when suddenly,
As if fast bound in chains, our chariot wheels
Refused to turn; and from the sky a flame
As of a mighty fire before us shone.
Their God, methinks, was there to succor them:
For they no sooner reached the farther shore,
Than close at hand we heard the mighty roar
Of surging waves; and one in terror cried:
Flee from the vengeful hand of the Most High,
For it is He that helps our enemies,
And works for our destruction. Then, the sea
Surged o'er our path, and overwhelmed our host.

WATCHER

See, my lord Moses, what a spot is found
Fanned by sweet airs from yonder shady grove.
For as thyself mayest see, there lies the stream,
And thence at night the fiery pillar shed
Its welcome guiding light. A meadow there
Beside the stream in grateful shadow lies,
And a deep glen in rich abundance pours
From out a single rock twelve sparkling springs.
There tall and strong, and laden all with fruit,
Stand palms threescore and ten; and plenteous grass
Well watered gives sweet pasture to our flocks.
Another living thing we saw, more strange
And marvelous than man e'er saw before.
The noblest eagle scarce was half as large:
His outspread wings with varying colors shone;
The breast was bright with purple, and the legs
With crimson glowed, and on the shapely neck
The golden plumage shone in graceful curves;

The head was like a gentle nestling's formed;
Bright shone the yellow circlet of the eye
On all around, and wondrous sweet the voice,
The king he seemed of all wingèd tribe,
As soon was proved; for birds of every kind
Hovered in fear behind his stately form;
While like a bull, proud leader of the herd,
Foremost he marched with swift and haughty step.

Special Laws of Passover[5]

PHILO OF ALEXANDRIA

The bread is unleavened either because our forefathers, when under divine guidance they were starting on their migration, were so intensely hurried that they brought the lumps of dough unleavened, or else because at that season, namely, the springtime, when the feast is held, the fruit of the corn has not reached its perfection, for the fields are in the ear stage and not yet mature for harvest. It was the imperfection of this fruit which belonged to the future, though it was to reach its perfection very shortly, that He considered might be paralleled by the unleavened food, which is also imperfect, and serves to remind us of the comforting hope that nature, possessing as she does a superabundant wealth of things needful, is already preparing her yearly gifts to the human race.

Another suggestion made by the interpreters of the holy scriptures is that food, when unleavened, is a gift of nature, when leavened is a work of art. For men, in their eagerness to temper the barely necessary with the pleasant, have learned through practice to soften by art what nature has made hard.

135

Since, then, the springtime feast, as I have laid down, is a reminder of the creation of the world—and its earliest inhabitants, children of earth in the first or second generation must have used the gifts of the universe in their unperverted state before pleasure had got the mastery—He ordained for use on this occasion the food most fully in accordance with the season. He wished every year to rekindle the embers of the serious and ascetic mode of faring, and to employ the leisure of a festal assembly to confer admiration and honor on the old-time life of frugality and economy, and as far as possible to assimilate our present-day life to that of the distant past. These statements are especially guaranteed by the exposure of the twelve loaves, corresponding in number to the tribes, on the holy table. They are all unleavened, the clearest possible example of a food free from admixture, in the preparation of which art for the sake of pleasure has no place, but only nature, providing nothing save what is indispensable for its use. So much for this (*The Special Laws,* Book II, 158-161).

Leaven is forbidden because of the rising which it produces. Here again we have a symbol of the truth, that none as he approaches the altar should be uplifted or puffed up by arrogance; rather gazing on the greatness of God, let him gain a perception of the weakness which belongs to the creature, even though he may be superior to others in prosperity; and having been thus led to the reasonable conclusion, let him reduce the overweening exaltation of his pride by laying low that pestilent enemy, conceit. For if the Creator and Maker of the universe, though needing nothing of all that He has begotten, has regard to your weakness and not to the vastness of His might and sovereignty, makes you a partaker in His gracious power and fills up the deficiencies that belong to your life, how ought you to treat other men, your natural kinsfolk, seedlings from the same elements as yourself, you who brought nothing into the world, not even your-

11. *Top:* Jethro, Balaam and Job Watch Moses Remove Pharaoh's Crown
   Bottom: The Testing of Moses

Kaufmann Haggadah

Nuremberg Haggadah

12. Moses Removing Pharaoh's Crown

13. Woman Praying Near a Passover Table

Crawford Haggadah

Frankfort Haggadah

14. Teacher and Pupil

Haggadah, British Museum

15. Reading the Haggadah in the Synagogue

self? For naked you came into the world, worthy sir, and naked will you again depart, and the span of time between your birth and death is a loan to you from God. During this span what can be meet for you to do but to study fellow-feeling and goodwill and equity and humanity and what else belongs to virtue, and to cast away the inequitable, unrighteous and unforgiving viciousness which turns man, naturally the most civilized of creatures, into a wild and ferocious animal! *(ibid.,* Book I, 293-295).

The Deeper Meaning of Unleavened Bread and Bitter Herbs[6]

PHILO OF ALEXANDRIA

[Why] does He say (Ex. 12.8) that they shall offer [eat] unleavened bread on bitter herbs together with the above-mentioned sacrifice?

Unleavened bread is [a sign] of great haste and speed, while the bitter herbs [are a sign] of the life of bitterness and struggle which they endure as slaves. That is the literal meaning. But as for the deeper meaning, this is worth noting [namely], that that which is leavened and fermented rises, while that which is unleavened is low. Each of these is a symbol of types of soul, one being haughty and swollen with arrogance, the other being unchangeable and prudent, choosing the middle way rather than extremes because of desire and zeal for equality. But the bitter herbs are a manifestation of a psychic migration, through which one removes from passion to impassivity and from wickedness to virtue. For those who naturally and genuinely repent become bitter toward

137

their former way of life and are vexed with their wretched life, weeping, sighing and groaning because they have given over the most necessary part of time to that seductive and deceitful mistress, Desire, and have spent the prime of their youth in being deceived by her when they ought to have renewed themselves and advanced in the contemplation of wisdom toward the goal of a happy, fortunate and immortal life. And so, we who desire repentance eat the unleavened bread with bitter herbs, that is, we first eat bitterness over our old and unendurable life, and then [we eat] the opposite of overboastful arrogance through meditation on humility, which is called reverence. For the memory of former sins causes fear, and by restraining it through recollection brings no little profit to the mind (*ibid.*, Book I, 15).

The Burning Bush[7]

PHILO OF ALEXANDRIA

Now, as he [Moses] was leading the flock to a place where the water and the grass were abundant, and where there happened to be plentiful growth of herbage for the sheep, he found himself at a glen where he saw a most astonishing sight. There was a bramble-bush, a thorny sort of plant and of the most weakly kind, which, without anyone's setting it alight, suddenly took fire; and, though enveloped from root to twigs in a mass of fire, which looked as though it were spouted up from a fountain, yet remained whole and, instead of being consumed, seemed to be a substance impervious to attack and, instead of serving as fuel to the fire, actually fed on it. In the midst of the flame was a form of the fairest beauty, unlike any visible object, an image supremely divine in appearance, refulgent with a light brighter than the light of fire. It might be supposed that this was the image of Him that is; but let us rather call it an angel or herald since, with a silence that spoke more clearly than speech, it employed as it were the miracle of sight to herald future events. For the burning bramble was a symbol of those who suffered wrong, as the flaming fire was of those who did it. Yet that which burned was not burnt up, and this was a sign that the sufferers would not be destroyed by their aggressors, who would find that the aggression was vain and profitless while the victims of malice escaped unharmed. The angel was a symbol of God's providence, which all silently brings relief to the greatest dangers, exceeding every hope. But the details of the comparison must be considered. The bramble, as I have said, is a very weakly plant, yet it is prickly and will wound if one do but touch it. Again, though fire is naturally destructive, the bramble was not devoured thereby, but on the contrary was guarded by it, and remained just as it was before it took fire, lost nothing at all but gained an additional brightness. All this is a description of the nation's condition as it then stood, and we may think of it as a voice proclaiming to the sufferers: "Do not lose heart; your weakness is your strength, which can prick, and thousands will suffer from its wound. Those who desire to consume you will be your unwilling saviors instead of your destroyers. Your ills will work you no ill. Nay, just when the enemy is surest of ravaging you, your flame will shine forth most gloriously." Again fire, the element which works destruction, convicts the cruel-hearted. "Exult not in your own strength," it says. "Behold your invincible might brought low, and learn wisdom. The property of flame is to consume, yet it is consumed, like wood. The nature of wood is to be consumed yet it is manifested as the consumer, as though it were the fire" *(Moses* I. 65-70).

At the Time of the Fall of the Second Temple[8]

FLAVIUS JOSEPHUS

The total number of prisoners taken throughout the entire war amounted to ninety-seven thousand—and of those who perished during the siege, from first to last, to one million one hundred thousand. Of these the greater number were of Jewish blood, but not natives of the place, for, having assembled from every part of the country for the feast of unleavened bread, they found themselves suddenly enveloped in the war, with the result that this overcrowding produced first pestilence and, later, the added and more rapid scourge of famine. That the city could contain so many is clear from the count taken under Cestius. For he, being anxious to convince Nero, who held the nation in contempt, of the city's strength, instructed the chief priests, if by any means possible, to take a census of the population. Accordingly, on the occasion of the feast called Passover—at which they sacrifice from the ninth to the eleventh hour, and a little fraternity, as it were, of not fewer than ten persons gathers round each sacrifice (feasting alone not being permitted), while the companies often include as many as twenty—the victims were counted and amounted to two hundred and fifty-five thousand six hundred; allowing an average of ten diners to each victim, we obtain a total of two million seven hundred thousand, all pure and holy. For those afflicted with leprosy or gonorrhea, menstrous women or persons otherwise defiled were not permitted to partake of this sacrifice; nor yet could any foreigners be present for worship, a large number of whom assemble from abroad. But now the whole nation had been shut up by fate as in a prison, and the city when war encompassed it was packed with inhabitants. The victims thus outnumbered those of any previous visitation, human or divine *(Jewish War* VI.9.3-4).

Anti-Judaism in Egypt[9]

FLAVIUS JOSEPHUS

Now the Egyptians were the first that cast reproaches upon us, in order to please which nation, some others undertook to pervert the truth, while they would neither own that our forefathers came into Egypt from another country, as the fact was, nor give a true account of their departure thence; and indeed the Egyptians took many occasions to hate us and envy us; in the first place because our ancestors had had the dominion over their country, and when they were delivered from them, and had gone to their own country, they lived there in prosperity. In the next place, the difference of our religion from theirs had occasioned great enmity between us, while our way of divine worship did as much exceed that which their laws appointed, as does the nature of God exceed that of brute beasts; for so far they all agree through the whole country, to esteem such animals as gods, although they differ from one another in the peculiar worship they severally pay to them; and certainly they are entirely of vain and foolish minds, who have thus accustomed themselves from the beginning to have such bad notions concerning their gods and could not think of imitating that decent form of divine worship which we made use of—though, when they saw our institutions approved of by many others, they could not but envy us on that account; for some of them

141

have proceeded to that degree of folly and meanness in their conduct, as not to scruple to contradict their own ancient records, nay, to contradict themselves also in their writings, and yet were so blinded by their passions as not to discern it.

And now I turn to one of their principal writers, whom I have a little made use of as a witness to our antiquity: I mean Manetho. He promised to interpret the Egyptian history out of their sacred writings, and premised thus: that "our people had come into Egypt, many ten thousands in numbers, and subdued its inhabitants"; and he further confessed that "we went out of that country afterward, and settled in that country which is now called Judea, and there built Jerusalem and its Temple." Now, thus far, he followed his ancient records; but after that he permits himself to write that rumors and reports passed abroad about the Jews, and introduces incredible narrations, as if he would have the Egyptian multitude, that had the leprosy and other distempers, to have been mixed with us and condemned to fly out of Egypt together with us *(Against Apion* I.25-26).

The Exodus and the Origin of the Feast of Unleavened Bread[10]

FLAVIUS JOSEPHUS

God, having revealed that by yet one more plague he would constrain the Egyptians to release the Hebrews, now bade Moses instruct the people to have ready a sacrifice, making preparations on the tenth of the month Xanthicus over against the fourteenth day (this is the month called by the Egyptians Pharmuthi, by the Hebrews

Nisan, and by the Macedonians termed Xanthicus) and then to lead off the Hebrews, taking all their possessions with them. He accordingly had the Hebrews ready betimes for departure, and ranging them in fraternities kept them assembled together; then when the fourteenth day was come the whole body, in readiness to start, sacrificed, purified the houses with the blood, using bunches of hyssop to sprinkle it, and after the repast burnt the remnants of the meat as persons on the eve of departure. Hence comes it that to this day we keep this sacrifice in the same customary manner, calling the feast Pascha, which signifies "passing over," because on that day God passed over our people when he smote the Egyptians with plague. For on that selfsame night destruction visited the first-born of Egypt, insomuch that multitudes of those whose dwellings surrounded the palace trooped to Pharaothes to urge him to let the Hebrews go. And he, summoning Moses, ordered him to depart, supposing that, once his people were quit of the country, Egypt's sufferings would cease. They even honored the Hebrews with gifts, some to speed their departure, others from neighborly feelings towards old acquaintances.

So they departed, amid the lamentation and regrets of the Egyptians for having treated them so hardly. They took the road for Letopolis, at that time desert, afterwards the site of Babylon, founded by Cambyses when he subjugated Egypt. Quitting the country by the shortest route they arrived on the third day at Beel-sephon, a place beside the Red Sea. Being bereft of any sustenance from the barren soil, they kneaded flour, baked it with merely a slight heating, and subsisted on the bread so made; on this they lived for thirty days, for they could make what they had brought from Egypt last no longer, notwithstanding that they rationed the food, limiting the portions to bare needs without eating to satiety. Hence it is that, in memory of that time of scarcity, we keep for eight days a feast called the feast of unleavened bread *(Jewish Antiquities* II.311-317).

The Prayer of Moses at the Red Sea[11]

FLAVIUS JOSEPHUS

He [Moses] led them towards the sea under the eyes of the Egyptians; for these were in view but, exhausted with the fatigue of the pursuit, judged it well to defer battle until the morrow. Then, when he reached the shore, Moses took his staff and made supplication to God, invoking His alliance and aid in these words: "Thou thyself knowest full well that escape from our present plight passes alike the might and the wit of man; nay, if there be any means of salvation at all for this host which at Thy will has left Egypt, Thine it is to provide it. For our part, despairing of other hope or resource, we fling ourselves upon Thy protection alone, and expectantly, if aught be forthcoming from Thy providence of might to snatch us from the wrath of the Egyptians, we look to Thee. May it come quickly, this aid that shall manifest to us Thy power; raise the hearts of this people, whom hopelessness has sunk into the depths of woe, to serenity and confidence of salvation. Nor are these straits in which we find ourselves without Thy domain; nay, Thine is the sea, Thine the mountain that encompasseth us: this then can open at Thy command, or the deep become dry land, or we might e'en find escape through the air, should it please Thine almighty power that after this manner we should be saved" (*ibid.*, II.333-337).

Introductory Note

The lessons drawn from the ancient Egyptian bondage of
the children of Israel and their Exodus from the land of
oppression were taught again and again by the Jewish
sages in the vast literature of the Talmud and Midrash.
Through commentary, interpretation and legend, the
Passover story was given new and added meanings. Especially true is this of the narrative portions of the Bible
which were embellished with ethical and moral teachings.

An entire tractate of the Talmud, containing one hundred and twenty folios, Pesahim (Paschal Lambs), details the laws of Passover and presents homiletic material.
Other tractates also include references to the account of
the Exodus and its significance.

Of the midrashim from which we quote, one of the
oldest is *Mekhilta de-Rabbi Ishmael*, an exposition of
portions of the Book of Exodus. *Midrash Shemot Rabbah*
is an extensive study and interpretation of the same biblical book. One of the important works of the rabbinic
pseudepigrapha, *Pirke de-Rabbi Eliezer*, contains many
interpretative renderings of the story of Passover. This
work, whose putative author is Rabbi Eliezer son of

145

Hyrcanus, of the first and second centuries C.E., was probably completed in the ninth century. *Midrash Tehillim*, according to a modern scholar, expanded "by accretion" from the third century C.E. to the thirteenth century. It consists largely of homilies upon passages in the Book of Psalms.

Sefer ha-Yashar (Book of the Righteous), first printed in 1552 at Naples, was an attempt by an unknown author to collate and present sundry biblical legends in a popular style.

BONDAGE IN EGYPT

A change in the relations of the Egyptians towards the Israelites had, indeed, been noticeable immediately after the death of Joseph, but they did not throw off their mask completely until Levi, the last of the sons of Jacob, was no more. Then the slavery of the Israelites supervened in good earnest.

The first hostile act on the part of the Egyptians was to deprive the Israelites of their fields, their vineyards, and the gifts that Joseph had sent to his brethren. Not content with these hostile acts, they sought to do them harm in other ways *(Sefer ha-Yashar Shemot* 118a, 122a-122b).

The physical strength and heroism of the Israelites were extraordinary and therefore alarming to the Egyptians. There were many occasions at that time for the display of prowess. Not long after the death of Levi occurred that of the Egyptian king Magron, who had been brought up by Joseph, and therefore was not wholly without grateful recollection of what he and his family had accomplished for the welfare of Egypt. But his son and successor Malol, together with his whole court, knew not the sons of Jacob and their achievements, and they did not scruple to oppress the Hebrews.

The final breach between them and the Egyptians took place during the wars waged by Malol against Zepho, the grandson of Esau. In the course of it, the Israelites had saved the Egyptians from a crushing defeat, but instead

146

of being grateful they sought only the undoing of their benefactors, from fear that the great strength of the Hebrews might be turned against them *(ibid.,* 112b, 125a-125b).

Even as a bird is held fast in the hand of the hunter who, if he wishes, slays it, or if he wishes, lets it live, so Israel was held fast in the hand of the Egyptians, as Scripture notes in saying (Ex. 3.8), *I am come down to deliver them out of the hand of the Egyptians (Midrash Tehillim* 107.4).

ADVICE OF THE COUNSELLORS

In the one hundred and thirtieth year after Israel's going down to Egypt, Pharaoh dreamed that he was sitting upon his throne. He lifted up his eyes, and he beheld an old man before him with a balance in his hand. He saw him taking all the elders, nobles, and great men of Egypt, binding them together, and laying them in one scale of the balance, while he put a tender kid in the other. The kid bore down the pan in which it lay until it sank lower than the other with the bound Egyptians. Pharaoh arose early in the morning, and called together all his servants and his wise men to interpret his dream. The men were greatly afraid on account of his vision. Balaam the son of Beor then spoke, and said, "This means nothing but that a great evil will spring up against Egypt. A son will be born unto Israel, who will destroy the whole of our land and all its inhabitants, and he will bring forth the Israelites from Egypt with a mighty hand. Now, therefore, O king, take counsel as to this matter, that the scheme of Israel be frustrated before this evil arise against Egypt."

The king said unto Balaam, "What shall we do unto Israel? We have tried several devices against this people, but we could not prevail over it. Now let me hear your opinion."

At Balaam's instance, the king sent for his two counsellors, Reuel the Midianite and Job the Uzite, to hear their counsel. Reuel spoke: "If it appears good to the

147

king, let him desist from the Hebrews, and let him not stretch forth his hand against them, for the Lord chose them in days of old, and took them as the lot of His inheritance from amongst all the nations of the earth, and who is there that has dared stretch forth his hand against them with impunity, but that their God avenged the evil done unto them?" Reuel then proceeded to enumerate some of the mighty things God had performed for Abraham, Isaac, and Jacob, and he closed his admonition with the words: "Verily, your grandfather, the Pharaoh of former days, raised Joseph the son of Jacob above all the princes of Egypt, because he discerned his wisdom, for through his wisdom he rescued all the inhabitants of the land from the famine, after which he invited Jacob and his sons to come down to Egypt, that the land of Egypt and the land of Goshen be delivered from the famine through their virtues. Now, therefore, if it seem good in your eyes, leave off from destroying the children of Israel, and if it is not your will that they dwell in Egypt, send them forth from here, that they may go to the land of Canaan, the land wherein their ancestors sojourned."

When Pharaoh heard the words of Jethro-Reuel, he was exceedingly angry with him, and he dismissed him in disgrace from before his presence. And Jethro-Reuel went to Midian.

The king then spoke to Job, and said, "What do you say, Job, and what is your advice respecting the Hebrews?" Job replied, "Behold, all the inhabitants of the land are in your power. Let the king do as it seems good in his eyes."

Balaam was the last to speak at the behest of the king, and he said, "From all that the king may devise against the Hebrews, they will be delivered. If you try to diminish them by the flaming fire, you will not prevail over them, for their God delivered Abraham their father from the furnace in which the Chaldeans cast him. If, perhaps, you think to destroy them with the sword, remember that their father Isaac was delivered from being slaughtered

148

by the sword. And if you try to reduce them through hard and rigorous labor, you will also not prevail, for their father Jacob served Laban in all manner of hard work, and yet he prospered. If it please the king, let him order all the male children that shall be born in Israel from this day forward to be thrown into the water. Thereby you can wipe out their name, for neither any of them nor any of their fathers was tried in this way" *(Sefer ha-Yashar Shemot* 128a-130b).

THE PLIGHT OF NEW-BORN BABES

A Tanna taught: Amram was the greatest man of his generation; when he saw that the wicked Pharaoh had decreed *Every son that is born ye shall cast into the river* (Ex. 1.22), he arose and divorced his wife [since all the male children would be killed, and the primary object of marriage was the procreation of sons]. All [the Israelites] thereupon arose and divorced their wives. His daughter said to him, "Father, your decree is more severe than Pharaoh's; Pharaoh decreed only against the males but you have decreed against the males and females. Pharaoh only decreed concerning this world but you have decreed concerning this world and the world to come [as unborn children would also be denied the Hereafter]. In the case of the wicked Pharaoh there is a doubt whether his decree will be fulfilled or not; whereas in your case, as you are righteous, it is certain that your decree will be fulfilled."

He then arose and took his wife back; and they all arose and took their wives back *(Sotah* 12a).

Rabbi Hanan said: The virtuous and chaste daughters of Israel adopted the plan of taking their infant sons and hiding them in holes [to save them from Pharaoh's decree]. So the wicked Egyptians used to take their young children and bring them into the houses of the Israelites and pinch them and make them cry. When an Israelite child would hear the other crying, he would commence to cry with him. Then the Egyptians took them and threw

149

them into the river. *(Midrash Shir ha-Shirim Rabbah II.15,2)*.

THE SAVING OF MOSES

Now Bithyah, the daughter of Pharaoh, was smitten sorely with leprosy and she was not able to bathe in hot water, and she came to bathe in the river and she saw the crying child. She put forth her hand and took hold of him, and she was healed. She said, "This child is righteous, and I will preserve his life." Whosoever preserves a single life is as though he had kept alive the whole world. Therefore she was worthy to inherit the life in this world and the life in the world to come *(Pirke de-Rabbi Eliezer 48)*.

THE CROWN OF PHARAOH

Pharaoh's daughter used to kiss and hug Moses, loved him as if he were her own son and would not allow him out of the royal palace. Because he was so handsome, everyone was eager to see him, and whoever saw him could not tear himself away from him. Pharaoh also used to kiss and hug him, and he used to take the crown of Pharaoh and place it upon his own head ...

The magicians of Egypt sat there and said, "We are afraid of him who is taking off your crown and placing it upon his own head, lest he be the one of whom we prophesy that he will take away the kingdom from thee." Some of them counselled to slay him and others to burn him, but Jethro was present among them and he said to them, "This boy has no sense. However, test him by placing before him a gold vessel and a live coal; if he stretch forth his hand for the gold, then he has sense and you can slay him, but if he makes for the live coal then he has no sense and there can be no sentence of death upon him." So they brought these things before him, and Moses was about to reach forth for the gold when Gabriel came and thrust his hand aside so that it seized the coal, and he thrust his hand with the live coal into his mouth, so that his tongue was burnt, with the result that he became slow of speech and of tongue *(Midrash Shemot Rabbah* 1.26).

ISRAEL IN SLAVERY

And he (Moses) *looked on their burdens* (Ex. 2.11). R. Eleazar, son of R. Jose the Galilean, said, "He saw great burdens put upon small people and light burdens upon big people, and a man's burden upon a woman and a woman's burden upon a man, and the burden which an old man could carry on a youth, and of a youth on an old man. So he left his suite and rearranged their burdens, pretending all the time to be helping Pharaoh. God then said to him, 'You have put aside your work and gone to share the sorrow of Israel, behaving to them like a brother; well, I will also leave those on high and below and only speak with you!' " *(ibid.,* 1.27).

Another interpretation of *And he looked on their burdens:* He saw that they had no rest, so he went to Pharaoh and said, "If one has a slave and he does not give him rest one day in the week he dies; similarly, if you will not give your slaves one day in the week rest, they will die." Pharaoh replied, "Go and do with them as you say." Thereupon Moses ordained for them the Sabbath day for rest *(ibid.,* 1.28).

THE TEST OF THE SHEPHERD

Moses was tested by God through sheep. Our rabbis said that when Moses our teacher, peace be upon him, was tending the flock of Jethro in the wilderness, a little kid escaped from him. He ran after it until it reached a shady place. When it reached the shady place, there appeared to view a pool of water and the kid stopped to drink. When Moses approached it, he said, "I did not know that you ran away because of thirst; you must be weary." So he placed the kid on his shoulder and walked away. Thereupon God said, "Because you have mercy in leading the flock of a mortal, you will assuredly tend my flock Israel" *(ibid.,* 2.2).

151

THE MERIT OF THE THORN-BUSH

A heathen once asked R. Joshua b. Karhah, "Why did God choose a thorn-bush from which to speak to Moses?" He replied, "If it were a carob tree or a sycamore tree, you would have asked the same question; but to dismiss you without any reply is not right, so I will tell you why: To teach you that no place is devoid of God's presence, not even a thorn-bush . . ."

R. Eliezer said, "Just as the thorn-bush is the lowliest of all trees in the world, so Israel were lowly and humble in Egypt; therefore God revealed Himself to them and redeemed them, as it is said: *And I am come down to deliver them from Egypt*" (Ex. 3.8).

R. Johanan said, "Just as one makes of thorns a fence for a garden so Israel is a fence to the world. Moreover, just as the thorn-bush grows near any water, so Israel grew only in virtue of the Torah that is called water, as it is said: *Ho, every one that thirsteth, come ye for water* (Isa. 55.1). Also, just as the thorn-bush produces thorns and roses, so among Israel there are wicked and righteous." R. Phinehas b. Hama the priest said: "Just as when a man puts his hand into a thorn-bush he does not at first feel it, but when he takes it out it scratches, so when Israel came into Egypt nobody perceived them, but when they went out, they departed with signs and wonders" *(ibid., 2.5)*.

MOSES AT THE BURNING BUSH

The bush burned with fire (Ex. 3.2). Why did God show Moses such a symbol? Because Moses had thought to himself that the Egyptians might consume Israel; hence God showed him a fire which burnt but did not consume, saying to him, "Just as the thorn-bush is burning and is not consumed, so the Egyptians will not be able to destroy Israel" *(ibid., 2.5)*.

Moses spoke before Him: "Sovereign of all worlds! Give me a wonder or a sign." He said to him, "Cast thy

152

staff to the ground." He cast his staff to the ground, and it became a fiery serpent. Why did the Holy One, blessed be He, show Moses a sign with a fiery serpent, and why did He not show it to him with something else? Just as the serpent bites and kills the sons of man, likewise Pharaoh and his people bit and slew the Israelites. He spake before Him: "Sovereign of all worlds! Give me another wonder." He said to him, *"Put now thy hand into thy bosom"* (Ex. 4.6). And he put his hand into his bosom, and he brought it out leprous like snow. Why did the Holy One, blessed be He, show Moses a sign by means of an unclean thing, and why did He not show it by means of a clean thing? But just as the leper is unclean and causes uncleanliness, likewise Pharaoh and his people were unclean, and they caused Israel to be unclean. Afterwards Moses became clean again and He spoke to him: "Likewise Israel shall become clean from the uncleanliness of the Egyptians" *(Pirke de-Rabbi Eliezer* 40).

MOSES AND JETHRO

And Moses went and returned to Jethro his father-in-law (Ex. 4.18). He went to get his wife and children. Jethro said to him, "Where are you taking them?" He replied, "To Egypt." Then came the rejoinder, "Those who are in Egypt wish to go out, and you would fain take them there!" He replied, "Tomorrow they will depart from there and stand near Sinai to hear from God *I am the Lord, thy God* (Ex. 20.2). Shall not my children also hear this?" Whereupon Jethro said to Moses (Ex. 4.19) *"Go in peace"* *(Midrash Shemot Rabbah* 4.4).

Moses sent his father-in-law Jethro back to his home shortly before the revelation on Mount Sinai. He thought, "When God gave us a single commandment of the Torah in Egypt, the Passover, He said: *There shall no alien eat thereof* (Ex. 12.47). Surely Jethro may not look on when God gives us the whole Torah." Moses was right: God did not want Jethro to be present at the revelation. He said, "Israel was in Egypt, bound to work with clay and bricks, at the same time as Jethro was sitting at home in peace and quiet. He who suffers with the community shall share their future joys, but he who does not share the sufferings of the community shall not take part in their rejoicing" (*Midrash Tanhuma ha-Kadom veha-Yashan* II, 74-75).

MOSES AND AARON BEFORE PHARAOH

That day [when Moses and Aaron came to Pharaoh] was Pharaoh's day for the reception of ambassadors, when all the kings came to pay him honor, bringing with them gifts of crowns wherewith they crowned him lord of the world, and also their idols they brought with them. After the others had placed their crowns on his head, Moses and Aaron were still standing at the door of Pharaoh's palace; whereupon his servants came and said, "Two elders are at the gate." The reply was, "Let them enter." When they entered, he looked at them as if expecting them to crown him or give him their credentials, but they did not even greet him. He said to them, "Who are you?" They replied, "We are the ambassadors of the Lord, blessed be He." "What do you want?" he asked. They replied, *"Thus saith the Lord the God of Israel: Let My people go"* (Ex. 5.1). Then Pharaoh became very angry and said, *"Who is the Lord, that I should hearken unto His voice to let Israel go?* (ibid., 5.2). Has He not the sense to send me a crown, that you come to me with mere words? *I know not the Lord, and moreover I will not let Israel go" (ibid.).* He added, "Tarry awhile, till I search in my records." So he went into his palace chamber and scrutinized every nation and its gods, beginning with the gods of Moab, Ammon and Zidon. He then said to them, "I have searched for His name throughout my archives, but have not found Him." Moses and Aaron then said to Pharaoh, "Idiot! Is it the way of the dead to be sought for among the living, or are the living among the dead? Our God is living, whereas those

154

you mentioned are dead; yes, our God is a living God and an eternal King" (*Midrash Shemot Rabbah* 4.14).

THE LESSONS OF THE PLAGUES

When a human being wishes to bring some sudden evil upon his foe, he usually tries to catch him unawares, but God warned Pharaoh with every plague, in the hope that he might repent *(ibid., 9.9)*.

R. Johanan said, "Does this not provide heretics with ground for arguing that he had no means of repenting, since it says: *For I have hardened his heart*?" (Ex. 10.1). To which R. Simeon b. Lakish replied, "Let the mouths of the heretics be stopped up. *If it concerneth the scorners, He scorneth them* (Prov. 3.34); when God warns a man once, twice, and even a third time, and he still does not repent, then does God close his heart against repentance so that He should exact vengeance from him for his sins. Thus it was with the wicked Pharaoh. Since God sent five times to him and he took no notice, God then said, 'You have stiffened your neck and hardened your heart; well, I will add to your uncleanness!'" *(ibid., 13.3)*.

During the night of the plague of the first-born, Pharaoh arose and went to Moses and Aaron, as is said: *And he called for Moses and Aaron by night* (Ex. 12.31). And in the night he knocked on the doors of Moses and Aaron, and said to them, *Rise up, get you forth from among my people (ibid.)*. They answered, "Fool, are we to arise in the night? Are we thieves that we should go forth by night? In the morning we shall leave. It was thus the Holy One, blessed be He, charged us: *None of you shall go out of the door of his house until the morning*" *(ibid., 22)*. Pharaoh said to them, "But by that time all the Egyptians will be dead!"—as is written: *They said: We are all dead men (ibid., 33)*. Moses and Aaron replied, "Do you seek to end this plague? Then say, 'Behold, you are free; behold, you are your own men, you are no longer servants of mine, you are servants of the Lord!'" (*Midrash Tehillim* 113.2).

As the plagues came down on the Egyptians, the Egyptians waited, wondering when the Israelites were going to leave; and the Israelites waited, wondering when the Holy One, blessed be He, would redeem them. After they went forth and were redeemed, the former were glad, and the latter were glad (*ibid.*, 105.11).

AT THE RED SEA

And the Lord said unto Moses: "Wherefore criest thou unto Me? Speak unto the children of Israel that they go forward" (Ex. 14.15). R. Eliezer says, "The Holy One, blessed be He, said to Moses, 'Moses, My children are in distress, the sea forming a bar and the enemy pursuing, and you stand there reciting long prayers; wherefore criest thou unto Me?' " For R. Eliezer used to say: "There is a time to be brief in prayer and a time to be lengthy" (*Mekhilta de-Rabbi Ishmael*, "Beshallah" 4).

The Holy One, blessed be He, does not rejoice in the downfall of the wicked. R. Johanan said, "What is the meaning of the verse, *And one came not near the other all the night* (Ex. 14.20, referring to Pharaoh and the Israelites at the Red Sea)? The ministering angels wanted to chant their hymns, but the Holy One, blessed be He, said, 'The work of my hands is being drowned in the sea, and shall you chant hymns?' " (Megillah 10b).

THE SONG OF MOSES

Who is like unto Thee, O Lord, among the mighty? (Ex. 15.11). When the Israelites saw that Pharaoh and his hosts perished in the Red Sea and that the kingdom of the Egyptians came to an end, and that judgments were executed upon their idols, they all opened their mouths and said, "Who is like unto Thee, O Lord, among the mighty." And not only Israel uttered song, but the nations of the world also uttered song (*Mekhilta de-Rabbi Ishmael*, "Shirata" 8).

The sea had no heart but a heart was ascribed to it, as it is said: . . . *in the heart of the sea* (Ex. 15.8). It was

156

fitting that the sea which had no heart but to which a heart was ascribed should come and punish the Egyptians, who had hearts but who nevertheless subjected Israel to all sorts of affliction *(ibid., 6)*.

THE MERITS OF ISRAEL

When Moses said to Israel, "In this month ye are to be delivered," they said to him, "Our teacher Moses, how can we be delivered, seeing that we have no good deeds to our credit?" He said to them, "Since God desires to deliver you, He disregards your evil deeds. What then does He heed? The righteous among you and their actions" *(Midrash Shir ha-Shirim Rabbah* II.8.1).

Israel was redeemed from Egypt on account of the righteous women of that generation *(Sotah* 11b).

For four reasons the children of Israel were redeemed from Egypt: they did not change their names; they did not change their language; they did not reveal their secrets; and they were not wanton *(Midrash Tehillim* 114.4).

THE CELEBRATION OF PASSOVER

It was related of Rabbi Akiba that he used to distribute parched ears of corn and nuts to children on the eve of Passover, so that they might not fall asleep but ask the questions.

Our rabbis taught: A man is in duty bound to make his children and his household rejoice on a festival, for it is said: *And thou shalt rejoice in thy feast* (Deut. 16.14). Wherewith does he make them rejoice? With wine. Rabbi Judah said, "Men with what is suitable for them, and women with what is suitable for them. Men with what is suitable for them: with wine. And women with what?" Rabbi Joseph replied, "In Babylonia, with colored garments; in the Land of Israel, with ironed linen garments."

It was taught, Rabbi Judah ben Bathyra said, "when the Temple was in existence there could be no rejoicing save with meat, as it is said: *And thou shalt sacrifice peace-offerings, and shalt eat there; and thou shalt rejoice*

157

before the Lord thy God (Deut. 27.7). But now that the Temple is no longer in existence, there is no rejoicing save with wine, as it is said (Ps. 104.15): *And wine maketh glad the heart of man"* (Pesahim 109a).

THE MESSIANIC EXODUS

Ben Zoma said to the sages, "Will the Exodus from Egypt be mentioned in the days of the Messiah? Has it not long ago been declared: *Therefore, behold, the days come, saith the Lord, that they shall no more say: 'As the Lord liveth, that brought up the children of Israel out of the land of Egypt'; but: 'As the Lord liveth, that brought up and that led the seed of the house of Israel out of the north country, and from all countries whither I had driven them'* (Jer. 23.7)?" They answered him: "[This passage does not mean] that the memory of the Exodus from Egypt is to be obliterated, but that [the memory of the release from] the servitude of the Kingdoms will be fundamental and the Exodus from Egypt secondary to it" (Berakot 12b).

PASSOVER IN MEDIEVAL JEWISH LITERATURE

Introductory Note

Jewish literature of the medieval period is rich in philosophy, poetry and works of scholarship. This age gave birth to numerous classics that have remained our literary heritage to this day. Foremost among the philosophical writings of this period are Saadia Gaon's *Book of Beliefs and Opinions*, Maimonides' *Guide for the Perplexed* and Judah Halevi's *Kuzari*. All three of the above books, written originally in Arabic, exerted a profound influence on Jewish thought and have become standard texts of Jewish philosophical teaching.

Saadia Gaon (892-942), who contributed to many branches of Jewish literature, was the first to attempt a systematic presentation of the compatibility of the Jewish religion with the then prevailing philosophy. The foremost Hebrew poet of the Middle Ages, Judah Halevi (1085-1142), affirmed the superiority of Judaism over other universal religions in his philosophic work, the *Kuzari*. Moses ben Maimon (1135-1204), popularly called Maimonides, and noted as a philosopher, codifier and physician, wrote the *Guide for the Perplexed,* in which, like Saadia, he sought to harmonize philosophy and religion.

Different in character is the *Zohar* which, while popularly attributed to Simeon ben Yohai of the second century, first made its appearance in the thirteenth century through Moses ben Shemtob de Leon. It is the basic work of Cabala, consisting mainly of discursive commentaries on the Bible, and teachings on mysticism.

The above medieval classical volumes are concerned with various phases of Passover, as is evident from the following selections.

The Israelites Depart from Egypt[1]

JUDAH HALEVI

The Israelites lived in Egypt as slaves, six hundred thousand men above the age of twenty, descendants of the Twelve Tribes. Not one of them had separated or emigrated into another country, nor was a stranger among them. They looked forward to the promise given to their ancestors, Abraham, Isaac and Jacob, that the land of Palestine should be their inheritance. At that time it was in the power of seven mighty and prosperous nations, whilst the Israelites sighed in the depths of misery under the bondage of Pharaoh, who caused their children to be put to death, lest they should increase in numbers. Notwithstanding their lowly position as compared to the tyrant in his might, God sent Moses and Aaron before Pharaoh with signs and miracles, allowing them even to change the course of nature. Pharaoh could not get away from them, nor harm them, neither could he protect himself from the ten plagues which befell the Egyptians, affecting their streams, land, air, plants, animals, bodies, even their souls. For in one moment, at midnight, died the most precious and most beloved members of their houses viz., every first-born male. There was no dwelling without dead, except the houses of the Israelites. All these plagues were preceded by warnings and menaces, and their cessation was notified in the same way, so that every one should become convinced that they were ordained by God, who does what He will and when He will, and were not ordinary natural phenomena, nor wrought by constellations or accident. The Israelites left the country of Pharaoh's bondage, by the command of God, the same night and at the same moment, when the first-born died, and reached the shores of the Red Sea. They were guided by pillars of cloud and fire, and led by Moses and Aaron, the venerated, inspired chiefs, then about eighty years of age. Up to this time they had only a few laws which they had inherited from Adam and Noah. These laws were not abrogated by Moses, but rather increased by him. When Pharaoh pursued the Israelites they did not have recourse to arms, being unskilled in their use. God, however, divided the sea, and they traversed it. Pharaoh and his host were drowned, and the waves washed their corpses towards the Israelites, so that they could see them with their own eyes. It is a long and well-known story *(Kuzari,* Part I.83).

Exodus and Creation[2]

JUDAH HALEVI

God commanded cessation of work on Sabbath and holy days, as well as in the culture of the soil, all this "as a remembrance of the Exodus from Egypt," and "remembrance of the work of creation." These two things belong

161

together, because they are the outcome of the absolute divine will, but not the result of accident or natural phenomena. It is said (Deut. 4.32-34) : *For ask now of the days past . . . whether there hath been any such thing as this great thing is, or hath been heard like it? Did ever a people hear the voice of God speaking out of the midst of the fire, as thou hast heard, and live? Or hath God assayed to go and take Him a nation from the midst of another nation, by trials, by signs, and by wonders, and by war, and by a mighty hand, and by an outstretched arm, and by great terrors, according to all that the Lord your God did for you in Egypt before thine eyes?* (*ibid.*, Part II.50).

Seven Days of Passover[3]

MOSES BEN MAIMON

Holy days are appointed for rejoicing and for such pleasant gathering as people generally need. They also promote the good feeling that men should have to each other in their social and political relations. The appointment of the special days for such purposes has its cause. The reason for the Passover is well known. It is kept seven days, because the period of seven days is the unit of time intermediate between a day and a month. It is also known how great is the importance of this period in nature, and in many religious duties. For the Law always follows nature, and in some respects brings it to perfection; for nature is not capable of designing and thinking, while the Law is the result of the wisdom and guidance of God, who is the author of the intellect of all rational beings.

The Feast of Weeks is the anniversary of the Revelation on Mount Sinai. In order to raise the importance of this day, we count the days that pass since the preceding festival, just as one who expects his most intimate friend on a certain day counts the days and even the hours. This is the reason why we count the days that follow the offering of the *Omer*, between the anniversary of our departure from Egypt and the anniversary of the Lawgiving. The latter was the aim and object of the Exodus from Egypt, and thus God said: *I brought you unto myself* (Ex. 19.4). As that great revelation took place only on one day, so we keep its anniversary only one day; but if the eating of unleavened bread on Passover were only commanded for one day, we should not have noticed it, and its object would not have been manifest. For it frequently happens that we take the same kind of food for two or three days. But by our continuing for a whole period [of seven days] to eat unleavened bread, its object becomes clear and evident *(The Guide, III.43)*.

The Redemption of Israel[4]

SAADIA GAON

The fact of Redemption is undeniable for various reasons:

(1) Because it is confirmed by the miracles performed by Moses, the first prophet, in announcing the message of Redemption, and because it is confirmed by the miracles which happened to the prophet Isaiah and to the other prophets who announced the Redemption of Israel. If God sent these prophets as His messengers, then undoubtedly He will fulfill His message, as is said: *That confirm-*

163

eth the word of His servant, and performeth the counsel of His messengers (Isa. 44.26).

(2) Because He is just and will not do wrong. Having inflicted on our people heavy and prolonged sufferings—some, no doubt, as punishment, and some as a test—He must certainly have set a time limit to them. It cannot be thought that they should be unlimited. When the end comes, He will assuredly punish those who oppressed us and reward those who suffered, as it says: *Bid Jerusalem take heart and proclaim unto her that her time of service is accomplished, that her guilt is paid off, that she hath received of the Lord's hand double for all her sins* (Isa. 40.2).

(3) He is a faithful keeper of His promises, His word endureth and His commandment stands for ever, as it says: *The grass withereth, the flower fadeth, but the word of our God shall stand for ever* (Isa. 40.8).

(4) We judge the promise of final Redemption from the first promise at the time when we were living as exiles in Egypt and God promised us in more precise terms that He would mete out judgment to our oppressors and reward us with great wealth, as it says: *And also that nation, whom they shall serve, will I judge; and afterwards they shall come out with great substance* (Gen. 15.14). Our eyes have seen the things which He performed for us in dividing the sea, in feeding us with the manna and the quails, in giving us the Law on Sinai, in causing the sun to stand still and similar things. For the future, He promised us wonderful and immeasurable bliss and happiness, and that honor, glory and distinction which He will bestow upon us as a double reward for all the humiliation and misery which He brought upon us, as it says: *For your shame which was double . . . therefore in their land they shall possess double* (Isa. 61.7). Of that which we endured in the past God speaks as of a brief moment, transient like the twinkling of the eye, but of the reward He will give us in the future He speaks in terms of a boundless compassion, as it says: *For a small*

moment have I forsaken thee, but with great compassion will I gather thee (Isa. 54.7). For the trials and ordeals of the past He will give us the double of our double share, which is over and above that which He promised, an amount of bliss not quickly or easily to be measured. Thus it is said: *And He will do thee good, and multiply thee above thy fathers* (Deut. 30.5). For this reason He mentions to us the Exodus from Egypt so frequently and in so many places. He wants us to remember the things we experienced. If anything which He did for us in the course of the redemption from Egypt is not explicitly included in the promise of the final Redemption, it is implied in the statement, *As in the days of thy coming forth out of the land of Egypt, will I show unto him marvelous things* (Micah 7.15).

For this reason one finds that we patiently endure our sufferings, and wait for Him without casting any doubt on His promise. We do not expire nor does our courage falter, but we grow in strength and in firmness, as it says: *Be strong and let your heart take courage, all ye that wait for the Lord* (Ps. 31.21).

Rejoicing Brings Forth Rejoicing[5]

ZOHAR

And the people took their dough before it was leavened. On the strength of this is founded the precept that the leaven should be burned on the Passover eve. "Leaven" and "unleaven" symbolize the evil and the good inclinations in man.

It is obligatory for every Israelite to relate the story of the Exodus on the Passover night. He who does so fervently and joyously, telling the tale with a high heart, shall be found worthy to rejoice in the *Shekinah* in the world to come, for rejoicing brings forth rejoicing; and the joy of Israel causes the Holy One Himself to be glad, so that He calls together all the Family above and says unto them, "Come ye and hearken unto the praises which My children bring unto Me! Behold how they rejoice in My Redemption!" Then all the angels and supernal beings gather round and observe Israel, how she sings and rejoices because of her Lord's own Redemption— and seeing the rejoicings below, the supernal beings also break unto jubilation for that the Holy One possesses on earth a people so holy, whose joy in the Redemption of their Lord is so great and so powerful. For all that terrestrial rejoicing increases the power of the Lord and His hosts in the regions above, just as an earthly king gains strength from the praises of his subjects, the fame of his glory being thus spread throughout the world ("Ray'a Mehemna," Bo,40b).

The Unbroken Bone

ZOHAR

With bitter herbs they shall eat it . . . neither shall ye break a bone thereof. The bitter herbs signify the *Shekinah's* exile with Israel in all their bitter afflictions in Egypt. Why were the bones of the Passover lamb not allowed to be broken? So that the dogs might drag them about and the Egyptians be thus made to realize the nothingness of that which they worshipped, and so be put to shame, and the Holy One be glorified (*ibid.*, 41b).

PASSOVER IN JEWISH LAW

Introductory Note

Tractate Pesahim of the Mishnah, compiled by Judah the Prince (about 135-220 C.E.), contains the Oral Law pertaining to Passover as preserved by many generations of Jews and recorded by the tannaim during a period of about four centuries. This tractate deals with laws concerning the paschal lamb offering, and it presents the original laws of the order of the Passover meal. Closely related to and supplementing the Mishnah is the Tosefta (literally, "Addition") which also embodies Passover rules. The vast body of Jewish law in these and other sources was systematized by Moses ben Maimon (Maimonides) 1135-1204, in his *Mishneh Torah*. Several centuries later, Joseph Karo (1488-1575), recognized as the last great codifier of rabbinical Judaism, prepared the *Shulhan Arukh*, accepted to this day as the basis for traditional practice. An abridged and popular version of Karo's monumental work was prepared by Solomon Ganzfried (about 1800-1886).

Interesting is the code of Karaite Law, written in Arabic by Samuel ben Moses al-Magribi (15th century), containing Passover customs strikingly akin to the rabbinic traditions.

167

The Passover laws, which go into minute details, are intended to make this festival a significant experience for young and old and, on occasion, to express to God gratitude for the bounteous freedom that He has given to His people.

Laws of the Seder[1]

MISHNAH PESAHIM

On the eve of Passover, from about the time of the Evening Offering, a man must eat naught until nightfall. Even the poorest in Israel must not eat unless he sits down to table, and they must not give them less than four cups of wine to drink, even if it is from the [paupers'] dish.

After they have mixed him his first cup, the School of Shammai say: He says the benediction first over the day and then the benediction over the wine. And the School of Hillel say: He says the benediction first over the wine and then the benediction over the day.

When [food] is brought before him he eats it seasoned with lettuce, until he comes to the breaking of bread; they bring before him unleavened bread and lettuce and the *haroset*, although *haroset* is not a religious obligation. R. Eliezer b. Zadok says: It is a religious obligation. And in the Holy City they used to bring before him the body of the Passover-offering.

They then mix him the second cup. And here the son asks his father (and if the son has not enough understanding his father instructs him how to ask), "Why is this night different from other nights? For on other nights we eat seasoned food once, but this night twice; on other nights we eat leavened or unleavened bread, but this night all is unleavened [some texts add: "on other nights we

168

Cincinnati Haggadah

16. The Seder

Kirchner, Judisches Ceremoniel

17. Preparations for Passover

Bernard Picart, The Religious Customs . . .

18. The Search for **Leaven**

Bernard Picart, The Religious Customs . . .

19. The Passover of the Portuguese Jews

20. Passover Festival

Painting. After Bodenschatz

eat all other manner of vegetables, but this night, bitter herbs"]; on other nights we eat flesh roast, stewed, or cooked, but this night all is roast" [some texts add: "on other nights we dip once, but this night twice"]. And according to the understanding of the son his father instructs him. He begins with the disgrace and ends with the glory; and he expounds from *A wandering Aramean was my father* ... until he finishes the whole section.

Rabban Gamaliel used to say: Whosoever has not said [the verses concerning] these three things at Passover has not fulfilled his obligation. And these are they: Pesach (Passover lamb), *matzah* (unleavened bread), and *maror* (bitter herbs). "Passover"—because God passed over the houses of our fathers in Egypt; "un-leavened bread"—because our fathers were redeemed from Egypt; "bitter herbs"—because the Egyptians em-bittered the lives of our fathers in Egypt. In every genera-tion a man must so regard himself as if he came forth himself out of Egypt, for it is written: *And thou shall tell thy son in that day saying, It is because of that which the Lord did for me when I came forth out of Egypt* (Ex. 13.8). Therefore are we bound to give thanks, to praise, to glorify, to honor, to exalt, to extol, and to bless him who wrought all these wonders for our fathers and for us. He brought us out from bondage to freedom, from sor-row to gladness, and from mourning to a festival-day, and from darkness to great light, and from servitude to re-demption; so let us say before him the Hallelujah.

How far do they recite [the Hallel]? The School of Shammai say to: ... *a joyful mother of children* [end of Psalm 113]. And the School of Hillel say to: ... *a flint-stone into a springing well* [end of Psalm 114]. And this is concluded with the Ge'ulah. R. Tarfon says: "... He that redeemed us and redeemed our fathers from Egypt and brought us to this night to eat therein unleavened bread and bitter herbs." But there is no concluding bene-diction. R. Akiba adds: "Therefore, O Lord our God and the God of our fathers, bring us in peace to the other set feasts and festivals which are coming to meet us, while we rejoice in the building-up of Thy city and are joyful in Thy worship; and may we eat there of the sacrifices and of the Passover-offerings whose blood has reached with acceptance the wall of Thy Altar, and let us praise Thee for our redemption and for the ransoming of our soul. Blessed art Thou, O Lord, who hast redeemed Israel!"

After they have mixed for him the third cup he says the benediction over his meal. [Over] a fourth [cup] he completes the *Hallel* and says after it the benediction over song. If he is minded to drink [more] between these cups he may drink; only between the third and the fourth cups he may not drink.

After the Passover meal they should not disperse to join in revelry. If some fell asleep [during the meal], they may eat [again]; but if all fell asleep, they may not eat [again]. R. Jose says: If they but dozed, they may eat [again]; but if they fell into deep sleep, they may not eat [again] (10.1-8).

Rabban Gamaliel's Seder²

TOSEFTA

A person is obligated to occupy himself with the laws of Passover (i.e., to relate the story of the Exodus) throughout the night, together with his son or even alone or with his pupil. It once happened that Rabban Gamaliel and the elders were reclining (at the Passover Seder) in the home of Boethus bar Zonin in Lud and were occupied with the laws of Passover all night until the rooster crowed (and the morning star appeared). They thereupon arose and arranged to go to the House of Study (10.7).

Removal of the Leaven[3]

MOSES BEN MAIMON

It is a positive commandment of the Torah to remove the leaven before the time when it is forbidden to eat it, as it is said: *the first day ye shall put away leaven out of your houses* (Ex. 12.15), and, on the basis of a tradition, it has been learned that this "the first" is the fourteenth day (of Nisan). Proof for this commandment is written in the Torah: *Thou shalt not offer the blood of My sacrifice with leavened bread* (*ibid.*, 34.25); that is to say: Do not slaughter the Passover sacrifice when the leaven is still in existence. The slaughtering of the Passover sacrifice is the afternoon of the fourteenth day.

What is this removal of which the Torah speaks? It is that one should annul the leaven in his heart and consider it as dust; and he should take to heart that there is no leaven at all in his possession and that all the leaven in his possession is as dust, and as something of which there is no need whatsoever.

According to the interpretations of the scholars, one is required to search for the leaven in hiding-places and holes and to remove it entirely from his property. Thus, according to the interpretations of the scholars, leaven is sought out and removed at night—at the beginning of the night of the fourteenth—by the light of a candle—because at night all the people are at home and the light of a candle is helpful in searching. Public study is not fixed at the end of the thirteenth day and even a sage should not begin to study at this time lest he continue and omit the

171

search for leaven at the beginning of its appointed time ("Laws of Leaven and Unleavened Bread," 2.1-3).

It is written in the Torah: *there shall no unleavened bread be seen with thee* (Ex. 13.7). One might argue that if he hid it or deposited it with a Gentile, he would not violate the law; hence, the text reads: *leaven shall not be found in your houses* (*ibid.*, 12.19), even if one deposited or hid it. One might think that he would not transgress the Law except if the leaven was in his house, but if it was distant from his house—in a field or in another city— he would not transgress; hence, the text reads: [neither] *shall there be leaven seen with thee, in all thy borders* (*ibid.*, 13.7), namely, in all your possessions (*ibid.*, 4.1).

Eating the Unleavened Bread[3]

MOSES BEN MAIMON

It is a positive commandment of the Torah to eat un- leavened bread on the night of the fifteenth (of Nisan), as it is said: *at evening ye shall eat unleavened bread* (Ex. 12.18), in every place and at all times. This eating (of unleavened bread) is not dependent on the Passover sacri- fice but is a law unto itself and its obligation lasts through- out the night. However, during the remainder of the festival, eating of unleavened bread is optional. If one desires, he eats unleavened bread or rice or millet or parched grain or fruit. However, only on the night of the fifteenth is it obligatory; and if one ate (a piece of un- leavened bread) the size of an olive, he has performed his duty (*ibid.*, 6.1).

All are obliged to eat unleavened bread, even women

and servants. A child who is able to eat a piece of bread should be educated in the commandments and be fed unleavened bread the size of an olive *(ibid., 6.10)*.

According to the interpretations of the scholars one must not conclude by eating anything after the unleavened bread . . . The sages have forbidden the eating of unleavened bread on the eve of Passover so that there be a recognition of its eating in the evening. . . . The early sages would hunger on the eve of Passover in order to eat the unleavened bread with good appetite *(ibid., 6.11-12)*.

The Narrative[3]

MOSES BEN MAIMON

It is a positive commandment of the Torah to relate the miracles and wonders that happened to our fathers in Egypt on the night of the fifteenth of Nisan, as it is said: *Remember this day in which ye came out from Egypt* (Ex. 13.3), and as it is written: *Remember the Sabbath day (ibid.,* 20.8). Whence do we know that it is the fifteenth? The text reads: *And thou shalt tell thy son in that day, saying: It is because of that . . . (ibid.,* 13.8)— at the time that unleavened bread and bitter herbs are set before you. Even one who has no son, and even a sage is obliged to narrate the Exodus from Egypt; and whoever expatiates on the events that occurred is praiseworthy.

It is one's duty to expound to his sons, even if they did not ask, as it is said: *And thou shalt tell thy son (ibid.,* 13.8). According to the intelligence of the son, his father teaches him. In what manner? If he is a young or foolish child, he says to him "My son, in Egypt all of us were slaves, just like this maid-servant or this man-servant; and on this night the Holy One, blessed be He, redeemed us and brought us to freedom." If the son is grown and wise, he makes known to him what happened to us in Egypt and the miracles that were performed for us by Moses our teacher. Everything is done according to the understanding of the son.

It is necessary to make a change on this night so that the sons will notice it and will ask, as follows: "Wherefore is this night different from all other nights?" Then he will reply and say to them: "Such and such happened." How does one make a change? He distributes among them parched grain and nuts; he changes the location of the table before they eat; they snatch unleavened bread one from another—and the like. If he has no son, his wife asks him; if he has no wife, the guests ask one another, "Wherefore is this night different from all other nights?"—even if they are all wise men. If he is alone, he asks himself, "Wherefore is this night different from all other nights?"

One should begin with disgraceful facts and conclude with glorious ones, i.e., he starts to narrate that in the beginning our ancestors in the days of Terah and before him were unbelievers, pursuing vanity and the worship of idols; and he concludes with the religion of truth to which the Lord brought us close and by which He distinguished us from the nations and brought us near to Him. Similarly, he begins by announcing that we were slaves to Pharaoh in Egypt. These things are called the Haggadah.

In every generation man is obliged to consider himself as if he personally went forth from slavery in Egypt, as it is said: *And he brought us out from thence* (Deut. 6.23). In this matter the Holy One, blessed be He, commanded in the Torah *And thou shalt remember that thou was a servant* . . . (*ibid.*, 5.15), namely, it is as if you yourself were a servant and have just been freed and redeemed (*ibid.*, 7.1-6).

The Bread of Poverty[4]

SAMUEL AL-MAGRIBI

As for the meaning of *bread of poverty,* scholars have uttered many different opinions concerning it, and we shall confine ourselves to the opinions of those who seem nearer to the truth.

Some say that this means, literally, the bread of the poor—because poor people, in the severity of their destitution, will take some flour, knead it, and bake it into unleavened cakes which they eat immediately, and because this is the sort of bread they have most often. Others say that it means bread that is injurious to the digestive apparatus of the body and causes harm to it. Still others say that it signifies bread suitable for the hardships of travel, since Scripture speaks of hardship in connection with travel, e.g., *He subjected my strength to hardship on the road* (Ps. 102.24) ; i.e., the traveler is hardly able to afford the delay of letting his dough ferment, since he is usually in a hurry to go on. This is confirmed by the words following the command to eat unleavened bread: . . . *for in haste didst thou come forth out of the land of Egypt* (Deut. 16.3).

Laws of Passover[5]

SOLOMON GANZFREID

WHEAT FOR UNLEAVENED BREAD

It is written: *And ye shall observe the unleavened bread*, hence it is inferred that it is requisite to observe the wheat intended for the unleavened bread for the purpose of performing the precept, to see that no water come thereon. According to the opinion of some of the great authorities such observation should take place from the time that it is taken off the field and thenceforth. However, the custom prevails in conformity with the view of those authorities who hold that it suffices to observe it from the time it is brought to the mill and henceforth. Only the zealous observe it from the time it was reaped, and this is the proper procedure. And it is advisable to note that the stalk should not remain attached to the soil until fully ripe and whitened, for then if rain descend upon them they become leavened even when attached, since they no longer need the soil. It is therefore best and most proper to reap them while they are still slightly green. It would be well if it were possible for one to use, during the entire festival, unleavened bread of wheat that was under observation from the time of reaping. If this is impossible, one should at least embellish the two Seder nights by using such unleavened bread thereon (*Code . . .*, 108.1).

BAKING OF THE UNLEAVENED BREAD

If one desires to bake unleavened bread in an oven where leaven had been baked, he is required to make it legally fit by glowing it, i.e., to heat it so much as to make sparks fly therefrom. For anything less than that would not constitute true glowing. Great care should be taken to spread the coals upon its entire surface; after glowing it is highly proper to remove the ashes and clean it carefully, waiting until it becomes slightly cooler. Thereafter he should make a new fire therein for baking unleavened bread, but not immediately after glowing *(ibid.,* 110.1).

Care should be taken not to let the dough lie for a moment without working upon it, and as soon as the dough is completed it should be distributed among those who roll it. Care should therefore be taken to make the dough only as big as those who roll it can take care of. And if a part of the unleavened bread remains in the hands of the kneader, the kneading of the dough should be kept up, as it should not lie idle for a moment *(ibid.,* 110.8).

Immediately after the unleavened bread was prepared it should be perforated quickly, not making any designs, and it should be put in the oven as quickly as possible. The utmost care should be taken not to delay it for a moment opposite the opening of the stove, as there it will quickly turn leavened. Hence it is necessary that the one handing the unleavened bread to the baker should be versed in the law and pay scrupulous attention to it *(ibid.,* 110.10).

It is proper for every God-fearing man to personally supervise the making and baking of his own unleavened bread and admonish the workingmen to use care and diligence. This was the method of the great men of Israel of blessed memory, and this is also the method of the pious in our own times *(ibid.,* 110.14).

The unleavened bread wherewith one fulfills the precept of eating *matzot* on the two first Passover nights, is called "the unleavened bread of the precept," and it should be made "for the sake of the precept" by an adult male Israelite of intelligence, aged at least thirteen years and one day, or by a female aged at least twelve years and one day, and at each stage of its process, even when drawing water, the worker should say "for the sake of the unleavened bread of the precept" *(ibid.,* 110.15).

FAST OF THE FIRST-BORN

The first-born, whether on the father's or on the mother's side, should fast on the day preceding the Passover, even if it occur on a Sabbath eve. While the child is small the father should fast in its stead. Whether at a feast given at the performance of a religious duty they are permitted to eat or not depends upon the custom of the locality *(ibid.,* 113.6).

SELLING OF THE LEAVEN

An Israelite having leaven in his possession during the Passover is perpetually transgressing the prohibition: "It shall not be seen nor shall it be found . . ." and out of such leaven he may never derive any benefit, even if he did annul it before the Passover. Therefore if one have in his possession much leaven which he is unable to clean away, he is required to sell it to a non-Jew before Passover while he is still permitted to derive benefit therefrom. And the matter of selling leaven shall not be considered just as a mere habit of formality, but one must bear it in mind that the sale he effects with the non-Jew is real and decisive, and he should not sell it at a higher price than it is worth. After the Passover he should make demand from the non-Jew that he repay him his debt, and when the latter replies that he has no money wherewith to pay it, he should request of him to resell to him the leaven (together with the room) for so much and so much. The transaction shall not be considered as a mere jest, but should be effected according to the true manner of merchants *(ibid.,* 114.1).

ENRICHED UNLEAVENED BREAD

In a case of necessity, as, for instance, for the requirements of a sick or an aged person, it is permitted to bake unleavened bread with extract of eggs or other extracts

178

such as fruit, milk, wine and so forth. This is called "unleavened bread prepared in a rich manner." Care, however, should be taken not to mingle any water with it, no matter how little. On the first two nights of Passover only the actual unleavened bread should be partaken of, and one does not fulfill one's obligation with the aforesaid *matzah (ibid.,* 118.6).

THE ORDER OF PASSOVER EVE

It is mandatory to acquire choice wine wherewith to perform the precept of drinking four goblets. If one can obtain red wine which is of the same quality as the white, and is also as valid for the use on Passover as the white, the former is to be preferred to the latter, for it is written: "Do not observe wine when it becomes red," from which it may be inferred that the value in wine lies in it being red.

For the first dipping, termed *karpas,* many are accustomed to take parsley, but it is best to take celery which also has a good taste when raw. And it is best of all to take radishes.

For the bitter herbs it is customary to take horseradish, but as it is very pungent, it may be grated; care, however, should be taken that it does not become entirely tasteless.

The *haroset* must be thick in commemoration of the clay, and when one needs dip the bitter herb therein, he should pour a little vinegar in it so that it be softened in commemoration of blood, and for the further reason that it may become fit to dip something therein. It is proper to prepare the *haroset* out of fruits to which the people of Israel are likened—for instance, figs, because it is written: *The fig-tree perfumeth its green figs* (Song of Songs 2.13) ; nuts, because it is said: *Into the nut-garden was I gone down (ibid.,* 6.1) ; dates, because it is said: *I wish to climb up the palm-tree (ibid.,* 7.9) ; pomegranates, because it is said: *Like the half of the pomegranate (ibid.,* 6.7) ; apples, in commemoration of what is said: *Under the apple tree have I waked thee* (*ibid.*, 8.5), where the women were accustomed to give birth to their children without pain; and almonds, because the Holy one, blessed be He, was anxious to bring about the end (the Redemption). One should put therein spices resembling straw, e.g., cinnamon and ginger which cannot be ground well and contain some threads resembling straw in commemoration of the straw they were accustomed to knead into the clay.

From the time the Temple was destroyed, the sages have enacted that during the recital of the Haggadah it is necessary that there be on the table two kinds of dishes, one in commemoration of the paschal offering, and the other in memory of the *Hagigah* offering which were sacrificed when the Temple was in existence. It is customary that one of the dishes be meat from the part called shoulder, in commemoration of the fact that God has redeemed them with an outstretched arm, and it should be roasted on coal in memory of the paschal lamb which was roasted on fire. The second dish should be an egg, because an egg in the Aramaic language is called *beah* [which also means *desire*]; that is to say, God desired to redeem us with an outstretched arm.

He should arrange his seat while it is yet day, using nice spreads to the full extent of his means, and place them in such a manner that he will be able to incline his body and recline on the left side. Even if he is left-handed, he should recline on the left side. The dish too should be set while it is yet day, in order that immediately on his arrival from the synagogue he may proceed with the Seder without any delay.

Although during the rest of the days of the year it is best not to display too many beautiful dishes in commemoration of the destruction of the Temple, yet on the night of Passover it is good to make use of as many vessels as one can afford. Even the vessels that one does not use for the meal, he should arrange on the table to beautify it and to symbolize freedom.

180

The "dish" should be set as follows: Three *matzot* should be placed upon the dish and covered with a nice cloth; near that, towards his right hand, the shank bone should be placed; the egg towards his left hand, the bitter herbs on which a benediction will be pronounced in the center, the *haroset* below the shankbone, the *karpas* below the egg, and the bitter herbs, to be eaten with *matzot*, in the center *(ibid.,* 118.1-10).

The Feast of Deliverance[1]

FRANZ ROSENZWEIG

The welding of people into a people takes place in its deliverance. And so the feast that comes at the beginning of its national history is a feast of deliverance. Because of this, the Sabbath can legitimately be interpreted as a reminder of the Exodus from Egypt. For the freedom of the man-servant and the maid-servant which it proclaims is conditioned by the deliverance of the people as a people from the servitude of Egypt. And in every command to respect the freedom of even the man-servant, of even the alien among the people, the law of God renews the awareness of the connection holding between the freedom within the people, a freedom decreed by God, and the freeing of the people from Egyptian servitude, a liberation enacted by God. Like the creation of the world, the creation of the people contains the final goal, the final purpose for which it was effected. So it is that the people have come to feel this feast as the most vivid of the three, including the meaning of the two others.

Among the many meals of the spiritual year, the evening meal of the Passover at which the father of the household gathers together all his family is the meal of meals. It is the only one that from first to last has the character of worship; hence the Seder (Order) is, from first to last, liturgically regulated. From the very start the word "freedom" sheds its light upon it. The freedom of this meal at which all are equally free is expressed in a number of rites—which "distinguish this night from all nights—among them the reclining of the participants on cushions. And even more vividly than in this reminiscence of the reclining of the guests in the symposia of antiquity, this particular freedom expresses itself in the fact that the youngest child is the one to speak, and that what the father says at table is adapted to this child's personality and his degree of maturity. In contrast to all instruction, which is necessarily autocratic and never on a basis of equality, the sign of a true and free social intercourse is this, that the one who stands—relatively speaking—nearest the periphery of the circle, gives the cue for the level on which the conversation is to be conducted. For this conversation must include him. No one who is there in the flesh shall be excluded in the spirit. The freedom of a society is always the freedom of everyone who belongs to it. Thus this meal is a symbol of the people's vocation for freedom. That this vocation is only a beginning, only the *initial* creation of the people, is shown in another aspect of this prominence of the youngest child. Since this youngest was permitted to speak for himself, the entire ceremony has, after all, to assume the form of instruction. The father of the family speaks, the household listens, and only in the further course of the evening is there more and more common independence until, in the songs of praise and the table songs of the second part of the meal, songs which float between divine mystery and the jesting mood begot by wine, the last shred of autocracy in the order of the meal dissolves into community.

The founding of the people affords a glimpse of its future destinies, but no more than a glimpse. All its further destinies are prefigured in its origin. It is not only today that enemies rise to destroy us; they rose to destroy us in every generation, back to the first, which went out of Egypt; and in every generation God saved us! And we should have been content with what He did for us when He delivered us from the servitude of Egypt, but He to whom He alone suffices did not consider it sufficient. He led us to Mount Sinai and on to the place of rest in his sanctuary. The texts read from the Scriptures on the last days of the feast give a survey from the origin on to what is latent in this origin, in this creation of the people: on to revelation and ultimate Redemption. The reading of the Song of Songs points to revelation. A distant view of Redemption is afforded by Isaiah's prophecy of the shoot that shall come forth out of the stock of Jesse and smite the land with the rod of his mouth, of the day when the wolf shall dwell with the lamb and the world shall be as full of the knowledge of the Lord as the sea is of water. But the stock shall stand, an ensign for the peoples, and the heathen shall seek it. And this is the deepest meaning of the farewell which those who participate in the evening meal bid one another: Next year in Jerusalem! In every house where the meal is celebrated a cup filled with wine stands ready for the prophet Elijah, the precursor of the shoot from the stock of Jesse, who is forever turning *the heart of the fathers to the children, and the heart of the children to their fathers* (Mal. 3.24), so that the flow of blood may not cease during the long night of time, and stream on towards a morning to come.

The Season of Joy[2]

KAUFMAN KOHLER

However burdensome the Passover minutiae, especially in regard to the prohibition of leaven, became to the Jewish household, the predominant feature was always an exuberance of joy. In the darkest days of medievalism the synagogue and home resounded with song and thanksgiving, and the young imbibed the joy and comfort of their elders through the beautiful symbols of the feast and the richly adorned tale of the deliverance (the Haggadah). The Passover feast with its "night of divine watching" endowed the Jew ever anew with endurance during the dark night of medieval tyranny and with faith in "the Keeper of Israel who slumbereth not nor sleepeth." Moreover, as the spring-tide of nature fills each creature with joy and hope, so Israel's feast of redemption promises the great day of liberty to those who still chafe under the yoke of oppression. The modern Jew is beginning to see in the reawakening of his religious and social life in western lands the token of the future liberation of all mankind. The Passover feast brings him the clear and hopeful message of freedom for humanity from all bondage of body and of spirit.

The Ethical Significance of the Passover[3]

MORITZ LAZARUS

Israel's experience was unique from the first, when it departed from Egypt. Again and again races have been subjugated, reduced to slavery or villeinage; but does history know of another horde of slaves that recovered itself, regained freedom, re-established its own civilization, its own government? It is eminently proper, therefore, that in the prophetic as well as the rabbinic cycle of ideas the Exodus from Egypt should occupy a prominent place. Its importance had been recognized still earlier, in

185

the code, the Torah. The most exalted moral statutes concerning the treatment of strangers are connected with the Exodus, and are, from a psychological point of view, impressively inculcated by means of the reminder: *Ye know the heart of the stranger!* (Ex. 23.9). It is remarkable how even the law of the Sabbath rest, at first sight unconnected with the story of Israel's slavery and redemption, is brought into relation with and illuminated by it. The fourth commandment in the second version of the Ten Commandments, in Deuteronomy, disregards the dogmatic reason attached to the first *for in six days the Lord made* . . . (Ex. 20.11). It emphasizes the ethical motive—that the man-servant and the maid-servant should be granted a day of rest—and employs the memory of the Egyptian experience to urge consideration for subordinates. This method, characteristic of the Bible and still more of the rabbis, of establishing a connection between the most important moral laws and the history of Israel in Egypt, at the same time illustrates how nations should draw instruction from their fortunes . . .

The prophets and psalmists employ the great historical event to give reality chiefly to the religious idea of God's providence and grace. The rabbis, finally, deduce from it the two fundamental elements of man's ethical education: the notion of liberty and the notion of man's ethical task.

Political and even civil freedom was lost. The Roman pharaohs, if they did not exact labor, the more despotically exacted property and blood, and aimed at the annihilation of ideal possessions—the Law, its study, and its execution. Yet the notion of liberty, inner moral and spiritual liberty, cherished as a pure, exalted ideal, possible only under and through the Law, was associated with the memory of the redemption from Egyptian slavery, and this memory in turn was connected with symbolic practices accompanying every act, pleasure, and celebration.

186

The Impregnable Rock of Holy Scripture** *⁴

WINSTON S. CHURCHILL

We must . . . examine briefly the whole question of the miracles . . . It is silly to waste time arguing whether God broke His own natural laws to save His Chosen People, or whether He merely made them work in a favorable manner. At any rate there is no doubt about one miracle. This wandering tribe, in many respects indistinguishable from numberless nomadic communities, grasped and proclaimed an idea of which all the genius of Greece and all the power of Rome were incapable. There was to be only one God, a universal God, a God of nations, a just God. . . .

We reject with scorn all those learned and labored myths that Moses was but a legendary figure upon whom the priesthood and the people hung their essential social, moral and religious ordinances. We believe that the most scientific view, the most up-to-date and rationalistic conception, will find its fullest satisfaction in taking the Bible story literally, and in identifying one of the greatest of human beings with the most decisive leaps forward ever discernible in the human story. We remain unmoved by the tomes of Professor Gradgrind and Dr. Dryasdust. We may be sure that all these things happened just as they are set out according to Holy Writ. We may believe that they happened to people not so very different from ourselves, and that the impressions those people received

* Reprinted with the permission of Charles Scribner's Sons from *Amid These Storms* by Winston Churchill; copyright 1932, Charles Scribner's flons; renewal copyright 1960.

were faithfully recorded and have been transmitted across the centuries with far more accuracy than many of the telegraphed accounts we read of the goings-on of to-day. In the words of a forgotten work of Mr. Gladstone, we rest with assurance upon "the impregnable rock of Holy Scripture."

Exodus[5]

BERL KATZENELSON

Passover! A nation has been commemorating for thousands of years the day of its Exodus from the house of bondage. Throughout all the atrocities of enslavement and despotism, of inquisition, forced conversion and massacre, the Jewish nation carries in its heart the yearning for freedom and gives this craving a folk expression which shall not pass over a single soul in Israel, a single downtrodden, pauperized soul!

From fathers to sons, throughout all the generations, the Exodus from Egypt is related as a personal reminiscence, thereby retaining its original lustre. "In every generation every man must regard himself as if he personally were redeemed from Egypt."

This is the peak of historic consciousness and history has no example of a greater fusion of individual with group than this ancient pedagogic command. I am not acquainted with a literary creation which can evoke a greater contempt for slavery and love of freedom than the narrative of the bondage and Exodus from Egypt. And I do not know of any other ancient memory so entirely a symbol of our present and future, as the "memory of the Exodus from Egypt."

188

The Modern Significance of Passover[6]

MORRIS JOSEPH

In keeping in view the agricultural aspect of the Three Festivals the modern Jew performs no unimportant duty. He realizes the fact that Israel was once a people that lived by tilling the soil, and that the commercial character which so largely distinguishes his people in these times is not, as is commonly thought, inborn, but is the result of the unkindly conditions in which they have been compelled to live. It is good for us and for the world at large to remember that the history of our race has its idyllic side, that there was a time when the Israelite lived the simple life of the husbandman and when his ideal of earthly blessedness was that which pictured each man dwelling in peace and security *under his vine and under his fig-tree* (I Kings 5.5).

But the chief significance of the Feast of Passover is derived from the special historical event it commemorates. That event is the Exodus from Egypt. Passover is, above everything, the commemoration of the great deliverance —a deliverance which transformed a horde of slaves into a people. It is, then, Israel's birthday. From one point of view it is the greatest of all the historical festivals. No other brings the Israelite into such close touch with his people's past. No other so powerfully appeals to his historic sympathies. He is one, for the moment, with his ransomed fathers; he shares with them the proud consciousness of the free, the dignified sense of nationality that is beginning to stir in their hearts. He shares their glowing hopes, the sweet joy of newly recovered manhood.

189

The events of the Exodus are impressive from yet another point of view. The Israelites were free not only from the degradation of bondage but from its agony. They were safe from the taskmaster's cruel whip. They were delivered from the fetters of despair. This thought intensifies the effect of the Passover. We feel all the suffering of our dead ancestors. We share their burdens with them. But we hear too the fateful signal which proclaims that the hour of their redemption has struck; we march forth with them from the scenes of oppression in gladness and gratitude. The ideal of the rabbis fulfills itself. "In every generation it is for the Jew to think that he himself went forth from Egypt" (Pesahim 10.5). So indestructible is the effect wrought by these moving episodes of a bygone day!

Moses the Artist[7]

HEINRICH HEINE

Formerly I felt little affection for Moses, probably because the hellenic spirit was dominant within me, and I could not pardon the Jewish Lawgiver for his intolerance of images, and every sort of plastic representation. I failed to see that despite his hostile attitude to art, Moses was himself a great artist, gifted with the true artist's spirit. Only in him, as in his Egyptian neighbors, the artistic spirit was exercised solely upon the colossal and the indestructible. But, unlike the Egyptians, he did not shape his works out of bricks or granite. His pyramids were built of men, his obelisks hewn out of human material. A feeble race of shepherds he transformed into a people bidding defiance to the centuries—a great, eternal,

190

holy people, God's people, an exemplar to all other peoples, the prototype of mankind; he created Israel. With greater justice than the Roman poet could this artist, the son of Amram and Yochebed the midwife, boast of having erected a monument more enduring than brass.

Moses the Leader[8]

HENRY GEORGE

The striking differences between Egyptian and Hebrew polity are not of form but of essence. The tendency of the one is to subordination and oppression, of the other, to individual freedom. Strangest of recorded births! from out the strongest and most splendid despotism of antiquity comes the freest republic. From between the paws of the rock-hewn Sphinx rises the genius of human liberty, and the trumpets of the Exodus throb with the defiant proclamation of the rights of man. . . .

Imagine what opportune circumstances we may, yet to organize and carry on a movement resulting in the release of a great people from such a soul-subduing tyranny, backed by an army of half a million highly trained soldiers, required a leadership of most commanding and consummate genius. But this task, surpassingly great though it was, is not the measure of the greatness of the leader of the Exodus. It is not in the deliverance from Egypt, it is in the constructive statemanship that laid the foundations of the Hebrew commonwealth that the superlative grandeur of that leadership looms up. As we cannot imagine the Exodus without the great leader, neither can we account for the Hebrew polity without the great statesman—not merely intellectually great, but

191

morally great—a statesman aglow with the unselfish patriotism that refuses to grasp a scepter or found a dynasty.

The Master of the Prophets[9]

AHAD HA-AM

On the threshold of Jewish history the figure of Moses, the greatest of our national heroes, stands like a pillar of light. As I read the Haggadah, on Passover eve, his image hovers over me and lifts me to a higher plane, where all the doubts and questions that have been raised about Moses do not trouble me in the least. Did Moses really exist? Did his life and activities really correspond with the traditional account? Did he really save the Jewish people and give them the Torah in the form in which it has been handed down to us? Questions there are in plenty; but I wave them aside with a short and simple answer. This Moses—I say to the erudite questioners— this man of antiquity, whose existence and character you are investigating, is no concern of anybody but learned antiquarians like yourselves. We have another Moses of our own, whose image has been enshrined in the hearts of the Jewish people for centuries, and who has never ceased to influence our national life from the earliest times to the present day. The existence of this Moses of ours is a historical fact which is wholly independent of your researches. Even if you succeeded in proving beyond all doubt that the man Moses never existed, or that the actual Moses was different from our picture of him, that would not in the slightest degree affect the historical reality of the ideal Moses—the Moses who not only led

192

us for forty years in the wilderness of Sinai, but has led us for thousands of years in all the wildernesses in which we have wandered since the Exodus . . .

A comprehensive view of what tradition tells us about Moses will enable us to discover what the Jewish people regard as the ideal type of a hero. Heroes are not, of course, all of one mold: there are warrior-heroes, thinker-heroes, and many other types. In considering any of these idealized national figures we have first of all to inquire what is the type of man that the creative imagination of the people has tried to represent.

Was Moses a warrior? No! In the whole traditional picture there is no reference to physical force. Moses never led an army to battle or performed deeds of valor on the field. It is only in the fighting with Amalek that he appears on the field of battle; and there he takes no part in the action, but only watches the course of the struggle and influences the fighting men of Israel by his *moral* strength.

Was he, then, a statesman? No! When he had to discuss political affairs with Pharaoh, he was helpless without Aaron for his mouthpiece.

Was he a lawgiver? Again, no! The lawgiver legislates for his own generation; he makes such laws as are required in a particular country at a particular time. Moses legislated for the future; he made laws for a generation as yet unborn and a country as yet unconquered. . . .

What, then, was Moses?

Tradition gives us a clear answer. "There hath not arisen a prophet since in Israel like unto Moses." A prophet—that is what Moses was. But he stands apart from the other prophets, whose first appearance as a distinctive type dates from the period of the monarchy. He is—to use a title of much later origin—"the Master of the Prophets": in other words, the ideal archetype of Hebrew prophecy in its purest and most perfect manifestation. . . .

As soon as Moses leaves the schoolroom for the world, he is confronted by an act of injustice; and he unhesitatingly takes the side of the victim. The eternal conflict between the prophet and the world breaks out at once. An Egyptian striking a Hebrew—the strong trampling on the weak—this first experience of his is an occurrence of every day. The prophet in him is roused to anger, and he helps the weaker. Gradually his knowledge of life widens, and he has an even more painful experience. He sees two Hebrews quarreling. Though they are brothers, though both are powerless bondsmen of Pharaoh, they nonetheless fight one another. Again the prophet's sense of justice is aroused, and he interferes in a quarrel which is none of his. And this time he discovers that it is no light matter to fight justice. The world is stronger than himself, and to oppose it is to imperil his life. But this experience does not teach him the worldly wisdom of caution. His passion for justice exiles him from his country; and as soon as he approaches another place of human habitation—even while he sits by the wall outside the city, without a friend to offer him shelter—he hears the cry of outraged justice, and immediately hastens to the rescue. This time the quarrel is not between Hebrews, but between people entirely unknown to him; but that makes no difference. The prophet draws no distinction between man and man, only between right and wrong. He helps the weak women against the shepherds who trample on their rights.

This is all that we are told about Moses before his first audience with Pharaoh, which did not take place till he was nearly eighty years of age. That period of his life, which was merely one of preparation, was not of sufficient importance to call for any detailed record. All the greater significance attaches to the selection of the three incidents of his early life which are recorded. Bearing in mind that their common characteristic is the prophet's revolt against injustice, we may confidently infer that the intention of the record was to throw that conflict into relief, and thus to show that the prophetic quality was there from the very beginning. We may also infer that throughout the long period of his wanderings Moses never ceased to fight for justice, until the moment came for him to become the savior of his people and to teach mankind justice— not for his age alone, but for all time.

That great moment dawned in the wilderness, far from the turmoil of life. The prophet's soul is weary of the endless struggle, and longs for peace and rest. He seeks the solitude of the shepherd's life, goes into the wilderness with his sheep, and reaches Horeb, the mountain of the Lord. But even here he finds no rest. He feels in his innermost being that he has not yet fulfilled his mission. Some hidden force within him urges him on; it bids him go forth to work and fight and thus fulfill himself . . .

Suddenly the prophet hears the voice of the Lord—the voice he knows so well—calling to him from some forgotten corner of his innermost being: *I am the God of thy father. . . . I have surely seen the affliction of My people that are in Egypt. . . . Come now therefore, and I will send thee unto Pharaoh, that thou mayest bring forth My people the children of Israel out of Egypt.*

The Penitent[10]

THEODOR HERZL

And so they went through with the Seder ceremony—half ritual, half family festival. This most Jewish of all the festivals dates back farther in history than any other civilized usage in modern times. For hundreds and hundreds of years it has been observed without change, while the whole world changed. Nations disappeared from history, others rose. The world grew larger. Undreamed-of continents emerged from the seas. Unimagined natural forces were harnessed for the pleasure and comfort of

195

man. But this one people still remained unchanged, retaining its ancient customs, true to itself, rehearsing the woes of its forebears. Israel, a people of slavery and freedom, still prayed in ancient words to the Eternal its God.

One guest at the Seder table pronounced the Hebrew words of the Haggadah with the zeal of a penitent. He was finding himself again, and his throat was often so tight with emotion that he had to master his longing to cry out aloud. It was almost thirty years since he himself had asked the Four Questions. . . . Then had come "Enlightenment," the break with all that was Jewish, and the final logical leap into the void, when he had no further hold on life. At this Seder table he seemed to himself a prodigal son, returned to his own people.

The first part of the ceremony ended, dinner was served. Kingscourt called across the table. "Fritz! I'd no idea you were so perfect a Hebrew scholar."

"I confess I did not know it myself."

Homesickness of the "Renegade" Jew [*11]

MAURICE SAMUEL

The death of a Jew to his people and his faith is (perhaps I say it because I am a Jew and know more about this instance) singularly tragic. I do not speak here of Jews who have been brought up without a tradition to overcome, but of those who were in the heart of the tradition and were compelled by "intellectual honesty" to break away. I cannot think of a parallel to the tragedy. A Jew leaving the faith under those circumstances leaves everything. . . .

* Copyright 1948 by Maurice Samuel.

And when, at stated seasons, there come round the days that are deeply implicated in the patterns of his life's responses, the anguish of his separation may become unbearable. Not to be home for the Passover ceremony of the Seder, for instance. How shall I convey that? Let me compare this man with a Christian who has repudiated all the "superstitions" of his faith and all the symbols associated with it, but a Christian in whose childhood the Christmas tree, the family reunion, the presents, the laughter, anticipation, loving-kindness—all the tenderness of a great, overriding redemptive idea—were living things. He too has made himself homeless by an act of the intelligence; for him too (let us assume) the personal, the religious, the artistic warmth of his early life is gone forever, never to be recaptured because it is of the essence of its enjoyment that it shall never have been challenged, never stained with a repudiation.

For the Christian thus self-exiled the reminders of the season, in windows, in streets, in public squares, and in shops, pursuing him all day long and all through the evenings, are painful in the extreme; this is the price he pays for remaining in a familiar world. But his case is still happier than that of the disbelieving Jew self-exiled from the Passover Seder, that unique family gathering round the dinner table, of the first and second nights of the festival.

There is no way of comparing the hold of the Seder on a Jewish child's memory with that of Christmas on a Christian child's; and the attempt would be tasteless, as well as pointless. But let it be said that the Seder ceremony has been specially devised by generations of pedagogues to appeal to children. Its ritual is charming, ingenious and powerful. Its folkloristic texts—historical and devotional—are of exceptional beauty. Some of them are deliberately amusing. The child who has sat through a few Seders carries into later years an unforgettable Passover nostalgia.

Yet this is not the point. For if a "renegade" Jew is homesick for the Passover as the "renegade" Christian for Christmas, and the two are in these respects equally miserable, there is a particular torment reserved for the Jew at Passover time. He too is surrounded by reminders, but they are of a terrible and ambiguous character. The Passover coincides with the time of the Christian Easter; and in certain lands Easter is the season for whipping up vengeful emotions round the death of Christ. Then the Jew must feel rising all about him that ancient, recurrent annual flood-tide of fury against his people. Let us assume that he has not accepted the Christian faith—he has lost only his Judaism, not his self-respect. Still he must feel he has betrayed someone. For the sake of "intellectual honesty" he is not there, in the beleaguered citadel. For the sake of intellectual honesty he is on the outside, living with safety (at least transient) among the armies of the besiegers.

And then he remembers incidents out of the past. There mingle in his mind poignant recollections of his own childhood Seder and the Seders of neighbors: the solemnity and the fun, the divinity and the earthliness; parents, brothers, sisters. His mind casts back to the antiquity of the ritual. He thinks of Seders in other climes, celebrants in other costumes; and, with the Seders, he remembers the lowering, threatening world outside.

The Exodus: A Historical Mission[12]

ANDRÉ NEHER

Passover contains a reproach and a challenge. It poses the question which is fundamental to the Jew and challenges him to answer that very question which God addressed to Adam: *Where art thou?* The mysticism of the

Passover is essentially tragic rather than romantic. The
Jew is always more or less a stranger in life. The reality,
the gravity, and the meaning of his alienation are measured by the Passover. No Jew can pass the Haggadah
untouched. For its style is not narrative, but interrogative.
Its story is not told like a legend, but like a problem. One
initial question is asked, and all the others follow from it:
"What is the difference between this night and all other
nights?" It is for the Jew to answer if he can, and if he
cannot, to feel that the question contains a challenge.

Like an unfinished play, the night of the Exodus continues through the centuries, seeking actors to relive it
perpetually, and to grasp its essential meaning.

> Every person in every generation must regard
> himself as having been personally freed from Egypt.
> The Holy One, blessed be He, has not only re-
> deemed our ancestors, but us also together with
> them. . . .

It is not the aesthetic attraction of the night alone
which causes so many writers to center their theme of
"the revival of Jewish consciousness" round the night of
the Passover; it is its spiritual significance. With a stroke
of genius Christopher Fry projected such a spiritual crisis
into his play *(The Firstborn)* on the first Exodus. Shendi,
the eldest son of Miriam and nephew of Moses, having
suffered with the other Hebrews, is promoted. He is a
soldier in the Egyptian army, a kapo in the camps, tortur-
ing his brothers even more than the Egyptians themselves.
But the night of the Exodus comes. Will he die with the
first-born, or will the cry, wrung from his very entrails,
"I am a Jew!" be heard? Christopher Fry only raises this
question. Yet the whole of Jewish history has answered
this cry, which may have been uttered by a Shendi of
flesh and blood in the days of Amenophis or Merneptah.
This unique moment of time, which once and for all separates the world into torturers and victims, into oppressors
and liberated, serves as a point of reference for all generations, so that in each generation every man, every Jew,

may rediscover his own essential place, even when he has denied and scorned it all his life. Jewish writers, too, could not but let their heroes, Jews who have strayed into neutrality or indifference, find the significance of their Jewishness in the brilliant light of the night of the Passover (Jo Sinclair, *Identity;* Sammy Tronemann, *Tohu Vabohu*). In almost all the novels dealing with the marranos the crypto-Jews take off their masks and reveal their identity during a Passover night. Moreover, is not the *Rabbi of Bacharach* a confession of a deep remorse? Was it not immediately after his formal conversion to Lutheranism that Heine wrote it? Only Israel Zangwill ends the play on a tragic note, when the Jew feels a stranger to the world of the torturers as well as the world of the tortured. In *Had Gadya* he describes the final situation of the Jew who is face to face with the Passover. During a Passover in which he takes part at Venice, a young emancipated Jew of the nineteenth century becomes so conscious of the failure and absurdity of his estrangement and, simultaneously, of his inability to identify himself completely with his brothers, that he commits suicide in the waters of the canal, while the last notes of the Passover Haggadah, which touched him to the quick, are ringing through the half-open windows above.

It is obvious—and the above examples, even though they are taken from literary and romantic works, underline the fact—that the center of the Jewish Passover is not the Jewish people as such. Its annual return does not resemble a patriotic festival like the fourteenth of July, the glory of which deserves enthusiasm and even sacrifice. So little is the Seder a national festival that the Haggadah does not even mention the name of Moses the Liberator. No human exploit is indicated. But what is shown as necessary is that the Jew should become conscious of his Jewishness. Not that the members of a nation should unite to celebrate a national liberation, but that the very ideas of liberation and Redemption should be removed from the sphere of abstract thought and be considered from the point of view of an experience, *which differs from all others,* the experience of the Jewish people in Egypt. *Every person in every generation must regard himself as having been personally freed from Egypt.* What then is the *human* significance of this liberty, to which those only can bear witness who accept the idea of having won it, like Moses, in Egypt?

The first idea that is expressed in the Jewish Passover is the certainty of freedom. With the Exodus a new age has struck for humanity: redemption from misery. If the Exodus had not taken place, marked as it was by the two-fold sign of the overriding will of God and the free and conscious assent of men, the historical destiny of humanity would have followed another course. This course would have been radically different, as the redemption, the *ge'ulah* of the Exodus from Egypt, would not have been its foundation. During the night of the Passover the Jew says: "Neither my fathers, nor I, nor my children would be free; we would still remain slaves forever." Inversely, the door opened by the Exodus cannot be closed again. "We are free with an eternal freedom." This is a para-doxical certitude, when it is proclaimed by the Jew, who is miserably immured in the ghetto, caught in the toils of persecution. However, the Jew cannot escape from this paradox by taking refuge in a dichotomy of freedom. He refuses to believe that only moral liberty is eternal, and that physical liberty might be lost for a time. The Jewish Passover respects the universal and indivisible quality of liberty. The Exodus was a physical, social and political event, a liberating of the body as well as of the soul (as a matter of fact rather of the body than of the soul, which was only fully set free on Sinai). The energy which then poured down upon the world like a torrent is inexhaustible and invincible. No barrier can resist it. All constraint is accidental; all misery is only provisional. The breath of freedom which has blown over the world since the Exodus can dispel them this very day. This is the conviction pro-claimed by the Jew when he "breaks bread and raises the

201

chalice of wine" in the night of the Passover: the bread of misery, and the wine of liberty, one vanquished by the other; proclaimed when in the era of the Temple he tasted the paschal lamb; when he tastes the bitter herbs, their bitterness overcome by the Passover today. The optimism of the Jewish people, their philanthropy during centuries of patriarchal government, their social dynamism in revolutionary ages, have their source and their impetus in the Passover, which retains the sense given it by Moses. "Whoever is hungry, let him come and eat. Whoever is in need, let him come and celebrate the Passover": this is the invitation at the beginning of the Jewish Passover night. By its "social" implications it appears to transcend the purely religious sphere, yet it is based on none other than the Pentateuch of Moses . . .

The event of the Passover allows all its depths and all its heights to be explored. From the dust of the most abject misery to the most fascinating miracle by which human dignity is restored to all its grandeur, the night of the Seder forces man to face and so fight himself. At the end of the dialogue this "vocation" becomes quite clear. It summons man to join his brother in the building of Jerusalem and, by that very fact, in the rebuilding of the world.

XIII

The Rabbi of Bacharach[1]

HEINRICH HEINE

Rabbi Abraham of Bacharach sat in the great hall of his house with his relations, disciples, and other guests, to celebrate the eve of the Passover. Everything in the hall was brighter than usual; over the table hung a gaily embroidered silk spread whose gold fringes touched the floor; the plates with the symbolic foods shone appealingly, as did the tall, wine-filled goblets adorned with the embossed images of many holy stories. The men sat in their black cloaks and black, flat hats and white ruffs; the women, in strangely glittering garments made of cloths from Lombardy, wore their diadems and necklaces of gold and pearls; and the silver Sabbath lamp cast its most festive light on the devoutly merry faces of old and young. Reclining, as custom enjoins, on the purple velvet cushions of a chair raised above the others, Rabbi Abraham sat reading and chanting the Haggadah, while the mixed choir fell in or responded in the prescribed places. The rabbi wore his black holiday garb. His noble, somewhat austere features seemed milder than usual; his lips were smiling out of the dark beard as if they had something

203

fair to tell; and in his eyes was a light as of happy memories and visions of the future.

Lovely Sarah, seated beside him on a similar high velvet chair, wore none of her jewelry, being the hostess; only white linen enclosed her slender form and pious face. It was a touchingly beautiful face, just as always the beauty of Jewesses is of a peculiarly moving kind—a consciousness of the deep misery, the bitter scorn, and the evil chances wherein their kindred and friends live, brings to their lovely features a certain aching tenderness and observant loving apprehension that strangely charm our hearts. So, on this evening, lovely Sarah sat looking constantly into her husband's eyes. But every now and then she also glanced at the quaint parchment book of the Haggadah which lay before her, bound in gold and velvet: an old heirloom with wine stains of many years on it, which had come down from her grandfather's time and in which were many bold and brightly-colored pictures that even as a little girl she had so loved to look at on Passover evenings. They represented all kinds of biblical stories, such as Abraham smashing his father's idols with a hammer, the angels coming to him, Moses killing the *Mitzri,* and Pharaoh sitting in state on his throne with the frogs giving him no rest, even at table. Also she saw how Pharaoh drowned, thank God! and how the children of Israel went cautiously through the Red Sea, how they stood open-mouthed before Mount Sinai with their sheep, cows, and oxen, how pious King David played the harp, and finally, how Jerusalem, with the towers and battlements of its Temple, shone in the glory of the sun!

The second cup of wine was poured, the faces and the voices of the guests grew brighter, and the rabbi, taking a piece of the unleavened bread and raising it in a gay greeting, read these words from the Haggadah: "Behold, this is the bread our fathers ate in Egypt. Whoever is hungry, let him come and share it! Whoever is in want, let him come and celebrate the Passover! This year we are here; the coming year, in the land of Israel! This year we are slaves; the coming year, free men!"

At this moment, the door of the hall opened and two tall, pale men entered, wrapped in very wide cloaks, and one of them said, "Peace be with you; we are men of your faith, on a journey, and wish to celebrate the Passover with you." And the rabbi, quickly and kindly, replied, "Peace be with you. Sit down here by me." The two strangers promptly sat down at the table, and the rabbi read on. Sometimes, while the others were saying the responses, he would throw an endearing word to his wife. Alluding to the old joke that on this evening the head of a Jewish house considers himself a king, he said to her, "Be happy, my Queen!" But she, smiling sadly, replied, "We have no Prince"—by which she meant the son of the house, whom a passage in the Haggadah requires to question his father in certain prescribed words about the meaning of the festival. The rabbi said nothing, only pointing with his finger to a picture just turned up in the Haggadah, on which was shown very charmingly how the three angels came to Abraham to announce to him that he would have a son by his wife Sarah, who with feminine cunning was listening to their talk from behind the tent door. This little hint sent a threefold blush to the beautiful woman's cheeks; she cast her eyes down, and then lovingly raised them again to her husband, who went on chanting the wondrous story of Rabbi Joshua, Rabbi Eliezer, Rabbi Azariah, Rabbi Akiba, and Rabbi Tarfon, who sat reclining in B'ne B'rak and talked all night long of the children of Israel's Exodus from Egypt, until their disciples came to tell them that it was daylight and the great morning prayer was being recited in the synagogue.

Now, as Lovely Sarah was thus devoutly listening and continually looking at her husband, she noticed that his face suddenly froze in horrible distortion, the blood left his cheeks and lips, and his eyes stood out like balls of ice. But almost at the same instant she saw his features returning to their former calm and cheerfulness, his cheeks

205

and lips growing red again, his eyes circling merrily—in fact, his whole being seemed seized by a mad gaiety that otherwise was quite foreign to his nature. Lovely Sarah was frightened as never before in her life. A chilling dread rose in her, due less to the signs of rigid terror which for a moment she had seen in her husband's countenance than to his present merriment, which gradually turned into rollicking exultation. The rabbi moved his cap from one ear to the other, pulled and twisted his beard comically, sang the text of the Haggadah as if it were a catch; and in the enumeration of the Egyptian plagues, when it is the custom to dip the forefinger in the full cup and shake the clinging drop of wine to the ground, the rabbi sprinkled the younger girls with red wine and there was much wailing over spoiled collars, and ringing laughter. An ever more eerie feeling overcame Lovely Sarah at this convulsively bubbling gaiety of her husband's; seized by nameless qualms, she gazed on the humming swarm of brightly illumined people, comfortably rocking to and fro, nibbling the thin Passover bread or sipping wine or gossiping or singing aloud, in the very happiest of moods.

The time for supper came and all rose to wash, and Lovely Sarah brought a great silver basin covered with embossed gold figures, which she held before each guest while water was poured over his hands. When she thus served the rabbi, he winked at her significantly and quietly slipped out of the door. Lovely Sarah followed on his heels hastily, the rabbi grasped her hand and quickly drew her away through the dark alleys of Bacharach, quickly through the town gate, out onto the highway leading along the Rhine, towards Bingen.

It was one of those nights in spring which, though soft enough and starry, raise strange shivers in the soul. The fragrance of the flowers was deathly. The birds chirped as if glad to vex someone and yet vexed themselves. The moon cast malicious yellow stripes of light over the darkly murmuring river. The tall, bulky rocks of the

206

cliffs looked like menacingly wagging giants' heads. The watchman on the tower of Castle Strahleck blew a melancholy tune, and with it, jealously chiming, tolled the little death bell of Saint Werner's. Lovely Sarah still held the silver ewer in her right hand; her left was held by the rabbi, and she felt that his fingers were icy and his arm was trembling. But she followed in silence, perhaps because she had long been accustomed to obey her husband blindly and without questioning—perhaps, too, because fear sealed her lips from within.

Below Castle Sonneck, opposite Lorch—about where the hamlet of Niederrheinbach stands now—a high cliff arches out over the bank of the Rhine. This Rabbi Abraham ascended with his wife, looked all about him and stared up at the stars. Lovely Sarah, trembling and chilled by fears of death, stood with him and regarded the pale face on which pain, dread, piety, and rage seemed to flash back and forth in the ghostly light of the moon. But when the rabbi suddenly tore the silver ewer from her hand and hurled it clanking down into the Rhine, she could no longer bear the awful anxiety—and crying out, "Merciful Shaddai!" she threw herself at his feet and implored him to reveal the dark secret.

The rabbi moved his lips soundlessly a few times, unable to speak; but finally he called out, "Do you see the Angel of Death? Down there he hovers over Bacharach. Yet we have escaped his sword. Praise be the Lord!" And in a voice still shaking with fright he told how reclining happily and chanting the Haggadah, he had chanced to look under the table and there, at his feet, had seen the bloody corpse of a child. "Then I knew," added the rabbi, "that our two late guests were not of the community of Israel, but of the assembly of the godless whose plan was to bring that corpse into our house by stealth, charge us with the murder, and incite the people to loot and murder us. I could not let on that I saw through the work of darkness; thereby I should have only speeded my destruction. Cunning alone could save our lives. Praised

207

be the Lord! Have no fear, Lovely Sarah; our friends
and relatives also will be saved. It was my blood after
which the villains lusted; I have escaped them, and they
will be content with my silver and gold. Come with me,
Lovely Sarah, to another land; we will leave misfortune
behind; lest it follow us, I threw the last of my possessions, the silver ewer, to it as a peace offering. The God of
our fathers will not forsake us."

Elijah's Goblet[2]

ISRAEL ZANGWILL

I

Aaron ben Amram removed from the great ritual dish
the roasted shankbone of lamb (symbolic residuum of
the paschal sacrifice) and the roasted egg (representative
of the ancient festival-offering in the Temple), and while
his wife and children held up the dish, which now contained only the bitter herbs and unleavened cakes, he
recited the Chaldaic prelude to the Seder—the long domestic ceremonial of the Passover evening:
"This is the bread of affliction which our fathers ate in
the land of Egypt. Let all who are hungry come in and
eat; let all who require come in and celebrate the Passover. This year here, next year in the land of Israel! This
year slaves, next year sons of freedom!"
But the Polish physician showed nothing of the slave.
White-bearded, clad in a long white robe and a white
skullcap and throned on white pillows, he made rather a
royal figure—indeed, for this night of nights, conceived
of himself as "King" and his wife as "Queen."
But "Queen" Golda, despite her silk gown and flowery

208

cap, did not share her consort's majestic mood, still less the rosy happiness of the children who sat round this fascinating board. Her heart was full of a whispering fear that not all the brave melodies of the father nor all the quaint family choruses could drown. All very well for the little ones to be unconscious of the hovering shadow, but how could her husband have forgotten the horrors of the Blood Accusation in the very year he had led her under the canopy?

And surely he knew as well as she that the dreadful legend was gathering again, that the slowly-growing Jew-hatred had reached a point at which it must find expression, that the *pritzim* (nobles) in their great houses and the peasants behind their high palings alike sulked under the burden of debts. Indeed, had not the Passover market hummed with the old, old story of a lost Christian child? Not murdered yet, thank God, nor even a corpse. But still, if a boy should be found with signs of violence upon him at this season of the paschal sacrifice, when the Greek Church brooded on the Crucifixion! O God of Abraham, guard us from these fiends unchained!

But the first part of the elaborate ritual, pleasantly punctuated with cups of raisin wine, passed peacefully by, and the evening meal, mercifully set in the middle, was reached, to the children's vast content. They made wry, humorous mouths, each jest endeared by annual repetition, over the horseradish that typified the bitterness of the Egyptian bondage, and ecstatic grimaces over the soft, sweet mixture of almonds, raisins, apples, and cinnamon, vaguely suggestive of the bondsmen's mortar; they relished the eggs sliced into salt water, and then—the symbols all duly swallowed—settled down with more prosaic satisfaction to the merely edible meats and fishes, though even to these the special Passover plates and dishes and the purified knives and forks lent a new relish.

By this time Golda was sufficiently cheered up to meditate her annual theft of the *afikoman*, that segment of Passover cake under Aaron's pillow, morsels of which,

209

distributed to each as the final food to be tasted that night, replaced the final mouthful of the paschal lamb in the ancient Palestinian meal.

II

But Elijah's goblet stood in the center of the table untasted. Every time the ritual cup-drinking came round, the children had glanced at the great silver goblet placed for the Prophet of Redemption. Alas! the brimming raisin wine remained ever at the same level.

They found consolation in the thought that the great moment was still to come—the moment of the third cup, when, mother throwing open the door, father would rise, holding the goblet on high, and sonorously salute an unseen visitor.

True, in other years, though they had almost heard the rush of wings, the great shining cup had remained full, and when it was replaced on the white cloth, a vague resentment as at a spurned hospitality had stirred in each youthful breast. But many reasons could be found to exculpate Elijah—not omitting their own sins—and now, when Ben Amram nodded to his wife to open the door, expectation stood on tip-toe, credulous as ever, and the young hearts beat tattoo.

But the mother's heart was palpitating with another emotion. A faint clamor in the Polish quarter at the back, as she replaced the samovar in the kitchen, had recalled all her alarms, and she merely threw open the door of the room. But Ben Amram was not absent-minded enough to be beguiled by her air of obedient alacrity. Besides, he could see the shut street-door through the strip of passage. He gestured towards it.

Now she feigned laziness. "Oh, never mind."

"David, open the street-door."

The oldest boy sprang up joyously. It would have been too bad of mother to keep Elijah on the doorstep.

"No, no, David!" Golda stopped him. "It is too heavy; he could not undo the bolts and bars."

"You have barred it?" Ben Amram asked.

"And why not? In this season you know how the heathen go mad like street-dogs."

"Pooh! They will not bite us."

"But, Aaron! You heard about the lost Christian child!"

"I have saved many a Christian child, Golda."

"They will not remember that."

"But I must remember the ritual." And he made a movement.

"No, no, Aaron! Listen!"

The shrill noises seemed to have veered round towards the front of the house. He shrugged his shoulders. "I hear only the goats bleating."

She clung to him as he made for the door. "For the sake of our children!"

"Do not be childish yourself, my crown!"

"But I am not childish. Hark!"

He smiled calmly. "The door must be opened."

Her fears lent her skepticism. "It is you that are childish. You know no Prophet of Redemption will come through the door."

He caressed his venerable beard. "Who knows?"

"I know. It is a Destroyer, not a Redeemer of Israel, who will come. Listen! Ah, God of Abraham! Do you not hear?"

Unmistakably the howl of a riotous mob was approaching, mingled with the reedy strains of an accordion.

"Down with the *Zhids!* Death to the dirty Jews!"

"God in heavens!" She released her husband, and ran towards the children with a gesture as of seeking to gather them all in her arms. Then, hearing the bolts shot back, she turned with a scream. "Are you mad, Aaron?"

But he, holding her back with his gaze, threw wide the door with his left hand, while his right upheld Elijah's goblet, and over the ululation of the unseen mob and the

211

shrill spasms of music rose his Hebrew welcome to the visitor: *Barukh ha-Ba!*

Hardly had the greeting left his lips when a wild figure in a rich furred coat dashed round the corner and almost into his arms, half-spilling the wine.

"In God's name, Reb Aaron!" panted the refugee, and fell half-dead across the threshold.

The physician dragged him hastily within, and slammed the door, just as two *moujiks*—drunken leaders of the chase—lurched past. The mother, who had sprung forward at the sound of the fall, frenziedly shot the bolts, and in another instant the hue and cry tore past the house and dwindled in the distance.

Ben Amram raised the white bloody face, and put Elijah's goblet to the lips. The strange visitor drained it to the dregs, the clustered children looking on dazedly. As the head fell back, it caught the light from the festive candles of the Passover board. The face was bare of hair; even the side curls were gone.

"Maimon the *meshummad!*" cried the mother, shuddering back. "You have saved the Apostate."

"Did I not say the door must be opened?" replied Ben Amram gently. Then a smile of humor twitched his lips, and he smoothed his white beard. "Maimon is the only Jew abroad tonight, and how were the poor drunken peasants to know he was baptized?"

Despite their thrill of horror at the traitor, David and his brothers and sisters were secretly pleased to see Elijah's goblet empty at last.

III

Next morning the Passover liturgy rang jubilantly through the vast, crowded synagogue. No violence had been reported, despite the passage of a noisy mob. The ghetto, then, was not to be laid waste with fire and sword, and the worshippers within the moss-grown, turreted quadrangle drew free breath, and sent it out in great shouts of rhythmic prayer, as they swayed in their fringed shawls, with quivering hands of supplication. The Ark of the Law at one end of the great building, overbrooded by the Ten Commandments and the perpetual light, stood open to mark a supreme moment of devotion. Ben Amram had been given the honor of uncurtaining the shrine, and its richly-clad scrolls of all sizes with their silver bells and pointers stood revealed in solemn splendor.

Through the ornate grating of their gallery the gaily-clad women looked down on the rocking figures, while the grace-notes of the cantor on his central dais, and the harmoniously interjected "poms" of his male ministrants flew up to their ears, as though they were indeed angels on high. Suddenly, over the blended passion of cantor and congregation, an ominous sound broke from without—the complex clatter of cavalry, the curt ring of military orders. The swaying figures turned suddenly as under another wind, the women's eyes grew astare and ablaze with terror. The great doors flew open, and—oh, awful, incredible sight—a squadron of Cossacks rode slowly in, two abreast, with a heavy thud of hoofs on the sacred floor, and a rattle of ponderous sabers. Their black conical caps and long beards, their great side-buttoned coats, and pockets stuffed with protrusive cartridges, their prancing horses, their leaded knouts, struck a blood-curdling discord amid the prayerful, white-wrapped figures. The ramble of worship ceased; the cantor, suddenly isolated, was heard soaring ecstatically; then he, too, turned his head uneasily and his roulade died in his throat.

"Halt!" the officer cried. The moving column froze. Its bristling length stretched from the central platform, blocking the aisle, and the courtyard echoed with the clanging hoofs of its rear, which backed into the school and the poor-house. The *shammash* (beadle) was seen to front the flamboyant invaders.

"Why does Your Excellency intrude upon our prayers to God?"

The congregation felt its dignity return. Who would

213

have suspected Red Judah of such courage—such apt speech? Why, the very rabbi was petrified; the elders of the *Kahal* stood dumb. Ben Amram himself, their spokesman to the government, whose praying-shawl was embroidered with a silver band, and whose coat was satin, remained immovable between the pillars of the Ark, staring stonily at the brave beadle.

"First of all, for the boy's blood."

The words rang out with military precision, and the speaker's horse pawed clangorously, as if impatient for the charge. The men grew death-pale; the women wrung their hands.

"Ai, vai!" they moaned. "Woe! woe!"

"What boy? what blood?" said the *shammash*, undaunted.

"Don't palter, you rascal! You know well that a Christian child has disappeared."

The aged rabbi, stimulated by the *shammash*, uplifted a quavering voice.

"The child will be found of a surety—if, indeed, it is lost," he added with bitter sarcasm. "And surely Your Excellency cannot require the boy's blood at our hands ere Your Excellency knows it is indeed spilt."

"You misunderstood me, old dog—or rather you pretend to, old fox. The boy's blood is here—it is kept in this very synagogue—and I have come for it."

The *shammash* laughed explosively. "Oh, Excellency!"

The synagogue, hysterically tense, caught the contagion of glad relief. It rang with strange laughter.

"There is no blood in this synagogue, Excellency," said the rabbi, his eyes a-twinkle, "save what runs in living veins."

"We shall see. Produce that bottle beneath the Ark."

"That!" The *shammash* grinned—almost indecorously. "That is the consecration wine—red as my beard," quoth he.

"Ha! ha! the red consecration wine!" repeated the

214

synagogue in a happy buzz, and from the women's gallery came the same glad murmur of mutual explanation.

"We shall see," repeated the officer, with iron imperturbability, and the happy hum died into a cold-heart-faintness, fraught with an almost incredulous apprehension of some devilish treachery, some mock discovery that would give the ghetto over to the frenzies of fanatical creditors—nay, to the vengeance of the law.

The officer's voice rose again. "Let no one leave the synagogue—man, woman, or child. Kill anyone who attempts to escape."

The screams of fainting women answered him from above, but impassively he urged his horse along the aisle that led to the Ark; its noisy hoofs trampled over every heart. Springing from his saddle he opened the little cupboard beneath the scrolls, and drew out a bottle, hideously red.

"Consecration wine, eh?" he said grimly.

"What else, Excellency?" stoutly replied the *shammash,* who had followed him.

A savage laugh broke from the officer's lips. "Drink me a mouthful!"

As the *shammash* took the bottle, with a fearless shrug of the shoulders, every eye strained painfully towards him, save in the women's gallery, where many covered their faces with their hands. Every breath was held.

Keeping the same amused incredulous face, Red Judah gulped down a draught. But as the liquid met his palate a horrible distortion overcame his smile, his hands flew heavenwards. Dropping the bottle, and with a hoarse cry, "Mercy, O God!" he fell before the Ark, foaming at the mouth. The red fluid spread in a vivid pool.

"Hear, O Israel!" A raucous cry of horror rose from all around, and was echoed more shrilly from above. Almighty Father! The Jew-haters had worked their fiendish trick. Now the men were become as the women, shrieking, wringing their hands, crying, "Ai, vai!" "Gewalt!" The

215

rabbi shook as with palsy. "Satan! Satan!" chattered through his teeth.

But Ben Amram had moved at last, and was stooping over the scarlet stain.

"A soldier should know blood, Excellency!" the physician said quietly.

The officer's face relaxed into a faint smile.

"A soldier knows wine, too," he said, sniffing. And, indeed, the spicy reek of the consecration wine was bewildering the nearer bystanders.

"Your Excellency frightened poor Judah into a fit," said the physician, raising the beadle's head by its long red beard.

His Excellency shrugged his shoulders, sprang to his saddle, and cried a retreat. The Cossacks, unable to turn in the aisle, backed cumbrously with a manifold thudding and rearing and clanking, but ere the congregation had finished rubbing their eyes, the last conical hat and leaded knout had vanished, and only the tarry reek of their boots was left in proof of their actual passage. A deep silence hung for a moment like a heavy cloud, then it broke in a torrent of ejaculations.

But Ben Amram's voice rang through the din. "Brethren!" He rose from wiping the frothing lips of the stricken creature, and his face had the fiery gloom of a seer's, and the din died under his uplifted palm. "Brethren, the Lord hath saved us!"

"Blessed be the name of the Lord forever and ever!" The rabbi began the phrase, and the congregation caught it up in thunder.

"But hearken how. Last night at the Seder, as I opened the door for Elijah, there entered Maimon the *meshummad!* 'Twas he quaffed Elijah's cup!"

There was a rumble of imprecations.

"A pretty Elijah!" cried the rabbi.

"Nay, but God sends the Prophet of Redemption in strange guise," the physician said. "Listen! Maimon was pursued by a drunken mob, ignorant he was a deserter from our camp. When he found how I had saved him and dressed his bleeding face, when he saw the spread Passover table, his child-soul came back to him, and in a burst of tears he confessed the diabolical plot against our community, hatched through his instrumentality by some desperate debtors; how, having raised the cry of a lost child, they were to have its blood found beneath our Holy Ark as in some mystic atonement. And while you all looked joyously at the Seder table, a bottle of blood lay here instead of the consecration wine, like a bomb waiting to burst and destroy us all."

A shudder of awe traversed the synagogue.

"But the Guardian of Israel, who permits us to sleep on Passover night without night-prayers, neither slumbers nor sleeps. Maimon had bribed the *shammash* to let him enter the synagogue and replace the consecration wine."

"Red Judah!" It was like the growl of ten thousand tigers. Some even precipitated themselves upon the writhing wretch.

"Back! back!" cried Ben Amram. "The Almighty has smitten him."

" 'Vengeance is mine, saith the Lord,' " quoted the rabbi solemnly.

"Hallelujah!" shouted a frenzied female voice, and "Hallelujah!" the men responded in thunder.

"Red Judah had no true belief in the God of Israel," the physician went on.

"May he be an atonement for us all!" interrupted the cantor.

"Amen!" growled the congregation.

"For a hundred rubles and the promise of personal immunity Red Judah allowed Maimon the *meshummad* to change the bottles while all Israel sat at the Seder. It was because the mob saw the *meshummad* stealing out of the synagogue that they fell upon him for a pious Jew. Behold, brethren, how the Almighty weaves His threads together. After the repentant sinner had confessed all to me, and explained how the Cossacks were to be sent to catch all the community assembled helpless in synagogue, I deemed it best merely to get the bottles changed back again. The false bottle contained only bullock's blood, but it would have sufficed to madden the multitude. Since it is I who have the blessed privilege of supplying the consecration wine it was easy enough to give Maimon another bottle, and armed with this he roused the *shammash* in the dawn, pretending he had now obtained true human blood. A ruble easily procured him the keys again, and when he brought me back the bullock's blood, I awaited the sequel in peace."

"Praise ye the Lord, for He is good," sang the cantor, carried away.

"For His mercy endureth forever," replied the congregation instinctively.

"I did not foresee the *shammash* would put himself so brazenly forward to hide his guilt, or that he would be asked to drink. But when the *apikoros* (atheist) put the bottle to his lips, expecting to taste blood, and found instead good red wine, doubtless he felt at once that the God of Israel was truly in heaven, that He had wrought a miracle and changed the blood back to wine."

"And such a miracle God wrought verily," cried the rabbi, grasping the physician's hand, while the synagogue resounded with cries of "May thy strength increase," and the gallery heaved frantically with blessings and congratulations.

"What wonder," the physician wound up, as he bent again over the ghastly head with its pious ringlets writhing like red snakes, "that he fell stricken by dread of the Almighty's wrath!"

And while men were bearing the convulsive form without, the cantor began to recite the Grace after Redemption. And then the happy hymns rolled out, and the choristers cried "Pom!" and a breadth of jubilant hope passed through the synagogue. The mighty hand and the outstretched arm which had redeemed Israel from the Egyptian bondage were still hovering over them, nor would the prophet Elijah forever delay to announce the ultimate Messiah.

Elijah the Prophet*[3]

SHOLOM ALEICHEM

It is not good to be an only son, to be fretted over by father and mother—to be the only one left out of seven. Don't stand here. Don't go there. Don't drink that. Don't eat the other. Cover up your throat. Hide your hands. Ah, it is not good—not good at all to be an only son, and a rich man's son into the bargain. My father is a money-changer. He goes about amongst the shopkeepers with a bag of money, changing coppers for silver, and silver for copper. That is why his fingers are always black, and his nails broken. He works very hard. Each day, when he comes home, he is tired and broken down. "I have no feet," he complains to mother. "I have no feet, not even the sign of a foot." No feet? It may be. But for that again he has a fine business. Mother is satisfied. So am I. "We shall have a Passover this year, may all the children of Israel have the like, Father in Heaven!"

That's what my mother said, thanking God for the good Passover. And I also was thankful. But shall we ever live to see it—this same Passover?

Passover has come at last—the dear sweet Passover. I was dressed as befitted the son of a man of wealth—like a young prince. But what was the consequence? I was not allowed to play or run about, lest I catch cold. I must not play with poor children. I was a wealthy man's son. Such nice clothes, and I had no one to show off before. I had a pocketful of nuts, and no one to play with.

It is not good to be an only child, and fretted over—the

* Copyright 1922, 1926, by Alfred A. Knopf, Incorporated.

219

only one left out of seven, and a wealthy man's son into the bargain.

My father put on his best clothes and went off to the synagogue. Said my mother to me, "Do you know what? Lie down and have a sleep. You will then be able to sit up at the Seder and ask the Four Questions!"

Was I mad? Would I go to sleep before the Seder?

"Remember, you must not sleep at the Seder. If you do, Elijah the Prophet will come with a bag on his shoulders. On the first two nights of Passover, Elijah the Prophet goes about looking for those who have fallen asleep at the Seder and takes them away in his bag." Ha, ha! Will I fall asleep at the Seder? I? Not even if it were to last the whole night through, or even to broad daylight. "What happened last year, mother?" "Last year you fell asleep soon after the first blessing." "Why did Elijah the Prophet not come then with his bag?" "Then you were small; now you are big. Tonight you must ask father the Four Questions. Tonight you must say with father—'Slaves were we.' Tonight, you must eat with us fish and soup and *matzah* balls. Here is father, back from the synagogue."

"Good *Yom-tov!*"

"Good *Yom-tov!*"

Thank God, father made the blessing over wine. I, too. Father drank the cup full of wine. So did I, a cup full, to the very dregs. "See, to the dregs," said mother to father. To me she said: "A cup full of wine! You will drop off to sleep." Ha! ha! Will I fall asleep? Not even if we were to sit up all the night, or even to broad daylight. "Well," said my father, "how are you going to ask the Four Questions? How will you recite Haggadah? How will you sing with me—'Slaves were we'?"

My mother never took her eyes off me. She smiled and said: "You will fall asleep—fast asleep." "Oh, mother, mother, if you had eighteen heads, you would surely fall asleep, if someone sat opposite you and sang in your ears, 'Fall asleep, fall asleep!'"

220

Of course I fell asleep.

I fell asleep, and dreamt that my father was already saying, "Pour out Thy wrath." My mother herself got up from the table, and went to open the door to welcome Elijah the Prophet. It would be a fine thing if Elijah the Prophet did come, as my mother had said, with a bag on his shoulders, and if he said to me, "Come, boy." And who else would be to blame for this but my mother, with her "fall asleep." And as I was thinking these thoughts, I heard the creaking of the door. My father stood up and cried, "Blessed art thou who comest in the name of the Eternal." I looked towards the door. Yes, it was he. He came in so slowly and so softly that one scarcely heard him. He was a handsome man, Elijah the Prophet, an old man with a long grizzled beard reaching to his knees. His face was yellow and wrinkled, but it was handsome and kindly without end. And his eyes! Oh, what eyes! kind, soft, joyous, loving, faithful eyes. He was bent in two, and leaned on a big, big stick. He had a bag on his shoulders. And silently, softly, he came straight to me.

"Now, little boy, get into my bag and come." So said the old man to me, but in a kind voice and softly and sweetly.

I asked him, "Where to?" and he replied, "You will see later." I did not want to go, and he said to me again, "Come." And I began to argue with him. "How can I go with you when I am a wealthy man's son?" Said he to me, "And as a wealthy man's son, of what great value are you?" Said I, "I am the only child of my father and mother." Said he, "To me, you are not an only child." Said I, "I am fretted over. If they find that I am gone, they will not get over it; they will die, especially my mother." He looked at me, the old man did, very kindly and he said to me, softly and sweetly as before, "If you do not want to die, then come with me. Say good-bye to your father and mother, and come." "But how can I come when I am an only child, the only one left alive out of seven?"

221

Then he said to me more sternly: "For the last time, little boy. Choose one of the two. Either you say good-bye to your father and mother, and come with me, or you remain here, but fast asleep forever and ever."

Having said these words, he stepped back from me a little, and was turning to the door. What was to be done? To go with the old man, God-knows-where and get lost, would mean the death of my father and mother. I am an only child, the only one left alive out of seven. To remain here, and fall asleep forever and ever—that would mean that I myself must die . . .

I stretched out my hand to him, and with tears in my eyes I said, "Elijah the Prophet, dear, kind, loving, darling Elijah, give me one minute to think." He turned towards me his handsome, yellow, wrinkled old face with its grizzled beard reaching to his knees, and looked at me with his beautiful, kind, loving, faithful eyes, and he said to me with a smile, "I will give you one minute to decide, my child—but no more than one minute."

I ask you. "What should I have decided to do in that one minute so as to save myself from going with the old man, and also to save myself from falling asleep forever? Well, who can guess?"

A Seder That Went Wrong[4]

MARTIN BUBER

Several weeks before Pesach there was a great tumult in the house of the Seer. Confidential messengers were sent forth to all the great *Tzaddikim* of the period, who had studied with him under the *Maggid* of Mesritsh or under Rabbi Schmelke of Nikolsburg or under Rabbi Elimelech.

A messenger was sent to only one of his own disciples, and that was the Yehudi. The message sent forth was a single message. All of its recipients were invited to fix their entire souls upon the coming of Redemption all during the celebration of the Seder, during each part of the ceremony and each utterance, and to do so in a very special way, according to very special attitudes and aims concerning which the Seer provided precise directions. In this message the beginning of the celebration and the time which was to be devoted to each part of it were determined by hours and minutes. With an emphasis which rose to a cry of adjuration, an appeal was made and a command was issued to the common will that, in spite of separation in space, all this should be done by universal consent, so that nowhere there should protrude a personal expression or gesture. Usually the conduct of this night was largely left to the impulses of the master of the house; this time a perfect circle unified in attitude, action and speech was to bind together place to far place. The thing which our narrator, Rabbi Benjamin, had perceived twice seven years ago, on the day of the battle of Megiddo, namely, that the souls of the assembled Hasidim, melting into one, stretched out mighty hands into the darkness of the decision, this thing was now to take place in the houses of the great Hasidim. But this time the concentrated soul of the community could not be fixed upon a simultaneously occurring event. The only way of offering to all a common goal of vision, upon which every soul could concentrate, was to offer them that which from the beginning was the aim of their common and passionate desire: the coming of Redemption, come as it may. At bottom, in fact, nothing other was demanded than that which everyone as a rule attempted on this night, namely, by the might of one's yearning to throw a bridge between that deed which God performed in the liberation from Egypt to that awaited deed of His, which as yet has no name. Only in this sense was it possible for the rabbi to address himself to all, including the Yehudi.

223

Many of the recipients of the message were not wholly unaware of the renunciation, though but for a single night, inherent in this kind of demand; all perceived that such a message could have been sent forth by none other than the acknowledged leader of the generation.

None of the messengers who returned brought a refusal. The *Maggid* of Kosnitz, to be sure, had received the communication in silence, but he had offered no objection. The Yehudi had said nothing but "Thank God that I may obey." One man only had reacted in an almost incomprehensible way. That was the Rabbi of "Kalev," which is the north Hungarian small town of Negy-Kallo. While the message was being communicated to him he had, according to his custom and seeming scarcely to listen, hummed to himself a little song. He gave the document which described the special attitudes desired only a cursory glance.

"Oh well, we do it just about that way," he had then said. With that the messenger had to content himself.

Rabbi Yitzhak Eisik of Kalev was a singer of love songs. The songs treated of love and of yearnings of parted lovers. He heard them from Hungarian shepherds, whose company he liked because in his childhood he had himself been a herder of geese. Then delicately he rewrought the songs. It was not his intention to add an alien element to them but to reconstitute their great original meaning which had been transformed among the shepherd people and which was this: that the origin of all love is God's love for His *Shekinah*—all love points to this love and may receive its consecration therein. The shepherds sang of their far-away sweethearts. Now it was a great dense forest which separated the lovers, and now it was a high steep mountain that arose between them; but always the song ended with the removal of the obstacle and the uniting of those who belonged together. Not much needed to be added to this imagery. Was not our exile in very truth a dark forest in which one wandered and wandered and saw no end; was it not an immeasurably high mountain which one climbed with wounded feet only to see arise above one more jagged crag?

"Were I but snatched from exile's pain,
So that we two might meet again!"

Thus sang the Rabbi of Kalev. But it was not his singing alone. Every gesture of his expressed the deeply felt desire that those who are parted be united again. Among all the periods of the year the night of Pesach was the most precious to him; for it was evident that this, above all others, was the time of liberating grace. The daughter of Rabbi Hirsch of Zydatshov, the disciple of the Seer, who had married a son of the Rabbi of Kalev, once told her father that on the last Pesach night her father-in-law had waited until eleven o'clock to begin the Seder ceremony. At that hour he had opened a window. "Thereupon," she narrated, "a carriage came driving up, drawn by two horses silvery white. In it sat three aged men and four aged women of princely aspect and clad in princely garments, and the rabbi went to them and I saw how they embraced him and kissed him. Then I heard the crack of a whip and the carriage clattered off. The rabbi closed the window and sat down at the Seder table. I did not dare ask him who they were."

"They were the arch-fathers and the arch-mothers," Rabbi Hirsch had explained to his daughter. "The *Tzaddik* of Kalev had not been willing to sit down before the breaking of the dawn of Redemption and besieged with his prayers the highest worlds. And so the Fathers and the Mothers had to come and make him understand that the time was not yet."

The Seer himself was accustomed to saying that in all the world there was no light such as the light which radiated from the Seder of the Rabbi of Kalev.

The Rabbi of Lublin celebrated the Seder more consecratedly and with all the attitudes and motivations which he had himself prescribed. During the repast he explained, as was customary, the eating of the paschal

225

lamb and ended his instructive discourse with the traditional saying: "This is the command concerning the eating of the paschal sacrifice. May the All-Merciful find us
worthy of partaking of it even in our days in the city of
our sanctuary and may thus be fulfilled the Scripture that
is written: 'For not in haste will ye set forth, nor in the
manner of flight will ye go. For before you goes the Lord
and your rearguard is the God of Israel!' As in the days
of our Exodus from the land of Egypt will He cause us to
see wonders. The word of our God will stand fast in
world time. His right hand is lifted up to perform dreadful things."

Scarcely had he uttered the last word than there issued
from his throat a wild and dreadful cry. Before anyone
knew what was happening all throats were beset by the
same loud cry. "It has failed!" he cried. "The Seder is
disturbed! The Seder is pain-riven! It was so from beginning!" Gasping he fell back in his seat. No one knew
what he meant. After a while he whispered: "Pshysha!"
And once again: "All is lost!" Long he remained without
stirring in his seat.

It was after midnight. According to the regulation he
brought forth the half of a cake of *matzah* set aside at
the beginning of the celebration for the dessert, the
afikoman, and said in a trembling voice before he ate
thereof and distributed it, "Herewith I am prepared and
arrayed to fulfill the command of the eating of the
afikoman to the unification of the Holy One, Blessed be
He, and his *Shekinah,* through Him, the Hidden One and
the Secret One, in the name of all Israel." Then, ever and
again forced to pause, he pronounced grace; he leaned
towards his left side, as it is ordered, for the purpose of
marking those who had been liberated from the Egyptian
yoke, grasped the beaker with still trembling hands, pronounced the blessing over it, drank of it and, singing the
songs of praise against his custom with but half a voice,
he completed the ceremony. It was evident to those about
him that all he spoke and did was spoken and done, con-

trary to his annual custom and especially to his attitude at the beginning of this night, without fervor or fixed inner direction. When he arose and went slowly forth, one saw that his steps were faltering and difficult. But he would have no one support him.

Immediately after the two festival days the Seer sent out the messengers to the same places to inquire how the Seder had gone.

The first news came from Pshysha. It crossed with the messenger sent thither. And this is what took place on the night of Seder there:

When the mother of the Yehudi prepared to take her seat, as she did every year, at his side, Schoendel flew into a rage.

"That is my place!" she cried. "I will no longer be pushed out of my place!"

"What are you talking about, daughter?" said the old woman. "Will you not let me sit beside my son?"

"I demand my due," Schoendel shrieked.

"If you feel in your heart that it is your due," answered the mother, "I shall yield the place to you in peace."

"It's too late now!" Schoendel shrieked again. "I won't sit down at all unless you leave the table."

They all stared at her, incapable of speech. She rushed forward, tore the cushions and covers from the seats around the table and threw them into an adjoining room. Then she ran in after them and shot the latch. For the first time the Yehudi was seen to weep. The Hasidim were about to remove their long coats in order to refurnish the seats with them, when Mendel of Tomashov hastened to the latched door of the adjoining room.

"*Rebbetzin,*" he cried, "come and look at your child!"

Instantly the latch was opened and Schoendel rushed forth. She looked at the boy Nehemya who, pale as death, trembling all over, was regarding his weeping father. Besides him his brother Asher, who was twelve years older than the little boy of six, sought in vain to soothe him. Nehemya uttered little cries of fright. They made one

227

think of the young of birds whose nest is menaced by a hawk. Schoendel ran up to the child. But so soon as she took him by the hand, he tore it away; he threw at her a glance of fear and anger. When she tried to approach him again he struggled wildly with his hands and feet. For an instant Schoendel stood stock still. Then she ran back into the other room and tugged at the pillows and covers and began to array the seats anew. The Hasidim helped her. Everyone sat down. There was still another delay because Schoendel now begged her mother-in-law to take the place of honor; the old woman was inclined to insist upon her renunciation; finally she was persuaded to take her place. Now the ceremony proceeded. The Yehudi sought to fulfill all the directions of the message from Lublin. But the lost time could not be retrieved.

The messengers who returned to Lublin brought one strange piece of news after another. Everywhere disturbances had taken place. In one single house, namely, the famous "Court" of the *Tzaddik* of Tshernobil, everything had gone well—up to the moment when the *afikoman* was to be eaten. No one could find it! But the strangest report of all came last on account of the long distance. It came from Kalev.

Superficially as he seemed to have listened and read, the Rabbi of Kalev had precisely followed the directions of the Seer. But he had spoken every word which was to be spoken in Hungarian, as was his custom. He used to say, "Not in vain is the totality of that which is spoken on this night called Haggadah, that is to say an account. An account must be communicated in such a manner that all who hear it understand it. I render this account to all, including the poor man who is my guest this evening and has crossed my threshold in order to eat and drink with me, as well as to the servants who join me and mine in this celebration. All are to understand the account, even as they all went forth from Egypt with us."

In Lublin this custom of the Rabbi of Kalev had either not been known or not thought upon. Only when the news reached the house of the Seer was there an old Hasid who remembered and whispered to his fellow, "Do you know that Rabbi Shmelke of Nikolsburg, the teacher of him of Kalev, would listen to all the places where on the Seder disciples of his recited the Haggadah? In the year after his disciple Yitzhak Eisik had been made Rabbi of Kalev, Rabbi Shmelke said, 'How does it happen that I do not hear the Rabbi of Kalev recite the Haggadah? Is it possible that he recites it in Hungarian?' "

The Seer had received the report from Pshysha with a singularly strained expression of countenance. "He looked," the bearer of the report said later on, "like a lion who was about to leap upon his prey."

"Do you know," it was objected to him, "how a lion looks?"

"I know it now," said the other, and that had to suffice them.

The Rabbi accepted all the later reports with great equanimity . . .

The Passover Celebrants*[5]

S. J. AGNON

There are many who have heard the tale of Reb Mechel, the beadle, and the wealthy Sarah Leah. At the same time there are as many who have not heard it; and for those who have not heard it, it is worth the telling.

This is the tale of Mechel the beadle. When Mechel the beadle left the House of Study on the first night of

* From: *The Bridal Canopy*, by S. J. Agnon, trans. by I. M. Lask. Copyright 1937 by Doubleday & Company, Inc. Reprinted by permission of the publisher.

Passover, his mood was cheerful. Blest be The Name, said he to himself, that the eve of Passover is over and done with so that I too can rejoice this night like other folk. But when he had locked the doors and found himself proceeding homeward his good mood left him. He knew that he went to no royal feasting hall but to a tumbledown dwelling; that he would be sitting not on a fine handsome couch but on a torn cushion unmended of woman's hand; and that he must trouble himself a deal to warm his food.

For at the time, Mechel the beadle was a widower; there was no woman in his home to prepare his table, make his bed or cook his meals. Truth to tell, many of the householders had wished to invite him to celebrate the Passover feast with them. Reb Mechel, they had said, tonight the whole world is rejoicing and all Israel feasts with their households, so why should you celebrate on your own? Be happy, Reb Mechel, that the demons have no power on this night; but even so there is a peril of sadness, which is as much prohibited on the Passover as leaven, the Merciful One deliver us. Yet Mechel refused all offers of hospitality, for he did not wish to burden another's table at the festival.

The streets had emptied, and all the houses of the town shone with Passover light. The moon was bright and gracious, and a spring breeze blew. Mechel began to turn his mind away from himself and enjoy the wonders of the Creation, jingling the keys of the synagogue like a bell. But hearing the sound of the keys he grew sorrowful and began to remind himself bitterly how he was the beadle of the House of Study, toiling hard and doing all sorts of work; and how, when he had completed his work and returned home, he remained cramped and lonely between the walls, never even tasting cooked food; since if he put food on to warm he would be asleep before it was cooked. So he would stay his hunger with an onion roll or some bread and radish, or the potato a woman might bring to the House of Study so that he should pray for the souls of her near ones to rest in peace. But what you may do all the year round, and rest satisfied, you may not do on a festival when we are bidden to rejoice.

On the way home he noticed that one house had a window open; looking again, he saw that it was a window in the house of Sarah Leah, the widow. She herself was standing at the window looking out. Mechel bowed to her with the greeting, "Festivals for joy, Sarah Leah."

"Holidays and appointed times for gladness, Reb Mechel," responded Sarah Leah. "Whence and whither, Reb Mechel?"

"I am coming from the House of Study," said Mechel, "on my way home to prepare my table and sit and celebrate."

Sarah Leah nodded her head and sighed. I see she would like to say something to me, said Mechel to himself, and stood waiting.

Seeing Mechel standing waiting, she said, "I just opened my window to see if it were time to leave, for I am celebrating at my neighbor's. I've prepared all sorts of good things, by your life, and I'm short of nothing in order to celebrate the Passover down to the last detail, and all the same I have to leave my own home and burden myself on others. It's not enough that I go burdening them every Sabbath and festival, when I suddenly appear among them for the Hallowing and the *Habdalah;* I have to go bothering them on Passover as well."

"Well, it may be a bother in your eyes," said Mechel, "but others regard it as fulfilling a commandment."

"A commandment, d'you say, Reb Mechel," responded Sarah Leah. "Do you suppose such commandments come easily to those who perform them? Here's a man who's busy all day long and never sees his wife and children; Passover comes, a time of rest; he wishes to sit quiet with his family when in jumps that widow all of a sudden, and sits down among them. May it be His Will that I shouldn't sin with my words, the years grow less and the world grows wearier and weaker. In times gone by a Jew would bring any number of guests home with him

231

and there'd be room enough, and nowadays there's no room even for a lonely widow like me. I remember Passover at father's, may he rest in peace, when we'd have ten Jews and more there. And was my husband, may he rest in peace, accustomed to celebrate Passover without a guest? And I have to leave my home now. And am I short of anything here? If it's wine a body wants, here's wine and enough to spare for an extra glass; and if it's *matzot,* here are the extra special *matzot;* if it's meat, here's a turkey cock whose wings were absolutely hidden by fat. Why, what did the neighbors say, 'Sarah Leah, don't tie him to the foot of your bed or he'll drag you across Sambatyon River. That's no bird, that's an aurochs.' But as long as a woman's in her husband's house it's all worth while; and once he's dead even the whole of the world isn't worth while. At first I was thinking of inviting a guest, only folk would say, 'That old woman's a fiend from Hell, wants a man for to serve her well.' "

Mechel smiled, sighed and quoted the Talmud, " 'Tis better to dwell in trouble than to dwell in widowhood."

And although the saying was in Aramaic, a tongue Sarah Leah did not understand, she nodded her head like a person saying, "You've said it well and true." Mechel's an upright man and assuredly has some good thought in mind. And she added, "There's everything here, but if there's no master in the house what is there in the house? I often ask myself, 'Sarah Leah, what are you doing here and whom have you here?' I have reared children to their full size and they forsook me, so now I am bereft and forsaken, as a table after a feast. I thought of ascending to the Land of Israel to be near the holy places, and not to be thinking all the time of my loneliness; but then I am again faced by the difficulty—how can a woman go alone to a place where she is not known? All Israel are brethren, but nevertheless my heart troubles me at the thought of ascending alone."

Mechel felt full of pity for her. He took hold of his right earlock and wished to say words of comfort to her.

232

Painting. Moritz Oppenheim

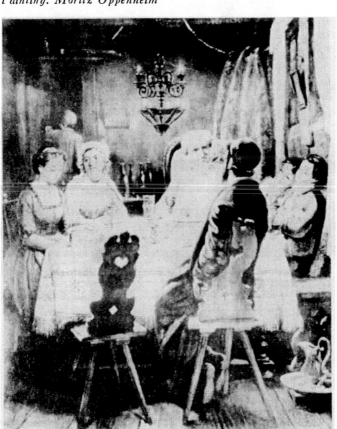

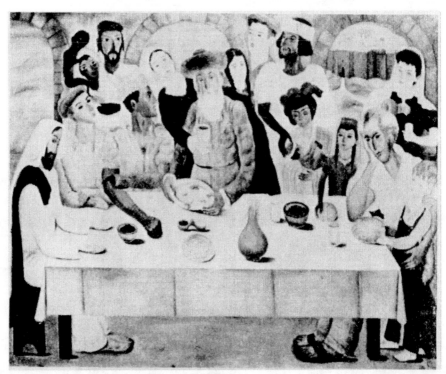

22. First Seder in Jerusalem

Painting. Reuven Rubin

Photograph. P. Gross

23. Family from Hadramaut

Pesaro, Italy, 1614

24. Seder Plate. Faience

Yet he could get nothing out, began stammering and at last said, "Woman, is my luck any greater than yours? You, God be praised, are adorned as a bride and eat fine foods, while I am chidden and mourning as a widower. But no man in Israel has other to depend on than the loving kindness of the Holy and Blessed One. What has any living person to grumble at? The festival should not be degraded."

And from seeking to comfort her he began to feel sorry for himself and he said, "And what is a man? Something bare in the waste. Blessed be He that did not make me a woman. Blessed be His Name that I know how to hallow the wine and prepare for the Passover according to the Law. But now go to a tumbledown dwelling and warm up half-cooked food and sit on a broken bed, and then sit on a torn cushion and think you're like a king. It was with good reason the *Yalkut* says, 'All sufferings are hard to bear, but those of poverty are hardest of all; all sufferings come, and once they are gone leave things as they were; but poverty dims the eyes of a man.' I'm only saying this to balance your saying, 'I'm a woman.' And what's more the Holy and Blessed One has brought a bad cough upon me, may you never know its like, which takes away my breath and steals the life from me and will drive me out of the world." And before ever he finished speaking he had begun coughing.

"Reb Mechel," said Sarah Leah to him, "don't stand out in the cold; winter may have gone but it's still chilly. Better come into the house and not stand about in the open."

Mechel bowed his head between his shoulders, entered and found himself in a fine dwelling with handsomely decked cushions to recline upon, and a table covered with silverware in the middle of the room, and a bottle of wine on the table, candles burning in all the candlesticks and every corner of the room gleaming and shining with festival. His first words were in honor of the place, for he said, "How fine this room is where the hands of a

233

woman have been employed." Sarah Leah at once rushed to show him all she had ready for the table. *Matzot* and bitter herbs lay there, parsley and *haroset*, eggs and a sheepshank and flesh and fish and a fat pudding and borsht red as wine.

"And who," said Sarah Leah to Mechel, "needs all this array? I'm just about to go off and bother somebody else, but it's hard for me to forget that I'm a housewife, so I prepared a Passover for myself as though my husband were still here and he and I were celebrating like all other folk."

Mechel's heart warmed within him, and he wished to say something, but a furious fit of coughing overcame him. Sarah Leah stared at him with her two eyes and said, "Don't eat too much bitter herbs and don't eat sharp foods, Reb Mechel; you cough too badly. You know what you need? It's a glass of hot tea you need. But who have you at home to make something hot? Wait a few minutes and I'll put the kettle on for you."

But scarce had she finished her sentence when she struck herself on the mouth, crying, "What a silly head I have, to forget that we have to hallow the festival first. Maybe you'll celebrate here?" And since the thought had found expression in words she repeated, "Maybe you'll celebrate here?"

Mechel saw all the goodness of the housewife and could not move, as though his limbs were fastened to the spot where he stood. He began stammering and swallowed his indistinct answer. And Sarah Leah began preparing the feast as had been her wont when her husband was still with her.

So Mechel took the keys of the House of Study and put them away somewhere, staring meanwhile at the white cushions that Sarah Leah had prepared for reclining on during the celebration as though the Higher Light shone from them. Within a few moments he had let himself down among them, by reason of the thought that the woman would again ask him to celebrate with her. When she saw him at his ease she filled a glass of wine. With one eye on the wine and one on the household ware, he thought to himself, "What a fine spot this is, where a woman's hands do the tending." While thinking, he found the glass of wine at his hand, and his lips of themselves began repeating the hallowing of the wine.

Sarah Leah sighed with satisfaction; her face grew bright; her clothes were suddenly filled with her body, as happens with a rejoicing person, and she thought to herself, "How fine is a Jew's voice when he utters holy words." And within a moment she had brought him a ewer of water. He washed his hands, took a leaf of green-stuff, dipped it in salt water, broke the *matzot* in half, put one half in a cloth and hid it away for the dessert, lifted up the dish and began reciting, "This is the bread of affliction, the which our fathers ate in the land of Egypt."

And Sarah Leah wondered at herself, saying, "Just a little while ago I was preparing to leave my house, and now here am I sitting at home." And she watched Mechel's hands, observing how accustomed his hands were in holy things, until her face grew red and she lowered her eyes in shame. Then she filled the glasses afresh and uncovered the *matzot*. Mechel made her a sign. Sarah Leah blushed like a child, dropped her eyes to the prayer book and recited the Four Questions to their close, "This night we all do recline."

Thereupon Mechel set the dishes back in place and repeated in a loud and joyful voice, "We were the slaves of Pharaoh in Egypt"; and he continued reciting the Relation of the Departure from Egypt as far as the feast, interpreting to her in Yiddish all that required interpretation and seasoning the entire narration with parables and tales of wonders. His sufferings and troubles far from him, his head resting on the cushion, sweat caressing his earlocks and the cushion growing deeper beneath him, he continued. His blood beat through his limbs and his heart

235

might have leaped forth; a single hour here was preferable to his whole life in This World.

The Order of Passover came to its appointed end. The whole town was silent; the moon spread a canopy of light over the house of Sarah Leah. Mechel tunefully sang, "May His House soon be built," and Sarah Leah responded, "Speedily, speedily, in our own day soon." From the other houses of the street came the chorus, "God rebuild, God rebuild, rebuild Thy House soon." And the fantasy that is root and branch of Man led them to imagine that here was a strip of the Land of Israel, and they were calmly and happily singing the Song of Songs.

The night passed. The morning birds rose to repeat their portions of song. In the home of Sarah Leah could be heard the voice of a man chanting the Song of Songs.

> Here ends the tale of Mechel,
>   On whom God did bestow
> The wealthy lady Mistress
>   Sarah Leah, the widow.

Warm Matzot[6]

ALBERT HALPER

I was walking down the street one afternoon—spring was in the air—when I passed Father Aiken coming out of St. Stephen's. Through the briefly opened door I could hear the boys' choir rehearsing, and their blended voices sounded pleasant to my ears.

"Hello, Dave," the priest smiled as he passed me.

"Lo," I answered, ducking my head briefly.

I knew the kids inside the church were practicing for

Easter services, and I was a little jealous because they were enjoying singing in the ornate gallery above the pulpit, where they could see the glittering architecture and trappings of the holy place. But I wasn't envious, really. I knew that at about this time of year our people had a big holiday, too—a whole week during which we celebrated and gorged ourselves on the best food in the world.

I trudged up Kedzie Avenue, where my father had bought a new grocery, warming over memories of past holidays in my mind. Up ahead, near Franklin, was the big, dull block of apartments in which my family lived.

I climbed the back stairs, whistling a song, and, coming into the flat, said, "Ma? Anybody home?"—which really meant, *how about a sandwich before supper, Ma?*

I found my mother in the kitchen where, bent over, she was engaged in her weekly battle with some intruders. She was spraying the cracks under the sink with some green powder, muttering, "Bandits, holdups!"—directing her phrases at some fleeing cockroaches. "Wait, wait," she told them. "I'll get you, where are you going so fast?"

I waited until the battle was over, then my mother washed her hands and made me a big jelly sandwich. I had planned to ask her a question about our big holiday which I knew was due soon, but the sandwich tasted so good I forgot all about it.

That night my father came home from his grocery a block away, stepped into the flat, and with an important look on his face, announced to my mother, "Etta, I looked at the calendar today. Passover is only a week off. I'll have to go for the *matzot* soon."

Then I remembered!

"Is that so?" asked my mother, who had been as cognizant of the date as her husband. "So soon—next week?"

And the following day my mother started cleaning the flat for the coming Passover holidays. It wasn't an ordinary cleaning. It was like tearing the house apart and putting it together again. She stood on a chair in the pantry and took down special sets of dishes, glasses, and silverware, which she used only once a year, during Passover week. She boiled and scalded them and shined them. She went to a special drawer in a bureau and drew out tablecloths and napkins which had reposed there for fifty-one weeks; these she tubbed and scrubbed and ironed. She gave my brother Irving and me twenty cents each for washing all the windows of the flat—nine windows. Afterward she hung fresh curtains. Of course she scrubbed the floors, twice.

It was a week of almost terrifying activity that wore her out, but I believe she loved it. It was something she did every year, and was something her mother and her mother's mother had done before her, annually, in Europe.

As the days of preparations continued, the flat grew shinier and shinier. My brothers, my sister, and I walked on tiptoe through the rooms; we didn't want to displace or soil anything. We were careful how we spoke, too.

"No rough talk in the house this week," our mother had warned us, which meant Irving, Louis and I couldn't face each other and say, "Give me that ball or I'll pin your ears back," or, "I'll spit in your eye and drown you!"

During that week of hectic preparations we often heard our parents talking at the supper table, after my father returned from his grocery. They spoke of Milt, who, at twenty, was making his first trip on the road as a traveling shirt-salesman.

"Here's another letter from Milt today," my mother said, showing the latest letter. "Tomorrow he's going to Cedar Rapids, Iowa. I hope he'll be able to come to the Seder, on Tuesday."

My father took the letter from my mother, putting on his gold-rimmed glasses, and read Milt's note.

"Hm, he writes business is good . . . opened up two new accounts in Muscatine." He cleared his throat. "Of course he'll come home for the Seder!" He stood there, short and stocky, his words booming powerfully in the flat. "Of course! He's still one of the family, the oldest son, isn't he? Of course!"

None of us dared to speak; we knew better than to challenge that stern note of authority.

"Sit down and write a letter," he commanded Ben. "Write Milt he has to come home for the holiday, even if he's out in California!"

And Ben, who had come home tired from his order-picker's job in a wholesale hardware concern, sat down and wrote while we crowded around him.

"How far is Cedar Rapids, Iowa?" my mother asked timidly, while Ben was scribbling away.

"One hundred miles, one *thousand* miles," my father answered clearly. "What difference does it make? Huh?" He pointed a finger at Ben. "Tell Milt we're expecting him!"

The violent house cleaning, the talk about Milt, and all the other preparations keyed us up. Two days before the holiday we watched our mother buying chickens, special flour, special salt, holiday candles, and new spices; and we saw her readying her biggest cooking pots and pans for action.

On the day of the Seder, the feast that celebrates the liberation of the people from Egyptian bondage, I was startled when my father addressed me.

"This year I want you to go with me to get the *matzot*. We're going this afternoon, in a little while. Irving will mind the store with your mother, Louis is too young to carry anything, and your sister Ruth is only a girl. So I'm taking you along. Go wash up now."

I tried to hide my excitement. I had never gone with my father for the *matzot* before.

In a little while, my face and hands scrubbed, I was ready to accompany my father. Mother was standing behind the counter with Irving. My sister Ruth was at the flat, watching the pots of food cooking on the stove and in the oven.

"Don't give him any heavy packages," my mother warned my father. "He's still a small boy."

"I know, I know," my father answered. "I always carry the large ones, don't I?"

"Twenty pounds of *matzot*, that's enough this year. We had too much last year again, remember? Twenty pounds, just buy twenty pounds."

"Yes, yes." My father was putting on his coat and hat. "Twenty, twenty." He scowled. "All right, we're going." He walked out of the grocery, still frowning and I followed obediently.

We rode a trolley east and transferred on Halsted Street. My father paid half fare for me. We transferred south on Halsted, riding past desolate junk-yards, factories, and rooming houses, and soon we approached Taylor Street, where the big Jewish settlement began. Having lived in Gentile neighborhoods all my life, I found this section fascinating. Retail stores crowded one another here, displaying all types of merchandise, while at the curbs stood pushcarts manned by aggressive men and women who advertised the good points of their wares, shouting in English and in Yiddish.

"Bargains today, big bargains! Look, mister, see, missus, feel the cloth! Half price, half price!"

We got off near Twelfth Street, where the hucksters stood thicker than ever, and made our way up the jammed sidewalk. My father pushed forward steadily and sometimes I had to run to keep up with him. In the middle of the block, he stopped before a building that resembled a garage, or a small warehouse. A six-pointed star was painted on a wooden sign overhead. "Pearlstein's *Matzot*. The World's Best."

"In here," my father commanded, and I stood behind him as he swung open a big, iron, fireproof door.

As we entered a long, low building, I felt warm waves of heat brushing my face. Suddenly, under strong overhead lights, I saw what looked like a hundred men working before big ovens. Actually, when I counted them later

240

on, there were only thirteen men in the place. Most of them wore long white aprons and small white cotton caps; their sleeves were rolled to their elbows, and their faces looked healthy and red from the heat. Near us, against the wall, was a sign: "No admittance. Wholesale only."

My father did not advance further, but stood hesitantly near the sign. The men at the ovens did not notice him. Looking around, I saw white *matzot* stacked on tables and on racks in tall, neat piles. The pleasant smell of the fresh *matzot,* different from the odor of new bread, filled every inch of the place.

Suddenly my father made a motion with his hand toward a tall, strongly built baker in a white apron. The workman didn't see the gesture as he bent near an oven to examine the gauges, after which he opened one of the iron doors, revealing the gas flames. When he shut the oven he turned and saw my father.

"Hello, hello!" he called above the hubbub of the place, grinning. *"Guten yom-tov, bruder!"* He came over briskly and shook hands vigorously with my father, then glanced smilingly at me. "Who is this one? Number three or four?"

"No, he's number five," my father said with a laugh. "He's the next-to-the-youngest. Shake hands with Mr. Kleinholtz. Go on, shake hands."

Shyly, I stuck my hand out and in a moment felt it swallowed in the large, warm, friendly paw of the broad-shouldered baker; he pumped it a few times, then released it, grinning at me.

"You came to help your Pa carry the *matzot,* right?"
"Yes."

"Good, good. This year it turned out better than ever. The flour is better."

"You said the same thing last year," my father remarked with a smile. "And the year before that."

"No, no. Did I? The *matzot* are really good this year." His broad smile reflected my father's. I could see they were fond of each other. They looked like brothers, only

241

Mr. Kleinholtz was much taller. "How's the missus, how're the other children?"

"Everybody is fine. Now I want some good *matzot,* not too well done but not underdone, either. Listen, I want it from the last batch, like I get it every year."

A side door opened and a little middle-aged man approached us excitedly. "What do you want here? Can't you see the men are working?" He continued shouting and waving his hands nervously. "It's against the rules of the union—it's against the rules!"

"Listen, Mr. Epstein," Mr. Kleinholtz lied calmly, "This man is my brother, my blood brother. He wants to buy some *matzot.* He buys here every year. He pays for it. So what's against the union? I'm the shop chairman, right? What's criminal about it?"

A phone began ringing somewhere and a young woman stuck her head out of the little office.

"Telephone, Mr. Epstein!"

"They're always pestering me, the union!" Mr. Epstein shouted. "Better working conditions, a new toilet! Yes, yes! Tomorrow you'll want showers!" He waved his small hands wildly, then disappeared into his office and slammed the door.

"So how much do you want this year?" Mr. Kleinholtz asked my father pleasantly, as though the owner had never made his appearance. "One hundred pounds? Three hundred pounds?"

My father chuckled. "That all? That all? The missus says not to bring home more than twenty pounds, but I think I ought to buy thirty. The boys are big eaters."

We began following Mr. Kleinholtz, who was heading for one of the big tables directly in front of the first oven. A minute later we stood before ten big piles of freshly baked *matzot* which had just been drawn from under the flames by one of the bakers; they were snow white, with here and there a faint, faint tint of tan at the edges. A wonderful smell rose from them. Mr. Kleinholtz smiled proudly at the piles but said nothing.

"I'll take thirty—" my father weakened—"no, make it thirty-five pounds from this batch," my father concluded simply.

"Good, good. They're the best. You won't be sorry."

Instead of calling over one of the young apprentices, Mr. Kleinholtz himself wrapped them in double thicknesses of smooth, shiny, white paper sheets. He tied the four bundles with strong, thick, hairy, yellow cord, two big bundles and two small bundles.

Afterward, my father and Mr. Kleinholtz stood talking together near the ovens. Their friendship was of a curious nature. They had met, accidentally, at the wedding of one of our distant cousins fifteen years ago, long before I was born, and for a time our families had been on friendly terms. My mother and Mrs. Kleinholtz, however, did not get on well together, so the family social calls had terminated. These annual pilgrimages to the *matzot* factory formed the sole contact between my father and the baker, who bowed their heads philosophically before the quarrels of the women.

At last my father picked up the two bigger bundles. Turning to Mr. Kleinholtz, he said, "Well, a good holiday, a good Passover. And may the next year be a healthy and prosperous one for you and your family."

"Thank you," the big, smiling baker boomed. "Same to you. And if that's not the best *matzot* you ever ate, bring it back and I'll eat it all up, together with the paper and the string!" He laughed and stroked my head. "I mean it. Swear to God!" He accompanied us to the door where he and my father shook hands again.

"Good-by," my father said. "We'll see each other soon. Why do we have to wait till next year? Soon, soon."

Nodding in agreement, the baker waved at us and then we were out on the chilly street. Darkness was coming and we hurried toward the corner. We got aboard a trolley, and as we rode home my father was silent, his wide face moody. Sitting on the cane seat, I began to feel the heat from the freshly baked *matzot* slowly working itself through the thick wrappings of paper. In the cold trolley the warmth was comforting.

When we reached the store, my mother threw up her hands when she saw the four bundles. "Every year," she cried, "every year it's the same! No, you bought too much!"

"Passover is a whole week," my father argued. "Listen, we'll eat it, we'll eat it."

Irving, Louis, and I carried the bundles of still-hot *matzot* to our flat a block away, while our father took over the duties of the store. When we reached our apartment, we smelled the wonderful odors of the holiday food coming from the stove; the rooms were filled with aromas.

"All right, children, change into your best clothes," our mother commanded. "But first wash yourselves good. Remember, you have to be real clean for the Seder."

We went to our bedroom where we found our best clothes had been placed on the bed for us. After washing and dressing, we came into the dining room.

A familiar but dazzling sight met our eyes. The big, square, mission-oak table, expanded to its utmost and covered with a snowy-white tablecloth, was already set. The water tumblers and cut-glass wine glasses sparkled like crystal. The Passover silverware gleamed. Neatly folded linen napkins—we never used even paper napkins during the rest of the year—were placed next to each large dinner plate. The decanter filled with home-made red wine stood on a glass tray in the center of the table, shining under the twin gasmantles overhead. As we stared, my sister Ruth came from the kitchen and set down tiny silver saltcellars, which we used one week each year.

The door opened and Ben came in, home from work. He went into the bathroom to clean up and to change into his best suit.

Then, at six, our father came home, closing the store a whole hour earlier tonight. He, too, washed up and began changing into his dark blue Sunday suit. As he struggled into a starched white shirt, he shouted towards the kitchen, "Isn't Milt home yet?"

He knew, of course, that Milt's train did not arrive until 6:09, that it was at least a forty-minute trolley ride from the railroad station, but he inquired about Milt just the same. "Isn't he home?"

"I'm so worried," my mother called in a high, nervous voice from the kitchen. "We can't start the Seder without him. Do you think something's wrong with his train?"

"Maybe an accident?" my father said, worried also.

"Look, what's all this talk?" Ben cut in, smiling but a little exasperated. "His train doesn't get in until after six, does it? Is this a night to talk of wrecks and accidents?" He turned to Irving. "How about putting on a dance record to liven up things?"

Irving cranked the phonograph and put on "Alexander's Ragtime Band," opening the little doors of the machine so that the strains emerged with strident force.

"No!" my father shouted. "Stop it! Tonight's a holiday—no ragtime!" He walked over and stopped the record. "Quiet!" he roared. "Let it be quiet!"

No one said anything. In the silence, the pungent smells of cooking drifted tantalizingly from the kitchen. Our appetites were increasing with the passing of each second. The doorbell rang.

"Milt!" my sister screamed happily.

We heard our oldest brother pounding up the stair, his heavy Gladstone bag bumping against the banister in his triumphant ascent. My mother rushed from the kitchen, shouted his name, and, when he reached our door, gathered him into her arms with a sob.

"So late?" she exclaimed worriedly. But a moment later, ashamed of her show of emotion, she wiped her eyes and smiled. "We were waiting so long, we thought maybe something happened—"

"What could happen?" Milt grinned. Though still a boy, he stood before us, tall, handsome, mature and magnetic. "I couldn't make the train go faster, could I? I even took a cab home."

"A taxi?" cried our father. "All the way from the station?" His face shone proudly, for he knew some of

the neighbors must have seen his son arrive like a poten-
tate from the railroad terminal. "Well, well!" He blew
his nose loudly into his handkerchief. "So how was the
trip? Did you do good business for the firm?"

Irving, Louis and I fought for the privilege of lugging
Milt's heavy bag into his bedroom.

"If I go over my quota by twenty per cent this trip,"
Milt said, "Mr. Liebman promised me Omaha and
Kansas City on the next trip."

"Is that right?" cried our father. "You really mean
it?"

"I'm running close to twenty-five per cent above quota
right now, Pa."

"You hear that, Etta?" my father shouted. "You hear
what Milt said?"

Fifteen minutes later, having changed into a clean
white shirt and sporting a brand new silk necktie he had
received from a necktie salesman in Peoria as a gift, Milt
joined us in the living room in his pencil-striped blue suit.
As he saw us standing assembled, as if rendering him
homage, he suddenly looked confused and warmly
pleased. For a moment he wasn't a traveling salesman
sleeping in strange hotels, but only a boy. The moment
passed, and he smiled with self-confidence. "Well, when
do we eat?"

My mother bustled in from the kitchen. "All right, sit
down, everybody. Everything is ready. I'll be with you in
a minute, so sit down please, everybody."

The male members of the family came to the dining
table wearing their hats, according to the orthodox tradition. Irving, Louis and I were too young to own hats, so
we put on our caps; wearing our hats and caps at table
lent us an air of solemnity. Ruth sat primly between Ben
and Milt, in a new pink dress, her blonde hair in neat,
beribboned braids down her back. At the head of the
table our father sat on two big white pillows. His nose
was twitching, for the luxurious smells of the food were
driving him half mad. All thoughts of his little grocery,

246

with its bills and disappointing business, were forgotten tonight.

"Well?" he said, turning impatiently towards the kitchen. "So?"

"One second, one second." Hastily our mother joined us, in a blue shot-silk shirtwaist and a new skirt, protected by an apron. She sat at my father's left, her happy face flushed, and gave her six children a quick, almost imperceptible nod of approval as, taking her place, she noticed that we were spruced to shining for the occasion.

My father reached for his big, heavy, old-fashioned prayer book, the Haggadah. Turning to Milt, he said, "Open the hall door, so that any stranger can come in and join us at this Seder."

Milt opened the hall door, the standard proceeding before the feast, and returned to his chair. My father bit his lip, lowered his eyes and, in a sing-song, semi-oriental monotone, began intoning the opening sanctification prayer, the *Kiddush*, in Hebrew. On the sideboard, two white Sabbath candles, which my mother had lit at sundown, burned steadily.

I sat patiently, my eyes alert, half-listening to my parent. As my gaze roved about the table my mouth began to water. The prospect of a solid week of eating the tasty, special, Passover dishes was almost more than I could bear. No matter how expensive meat or chicken was, this was one week when our mother went all out in her cookery.

My restless glance strayed to the shankbone of a lamb on a plate—symbol of the paschal sacrifice in biblical times; I saw the dishes of parsley and radishes, the hard-boiled egg, the bitter herbs floating in water—all religious and historical symbols which did not interest me, though I knew the bitter herbs were very important tonight because they were a reminder of the bitter years of bondage the Israelites had suffered under the yoke of the cruel Egyptians. Near the plate of bitter herbs stood a squat jar of red, home-made, powerful horse-radish that, tasted, instantly drew tears to the eyes as well as a stinging sensation inside one's nostrils.

Other plates held cut-up slices of cold meats, cold chicken wings, giblets and chicken hearts and livers. There was no bread and butter on the table; at my father's elbow was a plate covered with a snowy linen napkin, which we all knew hid three big unbroken squares of *matzot*, in keeping with the ritual. My gaze strayed to the left. Near the bulging wine decanter which was ringed by eight empty glasses that seemed to lift up their hollow cups like the open, beseeching mouths of baby birds, stood a large plate of homemade macaroons, a dish holding nuts and raisins, and a large, fluffy, uncut yellow cake made from *matzot* flour. From the kitchen, in waves, flowed the tantalizing, heavy odors of hot soup, roast chicken, simmering meats bedded in luscious sauces. Next to me Louis began to fidget and wriggle his knees under the table. Irving and I began to stir and move restlessly. Ruth, usually so proper, began to moisten her lips as the aromas continued to inundate the room. On the other side of the table, Milt and Ben grinned at each other; as kids, they, too, had squirmed during the lengthy ceremony.

My father continued his praying, peering over his glasses occasionally at us to see if we were listening. In a few minutes, as the spirit of the ceremony fastened its grip upon him, he began to rock up and back in rhythm, as the rich, Hebraic phrases issued from his lips.

"*I will bring you out from under the burden of the Egyptians, and I will rid you of their bondage, and I will redeem you . . .*" He wet his forefinger and turned another yellowed page of the Haggadah, and young as I was I began to feel the immediacy of the prayer. "*. . . and I will take you to Me for a people . . .*"

He looked up, bending his gaze upon little Louis. The table fell silently attentive. Fingering the heavy book, our father asked his youngest, in English, "Well? Well?"

Louis reddened as he struggled to recall what he had to say. He had been coached beforehand by Ben, but now

248

his memory deserted him. His lower lip trembled, but finally he remembered. In a high, faltering voice, he said, "Why is this—this night different from all other nights?"

"Because," our father answered, "on all other nights we eat leavened and unleavened alike, but on this night only unleavened bread. On all other nights we eat any kind of herbs, but on this night bitter herbs. On all other nights we do not dip even once, but on this night twice. On all other nights we sit either upright or leaning, but on this night we all lean." As we saw our father's face relax, we all smiled.

"Pop," Milt cracked, "how about hurrying the ceremony tonight? We're all starved."

Ignoring the request, my father returned to his singsong incantations, rocking up and back. He halted to dip his wine into the big, cut-glass rimmed base upon which the decanter rested, and we followed suit, dribbling a few drops of the red, red wine in unison as he intoned the command to dip. I stared at the large filled goblet of wine standing in the center of the table which was for the prophet Elijah. As an unseen guest in our home on this auspicious night, we welcomed him as a precursor of the Messiah.

As the lengthy ceremony continued and Ruth, Irving, Louis and I grew more hungry and fidgety, our father, we noticed, began to skip a few pages surreptitiously, after reading a few words at the top of a page. Our spirits rose, and we nudged each other under the table. Once or twice my mother put her finger to her lips, in an admonition for better behavior; but now we sensed our father was shortening the service for us, and we grinned and grew more restless than ever.

"Hurry up, Pa," Irving had the temerity to whisper. "Us guys are dying at the table."

After glaring at Irving for a moment, my father turned five pages of his Haggadah unobtrusively and continued his singsong. He finished by clearing his throat and raising his voice righteously, as a cover for his guilt at finishing

249

so quickly. The final phrases of the prayer died over our bent heads. The tall candles on the sideboard still gleamed steadily. Our father closed the heavy Haggadah.

"All right," he said in English. "So it's finished. Now we can eat."

"Yippee!" Louis and I cried, clapping our hands. "Food, food!"

My mother rose, smiling, and hurried toward the kitchen. "Ruth, Ruthie," she called. "Come help me."

A few minutes later we were bent over steaming plates of tasty chicken soup in which two giant *matzot* dumplings stood up like islands in each dish. Irving, Louis and I were the first to finish; we scraped the bottoms of the plates clean. My mother went into the kitchen and returned with a great platter of roast chicken; she made another trip and brought back a second platter holding a large, steaming, roasted stuffed veal. Ruth helped her bring bowls of string beans, potatoes, and apple sauce to the table, as well as two plates stacked high with *matzot* which we began eating.

With his napkin tucked under his chin, and still wearing his hat, our father proceeded to make the greatest inroads in the pile of food. Short and powerfully built, he had never suffered from a loss of appetite. He set us all an example and, except for Ruth who was a skimpy eater, we did not fail him. With every dish of food we continued to eat pieces of *matzot,* which the grownups washed down with wine.

Everytime our mother came from the kitchen with a fresh supply of *matzot* from the first of the opened bundles, she cried out, "Feel! The *matzot* is so fresh it's still warm!"

"You can thank Mr. Kleinholtz the baker," my father remarked proudly. "He gave me the best, right from the oven!"

Curious, Louis and Irving rose from their chairs and, walking into the kitchen, investigated the bundles. "Still warm!" they cried. "Gee!" They returned to their chairs and continued eating.

In the middle of the meal, when all of us were on our second helping of chicken and third helping of veal and apple sauce, the phone rang in the front room. Milt rose instantly, and as he left the room I saw my parents exchange a glance. We could hear Milt speaking cautiously a moment later, and when he returned his face was a mask.

As he sat down my mother asked, "Who was it?"

"Oh—somebody."

"A girl? That one on the North Side?"

"Yes—Anne."

"How did she know you came home?"

Milt bent to cut his chicken. "Gee, I don't know. I guess she took a chance and called."

My parents exchanged another glance. Of course he was lying; he must have sent the girl a letter from the road, notifying her that he'd be in Chicago for the Seder.

"Milt," our mother said with forgiveness in her voice, as well as gentle understanding in her eyes, "we don't see much of you now—with your traveling. Don't you think it would be nice to spend this evening with us at home here?"

"Gee, Ma." There was pain in Milt's voice, in his face. "You don't understand—"

My father reached for more wine, his wide face flushed. "The grapes were good this year," he blurted. He took a hearty swallow and speared another piece of veal. For a few moments there was silence around the table.

"Hey, look, I got the wishbone," Louis yelled. Turning, he gripped one part of it and I held on to the other. We pulled, there was a snap, and he got the bigger part. "I wish . . ."

"Don't say it!" Ruth cried to Louis warningly.

We ate until we could eat no more. Under the table I could feel my belly stretched tight as a drum. I felt uncomfortable but knew that in another hour I'd feel better.

My mother went into the kitchen to prepare tea for the grown folks. She returned with cups of very hot tea, pieces of lemon resting in the saucers. After setting down the steaming cups before Milt, Ben, my father and herself, she proceeded to slice the big, fluffy, yellow Passover cake. There wasn't any more room left in my stomach, but as I witnessed Louis and Irving accepting portions of cake, I did likewise and stuffed myself with it, adding three macaroons to my share.

Then Milt went into his bedroom where his Gladstone bag rested on the floor. Returning, he gave Louis and me five small cakes of beautiful-smelling soap taken from various Iowa hotels; he handed Irving a small, celluloid-handled pocket knife; he presented Ruth with a little genuine leather handbag; he gave our father a blue knitted necktie and Ben a shirt; and he held out a beautiful brown silk blouse to our mother.

Choking, our mother got up and kissed him. While Milt sat grinning, my father blew his nose, then took another big swallow of wine; his face was really overhealthy-looking by this time.

"All right," he remarked clearly, rising from the table. "This seems to be the night for presents." He glanced at our mother, who nodded. "Well," he said, "everybody here knows that when they reach the age of twenty-one they're going to get a present—from Ma and me." He glanced around the table. "For years I've told you about it, how my parents gave *their* children presents when they reached twenty-one. It's a good tradition. It makes you think—uh, it makes you think of growing up—uh, life . . ."

Listening, we all grew silent. Usually he was never at a loss for words, but now he was stumbling.

"But because Milt—because he—our oldest son—has always been such a good boy, your mother and I decided not to wait until Milt is twenty-one, which won't be for another eight months. We're going to give him his gift on Seder night—tonight."

To our surprise and delight, he drew a new, round, solid gold watch from his pocket, holding it by its gold chain. My mother was crying a little, looking at us—God knows why. Milt moved his lips, choked up himself. As he reached forward for his present, we all clapped.

"And let me add," my father shouted above the excitement, looking at the rest of us, "that I'll break the rule for you, too. If anybody here accomplishes something big, like going on the road before he's twenty-one, or winning a prize, they'll get their gold watch before they're of age, too!"

We stamped and clapped, then crowded around Milt to inspect the brand-new present. To cover up his confusion, my father tossed off another glass or two of wine.

Then the feast was over. Blowing her nose and happy, my mother, with Ruth's assistance, began clearing the table, and we all moved into the front room. Irving and Ben played a dozen of my father's favorite phonograph records, mostly scratchy Caruso discs which we had listened to hundreds of times. We sat patiently, hearing the scratchy bellowings of the world's greatest tenor. My eyelids had grown so heavy (it was nine o'clock already) I could hardly keep them open. Louis was already dozing in a chair, and Irving began yawning.

After the phonograph recital, my father interrogated Milt again concerning business conditions out of town, new accounts he had opened up, and the state of the crops.

"And what do the merchants think about the next elections?" he pressed Milt.

My mother merely sat quietly, staring hungrily at her oldest son who had been away from home for many weeks.

At last I noticed Milt growing more and more restive. Finally he got up, his eyes avoiding my mother's. "Well, I think I'll go and comb my hair."

He went into his bedroom and a few minutes later, he came out, holding his hat. "I won't be gone long, just for an hour or so," he began lamely. My parents did not say anything. "If that blouse is too small or too big, Ma, I can always exchange it. I want you to try it on tomorrow —I want it to fit you just right."

253

He walked over guiltily and kissed my mother, who offered him her cheek. Her mouth was twisted as she attempted to understand the first crack opened in the wall of her large family. She followed him out with her eyes.

When the door closed behind Milt, my sister went to our upright piano and played her latest practice piece, twice.

Then she returned to her chair and joined us in the uneasy evening silence. To make conversation, my father, who looked tired, began to talk about this year's good *matzot,* praising the factory that had made them.

"It pays to have a good friend like Mr. Kleinholtz. Just think, he went right to the ovens and got them hot for me!" Then he broke off and yawned, as if thinking of his grocery which he would have to open at six o'clock tomorrow morning for the railroad workers' trade.

In the silence, we could hear a Kedzie Avenue trolley swishing along the rails in the night. Suddenly my mother bent over cautiously and picked up Louis in her arms, preparatory to carrying him to his bed and undressing him. As she looked down at him gently, a tear glistened on her cheek. Louis was snoring lustily, like an exhausted bartender. After my mother carried him from the room, I grew restless.

Finally I stole towards the kitchen. I stood on a chair and lit the gas-mantle, which revealed the unwashed dishes in the sink. Then I got down and came over to the three unopened parcels of *matzot,* still tied with yellow, hairy cord. When I felt them I was keenly disappointed. They were no longer warm to my touch. They were cold now, like bundles of last week's newspapers.

XIV

PASSOVER PSALM[1]

SOLOMON IBN GABIROL

Who is like unto Thee to uncover the deeps,
    And who hath Thy power to raise and cast down?
Show Thy marvelous love to the captive who weeps,
    O Worker of wonders, of awesome renown!

Thy children belovèd intoned a new song
    When Egypt's proud host found a watery grave,
There was praise from the saints in their jubilant throng
    When the wheels of the chariots clogged in the wave.

Thy fondlings storm-tossed were all weeping and tired
    When the great roaring flood-tides before them
        arose,
But Thy hand led them safe to the haven desired
    And the waters returned, overwhelming their foes.

The chariots of Pharaoh and all that great host
    God cast in the billows and covered them o'er,
But His people trod sea-bottom, coast unto coast,
    He admonished the sea and it dried like the shore.

255

Thus, Lord, do Thou Zion support and uphold,
　　Arise, for the hour of her grace is at hand,
The day long appointed to sing as of old,
　　God reigneth, His Kingdom forever shall stand.

BY THE RED SEA[2]
Hymn For The Seventh Day Of Passover

JUDAH HALEVI

When as a wall the sea
In heaps uplifted lay,
A new song unto Thee
　　Sang the redeemed that day.

Thou didst in his deceit
O'erwhelm the Egyptian's feet,
While Israel's footsteps fleet
　　How beautiful were they!

Jeshurun! all who see
Thy glory cry to Thee
"Who like thy God can be?"
　　Thus even our foes did say.

Oh! let thy banner soar
The scattered remnant o'er,
And gather them once more,
　　Like corn on harvest-day.

Who bear through all their line
Thy covenant's holy sign,
And to Thy name divine
　　Are sanctified alway.

Let all the world behold
Their token prized of old,
Who on their garment's fold
　　The thread of blue display.

Be then the truth made known
For whom, and whom alone,
The twisted fringe is shown,
　　The covenant kept this day.

Oh! let them, sanctified,
Once more with Thee abide,
Their sun shines far and wide,
　　And chase the clouds away.

The well-beloved declare
Thy praise in song and prayer:
"Who can with Thee compare,
　　O Lord of Hosts?" they say.

When as a wall the sea
In heaps uplifted lay,
A new song unto Thee
　　Sang the redeemed that day.

SEDER-NIGHT[3]
ISRAEL ZANGWILL

Prosaic miles of streets stretch all round,
Astir with restless, hurried life and spanned
By arches that with thund'rous trains resound,
And throbbing wires that galvanize the land;
Gin-palaces in tawdry splendour stand;

257

The news-boys shriek of mangled bodies found;
The last burlesque is playing in the Strand—
In modern prose all poetry seems drowned.

Yet in ten thousand homes this April night
An ancient People celebrates its birth
To Freedom, with a reverential mirth,
With customs quaint and many a hoary rite,
Waiting until, its tarnished glories bright,
Its God shall be the God of all the earth.

A VOICE UNTO PHARAOH[1]

ARTHUR GUITERMAN

Pharaoh, Pharaoh, let my people go!
My fettered children toil with aching limbs
    And wearied fingers, brain and spirit bound,
Their puny forms are bent; the shadow dims
    Their straining eyes; their ears are choked with
        sound,
And thick with reek is every breath they draw.
    I gave them light to see and song to hear.
I gave them Truth for guide and Love for law;
    And thou hast given darkness, blight and fear.

Pharaoh, Pharaoh, let my people go!
In chains, unseen but strong, my children slave,
    Too dull for hopes or dreams, too dumb for prayers.
Thou hast robbed them of the youth I gave,
    The world I made, the joy that should be theirs.
Their lives are coined to swell thy shining store;
    Then darest thou plead, "Nay, Lord, I did not
        know,"—
Still heaping up their burdens more and more?
    The sand is running; let my children go.

Pharaoh, Pharaoh, let my people go!
Thy heart is hard. Be warned. The plagues may come.
    The wrong thou dost may breed yet fouler **wrong.**
Those lips may speak in flame that now are dumb;
    Those feeble hands, through wrath and hatred
        strong,
May rend where they have wrought. Yes, once again
    Disease, Revolt and Crime may overthrow
The Selfishness that bred them. Sons of men,
    For dread of vengeance, let my people go!

LET MY PEOPLE GO[5]
A Negro Sermon in Verse

JAMES WELDON JOHNSON

Then the Lord said: Listen, Moses,
The God of Israel will not be mocked,
Just one more witness of My power
I'll give hard-hearted Pharaoh.
This very night about midnight,
I'll pass over Egypt land,
In My righteous wrath will I pass over,
And smite their first-born dead.

And God that night passed over.
And a cry went up out of Egypt.
And Pharaoh rose in the middle of the night
And he sent in a hurry for Moses;
And he said: Go forth from among my people,
You and all the Hebrew Children;
Take your goods and take your flocks,
And get away from the land of Egypt.

259

And, right then, Moses led them out,
With all their goods and all their flocks;
And God went on before,
A guiding pillar of cloud by day,
And a pillar of fire by night.
And they journeyed on in the wilderness,
And came down to the Red Sea.

In the morning,
Oh, in the morning,
They missed the Hebrew Children.
Four hundred years,
Four hundred years
They'd held them down in Egypt land.
Held them under the driver's lash,
Working without money and without price.
And it might have been Pharaoh's wife that said:
Pharaoh—look what you've done.
You let those Hebrew Children go,
And who's going to serve us now?
Who's going to make our bricks and mortar?
Who's going to plant and plough our corn?
Who's going to get up in the chill of the morning?
And who's going to work in the blazing sun?
Pharaoh, tell me that!

And Pharaoh called his generals,
And the generals called the captains,
And the captains called the soldiers.
And they hitched up all the chariots,
Six hundred chosen chariots of war,
And twenty-four hundred horses.
And the chariots all were full of men,
With swords and shields
And shiny spears
And battle bows and arrows.

And Pharaoh and his army
Pursued the Hebrew Children
To the edge of the Red Sea.

Now, the Children of Israel, looking back,
Saw Pharaoh's army coming.
And the rumble of the chariots was like a
    thunder-storm,
And the whirring of the wheels was like a rushing
    wind,
And the dust from the horses made a cloud that
    darked the day,
And the glittering of the spears was like lightnings
    in the night.

And the Children of Israel all lost faith,
The Children of Israel all lost hope;
Deep Red Sea in front of them
And Pharaoh's host behind.
And they mumbled and grumbled among
    themselves:
Were there no graves in Egypt?
And they wailed aloud to Moses and said:
Slavery in Egypt was better than to come
To die here in this wilderness.

But Moses said:
Stand still! Stand still!
And see the Lord's salvation.
For the Lord God of Israel
Will not forsake His people.
The Lord will break the chariots,
The Lord will break the horsemen,
He'll break great Egypt's sword and shield,
The battle bows and arrows;
This day He'll make proud Pharaoh know
Who is the God of Israel.

And Moses lifted up his rod
Over the Red Sea;
And God with a blast of His nostrils
Blew the waters apart,
And the waves rolled back and stood up in a pile,
And left a path through the middle of the sea
Dry as the sand of the desert.
And the Children of Israel all crossed over
On to the other side.

When Pharaoh saw them crossing dry,
He dashed on in behind them—
Old Pharaoh got about half-way cross,
And God unleashed the waters,
And the waves rushed back together,
And Pharaoh and all his army got lost,
And all his host got drowned.
And Moses sang and Miriam danced,
And the people shouted for joy,
And God led the Hebrew Children on
Till they reached the promised land.

Listen!—Listen!
All you sons of Pharaoh.
Who do you think can hold God's people
When the Lord God Himself has said,
Let My people go?

THE DEAD OF THE WILDERNESS[6]
HAYYIM NAHMAN BIALIK

Sixty myriads of voices—a thunder of heroes—awaken,
Crash through the tempest and tear asunder the rage of
    the desert.

Round them is wilderness and blindness:

                              And they cry

"We are the mighty!

The last generation of slaves and the first generation of
    freemen!

Alone our hand in its strength

Tore from the pride of our shoulders the yoke of
    bondage.

We lifted our heads to the heavens and behold their
    broadness was narrow in the pride of our eyes,

So we turned to the desert, we said to the Wilderness:
    'Mother!'

Yea, on the tops of the crags, in the thickness of clouds,

With the eagles of heaven we drank from her fountains
    of freedom.

And who is lord of us?

Even now, though the God of vengeance has shut the
    desert upon us,

A song of strength and revolt has reached us, and we
    arise.

To arms! To arms! Form ranks! Forward!

Forward into the heavens and the wrath thereof.

Behold us! We will ascend

With the tempest!

Though the Lord has withdrawn His hand from us,

And the Ark stands moveless in its place,

Still we will ascend—alone!

Even under the eye of His wrath, daring the lightning
    of His countenance,

We will carry with storm the citadels of the hills,

And face to face in combat encounter the armed foe!

Listen!

The storm, too, calls unto us—'Courage and daring!'

To arms! To arms! Let the hills be shattered and the
    mountains blasted into dust.

Or let our lifeless bodies be heaped in countless calms.

Forward!

On to the hills!"

PESACH HAS COME TO THE GHETTO AGAIN[7]
(Warsaw, April 19, 1943)

BINEM HELLER

Pesach has come to the Ghetto again.
The wine has no grape, the *matzah* no grain,
But the people anew sing the wonders of old,
The flight from the Pharaohs, so often retold.
How ancient the story, how old the refrain!

The windows are shuttered. The doors are
    concealed.
The Seder goes on. And fiction and fact
Are confused into one. Which is myth? Which
    is real?
"Come all who are hungry!" invites the
    Haggadah.
The helpless, the aged, lie starving in fear.
"Come all who are hungry!" and children sleep,
    famished.
"Come all who are hungry!" and tables are bare.

Pesach has come to the Ghetto again,
And shuffling shadows shift stealthily through,
Like convert-marranos in rack-ridden Spain
Seeking retreat with the God of the Jews.
But these are the shards, the shattered remains
Of the "sixty ten-thousands" whom Moses led out
Of their bondage . . . driven to ghettos again . . .
Where dying's permitted but protest is not.
From Holland, from Poland, from all Europe's
    soil,
Becrippled and beaten the remnant has come.

25. Seder Plate. Majolica

Ancona, Italy, 1673

Master G. R. van Go, 1718

26. Passover Plate. Pewter

Germany, 1771

27. Passover Plate. Pewter

28. Passover Plate. Pewter

Baruch Schtecher of Fuerth, 1773

And there they sit weeping, plundered, despoiled,
And each fifty families has dwindled to one.

Pesach has come to the Ghetto again.
The lore-laden words of the Seder are said,
And the cup of the Prophet Elijah awaits,
But the Angel of Death has intruded, instead.
As always—the German snarls his commands.
As always—the words sharpened-up and precise.
As always—the fate of more Jews in his hands:
Who shall live, who shall die, this Passover night.
But no more will the Jews to the slaughter be led.
The truculent jibes of the Nazis are past.
And the lintels and doorposts tonight will be red
With the blood of free Jews who will fight to
    the last.

Pesach has come to the Ghetto again.
And neighbor to neighbor the battle-pledge gives:
The blood of the German will flow in the Ghetto
So long as one Jew in the Ghetto still lives!
In face of the Nazi—no fear, no subjection!
In face of the Nazi—no weeping, no wincing!
Only the hatred, the wild satisfaction
Of standing against him and madly resisting.
Listen! how Death walks abroad in the fury!
Listen! how bullets lament in their flight!
See how our History writes END to the story,
With death heroic, this Passover night!

PASSOVER EVE[8]

FANIA KRUGER

Beside his wife at Passover in spring
Jacob sits on pillows like a king.

Elijah may appear with flowing hair
To lift the dark and sing away despair.
That holy sage who utters truth in jest
May enter in the guise of unknown guest.
A cup of wine for him, and goblets too
Are set for absent ones. In sorrow's hue
Jacob, on such symbolic night of song,
Recalls his boys, slender and brave and strong.
His wife beholds the five dark handsome faces
Above the festive table's empty places.

As *matzot* lie uneaten, candles sputter:
What says the wind that whispers in the shutter?

The mother speaks: *"My prayer flies back and forth;*
Our boys lie east and west and south and north.
Each one has fallen in an alien land.
Prophet Elijah lift your holy hand
In succor . . . give us faith, dispel our fear
Our sons no longer sit beside us here."

Then suddenly the darkening shadow falls—
Upon the board, the floor, the dusky walls.
The Seder table lengthens and grows wide;
The sons come in and sit on either side;
The sons come in, as tall as pines are straight,
Elijah leading them. And from each plate
They lift the brimming goblets. Then like wind
Their voices echo, deep yet strangely thinned:
"Forever keep the vow: that men be free
Like rain which gives sustenance to a tree,
That pestilence and sword be gone this hour;
The air be sweet with peace, the hedge in flower."

While Jacob chants the psalms, the candles sputter
And winds are whispering in every shutter.

PASSOVER IN JERUSALEM°

AVIGDOR HAMEIRI

Voluptuous angels hummed today in Jerusalem,
Thousands of springs condensed in me today
And from its grave every dead skeleton breathes the
    sun.
"Welcome be, all fragrances, messengers of God's
    fruition—
I am waiting today, I wait for one,
The Messiah redeeming, seducing, whoever may
    come,
If only he comes:
Today is festive Passover and faith has no bounds."

A thousand ancient kisses resound today in
    Jerusalem,
The world sobs in the choking abundance of godlike
    burgeoning
And from the graves of my ancestors spurts the
    song of the blood.
"Jerusalem, Jerusalem, city of prayer and arid earth,
Will you spread out for me a warm nuptial couch
For the kiss of the husband of your youth, the
    bridegroom of blood,
For the mourner of blood,
To bring from under your heart, the King Messiah's
    birth?"

267

HAGGADAH[10]

ABRAHAM M. KLEIN

Etching

The sky is dotted like th' unleavened bread,
The moon a golden platter in the sky.
Old midget Jews, with meditated tread,
Hands clasped behind, and body stooped ahead,
Creep from the synagogue and stare on high
Upon a golden platter in a dotted sky . . .

Once in a Year

Once in a year, this comes to pass:
My father is a king in a black skullcap,
My mother is a queen in a brown *perruque*,
A princess my sister, a lovely lass,
My brother a prince, and I, a duke . . .
Silver and plate, and fine cut-glass
Brought from the cupboards that hid them till now
Banquet King David's true lineage here.
Once in a year this comes to pass,
Once in a long unroyal year . . .

Black Decalogue

Compute the plagues; your little finger dip
In spittle of the grape, and at each pest
Shake off the drop with the vindictive zest:
Thus first: the Nile—a gash; then frogs that skip
Upon the princess' coverlet; the rip
Made by dark nails that seek the itching guest;

The plague of murrained carcasses; the pest;
Full boils that stud the Ethiop, leg to lip . . .
The visitation of hot hail, the fists of God;
The swarm of locusts nibbling Egypt clean;
Thick darkness oozing from out Moses' rod;
And first-born slain, the mighty and the mean;
Compute these plagues that fell on Egypt's sod,
Then add: In Goshen these were never seen.

The Bitter Dish

This is the bread of our affliction, this
The symbol of the clay that built Rameses,
And that horseradish-root of bitterness,
And you, my brethren, yea,
You are the afflicted, the embittered, and the clay.

Song

Fill the silver goblet;
Make open the door-way;
Let there be no sob; let
Elijah come our way.

And let him come singing,
Announcing as nigh a
Redemption, and drinking
The health of Messiah!

Had Gadya

This is a curious plot
Devised for eager riddling:
My father had a kidling
For two good *zuzzim* bought.

269

Graymalkin ate it; and
A dog munched sleek Graymalkin,
Whereat a Rod did stalk in
Beating his reprimand

Upon the Dog's spine. Came
Red Fire and did sputter
His wrath on Rod; came Water
And, sizzling, quenched the flame.

And down a bovine throat
Went Water, which throat, tickled
By pious Shohet, trickled
Red blood upon his coat.

The Angel of Death flew
And smote the Shohet; whereat
The Lord gave him his merit—
The Lord the Angel slew.

In that strange portal whence
All things come, they re-enter;
Of all things God is center,
God is circumference.

This is a curious plot
Devised for eager riddling:
My father had a kidling
For two good *zuzzim* bought.

The Still Small Voice

The candles splutter; and the kettle hums;
The heirloomed clock enumerates the tribes;
Upon the wine-stained tablecloth lie crumbs
Of *matzah* whose wide scattering describes
Jews driven in far lands upon this earth.

270

The kettle hums; the candles splutter; and
Winds whispering from shutters tell rebirth
Of beauty rising in an eastern land,
Of paschal sheep driven in cloudy droves;
Of almond-blossoms coloring the breeze;
Of vineyards upon verdant terraces;
Of golden globes in orient orange-groves.
And those assembled at the table dream
Of small schemes that an April wind doth scheme,
And cry from out the sleep assailing them,
Jerusalem, next year! Next year, Jerusalem!

JUDITH K. EISENSTEIN

To garner the music associated with the festival of Pesach, and to assort it into categories of period, location, subject matter or function, is to view in microcosm the story of the music of the Jewish people. This most ancient festival carries with it a heritage of countless ages and many climes. Its two basic themes, the redemption from Egypt and the coming of the spring harvest, break up into numerous sub-themes and their variations, which occur in the music of the synagogue, of the Seder, of the folk and of the concert hall. These different themes and their music slip imperceptibly from one category to another. They overlap and enrich each other.

In many instances only the texts of songs remain extant, while the melodies have been lost along with the communities which sang them. This is true of the hymns of the First Temple. It is equally true, alas, of much of the folk song of East-European Jewry. We shall endeavor, here, to indicate only a sampling of the repertoire of the Passover which endures and remains relevant to our musical understanding and taste. At the same time we shall hope to demonstrate the vitality of the festival, which is still a source of inspiration, so that the repertoire continues to grow and to be enriched by both the folk composers of Israel and the skilled composers of many countries.

THE TRADITION OF THE SYNAGOGUE

The first or, perhaps more correctly, the oldest stratum in the music of the festival is found in the tradition of the synagogue. And of all the music of the synagogue, most basic is the simple chant which is applied to the reading of biblical texts in the course of the service. In addition to the ordinary cantillation of the prescribed chapters of the Torah and of the Prophets, we hear on Passover the special variant of the Torah chant which is applied to the song of Moses after the triumphant crossing of the Red Sea. (This chant is also used when the poem is read in its normal place in the year's cycle of Torah readings.) In the Ashkenazi tradition the melody holds a note of triumph, with reminiscences of the call of the shofar. It is customary for the congregation to rise during the recital, and to join the reader in singing out the jubilant cadences.

SONG OF MOSES

More particularly belonging to Passover is the cantillation of the Song of Songs. That lyrical book of the Bible is read in the synagogue only on this occasion. While one cannot accurately say of a system of cantillation that it has any subjective values, consisting as it does merely of progressions of fixed musical motifs, nevertheless the chanting of the *Shir ha-Shirim* in each local group is characterized by a joyous lyricism which distinguishes it from all other chants. Israel Rabinovitch, in his book *Of Jewish Music,* devotes a chapter to the Ashkenazi version of the chant, and claims to hear echoes in it of the song of the cuckoo.[1] While this may be more charming fancy than scientific musicology, it is easy to agree with the author's appraisal of the melody. It assuredly expresses the joy of springtime and of love.

SONG OF SONGS

Shir ha-shi-rim___ a-sher li-sh'lo-moh___
yi-sha-ke-ni mi-ne-shi-kot___
pi-hu ki to-vim do-de-ka mi-ya-yin.
Le-re-aḥ she-ma-ne-ka to-vim___ she-men tu-rak___ she-
me-ka al ken___ a-la-mot a-he-vu-ka.

No less beautiful and moving is the chant for the Song of Songs which was discovered by Lazare Saminsky in the state of Georgia in the Caucasian mountains. He arranged it with taste and skill for solo voice. The following is the bare unaccompanied chant as he heard and notated it.[2]

The second source of thematic material to be heard in the music of the synagogue is the cantillation of the liturgy itself. Prescribed modes within which the cantor improvises and the congregation responds vary, as do the biblical modes, from one community to another, so that the Ashkenazi, the Sephardi, the Yemenite and other services will bear only a remote resemblance to each other. In the Ashkenazi tradition we find fragments of melody which serve as "leitmotifs" replete with associations for the worshipper. A number of these fragments are shared by the Passover with the other pilgrim festivals, Sukkot and Shavuot. An important example is the *Hallel* mode, used for the set of Psalms of Praise which are recited on all three festivals. The essence of the chant is contained in the blessing which precedes the reading of the *Hallel* itself.[3]

HALLEL

Ba-ruḳ at - tah A-do-nai E - lo- he - nu me-leḳ ha - o -

lam a - sher kid - de-sha - nu be-mitz-vo - tav v'tzi -

va - nu li - k'ro et ha - hal - lel.

This melodic fragment becomes thematic material for other parts of the service, and its cadence becomes the "Amen" response for the congregation.[4]

Ki El me-leḳ ga-dol ve-ka-dosh___ at - tah. Ba-

ruḳ at-tah A-do-nai (Ba-ruḳ hu u-va-ruḳ she-mo) ha-

El___ ha - ka - dosh (A - men.)

Another unit of melody which is associated equally with the festival of *Shemini Atzeret* and Pesach occurs in the introductions to the Prayer for Rain on the former and the Prayer for Dew on the latter. The origins of this melody are somewhat less ancient and obscure than those of much synagogue chant. It is believed to have been a special song created for these special prayers in the days of the troubadours and minnesingers of western Europe.[5]

276

PRAYER FOR DEW

Be - da - a - to___ a - bi - ah___ hi - dot Be -
am___ zu___ be - zu ___ be-
tal___ le-ha - ha -dot. Tal ge u-d'sha-e-ha la-ha-
dot_____ da - tzim___ b'tzil-lo le-he-ha-dot.___
Ot yal -dut tal l'ha-gen le-to-la-dot.___

Like the *Hallel* mode, this melody becomes in turn the
theme for other parts of the service on the first morning
of Passover, the day when the Prayer for Dew is recited.
The following examples demonstrate how the *Kaddish*
and the *Abot* of the *Musaf,* which actually precede the
Prayer for Dew in the liturgy, take on its melody.

KADDISH

Yit - gad-dal ve - yit - kad -
dash___ she - me rab - ba (A - men) Be-

277

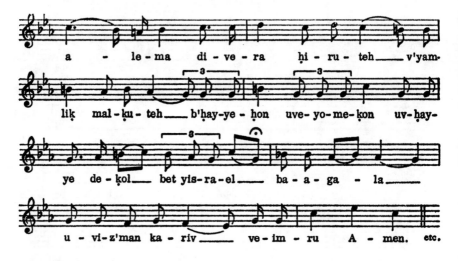

a - le - ma di - ve - ra hi - ru - teh___ v'yam-
lik mal - ku - teh___ b'hay-ye - hon uve - yo - me - kon uv - hay-
ye de - kol___ bet yis-ra-el___ ba - a - ga - la
u - vi - z'man ka - riv___ ve - im - ru A - men. etc.

MUSAF ABOT

Ba - ruk at - tah A - do - nai___ E - lo-
he - nu ve' lo - he___ a -
vo - te - nu E - lo - he av - ra - ham___ E - lo-
he yitz - hak___ ve - lo - he___ ya - a - kov. etc.

In traditions other than the Ashkenazi there occur a number of beautiful poems of Prayer for the Dew. Each of these has its own characteristic melody, deriving from the musical style of its own community, be it Sephardi, or

278

Yemenite, or Iraqi. One of these, a relatively uncompli-
cated verse in acrostic form, comes from the tradition of
the Yemenite Jews.[6]

Finally, associated with the second eve of Passover,
and thence on into the weeks which follow the festival,
is the first counting of the *Omer*. Here is a melody of
great dignity, proclaiming the blessing upon counting the
Omer, and declaring the first day of the *Omer*.[7]

COUNTING OF THE OMER

279

tzi - ... va - nu   al se - fi - rat___ ha - o - mer. Hay-

yom   yom e - ḥad___   la   -   o   -   mer.___

MUSIC OF THE SEDER

After the synagogue, the second important repository of
musical tradition is the home. Like the *zemirot* of the Sabbath, the music of the Seder has been carried down through
the generations by family tradition, and even within
each large geographic community there will be found
variations from family to family. Every tradition includes
a large portion of chant, applied to the narrative portions
of the Haggadah, to the *Kiddush,* the *Hallel* and the
Grace After Meals, plus a set of rhythmic and almost
childlike folk songs. The chant in oriental communities is
fairly monotonous, lying within a very narrow tone
range.[8] The Ashkenazi chant is subject to very free treatment, with only a few portions restricted by precedent.
The *Hallel* is generally chanted after the manner of the
synagogue. The *Kiddush* is chanted in the same manner
as on the other two pilgrimage festivals. The source of
the *Kiddush* chant is a very old melody, one which is originally applied to the metrical poem, *Akdamut,* from the
Shavuot service.

The *Kiddush* is a slight elaboration of the tune.

KIDDUSH

Ba- ruḵ at-tah A- do- nai E- lo- he- nu me-leḵ ha-o- lam
bo- re pe-ri__ ha-ga-fen. Ba-ruḵ at-tah A- do- nai E- lo-
he- nu me-leḵ ha-o- lam__ a-sher ba-ḥar ba-nu mik-kol
am__ ve-ro-me-ma- nu mik-kol la- shon__ ve-kid'-
sha-nu be-mitz-vo-tav__ va-ti-ten la-nu A-do-nai E-lo-he-nu be-
a- ha-vah mo-a-dim le-sim- ḥah__ ḥa-
gim u-z'man-nim le-sa-son__ et yom ḥag ha-ma-tzot ha-zeh__
Z'man ḥe-ru-te-nu mik-ra ko-desh ze-ḵer li-tzi-at mitz-ra-yim ki
va-nu va-ḥar- ta ve-o-ta-nu kid-dash-ta mik-
kol ha-a- mim__ u'mo-a-de kod-she-ḵa__ be-sim-

281

ḥah u-ve-ṣa-ṣon.__ hin-ḥal- ta - nu. Ba-ruḳ at-tah A-do-
nai.__ me- kad-desh yis-ra-el.__ ve - ha-z'man-nim.__

The Four Questions are traditionally sung to the melody which students have been wont to use in studying the Mishnah. In the Ashkenazi version we can recognize the question and answer of the mishnaic discussion or, perhaps more vividly, the pointing upwards and then downwards of the logical talmudic thumb.

THE FOUR QUESTIONS

Mah   nish-tan-nah ha-lai-lah ha- zeh.__   mik-kol ha-lay- lot.__
she-be-ḳol ha-lay-lot   a- nu o'ḳe-lin   ḥa-metz   u- ma- tzah.__
ha - lai - lah ha - zeh.__   ku - lo.__   ma - tzah.__   etc.

The songs which comprise the closing section of the Haggadah are among the most widely-known and beloved of the whole Jewish repertoire. The most popular of these may be found in a number of Haggadahs and song collections published in the United States. They are of great age, having originated in Germany and bearing a strong resemblance to German folk song. Even their texts seem to be of German Jewish origin, inasmuch as they do not appear in the Haggadahs of Sephardi and Eastern com-

282

munities. However, they have apparently been taken over by these communities, for we find that Idelsohn has notated a number of melodies from the Babylonian community. The following is an eminently singable version of the delightful cumulative song, *Had Gadya*.[9]

HAD GADYA

From the point of view of the folklorist, the song *Ehad Mi Yode'a* is probably one of the most interesting of all. Its similarity to the counting songs of other ethnic groups is striking, particularly where the numbers stand for religio-historical symbols and personalities. The English song, "Who'll sing me One, ho, Green grow the rushes, oh!" is an especially notable example, with its refrain of: "One and one is all alone and ever more shall be so." In some Jewish communities the song is sung not only in Hebrew, but in the vernacular. It appears, for example, in the Ladino or Judeo-Spanish of the western Sephardim.[10]

283

WHO KNOWS ONE?
(Ladino)

quen su - pie - sey en - te - dien - se a - la - ver al
Dio cre-en-se cua - lo es la u - no u - no es el
Cre - a - dor, Ba - ruḳ hu va - ruḳ she-mo quen su - pie - sey
en - te - dien - se a - la ver al Dio cre - en - se

Cua -los son los dos? Dos__ Mo - she y A - ron
Cua -los son los tres? Tres__ pa - dres mues-tros son
Cua -los son los qua-tro? Qua - tro ma - dres mues-tros son

D. S.

U - no es el Cre- a - dor Ba - ruḳ hu va -ruḳ she-mo etc.
Av - ram, Itz - ḥak y Ya' kov
Sarah, Riv-kah, Le - ah, Ra-ḥel

The song also occurs in the vernacular of the Bukharan Jews.[11]

284

Ya - ku-min ki me - da - nad ya - ku - min man
me - da nam Ya - ku - min ku - da i
ra - bul o - la - mim___ Du___ yu - min ki
me - da - nad Du___ yu - min man me - da-
nam du___ yu - min du lai ḥi gav - har___
___ ya- ku- min ku - da i ra - bul___ o - la- mim etc.

An amusing variant of *Ehad Mi Yode'a* is sung in
Yiddish. In this version each question and answer is preceded by the words "Mah adabberah, mah asappera
oteka?" (What shall I say, what shall I speak unto
Thee?).[12] In East-European folk song, moreover, we find
a number of parodies on this song, ranging from a
mnemonic of phrases from the Talmud to some highly
irreverent wedding songs.

A significant contribution to the music of Pesach, and
of the Haggadah in particular, has been made by the
Hasidim. In fact, a large number of songs which have
been incorporated into the ritual by the Ashkenazi community are the creations of that group, which raised the
status of melody to unprecedented heights as a medium of
religious expression. They made a great deal more, in the
first place, of the chant in the narrative portions of the

Haggadah, drawing on the *nusah* of other liturgies to express shades of meaning and varieties of mood. A telling illustration of this is their employment of the traditional chant for the reading of the Torah on the High Holy Days, in the long discussion of the ten plagues in the Haggadah.[13]

THE TEN PLAGUES

Reb-bi E-li-e-zer o-mer min-na-yin she-kol mak-kah

u-mak-kah she-he-vi ha-ka-dosh ba-ruk hu al ha-mitz-rim

be-mitz-ra-yim ha-ye'tah shel ar-ba mak-kot she-ne'-mar

ye-sha-lah bam ha-ron ap-po ev-rah va-za-am ve-

tza-rah mish-la-hat mal-a-ke ra-im ev-rah a-hat va-za-am

shta-yim ve-tza-rah sha-losh mish-la-hat mal-a-ke ra-im

ar-ba e-mor me-a-tah be-mitz-ra-yim la-ku ar-ba-im

mak-kot ve-al ha-yam la-ku ma-ta-im mak-kot.

286

Other passages in the Haggadah have been given folk-song settings by the Hasidim. The well-known melody for *Vehi she-Amedah* is a prime example of giving rhythmic musical form to an unrhythmic passage, so characteristic of the Hasidim. A number of the *piyyutim* which are part of either the synagogue service or of the Haggadah do have their own inherent rhythm. Traditionally, even these were chanted in free rhythm by the Ashkenazim. The Hasidim, however, have made true songs of them. It must be noted, however, that the melodic rhythms are, like the melodic lines, Slavic in character and do not derive from the original Arabic meters of the poems. The first of these occurs in the synagogue liturgy.

PESACH EMUNIM

The second illustration is drawn from the Haggadah, but has become a popular song for other occasions than Pesach.

KAREV YOM

One special category of traditional folk song has come in more recent times to be associated with the Seder. This is the set of songs expressing love and longing for Elijah the Prophet. In the tradition these have actually been sung at the closing of the Sabbath. It has become customary in many places to sing them at that point in the Haggadah when the door is opened for Elijah. Symbolizing the messianic dream of the Jewish people, Elijah is a beloved legendary figure. Songs and poems in his praise abound in every locale where Jews have lived. In addition to the very popular *Eliyahu ha-Navi,* the following is a good example from the East-European *shtetl.*

YOVO ADIR

The same *shtetl* produced a number of folk songs which, while not religious in character, are inspired by the festival of Passover. Most of these have remained unnotated, only their texts having been preserved in some instances and embellished with comments in others. They deal largely with the preparations for the holiday, the special concerns of the housewife, the *matzah*-baker, the children. One song appears in collections in several forms, seeming to indicate that it had achieved a certain popularity. It speaks of the universality of the joy of Pesach, when both the revered *rebbe* and the *baal agalah* (teamster) relax on their couches, so that they can obey the injunction to recline at the Seder table, each alongside of his wife, and each gleefully singing *Had Gadya*.[14]

THE RABBI AND THE TEAMSTER ON SEDER NIGHT

Es is a sim - ḥe mit un - zer reb - ben az es
kumt di se - der nacht___ Er shpringt un ḥul - iet un
is tzu - fri - den, un shpringt un ḥul - iet un lacht. Mit zei - ne
klo - re ze - ke - lach kricht er oif oif dem he - sev - bet___ un
nemt a - rum di ko - she - re mal - keh, git a glet___ un
zitz tzu - legt un zingt mit freid Ḥad gad - yo un di
mal - keh si helft im tzu, Ḥad gad - yo.

290

Es is a simhe mit unzer balagoleh
Az es kumt di seder nacht.
Er shpringt un huliet un is tzufriden
Un shpringt un huliet un lacht.
Mit zeine shtivel kricht er oif oif dem hesevbet
Un nemt arum di veibele un git a glet,
Un zitzt tzulegt un zingt mit freid, "Had Gadyo,"
Un di veib helft im tzu, "Had Gadyo."

THE ART MUSIC OF PASSOVER

These last items in the roster of Passover song, historically viewed, are actually a miniature offshoot of a much larger aspect of Passover music. It is only since the Enlightenment, at around the turn of the nineteenth century, that trained composers have been devoting their talents to the creation of music for trained performers, which provides more or less heightened expression of the emotional values of the festival. Approximately a century and a half have gone by. This is but a moment in the long history of our people, and but a moment, too, in the long development of Western music. When Handel wrote his great oratorio, *Israel in Egypt,* very few Jews anywhere in the world were aware of it. Their own great epic of emancipation was being sung in the outside world, while they were shut away behind ghetto walls. Even after Jews emerged from the ghetto, and the talented among them acquired the tastes and skills of the Western composers, they were a long time at work before anyone attempted a full scale celebration in music of the Passover.

The first efforts of composers were confined to synagogue music. There they found texts which cried out for choral arrangements, and eventually for organ accompaniment as well. The psalms of the *Hallel,* the processional psalm "Lift up your heads, O ye gates," and others found settings in the then prevalent Romantic style, with some obeisance to the baroque of Handel. Lewandowsky and Sulzer were the pioneers of the movement to create new synagogue music which continues into our own time.

291

It must be admitted that, unlike the music of the Sabbath service, that of the Passover service seems to have remained largely in the nineteenth century idiom. (There may be a purely practical explanation for this. Commissions for new compositions in recent decades have been offered by synagogues and other institutions largely for Sabbath music.) One notable exception is the *Hallel* service by Tzippora Jochsberger, for *a capella* chorus, soloist and children's chorus. This work, though written in the United States, shows the unmistakable influence of contemporary Israel vocal music.

In addition to the few original compositions for synagogue, composers have been called upon to arrange the traditional modes for organ accompaniment and for choral singing along with the cantor. Most of this music is adaptable to the liturgies of all three pilgrimage festivals. Occasionally the composer has introduced slight variations, using what are considered characteristic themes of the individual holidays as inserts into the body of the compositions. This has left Pesach to some extent the poorest, since the "theme" usually selected to represent it has been the *Addir Hu* of the Seder, probably one of the least distinguished tunes in itself, and least dynamic in its potentialities.

The story of the Exodus has received its first Jewish musical treatment in our own century, and for the concert hall rather than the synagogue. We have the score (piano) of an oratorio, *The Song of Moses*, by Max Ettinger of Switzerland. This oratorio for four solo singers, chorus and orchestra has a text drawn directly from the Bible, in its German version. (An English translation is also provided.) The full-length work is divided into three sections, "Exodus out of Egypt," "In the Wilderness" and "In Sight of the Promised Land." While the composer has utilized a number of Yemenite melodies, the total effect of the oratorio is entirely European. It is a dramatic piece, and shifts in style from the romantic to the more contemporary. To our knowledge it has not

292

been performed in America. The orchestra score, as well as the copyright, remains in the hands of the composer.

A second large work, which combines the Exodus theme with the Seder theme, is called *Haggadah*. It was composed in 1938 by Paul Dessau, who was at that time still in Europe. This work, for solo, chorus, children's chorus and orchestra, is based on a libretto by Max Brod, translated into Hebrew by Georg Mordecai Langer. The score remains in the composer's possession, but has been performed in recent years on the West Coast. What we know of it is only Max Brod's own eloquent description which serves to whet the reader's appetite for hearing the oratorio.[15] "The work bears the stamp of its purpose, which was to reflect all the aspects of the Feast of Passover, at once the family feast, a spiritualized banquet, and, finally and most important, a feast of remembrance of a great historical event, on which splendor is cast by the idea of God and of eternal symbols." Brod goes on to describe how the oratorio begins with the Seder itself, the questions and answers of the children, up to the discussions of the Sages of B'ne B'rak. It moves out then, into the re-enactment of the Exodus story, drawing on both biblical and midrashic sources for the narrative, with dramatic, pastoral and triumphant passages. Then comes the reminder of the pupils: "Masters, it is time to say the morning prayer." The historical passages fade away, and the oratorio returns to the Seder table, ending with a merry *Had Gadya* by the children.

The life and personality of Moses have inspired some of the greatest works of art, literature and drama. Although it can hardly be labeled a "Passover" work, one cannot fail to mention in this connection the unfinished opera of a most important composer of our century, Arnold Schoenberg. *Moses and Aaron* is based on a libretto written by the composer himself and contains his own highly personal interpretation of the Bible story in terms of a conflict between two great archetypes. Musically it is cast in the twelve-tone system, and is based on

Schoenberg's characteristic "tone-row." It uses speaking voices, both solo and choral, as well as singing voices, sometimes having both going on simultaneously. It is intense and difficult for both performance and appreciation, but so vital that it is well worth turning one's attention to at the Passover season.[16]

One or two smaller items will close the listing of Passover art music. A ballet suite, *Opus Americanum No. 2— Moses*, by Darius Milhaud, is an orchestral depiction of the life of Moses. This is an odd composition, combining French elegance with Hebraic grandeur, and is very appealing. It offers a variety of moods, austere, lyrical, triumphant and bacchanal. The sections called "The Infant Moses" and the "Crossing of the Red Sea" have been especially attractive and stimulating to the imagination of young people.[17]

The Song of Songs has had innumerable settings: a women's chorus by Paul Dessau, solo songs by Castelnuovo-Tedesco (intended by him for performance at the marriage ceremony, but appropriate for use at Passover), and others. Included in a Sabbath cantata by Mordecai Seter, the Israeli composer, is a very beautiful and interesting setting of passages from the Song of Songs which could very easily be extracted for use in connection with Passover as well.

The spring-harvest element of the festival has not yet been expressed in seriously composed music, and certainly not in the larger forms. One may hazard a guess, however, that such music is very likely to grow out of the revived recognition of this aspect of the marvelously complex structure which is the Passover.

BY RACHEL WISCHNITZER

Medieval Haggadah Manuscripts

The festival of Passover has been a strong incentive for the artistic creativity of our people. The Passover Haggadah, the little book recited at the home celebration of the festival, has offered rich material for pictorial illustration.

The illustrated medieval Haggadah manuscripts represent two types: the Sephardi or Spanish, and the Ashkenazi or Franco-German. Those of Italian provenience exhibit some characteristics common to both. The printed Haggadahs produced in the 16th-17th centuries in Prague, Mantua and Venice were illustrated with woodcuts. By the end of the seventeenth century a Haggadah with copperplate engravings was produced in Amsterdam. The woodcuts of the Venice Haggadah and the engravings of the Amsterdam Haggadah, particularly the latter, exercised a tremendous influence on Jewish folk art. In various places, chiefly in Bohemia and Moravia, self-taught Jewish artists copied by hand the texts and the pictures, redesigning them in their own way and touching them up with color. A number of these charming Haggadah manuscripts dating from the

295

eighteenth century have survived. Illustrations are usually inserted in the text, at the beginning of the paragraph. In some Haggadah manuscripts, however, whole sets of full-page pictures are appended at the beginning or at the end. In the printed Haggadahs the pictures are generally placed in the borders.

The study of the illustrated Passover Haggadah may be conveniently divided into the following topics: the Sages at B'ne B'rak, the family Seder, the parable of the Four Sons, the Exodus and other biblical motifs, and miscellaneous subjects. Because of the different pictorial interpretations of the various topics, it is the delight of the art student to detect trends and preferences and to relate them to their background.

THE SAGES AT B'NE B'RAK

The names of ten commentators on the festival of Passover and its manner of celebration are mentioned in the Haggadah. These men belong to the tannaitic period, comprising the last years of the Second Temple, which was destroyed in 70 C.E., and continuing to the uprising of Bar Kokhba, about 130 C.E.

Five of the sages—Eliezer, Joshua, Elazar ben Azariah, Akiba and Tarfon—appear early in the story. They are gathered in B'ne B'rak, a city near Jaffa where Rabbi Akiba had his academy, and are "reclining" and discussing the Exodus from Egypt. "Reclining" (*mesubbin*) is a term used to indicate the posture of men at a meal, usually in company. From the theme of the discussion one gathers the impression that the occasion was a Passover celebration. We learn that it lasted all night, until the students came to remind the rabbis that it was time to recite the morning prayers.

The ancient custom of eating in a reclining position is illustrated in an Assyrian relief of the seventh century B.C.E., showing Assurbanipal drinking wine while leaning on a couch.[1] His queen sits on a chair at his feet. A similar scene is carved on a sarcophagus from Sidon, fifth century B.C.E.[2] In the next century, Plato in his *Symposium* gives a vivid description of a banquet attended by Socrates, with the participants reclining on couches while conducting a spirited discussion on a topic of general interest. The Romans took over the table-manners of the ancients. In their dining rooms, called *triclinia,* they had three couches around the room, for reclining at meals.

Although we have no early representations of Jews attending the Passover meal, there exists a relatively early portrayal of the Last Supper, which was probably a Passover meal. In a miniature of a sixth century Gospel book at the Cathedral in Rossano, Italy, Jesus and his disciples are shown reclining on couches around a table on which there is a fish in a bowl.[3] The custom of reclining at a meal was still a vivid memory, even though it was no longer practiced. For the Jew, it became symbolic of the way of life of a free citizen in contrast to an Egyptian slave. The word *mesubbin* in the text is a reminder of it.

The medieval illustrator took pains in trying to visualize the B'ne B'rak scene. He knew of the Passover feast as it is described in the twelfth chapter of Exodus, with the men standing and eating the Passover lamb "in haste" to reproduce and evoke the original situation at the actual Exodus. He knew how it was celebrated at the time when the sanctuary existed. According to Deuteronomy 16, the lambs were offered on the grounds of the Temple, and roasted and eaten there. Only the *matzot* were eaten in the tents where the pilgrims from all over the country lived throughout the feast.

The meeting at B'ne B'rak was not, however, a pantomime portrayal of the Exodus, nor was it a pilgrims' feast. It was obviously not a Seder with women present, as the medieval illustrator knew it from his own experience. Yet he had to depict the men emphasizing the leaning pose, unrelated as it seemed to anything familiar to him.

In the fourteenth century Haggadah, written and illuminated in Spain (British Museum, Add. 14761), we see a masonry house with the five rabbis in the windows. Each sits at a window resting his head on his arm. The students, standing outside, have just opened the door; they point to the rabbis, reminding them that it is time for the morning prayers. Pesahim 108a asserts that one should not recline on his back nor lean on the right side at the Passover meal. The correct attitude was, of course, to rest the left elbow on the couch so as to be able to take the food with the right hand. However, while sitting on a chair at a table, one would rather rest the arm on the table. The medieval artist, to whom eating in a recumbent position was unfamiliar, portrayed the rabbis with one hand supporting the chin.

In a late fifteenth century Ashkenazi Haggadah, Darmstadt II (Landesbibliothek, Darmstadt), the rabbis are in a tower. Here again the Seder is avoided because of the inability of the artist to visualize the scene.[4] In another fifteenth century Ashkenazi Haggadah (British Museum, Add. 14762), the rabbis are shown, with gestures expressive of speech, standing around a pulpit on which there is a Haggadah (fig. 5). It occurred to the illuminator of the French Haggadah (Bibliothèque Nationale, Ms. hebr. 1388), written in 1583, to seat the five rabbis on a comfortable sofa.[5] The artist may have seen Gottfried Schedel's *Weltchronik* with woodcuts, published in Nuremberg in 1493. The seven sages of antiquity are shown there seated on a sofa.[6]

Among the Haggadahs of the Ashkenazi type with German or Franco-German character of illustration, the Darmstadt I manuscript (Landesbibliothek, Darmstadt) dating from the 1420-1430s has puzzled students of Hebrew iconography. This magnificently executed work shows men and women, in various attitudes and settings, raising their cups of wine or reading with expressive gestures of speech. Only one scene is directly related to the subject matter of the Haggadah—the Seder (fig. 6). This scene is inserted in the decorative framework of the

text beginning with *Pour out thy wrath upon the heathen.*
It is a peculiar Seder. There are no women present—only
nine men. Of these, six are seated and three are partly
hidden behind those seated, but their faces are seen very
clearly. Five of the seated men hold one hand on a book
and the other raised in speech. They are evidently the five
rabbis mentioned above. The sixth man, who is young,
holds one hand on a book and the other in his lap under
the table. He is the wise son. He touches the book while
asking his questions, but does not gesture because he is
not required to reply. The three in the rear have strikingly
moronic faces. Their hands are not visible, nor do they
sit at the table. They are inarticulate and are excluded
from the symposium. There are *matzot* on the table, but
no wine. While the interpretation of the five figures representing the rabbis at B'ne B'rak is offered here for the
first time, the four others were correctly identified as the
Four Sons by August L. Mayer, co-author of the
Darmstaedter Pessach Haggadah. However, Bruno
Italiener, the editor of the work, rejected his suggestion
without elaboration.[7]

In some Haggadahs only four of the sages of B'ne
B'rak are portrayed in a group; in others each one is
depicted separately. An example of a recumbent position
on a couch is the posture of Rabbi Eliezer in the sixteenth
century Italian Haggadah, formerly at the Stadtbibliothek at Frankfort a.M., 725/17. He reclines on a bolster
or mattress.

While some illustrators gave serious thought to the
problem of portraying the B'ne B'rak meeting, others
employed the figure of a scholar sitting with a book for
any of the sages, without individualizing them. This figure
also delineated the other commentators who are mentioned in the Haggadah. Outstanding among them is
Rabban Gamaliel, particularly important because he
formulated the three basic symbols of the festival. He
appears in the early fourteenth century Spanish Haggadah
in the National Museum at Sarajevo, Yugoslavia, as a

teacher seated in a chair and holding a scourge, the medieval emblem of the teacher.[8] Three students are seated facing him. It is he and the Elders who are associated in Tosefta Pesahim X.12 with the story of the all-night Seder. They were "reclining" in the house of Boethus son of Zenon, in Lydda, studying the prescriptions for Passover until the cock crowed. Then they "shook off the remainder of the food and went to the *Bet ha-Midrash.*"[9] From this version it is evident that the meeting was held at a meal.

After the destruction of the Temple, while the Haggadah was still in flux, Passover was celebrated in the houses of men versed in Scripture. Obviously, the women did not take part in these meetings.

THE FAMILY SEDER

The medieval Haggadah illustrators in Spain directed particular attention to the portrayal of the Seder. This was not a scene of the biblical Passover meal with *your loins girded, your shoes on your feet, and your staff in your hand; and ye shall eat it in haste* (Ex. 12.11), which was popular with the illustrators of Christian Bibles. The Haggadah illustrator was interested in the family Seder of his own time and place. He depicted every detail of the ceremonial with delight and with pride in its beauty. In a miniature of the Sarajevo Haggadah we see the master of the house at the head of the table resting his left arm on a pillow and holding a cup of wine in his right hand. His little son stands facing him, evidently asking the Four Questions. At the other end of the table are the mistress of the house, another young woman and a man. In medieval manuscripts figures at a table are usually shown "behind" the table facing the spectator. Figures seated on the front side of a table necessarily had their backs to the beholder; they were not easy to draw and were therefore avoided. In our scene a dark-skinned servant girl is seated at this side of the Seder table, but the rear view is skilfully avoided as she is shown in pro-

300

file. On the table are *matzot,* a wine decanter and a bowl of eggs. The white tablecloth is laid in dainty drapery folds, and a brass lamp and a Moorish glass lamp are suspended from the ceiling. The colors used are shades of light brown, brick red, olive green and a dark purple blue.[10]

Particularly rich in Seder scenes is the British Museum (Add. 14761) Haggadah of Spanish provenience, mentioned previously. The series starts with a procession of men displaying the symbolic foods (fig. 7). One carries a tray with *matzot,* another an egg container, still another a radish, and the leader of the procession holds a bunch of bitter herbs. The fifth man (the one before the last) performs the rite of washing the hands. In one Seder scene the emphasis is on the leaning gesture. Even the mistress of the house rests her head on her hand. This is contrary to Pesahim 108a, which exempts the wife from the duty of reclining. She is enjoined, however, to drink the four cups of wine, because "women are subject to the law of the four cups since they too were included in the miracle." In another Seder scene of this Haggadah, illustrating the passage "This is the bread of poverty," the father takes the cloth-covered basket from a servant girl who is carrying it on her head, perhaps to illustrate the custom of lifting the *matzot.* The daughter is on the mother's right and the son on her left; and there is also a guest. There are three Haggadahs and wine on the table. A green curtain, spangled with golden stars, drapes the wall, and three brass lamps are suspended from the Gothic vaults. A framework of grotesques, peacocks, pine-cones and pomegranates decorates the page. Other scenes illustrate the benedictions, the *Kiddush* and *Habdalah.*

In other Haggadahs the emphasis is on the preparation for Passover. In the small Spanish Haggadah (British Museum, Or. 2737), a series of scenes is devoted to cleansing, scouring (fig. 9) and baking.

One should not expect a strict division of ritual and

301

historical episodes in Haggadah illustration. In the thirteenth century Spanish Haggadah (Crawford I, formerly Earl of Crawford Collection, now in the John Rylands Library, Manchester), we find on one page the following scenes: in the upper part, slaughtering and roasting the lamb and painting the doorposts with the lamb's blood; in the lower part, two contemporary family Seders.[11] The lamb has not been eaten at the Passover meal since the destruction of the Temple, nor has the painting of the doorposts been observed. (The Samaritans are the only group which still celebrates Passover in the ancient manner.)

THE PARABLE OF THE FOUR SONS

Biblical passages (Deut. 6.20; Ex. 12.26,13.14 and 13.8, in that order) contain injunctions addressed to the father to teach his sons the meaning and significance of Passover as a commemoration of the liberation from Egyptian bondage. There are slight variations in the wording of these injunctions, which the authors of the Haggadah ingeniously used to portray four types of sons reflecting different intellectual levels, as well as different emotional and social attitudes. The four types of the Haggadah are: the wise, the wicked, the simpleton and the child who "knows not how to ask" intelligent questions. In the Haggadah, the wise son asks what the festival means to "us"; he clearly identifies himself with his ancestors. The wicked son asks what the service means to "you"; he dissociates himself from the community. In the biblical passages this difference is less apparent because both sons use the words "you." In the third biblical reference the son asks, "What is this?" The abruptness of the question was interpreted by the Haggadah author as the son's inability to express himself articulately. In the fourth passage, there is no dialogue. The text reads: *And thou shalt tell thy son* . . . (Ex. 13.8). The failure to ask was connected with the limited mentality of an innocent child. Basically, the Four Sons are types of students with different abilities to learn. The wicked, however, has become a product of the social pressures upon a minority. He is hostile to the group and is ready to desert it.

As depicted in the illustrations, the wise son is generally a scholar; he therefore resembles the sages in appearance. The wicked is more pointedly characterized. In the Spanish Haggadah (Crawford I) [12] he is a Moor with helmet, curved sword and shield. Only the wise and the wicked are portrayed in this Haggadah. In Ashkenazi Haggadahs the wicked son is a German soldier (fig. 8). The simple-minded son, more difficult to portray, is sometimes shown raising his hands in helpless astonishment. In the fifteenth century Haggadah, known as the Washington Haggadah (Library of Congress, Washington, D.C.),[13] with Italian features in lettering and illustration, the simpleton is, curiously enough, a man sitting with an open book. Only in contrasting him with the wise son, also sitting with an open book, do we discern the difference. The inquisitive mind of the wise son is associated here with vigor and self-discipline. He sits on the cushioned seat of a straight-backed chair, his feet on a footstool, the book spread in his lap, presenting a neatly dressed, serene and composed figure. The simple son, his head and body wrapped in a heavy cloak, sits huddled, with his book clumsily held before his near-sighted eyes.

The child in Haggadahs is usually portrayed as a fool. In the fifteenth-century German Nuremberg II Haggadah (Germanisches Nationalmuseum, Nuremberg), he wears a fool's cap, a yellow coat and red trousers, and hops around like a clown. His behavior is that of an irresponsible child.[14]

We have seen how the illustrator of the Darmstadt I Haggadah has converted the four different sons into students (fig. 6). The wise student is admitted into the company of the teachers, while the three others are excluded. There are certain telltale facial expressions in the three poor students. The student on the left with shifting eyes may be intended as the wicked son. The one with a

303

chin band attached to his headdress may be the feeble-minded, while the figure on the right listening intently but unable to understand, seems to be the student whose mind is not yet mature enough to absorb and digest. The two rabbis to whom he listens ignore him completely. The Four Sons presented a psychological problem with which the artist could not always cope. He therefore sometimes portrayed only two or three of them.

THE EXODUS AND OTHER BIBLICAL MOTIFS

The passage *And the Lord brought us forth out of Egypt with a mighty hand, and with an outstretched arm* (Deut. 26.8) is amplified in the Haggadah by the words: ". . . not by the hands of an angel, and not by the hands of a seraph, and not by the hands of a messenger, but by the Holy One Himself." In keeping with this statement, the Haggadah mentions Moses only once, in passing. The illustrator usually portrays two, sometimes more, phases of the Exodus. Obviously referring to Exodus 14.8 *(The children of Israel went out with a high hand)*, He shows the fugitives on the move with their arm raised to heaven. Moses is not recognizable in the crowd; he receives due credit, however, in the second scene. This depicts the crossing of the Red Sea, based on the biblical text: *And the Lord said unto Moses: "Wherefore criest thou unto Me? Speak unto the children of Israel, that they go forward. And lift thou up thy rod . . ."* (Ex. 14.15). Upon God's command Moses then takes over. In the scene of the crossing and pursuit he is clearly identified by his imposing figure and his rod. In the Spanish Haggadah (British Museum, Add. 27210), a late thirteenth century manuscript illustrated in the French style of the period, both scenes appear on one page (fig. 10). The conception of "Exodus" and "Crossing" is similar in the Haggadah of Sarajevo in the sense that Moses is identified only in the scene of the "Crossing."

A figure entirely missing in the text of the Haggadah is Miriam, Moses' sister. After the defeat of the Egyptian pursuers, she and her maidens celebrated the victory with timbrels and with dances (Ex. 15.20-21). The group of young women is depicted in the above-mentioned British Museum Haggadah (Add. 27210),[15] in the small Spanish Haggadah (British Museum Or. 2737), in the Sarajevo Haggadah, in the much cited British Museum (Add. 14761), and in the Spanish Kaufmann Haggadah (David Kaufmann Collection, Hungarian Academy of Sciences, Budapest),[16] which is closely related to Add. 14761. Very popular also was the episode of the "Finding of Moses," with Miriam watching the maidens of the Egyptian princess wade in the nude in the Nile River to pick up the infant Moses. This scene appears in Add. 27210[17] and in the Kaufmann Haggadah.

Besides the amplifications of the Exodus story, some Haggadahs offer an extension of the narrative cycle to include the book of Genesis. Julius Schlosser suggested that the Creation pictures in the Haggadah of Sarajevo may have been inspired by the Sabbath *Kiddush* recited on Passover when the festival falls on a Sabbath.[18] The first part of the Sabbath *Kiddush* reads: . . . *the sixth day. And the heaven and the earth were finished, and all the host of them. And on the seventh day God finished His work which He had made; and He rested on the seventh day from all His work . . .* (Gen. 1.31-2.2).

The illustrator of the Sarajevo Haggadah completes his series of the days of creation with a "picture" of the Lord, a seated figure resembling the figures of the rabbinical sages, facing the depiction of the sixth day. It would be difficult to explain why the Spanish Haggadahs (British Museum, Add. 27210 and Or. 2884) start with illustrations of Adam and Eve, unless we simply invoke the tendency of human nature to trace events to their beginnings. There was, in addition, the temptation for the Haggadah illustrator to borrow from the contemporary historiated Christian bibles with their meticulously detailed pictures. The historically conceived biblical cycle

305

ends in the Haggadah of Sarajevo with pictures of the Temple, the distribution of *matzot* and the synagogue.

While the Haggadah illustrator of the thirteenth and fourteenth centuries in Spain delights to dwell on the historical background of the Passover story, the illustrators of the French, German and Italian Haggadahs of the fifteenth and sixteenth centuries become interested in the psalms and in poetical pieces which were gradually added to the text of the Haggadah. Such figures as Daniel, Esther, Belshazzar, Sihon and Og, and others, lent themselves to attractive pictures, but their presence is justified only by the casual references to them in the supplementary hymns. As the chronological series beginning with Genesis were being dropped, figures and episodes from the later biblical books, often inserted in the text, became popular. To this type of illustration belongs, for instance, the figure of the psalmist who invokes the Lord: *Out of my straits I called upon the Lord* ... (Ps. 118.5). In the late fifteenth century Italian Haggadah, formerly Rothschild Haggadah, Nr. 24, now in the Bezalel Museum, Jerusalem, the man, obviously King David, is seen literally squeezed between steep rocks.

Some biblical figures owe their inclusion in the illustrations of the Haggadah to legendary episodes associated with them. Such is the "Test of the Infant Moses" which appears in the Ashkenazi fifteenth century Haggadah (Nuremberg II) as well as in the Spanish fourteenth century Kaufmann Haggadah. In the epic narrative style of the Spanish illustrator, the story occupies two scenes on a separate page. In the upper scene the infant Moses puts Pharaoh's crown on his head, to the consternation of Pharaoh's counsellors identified by inscriptions as Jethro, Balaam and Job (See above, p. 147). In the lower scene Moses is put to a test with coals and onyx stones. As the story is told in *Sefer ha-Yashar*, Moses reached out for the onyx stones. This would have cost him his life, for his choice would have proved that he had acted with discrimination when he removed Pharaoh's crown. The angel

Gabriel guided Moses' hand toward the pan with the burning coals, which burnt the hand. As he touched his mouth to ease the pain, he also burnt his tongue, and this accounts for his speech defect. Thus, in the scene below, the infant Moses is seen guided by the angel toward the coals (fig. 11). In the fifteenth century Nuremberg II Haggadah, the episode is recounted in a little drawing inserted in the text in the sketchy, humorous style which has become characteristic of the group of Haggadahs referred to as the Nuremberg type (fig. 12).

Another motif inspired by legend, recounted in *Midrash Bereshit Rabbah* 44, is Abraham's miraculous escape from a burning furnace. It is to be found in the sixteenth century Paris Haggadah (Bibliothèque Nationale, cod. hebr. 1388).[19] The motif of the prophet Elijah as the forerunner and herald of the Messiah, although based on Malachi 3.23, was inspired by folklore, as was the figure of the Messiah, educed from Zechariah 9.9. They appear in a number of fifteenth century Haggadahs and are together in the Munich Haggadah (cod. hebr. 200, Staatsbibliothek, Munich).

The difference in interpretation and emphasis between a Sephardi and an Ashkenazi Haggadah is particularly striking in the treatment of the problem of drunkenness. The restriction against having more than four cups of wine at the Passover meal must have provoked merriment and humor at the Seder table. Inevitably Noah's drunkenness was recalled. In the Haggadah of Sarajevo (fol. 6), Noah is depicted reclining *uncovered within his tent* (Gen. 9.21). It is the moment before the sons brought him a garment to cover his nakedness. The scene is part of the biblical series, and no attempt is made to draw a lesson from it, jestingly or otherwise.

In the German Haggadah (Nuremberg II), we find allusions to the story of Noah's planting a vineyard (Gen. 9.20), as it is told in Midrash Aggadah to this passage.[20] Satan had a hand in the planting. He slaughtered a lamb, a lion, a pig and a monkey over the planted seeds. The vine, fed with the blood, acquired the characteristics of the animals, and transmitted them to those who tasted of its fruit. A person would be like a lamb when he took a little wine; he would feel strong as a lion when he drank moderately. However, if he drank excessively he would become like a pig wallowing in mud; and if he drank to the point of intoxication, he would become like a gamboling monkey—singing, telling obscene jokes, unaware of what he was doing. Thus in the Nuremberg II Haggadah, the man drinking his second cup sits in a little house which looks like a spice box being carried by a pig. For those familiar with the legend, the picture did not need any comment. There is allusion to another phase of the story in the picture of a lion with a bird's head being attacked by a small child. The lion appears to be a very weak support for the house and there are other subtle suggestions in this Haggadah pertaining to the tale and its moral.

WOMEN IN THE HAGGADAH

Women are not mentioned in the Haggadah except in some of the directions for the Seder which were added at a later date. Evidently, the reason was that in the mishnaic period the Passover meal was attended only by men, and the Haggadah was created for fathers to relate to their sons and for teachers to instruct their students. The Haggadah illustrator sought to bridge this gap. This is readily understandable, since there is a considerable difference in social background between the period when the text of the Haggadah was compiled and the time the illustrations were first conceived, not earlier than the thirteenth century.

In the illustrations it is the family meal which is the center of interest, whereas the all-male party at B'ne B'rak is often not quite understood. The illustrated medieval Haggadah shows the mother, the daughter and even the servant girl participating in the Seder. Women are prominently represented also in the gallery of biblical figures created by the illustrators—figures not found in the text, or mentioned only in later supplementary hymns.

In some fifteenth century Haggadahs a woman is shown reading a book. Although several copies of the Haggadah are shown on the Seder table of the family in earlier illustrations, one may now see a woman with her own book. The sight was not unusual in a period when fictional and edifying literature existed in Judeo-German and other Jewish dialects intended for a female audience. The reading zeal of the women in the Darmstadt I Haggadah may be somewhat exaggerated, but we meet the new type of woman also in other Haggadahs, such as the late fifteenth century Ashkenazi Haggadah, Crawford II (formerly Earl of Crawford Collection, now John Rylands Library, Manchester) (fig. 13).

The sixteenth century Italian Haggadah introduces a more worldly type of woman. We find her for instance, in the Haggadah no. 750, dated 1515, of the Elkan Adler collection at the Jewish Theological Seminary of America, as the elegant and poised mistress of the house at the Seder table. In another Haggadah (formerly of the Stadtbibliothek Frankfort a.M., 725/17), she appears on the title page. This reflects the influence of the printed book, since in manuscripts the information about the book is given by the scribe in a colophon at the end of the text. Here we find a beautiful young woman, dressed in the taste of the High Renaissance, standing before a seated older man and holding up a large book to him. Wearing eyeglasses, he points out to her, with visible enjoyment, some passage in the book (fig. 14).

With this background in mind, it is amusing to find in fifteenth and sixteenth century Haggadahs a jest of which the butt is a woman. While lifting his hand and exhibiting the bitter herb, the man points to the woman. In the German fifteenth century Haggadah (Munich, cod. hebr. 200), the little picture is inserted on the right margin, close to the word *maror*. The man and woman, obviously a couple, sit on a bench together. Holding the bitter herb

309

in his lap, he extends his hand and points to her head, while she recoils from him in mock indignation. This little scene is also found in the sixteenth century Haggadah Rothschild, Nr. 24.[21] It obviously refers to Ecclesiastes 7.26: *And I find more bitter than death the woman whose heart is snares and nets.* Somewhat different is the picture in the Italian Washington Haggadah, dated 1478. Here both the man and the woman are standing, and he is so much taller than she that they appear to be an incompatible couple. He carries a bunch of bitter herbs in one hand and holds his other on her head, while she grasps a sword. According to an interpretation by Dr. Irving Levey, cited by Landsberger, this scene refers to Proverbs 5.4, where the "strange" woman is said to be *bitter as wormwood, sharp as a two-edged sword.*[22]

The printed Prague Haggadah of 1527 is careful enough not to include such a picture. However, above the woodcut depicting a man holding the *maror,* there is an annotation that in some places there is a custom (*minhag*) for the man to point at the woman while exhibiting the bitter herbs in order to demonstrate the biblical caution that a wicked wife is more bitter than death. The custom must have disappeared, as did the picture.

MONKEYS AND HARES

While most of the pictorial images of the Haggadah were derived from the Bible and from its paraphrases and legendary amplifications, some of the illustrative topics were garnered from heterogeneous sources. The Franco-German Haggadah (Crawford II) indicates the dangers of excessive drinking through a fable about the capture of monkeys, from Aelian's "On the Nature of Animals" (*De natura animalium,* VII. 25), which is also found in a French bestiary.[23] According to this tall tale, all the huntsman needs to do to capture monkeys is to leave boots and wine where they congregate. Intoxicated with wine, the monkeys put on the boots and cannot escape. The story must have been popular enough to prompt the artist to illustrate it.

A common subject for illustration in the Haggadah of German-speaking areas was the hare chase. The picture of the hare hunt is to be found, among others, in the fifteenth century Cincinnati Haggadah of the Hebrew Union College.[24] Above the picture are inscribed the words יין, קדוש, נר, הבדלה, זמן. The German transliterated initials of the Hebrew form the words *Jag' den Has* (*Jknhs*), that is, "Chase the hare." These words are a mnemonic for the sequence of the benedictions to be recited when the evening of the Seder and the termination of the Sabbath coincide. Usually the inscription over the picture is omitted, for the reader mentally associates the words with the picture.

PICTURES OF THE SYNAGOGUE

A pictorial image, whatever its source, was usually in some way related to the content of the Haggadah. Either it represented a figure referred to in the text or it emphasized some feature of the ritual. Pictures of the synagogue do not seem to belong in the iconography of the Haggadah. The Temple, whose restoration is the theme of several prayers in the Haggadah, appears there as a matter of course, either as a building alone, as in the Sarajevo Haggadah, or in the scenes depicting the arrival of Elijah or the Messiah. However, the link with the synagogue is not apparent, for the Passover synagogal liturgy belongs to the *Festival Prayer Book*. The presence of a synagogue interior in some Haggadahs is accounted for by an inscription in the fourteenth century Spanish Haggadah (British Museum, Or. 2884), which runs above the miniature portraying a synagogue (fig. 15). The picture shows men, women and a child seated in a vaulted hall illumined by Moorish glass lamps. On the *bimah,* the reader stands holding a book, which according to the inscription is a Haggadah.[25] In the group of worshippers we discern a man and a little boy each holding a book, and the elder raising his left hand to point out a passage to the child. Thus it appears that the Haggadah or portions of it were being recited in the synagogue in the Middle Ages in Spain.

The position of the synagogue picture in the Spanish Haggadahs varies. In the Haggadah of Sarajevo it is included in the full page set of miniatures, where it is preceded by pictures of the Temple and of the distribution of *matzot*.

In the Spanish Haggadah (British Museum Add. 14761) and in the related Kaufmann Haggadah, a synagogue scene is set in the text of Psalm 113, which shows the reader lifting a Torah scroll(!). The two pictures are similar in conception but different in design. According to the Mishnah, the *Hallel* was chanted in the period of the Temple during the sacrifice of the paschal lamb.[26] Was the picture of the synagogue intended to replace that of the Temple at this point of the recital of the Haggadah, or was the *Hallel* during Passover read in the synagogue from the Haggadah? Here is a question for the ecclesiologist.

THE ARTISTS OF HAGGADAH MANUSCRIPTS

A study of the Haggadah illustration shows a certain basic pattern which was sometimes amplified and enriched. The variable element was the biblical material not directly connected with the Exodus. The naive, narrative presentation of the pictorial matter, characteristic of the thirteenth and fourteenth century Spanish Haggadahs, gives way to the more subtle, witty and sketchy style of the Ashkenazi Haggadahs of the fifteenth century. Under the influence of the Italian Renaissance, however, the northern linear style softens again. The history of the illustrated manuscript Haggadah of the thirteenth up to the sixteenth century reflects a certain cultural and population trend in Jewish history. Spain, Germany and Italy mark the stations along the road. Actually, French and Italian influences may, on closer scrutiny, be discerned already in the Spanish Haggadahs. But the specifically northern, skimpy, dry and ironic style was the product of a *Galgenhumor* the Jew acquired in the fifteenth century under the impact of his political experience. Only the contacts with Italy and its more mellow style could soften the crudity and harshness of the "German" style. This raises the question of the identity of the artists who illustrated the Haggadah manuscripts. Medieval artists, illuminators of books in particular, seldom signed their works. It was usually the scribe who wrote the dedication to the patron who had commissioned the work, and if he himself was not also the illustrator, he was likely to omit mention of his collaborator. The Bible of the Bodleian Library in Oxford (Kennicot I), completed in 1476 in Coruna, Spain, is unique in possessing two colophons—one of the scribe, and the other of the illuminator, Joseph ibn Hayyim.[27]

The colophons in Haggadah manuscripts usually mention the scribe and the scribe's work. One scribe, Joel ben Simeon Ashkenazi of Cologne, called Feibush (Phoebus), has been identified in a number of manuscripts. In two instances he calls himself the designer and painter. The works signed by this name or a variation of it, show German and Italian influences characteristic of a number of fifteenth century Haggadahs. A whole literature has arisen around this name, and the question was raised if it represented the same person in all cases and if the ornamental and figure designs were by the same hand.[28] We still lack a well-organized photographic collection of material from illuminated Hebrew manuscripts—a prerequisite for thorough research.

The Illustrated Printed Haggadah

THE HAGGADAH OF PRAGUE

The first complete Haggadah with woodcut illustrations was published in 5287 (1527) in Prague, by Gershom ben Shelomoh ha-Kohen and his brother Gronem.[29] The late Lazarus Goldschmidt had in his possession a Haggadah which he regarded as a somewhat earlier version brought out by the same printers. The woodcuts are inserted on the margins of the pages; the tall designs are on the side borders and the broad ones on the lower margins. Some woodcuts are used to illustrate more than one figure or episode. The man reciting the *Kiddush* reappears as Rabbi Elazar ben Azariah. The wise son stands also for Rabbi Akiba. Rabbi Eliezer and Rabban Gamaliel are portrayed by the same figure. To cut new wood blocks for every figure was more expensive and more time consuming than to draw or paint a figure by hand. Thus, the printed book brought about an impoverishment of illustration, while conferring the great advantage of accessibility to the average person. The relationship to non-Jewish book production became closer when cuts made for Christian Bibles and for other books could be borrowed from printing shops and re-used, although in some cases they had to be redesigned, and this involved cutting new blocks. Thus we find in the Prague Haggadah such popular pairs as Adam and Eve, David and Goliath, Samson and Judith (not Jacob and Esau, as has been suggested)—the latter representing male and female heroes of the Bible—figures familiar from German woodcut books. These standard figures were used, however, in the outer framework of the pages, merely for embellishment.

The figures illustrating the text were fairly well adapted and treated more individually. The illustrator, evidently familiar with some manuscript Haggadahs, was anxious to follow certain traditions. The passage *And thou didst increase and grow up, and thou camest to excellent beauty: thy breasts were fashioned, and thy hair was grown; yet thou wast naked and bare* (Ezek. 16.7), applying to the city of Jerusalem, is illustrated in the Prague Haggadah by a young woman with luxuriant long hair, her body slightly draped. This allegorical portrayal of Israel is already found in a fifteenth century manuscript Haggadah (Munich, cod. hebr. 200).[30]

A new feature inspired by the passage *I took your father Abraham from beyond the River* (Josh. 24.3) is a little scene showing a young oarsman in a boat with an older bearded man. The publishers of the facsimile edition of the Prague Haggadah did not recognize the relationship of this picture to the lines printed just above the woodcut.

The Four Sons are typified in the usual way. The jest mentioned above about the wife and the bitter herb is not illustrated. There is a charming little Seder scene with the grandfather presiding at the table. The father sits on the far side in the center, with a guest on his right; and the little son is with his mother at the other end facing the grandfather. The roasted lamb on a platter does not actually belong in the family Seder; it may have been copied from a Passover meal in a Christian Bible. The paragraph beginning with "Pour out thy wrath" is illustrated in the traditional way by the prophet Elijah riding on a donkey.

Despite the borrowings from Christian materials, the illustrations were patterned, on the whole, on an Ashkenazi fifteenth century Haggadah manuscript. The type is of remarkable beauty, closely approximating Ashkenazi manuscript Hebrew characters. Some of the initial words are ornamented with conventional Renaissance foliage and with animal and human forms. The architecture in the framework and the costumes are typically German Renaissance. The Prague Haggadah has a printer's colophon at the end and no title page—still in keeping with the practices of the scribes.

THE MANTUA HAGGADAH

A new set of illustrations was created in a woodcut Haggadah published in Mantua in 1560. A number of scenes were taken over from the Prague Haggadah but were redesigned. The allegorical female nude is there. Abra-

315

ham with an oarsman in the boat has been placed in a seascape. David with his harp and Elijah were borrowed, but not exactly copied. The Seder preparation scenes were enriched by adding the baking of *matzot* to the search for the *hametz*. A second Seder scene was added, with the rising sun visible through the open door. One would think this might be the B'ne B'rak scene; however, among the seven figures seated at the table there are women. The hare chase appears in both the Prague and the Mantua Haggadahs.

Some of the models of the Mantua Haggadah have been identified. Such discoveries are, of course, a matter of chance, particularly when the model is not one of the famous works of art. Julius Schlosser[31] readily recognized the model of one of the rabbis of B'ne B'rak, represented as a single figure (in the edition of 1560 it is Rabbi Akiba), as the Jeremiah from Michelangelo's Sistine Chapel. The Haggadah illustrator placed a hat on the figure's head. The simpleton son in the Haggadah has his prototype in the fool mentioned in Psalm 53.2, in Holbein's *Historiarum Veteris Instrumenti Icones* (Lyons, 1538).[32] The title page of the 1568 edition of the Mantua Haggadah, with Mars and Minerva in the framework, turned out to have been used in various publications, and originally appeared in a non-Jewish book about 1500.[33]

THE EDITIONS OF THE VENICE HAGGADAH

The culmination of the efforts of the illustrators of the woodcut Haggadahs was reached in the Haggadah published in Venice in 1609. It appeared that year in three editions with identical pictures, but with the captions to the woodcuts in different languages—Italian, Spanish (Ladino) and Yiddish (Judeo-German)—printed in Hebrew characters. A detailed description of the illustrations would require a special study. We mention the further expanded Seder preparation scenes and the arrangement in the margins of biblical heroes in pairs—Moses and Aaron, David and Solomon, to whom in later re-issues

316

Isaiah and Jeremiah, as well as Samuel and Elijah were added. There are thirteen little Seder scenes, all placed on one page of this folio Haggadah. These scenes are arranged in two columns of six in each, with a broader one underneath as a base. The ten plagues are arranged in similar fashion. Most charming is the B'ne B'rak scene with the rising sun visible in the window. The five rabbis sit around a table with books and wine, but no *matzot*. Some lean in the traditional way, while others raise their hands in gestures of speech. Two students have entered the room; one points to the sun, the other to the outside, reminding the rabbis that it is time to leave for the synagogue.

Many scenes of the Venice Haggadah form the background of the initial letters which are inscribed in square panels. There we find the little son asking the Four Questions and also the four types of sons characterized in an entirely new way. The wise son is a young fellow dressed like the student in the B'ne B'rak scene. He carries something that looks like a scripture scroll, with a lamb walking meekly at his side. The wicked son is an unruly boy who mischievously kicks the lamb his father is about to slaughter. The simpleton, a smaller lad, watches his father working on the slaughtered lamb, but does not help him. The "child" runs after a hobby-horse his father points out to him, for all he can be expected to do is to play with toys. It is striking that the social undertone in the characterization of the wicked son is completely lacking here.

There are numerous scenes from the story of Abraham. In the scene of the sacrifice of Isaac, the postures of Abraham, Isaac and the angel were inspired by Ghiberti's famous relief, evidently known from prints. It also shows some original features inspired by Jewish legend.[34] Most amusing is the double scene depicting on one side the drowning of the sons of the Israelites by order of Pharaoh, and on the other a couple practicing abstinence so as not to have children. Bruno Italiener has found this motif

317

more symbolically treated in the sixteenth century Italian Haggadah (Bibliothèque Nationale, cod. hebr. 1388).[35] Another woodcut shows the Temple of Jerusalem, looking like the Dome of the Rock, surrounded by the booths of the Twelve Tribes. In the foreground of this scene the Messiah is riding on a donkey, preceded by the prophet Elijah sounding his horn.

THE AMSTERDAM HAGGADAH VARIATIONS

The Venice Haggadah marks the end of the supremacy of Italy as a center of Hebrew book production. Amsterdam, with its important Spanish and Portuguese Jewish community and its German group gaining strength and status, takes the lead in the second half of the seventeenth century. The Haggadah printed in Amsterdam in 1695 was intended for both the Sephardi and the Ashkenazi rituals. The reader is informed on the title page that the pictures previously printed from woodcuts "were not so pretty." They are now printed from engraved copperplates. It is pointed out that everyone can see the difference is "like light and dark." The title page of this edition carries the name of Abraham bar Jacob, "from the seed of our patriarch Abraham," and states that he engraved the picture of the Temple and the map of Palestine marked with the wanderings of the tribes. The expression "from the seed of our patriarch Abraham" is held to imply that he was a proselyte. Abraham bar Jacob is said to have been a Protestant pastor from the Rhineland. Although no further data about him have ever turned up, his name appears on some other engravings in Jewish books.

The character of the illustration of the Amsterdam Haggadah seems to confirm the belief that the artist was not born in the Jewish faith. Most striking from the outset is the total absence of ritual scenes. The family Seder is missing. The episodes illustrated could have been taken from the Bible. There is, however, the scene of the rabbis at B'ne B'rak and also the Four Sons. As I was able to prove elsewhere, the illustrations were borrowed from engravings of Matthaeus Merian of Basel.[36] Merian the Elder was the head of a thriving workshop in Frankfort-on-the-Main. He produced, with his sons and assistants, a considerable number of illustrated Bible editions, among them Old and New Testament selections (*Icones Biblicae*) and a folio Luther Bible which appeared in Strasbourg between 1625 and 1630. Dutch editions were published about 1650, without date. The popular engravings were often copied. While some of the biblical scenes in the Haggadah were outright borrowings, others were modified to harmonize with the requirements of the Haggadah text. The episode of the five rabbis at B'ne B'rak offered some difficulties. For his purpose, the engraver adapted Merian's illustration of Joseph entertaining his brethren. The engraver was in a dilemma because of too many figures at the banquet table. He therefore removed some. There are nine men in his B'ne B'rak scene. The Four Sons presented another problem as it was not easy to find models for them. The wise son could be any figure wearing a stately long garment. The engraver showed some ingenuity in selecting the appropriate figure for the simpleton from Merian's vast opus. "Saul anointed by Samuel" served the purpose. With his head bent to receive the anointing oil, Saul looked the part. Samuel was, of course, deleted. A Roman soldier from Merian's set for biblical and profane history was an appropriate model for the "villain": the wicked son. The "child" was originally "Hannibal vowing eternal enmity for the Romans," from *Historische Chronica* by Johann Ludwig Gottfried, published in Frankfort in 1657 with Merian's engravings. In lifting the figures out of their context but retaining their postures and grouping them all together in a row, the illustrator achieved a strange and rather quaint effect. It was this strangeness that made the figures so impressive. They have ever since become the pattern for the Four Sons of the Haggadah.

The family Seder is wanting in the Amsterdam Haggadah, as has been previously mentioned. Instead, we have the biblical Passover meal, consumed "in haste." This scene reconciles us somewhat to the illustrator's manipulations; for Merian, too, had taken it from another source. His model was the Passover meal by Hans Holbein, from the Luther Bible, Basel, 1523. As a matter of fact, pirating was common practice. It is rather our engraver's vast knowledge of Merian's publications that we find amazing. Although he is credited on the title page only with the picture of the Temple, which he also took from Merian's Bible, and with the map, he obviously produced all the engravings. The publishers may have regarded the Temple and the map as more likely to attract customers.

As interesting as was this new Haggadah, the users could not remain unaware of its shortcomings. Another Amsterdam printer undertook in 1712 a new edition with the same engravings, redesigned and slightly modified and, what was most important, with the inclusion of the three sets from the Venice Haggadah: the Seder scenes, the plagues and the initials. Aside from the initials, which were printed from woodcuts, the two other sets were printed from copperplates, especially engraved for the new edition. Thus was created the most popular Haggadah, known to everyone from numerous versions and re-issues—including many recent editions printed by commercial firms for advertising purposes.

The Amsterdam Haggadah became the manual for the self-taught Jewish artists who were now emerging everywhere. The texts were copied by hand and the engravings redesigned and touched up with colors. The hand-painted Haggadahs of the gayer eighteenth century possess the charm of the provincial baroque and rococo styles. The facial types and the costumes became Judaized, and dainty little details of domestic life were added. In these Haggadahs appear illustrations of the latest text additions— the songs "One Kid" and "Who Knows One." A rather coarse attempt to illustrate "One Kid" is already found in a Haggadah manuscript of 1693 produced in Darmstadt by a Joseph Leipnik.[37] He is evidently identical with Joseph son of David from Leipnik, in Moravia, who produced a Haggadah in Altona in 1705.[38] A hand-painted Haggadah owned by Lazarus von Geldern, the great-grandfather of Heinrich Heine, was the model of the Haggadah described by Heine in his famous story *The Rabbi of Bacharach.* The Von Geldern Haggadah is dated 1723. It is signed by the scribe Moses Judah, called Loeb, son of Benjamin Wolf Broda from Trebitsch in Moravia.[39] An earlier version of 1716-1717 is the so-called Second Cincinnati Haggadah (Hebrew Union College-Jewish Institute of Religion, Cincinnati) signed by the same scribe (fig. 16).[40] The fine miniatures of these manuscripts were evidently the work of this scribe.

A particularly interesting Haggadah with hand-drawn illustrations, partly copied and partly inspired by the engravings of the Amsterdam Haggadah, was produced in Amsterdam in 1738. It is in the Kunstgewerbe Museum in Frankfort. Another, dated 1740, is in the British Museum.[41]

Revival of Haggadah Illustration

With the revival of the graphic arts in the twentieth century, attempts were made by some Jewish artists to recast the illustrations of the Haggadah. Joseph Budko's etchings (1921) were rather timid and too gentle for the folksy little book. More convincing were Jacob Steinhardt's expressionist wood engravings (1923) which had the merit of conveying the mood of frustration engendered by World War I. Menachem Birnbaum devoted a whole volume (1920) to the *Had Gadya* song which offered him an outlet for his riotous colors. Siegfried Guggenheim's Haggadah, with woodcuts by Fritz Kredel of Offenbach (1927), breathes the rarefied air of the Nazarene paintings of a hundred years earlier. Arthur Szyk was hailed as the rediscoverer of the technique of medieval illumination (1941). He did not avoid a certain prettiness typical of most revivalisms. Some Haggadahs

321

were illustrated in a pseudo-Egyptian style; others exhibit simple, unpretentious pictures strictly for children. The Reconstructionist Haggadah, designed by Leonard Weisgard (1941), offers schematized, precisionist figured scenes.

The modern Haggadah illustrator finds his resources greatly enriched. He has access to the public collections of manuscripts and prints, the scholarly publications, and the re-issues of Haggadahs which appear at an undiminished pace every year. It remains for him to follow the traditional pattern or to set out to create something new. The Haggadahs published in Israel are still in an experimental stage. The experience of statehood should give the artist in Israel a new outlook, a new evaluation of the meaning of the Passover Haggadah, and a new interpretation of its images.

Passover Ritual Appurtenances

Some of the pictures of the Haggadah cycle found their way into the decoration of the plates for the symbolic dishes used at the Seder. Fewer than a dozen Italian majolica plates are extant; they are painted with scenes from the Venice Haggadah and from other sources. The plates have concavities around the border for the prescribed foods. The shallow, flat depressions have molded rims which make them appear deeper than they are. While the center of the plate is inscribed with a prayer or a psalm from the Haggadah, the concavities on the border are decorated with floral designs and figured scenes. A plate signed on back "Jacob Kohen Ancona 5414" (1654), exhibits in the broad oval cavities the Passover meal of Exodus and the sacrifice of Isaac. Both are from the Venice Haggadah. In the narrower compartments are the figures of Moses and Aaron, and of David and Solomon, from the same Haggadah. The text in the center of the plate begins with "This is the bread of poverty." The biblical scenes on one seventeenth century plate were taken from the vault paintings of the loggias in the Vatican, executed by pupils of Raphael in 1519 (fig. 25).[42]

Plates made of pewter, regarded as the poor man's silver, were much used for the Seder in Germany and in Holland. They were often decorated with engraved scenes from the Amsterdam Haggadah.[43] The nineteenth century marks the decline of this production; the engraved scenes become coarser. China plates appear, painted with Jewish scenes from Moritz D. Oppenheim's well-known series (1800-1882). In that more prosperous age, silver trays and plates, usually with chased flower decoration, were also used. For the prescribed three *matzot*, three-tier plates were produced in silver with fixtures on top for cups and other containers.

Perhaps the most interesting and rarest pieces are the pottery bowls and jugs inscribed "L'Pesach," of which only a few are known. A blue-gray glazed jug in Nassau pottery in the Gewerbemuseum, Stuttgart, first half of the nineteenth century, bears the inscription "Moshe Segal, for Pesach" in a heart-shaped frame surrounded by doves.[44] A small German faience bowl, eighteenth century, and another of Italian provenience, both inscribed "L'Pesach," turned up at an auction in New York in 1956.[45] Wine cups used at the Seder are actually *Kiddush* cups and are usually so designated. Wine cups inscribed for the prophet Elijah seem to be of later date.

A particularly interesting object is the *Laantuch* at the Landesmuseum in Kassel (German, seventeenth century). It is a piece of white linen with woolen embroidery in red and blue, measuring 35 by 165 cm., with an attached piece of damask. According to Rudolf Hallo, it is a case for the Seder pillow. Hallo believes that the name *Laantuch* was derived either from *Leinen* (linen) or from *sich anlehnen* (to lean). The embroidered decoration consists of lions flanking a vase and parrots. A similar piece of linen, with wool embroidery in dark green, brown and yellow (German, about 1700), is inscribed in Hebrew on the borders, "This is the bread of poverty . . ." The cen-

323

ter is decorated with a hare chase.[46] Unusual is a printed red linen tablecloth inscribed with blessings for the Sabbath and the holidays, measuring 5 ft. 8 in. by 3 ft. 1 in. and made in Augsburg, 1765.[47]

Linen Seder towels of the eighteenth and early nineteenth century, with wool embroidery depicting biblical motifs, were shown in 1932 in Marburg at the Exhibition of Religious Art from Hessen and Nassau.[48]

After its historic transformations, the Passover Seder was established as a family meal with the participation of parents, children, relatives and guests. It is both a solemn occasion because of its commemorative character and a gay one because of the presence and active participation of the children in the ritual. The table is laid with the best tablecloth, often especially made for the occasion. Plate and glass, down to the tiny wine cup of the youngest child, is different, beautiful and meaningful. No wonder the family Seder is one of the fondest recollections of childhood!

BOOK THREE

Passover for Young People

When thy son asketh thee in time to come, saying: "What mean the testimonies, and the statutes, and the ordinances, which the Lord our God hath commanded you?" Then thou shalt say unto thy son: "We were Pharaoh's bondmen in Egypt; and the Lord brought us out of Egypt with a mighty hand."

Deuteronomy 6.20-21

The Train that Knew about Pesach[1]

(age level four to six)   SADIE ROSE WEILERSTEIN

Daniel was going to Grandpa's for Pesach and there wasn't anything he liked better than going to his Grandpa's for Pesach.

First there were the *matzot,* and the wine and nuts, and the Pesach candy Grandma made. *Then* Grandpa lived in a far-away city, and you had to ride there on a train with an engine and smoke and steam. And *then* there was the Seder, and Daniel would sit on cushions and look at the queer pictures in the Haggadah, and stick his tongue into his little silver wine cup, and *then*—and this was most important of all—there were the Four Questions, and *Daniel* was going to ask them.

"*Mah nish-ta-nah ha-lai-lah ha-zeh.*"

Daniel said it over and over. He said it while Daddy was buying their tickets in the station. He said it while they were getting on the train. He said it while Daddy was lifting the suitcase—with Daniel's new Pesach shoes in it and his new Pesach suit—and setting it on the rack. He was saying it when the train man called "All aboard," and he was saying it when the train started off.

Then all of a sudden Daniel stopped saying *mah nish-*

327

ta-nah, and sat right up straight. From under the train where the wheels were going round and round, the queerest sound was coming:

Matzah, Matzah, Matzah, Matzah,
Matzah, Matzah, Matzah, Matzah.

Daniel listened to make sure. There it was over and over:

Matzah, Matzah,
Matzah, Matzah.

"Now, do you suppose," Daniel thought, "this old train knows about *Pesach*?"

The wheels answered as plainly as can be:

For Pesach,
For Pesach,
For Pesach,
For Pesach.

Then suddenly there came a S-S-S-S-S of steam, and the train was saying:

S-S-s-e-der.

Like that.

S-S-s-e-der.

Danny jumped from his seat. He was so excited.

"Did you ever see such a wise old train?" he cried. "It knows about Pesach; it knows about *matzah*; it knows about the Seder. What else does it know?"

At that moment the wheels began another song:

Mah nish-ta-nah,
Mah nish-ta-nah,
Mah nish-ta-nah,
Mah nish-ta-nah.

"If it doesn't know about the *mah nish-ta-nah,* too!" cried Danny. He was so astonished.

"But there is one thing you don't know, Mr. Train. Who's going to ask the *mah nish-ta-nah*?"

At that very moment and second the engine opened its deep throat, and the whistle called:

Toot-too-OOO-OO
You-you-ou-ou.

29. Passover Plate. Pewter

Alsace-Lorraine, 18th century

Germany, 19th century

30. Seder Plate. **Silver**

31. Seder Plate. Silver

Vienna, 1807

32. Seder Plate. Silver

After that Danny didn't ask any more questions. He just sat still and listened; and all the way the wheels kept singing:

Matzah, Matzah, Matzah, Matzah,
For Pesach! For Pesach!
S-S-S-se-der.
Mah nish-ta-nah, Mah nish-ta-nah,
Mah nish-ta-nah, Mah nish-ta-nah.
Who-oo-oo?
You-ou-ou-ou!

Until the trainman called, "Rochester!" And there was Grandpa waiting to lift him from the train.

The Story of K'tonton, A Mouse and a Bit of Leaven[2]

(age level five to seven)   SADIE ROSE WEILERSTEIN

Pesach was coming. K'tonton* sat on the rim of a basket swinging his legs. It was a big bushel basket filled with all-the-year-round dishes waiting to be carried to the basement. "Clitter, clatter, clitter, clatter!" went the dishes. K'tonton liked the sound. It made him think of the special Passover dishes that would soon be shining on the shelves, Seder plates, bowls for salt water, silver wine cups. It made him think of the special things he would eat in the special dishes—*matzah* and *matzah* balls, nuts and preserves and Passover candies. It made him think of the gleaming Seder table and the Four Questions he would ask.

"*Mah nishtanah ha-lai-lah ha-zeh?* Why is this night different from all other nights?"

* K'tonton was a tiny boy, no bigger than your thumb.

329

K'tonton's body swayed in rhythm to the words. He lifted his hands from the rim of the basket—and plump! He had tumbled from his seat and was in among the dishes. Down, down he went, past cups and saucers and frying pans and kettles. As he reached the bottom he heard his mother's voice.

"This way, Joe! Take the basket down to the basement and leave it there. Here's the key."

K'tonton felt the basket lifted. He was being carried off.

Clump! Clump! Clump! went Joe's feet down the stairs.

"Joe! Joe!" called K'tonton. His voice was lost in the clatter of dishes.

Clump! Clump! Clump! went Joe's feet from the landing to the basement.

The basket was set down.

"Joe! Joe!" called K'tonton, his voice growing shriller.

But Joe was whistling a gay tune.

K'tonton heard the scraping of a key in the lock. The whistling died away. He was alone, locked into the basement in a basket of dishes. Passover near and he in a basket of *hametzdik* dishes! And he'd have to stay there! No one would think of coming down until Passover was over. Father and mother would have to have their Seder alone. K'tonton thought of the little seat Father had made him piled high with wee cushions so that he too might lean like a free man. Mother always set it on the arm of Father's couch. He thought of the Seder dish with the bitter herbs and *haroset*, the roasted egg and lamb bone and parsley. Who would ask Father the Four Questions? Even a king and queen couldn't be happy on Passover with the prince away.

K'tonton pressed his cheek against the side of the basket. He was too sorry for himself to think, too sorry for himself even to try to escape. And then—something tickled his cheek. There was a queer sound in the room. Squeak! squeak! K'tonton sprang to his feet and peered out through a hole in the basket. A mouse! A little grey mouse had brushed past him with its whiskers. There it was underneath an old broom talking away to another mouse.

"Well, I dropped that crust and scurried off faster than the twinkle of a tail. You can feel my heart thump yet."

"Tsk, tsk, tsk!" squeaked the other mouse. "So the crust is up there on the shelf? I wouldn't mind having it right now. Since they began that housecleaning upstairs, I haven't dared venture out of my hole. That terrible woman with the rag round her head! Always opening drawers and shutting them and sweeping out corners and letting in the light. I'm that thin, you can feel the bones in my body."

The two mice went off shaking their heads about the dreadful state things had come to.

But K'tonton wasn't listening any longer. He was too excited about the first bit of information. The mouse had said it had left a crust on a shelf. It must be the shelf in the back pantry. Mother had said there was a mouse hole there that had to be stopped up. Passover coming and a crust on the shelf! Leaven in the house on Passover. And the Bible said as plainly as can be, *Seven days there shall be no leaven found in all the borders of thy house.* No, no! It couldn't be! He must escape somehow, out of the basket, out of the basement! Father wouldn't make the final search for leaven until that night. If he could reach the shelf in the pantry before sundown there would still be time.

K'tonton's eyes ran quickly along the sides of the basket. One opening was larger than the rest. He stuck his head into the hole and squeezed. The rough wood scratched his arms, it tore his trousers, but he pushed through. He was out of the basket. Now to escape from the basement.

A glimmer of light came down from a grated window high above. A fishing pole leaned against the grating. K'tonton hurried to the pole, grasped it firmly and began climbing up. Up and up he went, hand over hand, hand over hand. The pole was slippery. K'tonton began sliding back. He pressed his knees more firmly against the pole and went on. He must reach the top. There would be no leaven in the house on Passover if he, K'tonton, could help it. The window at last! K'tonton grasped a bar and slipped through the grating. He was safe in the spring sunshine. A dandelion nodded a greeting, but K'tonton had no time to answer, not with *hametz* lying on the shelf.

Skippety, hop, run, hoppity, skip, run went K'tonton to the doorway of the house. The door was open—good! But the stairs! How was he to climb those stairs? K'tonton stood at the foot of the lowest one and threw back his head. The step rose before him like a stone wall. And the sun had already reached the house tops. He must do something quickly! But what?

Someone was running down the walk! The grocer's boy with a basket in his hand! K'tonton sprang up on the boy's shoe. Up the stairs went the grocer boy, two steps at a time, and up the stairs went K'tonton holding fast to his shoelace. The grocer boy banged on the door, left the basket and turned. K'tonton slid from his shoe and slipped in through the open door. There was no time to look for Mother. Evening was coming on.

K'tonton hurried across the shadows on the kitchen floor, down the hall, into the pantry. Up the packages of *matzah* he climbed, holding on to the string, over the *matzah* meal sack, round a wine jug to the shelf. The mouse had been right. A wee bit of bread lay in a corner. K'tonton seized it in his hand. His heart was going pit, pat, patter, as fast as the mouse's had gone. How tired he was!

He sank down on the shelf to rest for a moment. His eyes closed. He was asleep.

K'tonton's mother looked up anxiously as Father entered the room.

"Any news?"

"None! And you?"

"None! I've hunted everywhere."

Even in the darkness Mother's face looked tired and anxious.

"We'll have to make the search for leaven without him, Father. See, it's already dark."

Mother lit a bit of candle. Father picked up a feather and a wooden spoon. They sighed. The search began. A bit of bread lay on a table. Whisk! Father brushed it into his spoon. Another one on the bookcase! One on a bureau, a chair! Now they were in the living room. Now in the kitchen. Now in the pantry. What was that queer looking crust in the shadow at the back of the shelf? Father touched it with his feather. It sprang to its feet. It wasn't a crust at all. It was K'TONTON! There he stood in the circle of light made by Mother's candle.

"K'tonton! K'tonton! My precious one!" cried Mother. "What happened? How did you get here?"

But K'tonton was too busy to answer.

"Bring your spoon quick, Father. There's *hametz* here!"

He opened his grimy little palm and dropped into Father's spoon the wee bit of leaven.

Only then did K'tonton tell Mother and Father the story of his day's adventures.

The Story of Passover

(age level six to nine)   DEBORAH PESSIN

Many many years ago the Jews were slaves in the land of Egypt. A cruel and mighty Pharaoh, who wanted to make his land beautiful with palaces and monuments of stone, ruled over the land. And Pharaoh said, "Let the Hebrews make bricks for my palaces and buildings."

Now the Hebrews were a shepherd people. They had come to Egypt from Canaan or Palestine many years before, when there was a famine in Canaan. They built their homes in Goshen and grazed their flocks of sheep. And now Pharaoh said, "Let the Hebrews be my slaves."

The soldiers of Pharaoh marched into Goshen and gathered the men and the strong lads. The women and children wept as the soldiers led off the men and boys. All day the Hebrews made bricks and worked at building. At night they returned and fell on their mats and wept. They were no longer free men. The new Pharaoh had forgotten that Joseph, a Hebrew, had saved Egypt from famine.

Pharaoh became more and more cruel. He feared that the Hebrew slaves would rise up against him. So one day he ordered that all boys born to the Hebrews were to be cast into the Nile River. Without men, thought Pharaoh, the Hebrews would become weaker and weaker.

Then there was much sorrow in Goshen. The Hebrews wished they had never come to Egypt and they longed for Canaan, the land of Abraham, Isaac and Jacob.

One day a Hebrew woman called Yochebed had a child, a strong and beautiful boy. She hid him carefully and watched over him day and night. But Yochebed feared that Pharaoh's soldiers would discover the child. So she took a basket and filled the cracks with tar. And she wrapped her little boy in a blanket and put him into the basket and covered him, took the basket with the child to the bank of the river and placed it among the rushes.

"Hide behind a tree," Yochebed said to her daughter, Miriam, "and see what happens to the child. Perhaps he will be saved by some kind Egyptian. May the God of Israel guard him and watch over him."

Miriam hid and waited. Suddenly she heard soft gay voices. She peeped out and saw a group of maidens in beautiful gowns. They came closer and closer, and at last

334

Miriam could see who they were. The princess, daughter of Pharaoh, had come to the river with her maidens to bathe.

"What is that thing I see there in the rushes?" she asked.

"It looks like a basket," one of the maidens answered.

"Fetch it for me," said the princess.

Miriam's heart pounded as a maiden waded out to the rushes for the basket. And when she returned with it the princess lifted the blanket and saw the child.

"A baby! It must be a Hebrew child. I am going to keep him," said the princess, looking into the little boy's eyes. "I will raise him in the palace, as I would my own son. And I am going to name him Moses, for I drew him out of the water."

"But you need a nurse for the child," said one of the maidens.

"Yes," said the princess, "I must find a Hebrew nurse."

Then Miriam ran from her hiding place and rushed to the side of the princess. "I know a nurse," Miriam said eagerly, "a Hebrew woman."

"Bring her here," the princess said.

Miriam ran off, and soon she returned with her mother Yochebed.

"Take this child," said the princess, "and nurse him for me."

"I will care for him as if he were my own son," said the happy Yochebed. And Yochebed took her son home with her and nursed him. As Moses grew up, his mother told him about his people, and of the land of Canaan where they had once lived.

"You will soon go to live in the palace," Yochebed would say. "But you must never forget that you are a Hebrew. Perhaps, when you are a man, you will be able to help free your people."

When Moses went to live in the palace, he did not forget what his mother taught him. The fine glittering palace, the beautiful horses and chariots that the princess gave him, did not make him forget that his people were slaves. He wanted to help them, but he did not know how.

So Moses grew to be a young man in the palace. And one day he went out to the fields where the Hebrews were making bricks, for he wished to see his people.

The sun shone hot on the large fields. Stripped to their waists, the men and boys toiled on, without stopping for rest or food. Over them stood the taskmasters, their whips in their hands. Moses saw an old man lift a pile of bricks to his back. The man took a few steps, stumbled and fell to the ground. A whip came down on his back, again and again. With a cry of anger, Moses sprang forward and tore the whip from the hand of the taskmaster. Then he struck the taskmaster with all his might. And to his great surprise, the man fell to the ground, dead.

MOSES FLEES FROM EGYPT

The next day, when Moses returned to the fields, he heard many people talking about him and the taskmaster he had slain. Moses feared that if Pharaoh learned that he had killed an Egyptian, he would be thrown into prison, or perhaps be killed. And Moses decided to flee from Egypt.

That night he left the palace, and he went to the wilderness. For many days he wandered on and on and at last he came to Midian.

Now in Midian there lived a kind priest called Jethro. Jethro's daughters were shepherdesses who grazed their father's sheep. And it happened that when Moses reached Midian and sat down near the well to rest, Jethro's daughters came there with their sheep. Moses was very kind to the shepherdesses. He lifted the heavy rock from the well and helped them draw water for the flock. When Jethro heard of the kind stranger at the well, he sent for him and Moses lived in Jethro's home.

Moses remained in Jethro's home for many years. He became a shepherd, and every day he took Jethro's sheep to the grassy places at the edge of the desert. And he married Zipporah, one of the daughters of Jethro, and was very happy. But often he would think of his people in Egypt and he wondered whether he would ever be able to help them.

One day, when Moses was near Mount Horeb with his sheep, he saw a bush in flames. The bush burned and burned, and still it did not burn up. Moses came closer to the bush, to see why the flames did not burn it. And suddenly he heard a voice come from the burning bush.

"Take your shoes off, Moses," said the voice, "for the ground on which you are standing is holy."

Moses took off his shoes and bowed his head, for he knew that the voice was the voice of God.

"I wish you to return to Egypt," said the Lord, "to free My people from slavery and lead them to the promised land of Canaan."

But Moses was afraid to go, for he feared Pharaoh.

"Do not fear, Moses," said the voice, "for I will be with you. You will take Aaron, your brother, with you and you will speak to Pharaoh in the name of the God of Israel."

MOSES, THE LEADER OF HIS PEOPLE

The next day Moses set out for Egypt. When he came to Egypt he and his brother Aaron went to the palace of Pharaoh.

"We have come in the name of the Lord of Israel to ask you to let the Hebrews go to the wilderness to worship their God," Moses and Aaron said.

But Pharaoh laughed and said, "Why should I let the Hebrews go? They may not want to return. No, they shall not leave the land."

"The Lord has commanded that you let them go," said Moses.

"I am not afraid of you or your God," said Pharaoh. "I will not let the Hebrews go."

And Moses and Aaron left the palace of the king.

Then many plagues came upon Egypt. There were

337

grasshoppers and insects who came in great clouds and ate the crops. There were frogs, and darkness, and hail. Each plague became worse and worse. Cattle grew sick and died. The Egyptians cried out to Pharaoh to let the Hebrews go. And each time Pharaoh promised to let the Hebrews go if Moses would remove the plague. But when the plague was lifted from the land, Pharaoh's heart became hardened, and he refused to allow the children of Israel to leave the land.

One day God spoke to Moses and said, "I have brought nine plagues upon Egypt. I will bring one more, a dreadful plague, and then Pharaoh will beg you to take the Hebrews out of the land. Therefore, tell My people to be ready to leave Egypt.

"Tell them also to prepare a lamb each for every family. And let them have a family feast and eat the roasted lamb with *matzot* and with bitter herbs. Every year, at this time, in all the many years to come, they must eat *matzot* for seven days to remember the time they were slaves in Egypt. And I will take My people out of the land of Egypt in the middle of the night."

Then Moses told his people all that the Lord had said. And that night, a terrible plague came upon Egypt—the first-born son in every Egyptian family died. But the plague passed over the homes of the Hebrews.

In the middle of the night Pharaoh called Moses and said, "See, my own son has died of the plague, too. Now take your people out of Egypt, quickly."

FREE AT LAST

And Moses hastened to take his people out of the land of suffering and slavery. The children of Israel were very happy to leave. At last, they were free again. Each family roasted a lamb and ate it as Moses had told them. Then, in the middle of the night, they left Egypt. And because they had no time to wait until their dough leavened, they baked unleavened bread or *matzot*.

On and on the Hebrews traveled in the wilderness until

338

they reached the Red Sea. Then they looked back, and they saw the army of Pharaoh following them on their horses and in their swift chariots.

And the people were frightened and said to Moses, "Why did you take us out of the land? Is it to die here, in the wilderness?"

But Moses said, "Do not fear, for the Lord is with us."

Then Moses held his staff out over the Red Sea, over the tumbling waters. And suddenly the water parted and became two towering walls. Between the walls there was dry land. Quickly the Hebrews passed through the Red Sea on the dry land. When they reached the opposite shore they looked back and saw the army of Pharaoh rushing toward them between the walls of water. Then the walls of water began to sway and tremble, and with a roar they fell on to the dry path between them. The rushing waters covered the army of Pharaoh. Horses and riders were covered by the waters of the Red Sea.

Safe on the shore stood the children of Israel. They danced and sang hymns of praise to their God who had freed them from the slavery of Egypt. Then they turned, and with Moses leading the way, they began their long, long journey to the land of Canaan, to Palestine.

Habibi and Yow Go to Grandfather's for Seder[4]

(age level seven to ten)   ALTHEA O. SILVERMAN

"So many people!" exclaimed Habibi, counting the silver winecups on Grandmother's Seder table. "It looks as though all our aunts and uncles and cousins are coming to the Seder."

339

Habibi and his little spaniel, Yow, had come to Grandmother and Grandfather for the first Seder. Tomorrow night they would go for Seder to the other Grandmother and Grandfather.

"What would we do if there were three Seders?" Habibi had asked. "We only have two grandmothers and two grandfathers."

Grandmother's table was already set with wine cups and Haggadahs and a beautiful olivewood *matzah* holder for the three whole *matzot* that Grandfather would use for the Seder service.

Yow, Habibi's little black spaniel, was frisking about the room, excited and eager for the relatives to arrive. He liked holiday gatherings, for at these gatherings he was allowed to sit with the guests at the table and to show off some of the tricks Habibi had taught him.

"We're going to have a special guest," Grandmother said. "His name is Eliyahu, Elijah, the Prophet."

"Elijah the Prophet?" Habibi gasped. "Is he coming here tonight, Grandmother? I always wanted to see Elijah the Prophet. Uncle Peter told me that, with four strokes of his wings, Elijah can travel all over the world. He can be everywhere at the same moment. And he doesn't always dress the same or look the same. Sometimes he looks like an old man, sometimes like a beggar, and sometimes he may even be dressed as a prince."

"That's right," said Grandmother, "but the thing to remember is, that wherever Elijah goes, he makes people happy."

Grandmother put the largest silver wine cup next to the olivewood *matzah* holder at Grandfather's place.

"For a special guest like Elijah, we must have a special wine cup," she said.

"Elijah, Elijah the Prophet," marveled Habibi, his eyes gazing rapturously upon Elijah's special silver wine cup.

Into the dining-room came Mother, carrying a large Seder dish. On the Seder dish were grated horseradish

340

and fresh green sprigs of parsley and a roasted shank-bone and a roasted egg.

"All we need now is *haroset*," said Grandmother, and she went into the kitchen to mix some fresh *haroset*.

"I'd like to help you, Grandmother," said Habibi stirring the reddish-brown mixture in the bowl.

Grandmother added a dash of this and a dash of that.

"Chopped apples and nuts and sweet, red wine,
I put in a bowl to mix, mix, mix.
I then add some cinnamon,—and guess what I have?
Haroset—the color of deep red bricks."

She gave Habibi a teaspoonful to taste. It was sweet and delicious.

One by one the aunts, uncles and cousins began to arrive, and soon it was time for the Seder to begin.

The table stretched from one end of the room to the other and was set with Grandmother's beautiful blue and gold Pesach dishes which she used only during the week of Pesach. The candles gleamed and the spring flowers in the center of the table were pink and golden and purple. Habibi's cheeks were flushed and Yow's eyes twinkled as he sat perched high on a stool right next to Grandfather.

At the head of the table sat Grandfather, dressed in a white robe which he called a *kittel*. On his snow white head was a white skullcap, at his left, a fluffy-white pillow.

Father helped pour the Pesach wine into the silver wine cups.

"We'll give a full cup of wine to Elijah," he said, filling Elijah's cup to the very brim.

"Will he drink it all?" asked Habibi, wide-eyed with wonder.

"He may just take one sip," said Father. "After all, he must drink Pesach wine at each Seder all over the world, and a full cup of wine at every Seder might be too much, even for Elijah."

Grandfather raised the first cup of wine. They all rose for *Kiddush,* even Yow.

After *Kiddush* came the moment for which Habibi waited!

Grandfather took part of the middle *matzah* from the middle compartment of the olivewood *matzah* holder and hid it carefully under the fluffy-white pillow at his left.

"The *afikoman!*" exclaimed Habibi.

"Yes, the *afikoman,*" said Grandfather, a twinkle in his eye. "And I intend watching it all evening, so don't anyone get a notion to try and take it."

Habibi winked at Uncle Peter. Uncle Peter winked back in a wise, understanding way. They had arranged to work together to secure that piece of *matzah* from under the fluffy-white pillow, and Habibi knew, that with Uncle Peter's help, the *afikoman* would surely be his. He had already decided on the reward he would ask for its return.

Ruth, Habibi's cousin, opened the front door wide.

"All who are hungry, come in and eat," Grandfather read from the Haggadah. "All who are in need, come in and celebrate the Seder with us."

"Now for *mah nishtanah,* the Four Questions," said Grandfather when the door was closed. "Who will say the *mah nishtanah?*"

All eyes turned to Habibi. He was the youngest at the table.

"I will say the *mah nishtanah,*" said Habibi, and without another word he rose and chanted the *mah nishtanah.* He knew the Four Questions by heart.

"*Mah nishtanah ha-lailah ha-zeh mi-kol ha-laylot?* Why is this night different from all other nights? Why must we eat only *matzah?* Why must we eat bitter herbs? Why must we dip parsley in salt water and bitter herbs in *haroset?* Why must we lean as we sit at the table?"

And this is how Grandfather answered Habibi's Four Questions:

"Our forefathers were slaves to Pharaoh in Egypt," he explained. "Tonight we celebrate their freedom from bondage. They had to leave Egypt in great haste and therefore had no time to bake bread, so they took their dough with them and the hot sun baked the dough into flat cakes which they called *matzot*. That is the answer to your first question.

"And now for the answer to your second question. We eat bitter herbs because the Egyptians made the lives of our forefathers very bitter. When we eat the bitter herbs —the horseradish—our eyes fill with tears to remind us of the tears they shed when they were forced by cruel masters to make bricks.

"We dip the parsley in the salt water to show that in the springtime, green things begin to sprout from the earth, and we dip the bitter herbs into the sweet brick-colored *haroset* to show that even though life was bitter for our forefathers when they made bricks in Egypt, the hope of freedom was sweet. That, Habibi, answers your third question.

"And now for your fourth question. We lean at the table tonight because our forefathers became free men, and free man, in olden times, reclined when they ate."

When the first part of the Seder service was over, a delicious Pesach dinner was served. There were hard-boiled eggs and *gefilte* fish and *knaidel* and roast lamb and chicken and *tzimmes* and so many other good things to eat that Habibi felt as stuffed as a goose. Yow ate and ate so much that he had to get down from off his stool and stroll through the rooms for exercise.

At last Habibi saw his chance!

Grandfather was telling a story. Father and all the aunts and uncles and cousins were listening to grandfather and had quite forgotten the *afikoman*. Now his time had come!

Quietly, without a sound, Habibi edged down from his chair and crept softly, slowly, towards the head of the table, towards the place where the fluffy-white pillow lay at Grandfather's chair.

He slipped his hand underneath, cautiously, stealthily,

343

farther and farther. He felt with his fingers. He felt with his hand. He reached upward and downward, to the right and to the left. But there was no *matzah*. There was no *afikoman!*

For a moment his heart seemed to have stopped beating.

"Who could have taken that *afikoman?*" he wondered.

He hadn't seen anyone go near the fluffy-white pillow, and he had watched closely all evening long.

As he made his way back to his chair, sad and disappointed, he caught Uncle Peter's gaze. Uncle Peter smiled and winked his eye.

Habibi's face brightened. "Uncle Peter must have taken the *afikoman*," he thought. "That's all right. He said he would help me get it." The boy began to feel happy again.

After what seemed ages to Habibi, the meal ended. Grandfather was ready to say grace. But first they must all eat portions of the *afikoman*.

Grandfather stuck his hand underneath the fluffy-white pillow.

"It's gone!" he announced. "The *afikoman* has been taken."

Habibi's eyes sparkled. He knew who had the *afikoman*. Soon he would ask for his reward, and Grandfather would have to give it to him, for otherwise he would not return the *afikoman* and then how could Grandfather conclude the Seder? He smiled at Uncle Peter. Uncle Peter smiled back.

"We must have the *afikoman*," said Grandfather. "We can't proceed without the *afikoman*."

No one said a word.

"Ruth," asked Grandfather, "did you take the *afikoman?*"

"No, Grandfather," replied Ruth. "I didn't take the *afikoman*."

"Aunt Judith," asked Grandfather, "did you take the *afikoman?*"

"No, I didn't take the *afikoman*," said Aunt Judith.

"Cousin Elaine, did you take the *afikoman?*" asked Grandfather.

"No, I didn't take the *afikoman*," said Cousin Elaine.

"Who then took the *afikoman?*" asked Grandfather. "Someone at this table must have taken the *afikoman*. We've got to get it back or we can't proceed with the service. Whoever took the *afikoman*, speak up!"

Everyone looked at Habibi. He flushed to the roots of his curly red hair.

"Habibi has the *afikoman!*" they said.

Habibi was embarrassed. He really should have gotten ahead of Uncle Peter. He wished he had taken the *afikoman* himself.

He went over to Uncle Peter and whispered in Uncle Peter's ear. Uncle Peter's face dropped.

"I haven't got the *afikoman*," he said. "I thought you took it."

"It wasn't there when I tried to get it. I was so sure that you had it, Uncle Peter." The boy's voice quivered. He was very close to tears.

"Well, where is the *afikoman?*" everyone asked.

No one at the table seemed to have the *afikoman* and no one seemed to know what had become of it.

"This is a nice fix," Grandfather said. "We can't say grace without first eating the *afikoman*, and we can't open the door for Elijah the Prophet until after we have said grace."

No one knew just what to do. They searched around the chair and under the chair. Perhaps the *afikoman* had slid down from under the fluffy-white pillow. But the *afikoman* was nowhere in sight.

Habibi gazed at the cup of Elijah filled to the brim with Pesach wine.

"How can we keep Elijah the Prophet waiting?" he thought bitterly. "Oh, how can we keep him waiting?" He minded that even more than the reward which he now would not receive.

345

"I guess we'll have to sit here until morning," said Grandfather.

Everyone was puzzled. No one knew what to do. They had given up all hope of finding the *afikoman* when suddenly, out of the kitchen, came the little black spaniel with a half cake of *matzah* in his little black mouth.

"YOW ! ! !" they all cried together. "Yow, was it you who took the *afikoman?*"

A smile seemed to flit across Yow's face. He walked directly over to Grandfather with the half cake of *matzah*.

Everyone was relieved. Everyone was amused. Yow, the little black dog, had poked his nose under the fluffy-white pillow and had taken the *afikoman*.

A shout of laughter went up from all at the table. Whoever heard of a dog taking the *afikoman?* Even Habibi forgot his disappointment and laughed and laughed until the tears rolled down his cheeks.

"That little dog," he said. "That little dog! What will he do next?"

"Who will get the reward?" Grandfather asked.

"Why, the dog, of course," everyone replied in unison.

"What can we give a dog?" Grandfather asked.

"I saw the nicest brass collar," Habibi said. "Won't you get that collar for Yow, Grandfather, please?"

Suddenly, from the street, came the sound of dogs barking. It seemed as if all the dogs in the neighborhood were barking together in one voice. Yow heard, and ran to the door.

"Elijah!" said Mother. "When Elijah the Prophet walks through the streets, even the dogs are happy. They bark for joy."

It was then that the door was opened for Elijah the Prophet.

Though Habibi strained his eyes and stared with all his might, he did not see Elijah enter. Cousin Ruth and Aunt Judith insisted they saw him sip some wine from his special wine cup, but Habibi, admitting that the cup did not seem as full of wine as before, was disappointed that he did not get even one glimpse of Elijah.

"It's because you didn't watch closely enough," Uncle Peter said. "Elijah must appear at every Seder in the world tonight and so he goes out so swiftly, that if you wink an eyelash, you're apt to lose sight of him."

"*Addir Hu, Addir Hu,*" sang Grandfather and all the aunts and uncles and cousins.

Habibi's eyes were beginning to get heavy. Before the *Had Gadya* was finished he was fast asleep.

Mother took him in her arms and carried him to bed.

"No night prayer tonight," she whispered. "On the night when Elijah the Prophet is about, we do not need to say our night prayer. He takes care of all of us."

"Elijah the Prophet," Habibi mumbled, "Elijah the Prophet. Tomorrow night at the second Seder, I won't—even—wink an eyelash. Then I'll be sure to see him, won't I, Mother?"

Mother kissed him and turned out the light. Soon Habibi was fast asleep.

And Habibi dreamed that at the second Seder, Elijah came and took the *afikoman.*

The Breakfast of the Birds[5]

(age level eight to twelve)   JUDAH STEINBERG

Two hundred and ten years were our fathers slaves, absolute slaves, to Pharaoh in Egypt. Everything that their masters commanded them, whether to break stones or to dig sand, whether by day or by night, that had they to do. Nor did they hope for pay, or dream that when their toil was over they could go free. They were bondmen.

Whenever the master bade the slave do two day's work in one, in that time it had to be done. Over him always was

347

the rod of the taskmaster to hasten his toil. His days were the days of his owner, who used them at will.

Should a man order his slave, "Cast thyself into the sea and drown," the slave did so. The life of a slave was the property of his master, by whose whim it was shortened or permitted to run its course.

Did the command come, "Part thy wife from her sons and slay thy daughters, that I may mix my wine and dye my apparel in their blood," even this also must the slave do. For whose are a slave's sons and daughters? The chattels of his master, bought with gold, even as are flocks and herds.

Such was the bondage of Israel in Egypt.

From morning until night did Israel toil, and darkness brought no rest. At daybreak there would sound a rapping at the door, and there stood the taskmaster whirling a scourge. The men arose from their couches and went out to hard labor. The women also arose and sod pottage which they fetched to their unhappy husbands in the fields. The little children were left at home; forlorn and lonely, they stole out of doors to look upon the sun.

Birds gathered and circled about their heads.

The little ones ran to gather the crumbs from the breakfast their mothers had left for them, and they fed the birds. The grateful songsters regaled them with tales of the land of the palm beyond the mountains. In their notes was the lapping of waters of the Jordan, in their chirping was the gossip of the rose of En-gedi. The cadence of their songs was as the lowing of the flocks pasturing on mount Gilead; they voiced the mysterious converse in the forest of Lebanon.

The birds sang laments over slavery, and chanted paeans to freedom. The children heard in awe, and questioned:

"Lovely birds, slaves are ye, or free?"

Joyful caroled the birds:

"Free, free, dearies, free;
 Where we list there fly we."

348

"This freedom ye sing of, birds, is it good?"
"Good!" echoed the birds:
  "Never let this be forgot:
  There's no good where Freedom's not.
  Starve and go an instant free;
  Feast not, slaves eternally!"
The birds lingered with the children, delighting the hearts of their lonesome playmates. When the fathers and mothers came home from the fields and prepared supper, the birds were again the guests of the children.
"God bless you!" called the children.
"The Lord shower you with blessings!" sang the birds as they flew away to their nests.
From the wing the birds counseled:
  "Think, oh think on what we say:
  Freedom learn to love alway.
  If they but determine so,
  Forth from bondage slaves can go."
Every day this happened, until the birds and the children became the closest of friends, and told their woes to one another.
Mourned the birds:
  "By an arrow Goldwing's slain;
  She will never sing again."
The children wept. Then they poured forth their sorrow. "Birdies dear! Little Naaman was taken to the palace. They will slit his throat that Pharaoh's leprosy may be cleansed in our playmate's blood."
Birds and children wailed in chorus for Naaman.
Days lengthened into years. Years became centuries. The children grew up slaves. The birds died or were slain.
The friendship descended through the generations. The birds loved the children and freedom. The children loved the birds, and yearned for freedom.
"Lovely birds, slaves are ye, or free?" questioned the children.
  "Free, free, darlings, free!
  In the cage dwells misery.

349

Above all, prize liberty."

Thus, morning after morning, they met and talked and separated. The children fed the birds with open hand, and the birds ate and were satisfied.

At length there dawned a morning when the birds sought their comrades, and lo! a new vision was before their eyes. Men and women with loins girt, staves in their hands and kneading-troughs on their backs, were hastening out of Egypt, leaving bondage forever.

The children saw the birds. They shouted:

"We're free! Birdies, we're free!

Forth we go to liberty."

How the birds clapped their wings and twittered: "Hurrah! Hurrah!"

One boy was heartbroken and cried and did not shout, for neither he nor his companions had bread crumbs for their friends.

The birds comforted him, saying that their breakfast could wait; then they trilled a gladsome lay:

"Better to hunger with the free
Than feast at board of slavery;
Follow where the fire-cloud leads
Freedmen's sons to freemen's deeds!"

Now the fathers were so hurried and walked so fast that little legs could not keep up with them, and the children lagged and lost the way.

Then the birds gathered together and flew before them to show the way, until they overtook their parents at the edge of the wilderness beside the sea.

It happened that the mixed multitude that had followed Israel felt a lusting in the desert for meat, and they cried, "Would that we were given flesh to eat!" The children of Israel all wept, and thought to return to the land of bondage and of flesh-pots.

Quickly the birds who heard gathered together, and twittered and twittered, uttering sounds that no human ear could understand. They took counsel, and this was the result: hosts of quail fell from the skies and came of glad purpose to the hands of men, that the lust of Israel for flesh food might be satisfied.

Thus the birds prevented the return to the land of slavery.

Even then the children mourned, for they had not a morsel of food for their loyal friends.

Sang the birds:

"No matter, dearies. Birds do not cry
For crumbs of bondage. They'd rather die.
Of Freedom's breakfast we'll take full share
In the days to come, in that land so fair."

Upon *Shabbat Shirah* the *Sidrah* of quails is read in the synagogue, retelling the story of the way in which the birds gave their lives to keep Israel's children free.

On that Sabbath it is the privilege of every Hebrew child to scatter crumbs for the birds. It is the breakfast of Egypt—the breakfast Israel's little ones owe the birds because they were unable to feed their saviors during the journey into the land of freedom.

Now must they pay the debt.

Today the songsters flutter at our windows. They eat out of our hands. They fly away.

Hark! Their song!—

"Sweet though feasts of the cage may be,
Sweeter to hunger and perish free."

It Is Good[6]

(age level ten to thirteen)   ISAAC LOEB PERETZ

On Passover I am always reminded of the hasidic rabbi, the *Zayde* (Grandfather) of Shpol.

In Russia, where I was born, many years ago, they had

351

a law which permitted the police to seize a young boy from his home and parents and enroll him in the army for twenty-five years. Well, you can imagine that being among non-Jews in the army for a quarter of a century made it pretty difficult to remain a Jew, and since I was one of those young boys, known as "cantonists," who were kidnaped and enrolled in the army, I know what that means.

If I am a Jew today it is only because of the *Zayde* of Shpol. Of course, when I knew him before I was kidnaped, he was only a young man who had come to our town as a *shohet*. He used to come to our house to slaughter cattle and poultry and sometimes just to pass the time of day. I loved him. He had a wonderful way with children and could tell the most interesting stories.

After a while, for some reason or other, he decided to leave town. He came to our house to bid my father goodbye and I cried and cried, and after he had left, I felt so bad, that I followed him. I wanted to stay with him. Just how that could be managed, I did not know; nevertheless, I followed him. It was not easy for a small fellow like me to keep up with him. He walked briskly and soon he was lost from sight. I entered the woods, but since I could not see him, I sat down under a tree to rest. Suddenly I heard a voice nearby. It sounded like his voice; I walked a little and soon caught sight of him. He was standing under a tree chanting *Shir ha-Shirim,* the Song of Songs.

When he had done, he returned towards me and said, "Listen, Yudel"—that's my name—"I have a request to make of you.

"I want you to remember your name, Yudel, for it comes from the Yiddish word that means 'Jew.' They are making you a cantonist. You will be going on a long journey. They will try to make you forget the Torah, your home and your parents. Probably they will succeed. But one thing I want you never to forget: always remain a Jew."

With that he turned and swiftly vanished.

Two weeks later, they came for me and hustled me off

to the army. I served far away from home, deep in the Russian wasteland and never set eyes on a Jew.

As time passed, I often thought of making things easier by taking another name, but whenever such a thought came into my head, the rabbi appeared before me in my thought, saying: "Keep your name; remain a Jew!"

Once they flogged me and his image stood by me and seemed to wipe the cold sweat off my forehead; he stroked my face, and said softly, "Don't cry out! Suffer in silence! Remain a Jew!" I bore the punishment without a cry, without a moan.

Once I was standing sentry duty. It was evening and a bitter snowstorm was raging. I saw some people walking past me in the blinding snow, and one of them said in Yiddish, "This is the first night of Passover." The words fell on my heart like lead and a longing came over me, a sort of heartache that is impossible to describe. I wanted to recite the Haggadah, but I couldn't recall a word of it. Not even the Four Questions which I used to ask my father. I had known them when I was only six years old. If only I could have recalled a single word, the rest would have followed. But my mind was blank. I couldn't remember.

"Lord of the universe," I cried, "one word; help me with only one word!" Just then the phrase *"Avadim hayinu*—we were slaves," came into my head. I was overjoyed. My prayer had been answered. And then the rest all came back to me, and as I paced up and down on my watch, with my musket on my shoulder, I recited and sang the Haggadah to the snowy world around. It poured out of me, word after word, like the links of a golden chain, like a string of pearls.

Meanwhile, the wind had died down. The snow had stopped falling and the sky became clear. It was quiet and there was a peaceful, shimmering whiteness all around. Suddenly something bright and shining appeared. It was the figure of a man in a *tallit*. A silvery beard gleamed in the moonlight and, above the beard, two shin-

353

ing eyes and a wrinkled forehead. As it approached and passed me, it said, *"It is good."*

The words sounded like the strains of a violin. The figure vanished. But it was the eyes and the voice of the rabbi whom I had known when I was a child.

I went to Shpol when I was released from the Army. I went right to the *Zayde* of Shpol, and told him my story. And he did not seem at all surprised.

A Passover in Spain[7]

(age level ten to fourteen)   BY CURTIS LUBINSKI

The sun shone down brightly on Seville. It was spring, and the proud capital of Andalusia was filled with a hum of excitement. Easter was coming, and the people of Spain loved holidays.

In the market place, a man slowly walked past the stands of the country merchants and turned into one of the side streets leading off the square. His eyes scanned the old building that stood well back from the street. He dipped down into a little bag he was carrying and checked a description. Good. This was the house. So far Providence had not failed him. He quickened his step. Now he was at the large, oaken door. He tapped sharply. The door opened an inch, and a pair of dark eyes peeped out.

"Yes?" It was a little boy's voice.

"Is this the home of Diego de Susa?"

"Y-yes."

"And you are his son, Fernando. Is that not so?"

The boy's eyes widened in surprise.

"Tell your father that I bring greetings from—Antwerp."

354

"Oh, come in!" The door swung open and the stranger slid in swiftly. "We have been waiting for you for so long. We thought you'd never come."

"I thank the Almighty," said Fernando's father, a tall, bearded Spanish grandee, who had been right behind his son. "You have arrived safely. You must be very tired. Come inside. Fernando! Bring us some wine."

The two men retired to the study. Fernando burned with curiosity, but there was nothing he could do about it, so he rushed into the kitchen to get the wine. When he returned, his father changed the subject of conversation. But at least the stranger had a name now. It was Abraham Mendes, and Fernando's father was telling him what it meant to be a Jew in Spain in 1510.

"It has been this way for eighteen years, you know. Little Fernando does not remember, of course, but we remember too well that second day of August in 1492 when we were exiled from Spanish territory by royal decree. Every Jew discovered on Spanish soil after that day was to be burned alive. But there is no need to tell you all this. You know it—else you would not be here."

Abraham Mendes put his arm around Fernando's shoulder. "Soon it will be different, young man." Fernando hungered to know more, but his father broke in.

"Is everything prepared, Mendes? There are many of us, you know."

"The arrangements are complete to the last detail. And it will be most fitting, since tonight is the eve of Passover." He paused. "Tell me, Señor de Susa, how did you know the date of Passover? I know that you marranos keep your faith alive within you, but I also know you dare not keep a Hebrew calendar, nor any Hebrew books."

Diego de Susa sighed. "That is true. But we have learned to watch for other signs, much like a blind man who develops his sense of hearing. This is March and tonight will be the full moon. Thus the heavens tell us that Passover has come."

355

"Truly amazing," Mendes said, almost to himself. "And thus you keep all our Jewish customs?"

"As many as we humanly can," De Susa replied. "Wait. I have an idea. Why don't you walk with us? You will observe how we Jews prepare for the Passover. And you will meet—at a distance, it is true—some of those whom you will get to know much better—in a little while." Fernando's father ended in a whisper, as though he were afraid the walls might have ears.

"May I go, too, Father?" Fernando spoke up bravely.

The two men looked at each other. "There will be no harm in that," said De Susa. "Fernando has known how to fool the king's guards almost since birth. Come along, my son."

They left the house and walked to the gardens which flanked the river Guadalquivir. In their broad berets and wide-sleeved velvet jackets they looked like any good citizens of Seville. Nobody paid any attention to them when they climbed down to the river bank. De Susa nodded to an old friend who stood at the water's edge. "It's all right," he whispered. "My companion is one of us." Abraham Mendes watched the old man cut a few willow branches and start to beat the waters of the river. A royal soldier passing by laughed loudly. "Ho, there," he shouted. "You won't catch any fish *that* way."

The soldier moved on. "You see," Fernando's father said, "the soldiers never even suspected our fellow-Jew. As you know, he wasn't fishing. Now he has observed our old Spanish custom of beating the waters to remind us of how the waters of the Red Sea gave way to Moses and his people when they left Egypt. And no one is the wiser. But it is hard. Very hard."

Together they moved through the winding streets. At last they reached the market place.

"Here we have to be most careful," Fernando said to the visitor. "You see, there are signs up all over the city telling people how to identify Jews. The posters are on

356

all the public buildings. And one certain way is to catch them buying food for Passover."

"And yet," the elder De Susa interrupted, "if you look sharply, you will see what Fernando and I see. But please pretend you are glancing about casually."

Abraham Mendes let his eyes rove over the crowd that thronged the merchants' stalls. People were buying food —a little parsley here, some nuts there, a head of lettuce, an apple or two. Never more than one fruit or vegetable at one stall, and always in tiny quantities.

"In that way no one suspects us," he said softly. "And this has been going on for eighteen years. Thank God that for many of us in Seville this awful secrecy will end —tonight."

Nearly a hundred people had assembled in the patio of the De Susa home when they returned there. Careful not to make any noise, they greeted each other with silent gestures. The only source of light in the patio was the pale glow of the full moon. The guests could barely be seen by its light. They wore heavy traveling shoes, held staves in their hands, and had a bundle thrown over their shoulders. They were observing another Spanish-Jewish custom, a custom that required that people dress for the Seder the way the Jews dressed when they left Egypt.

"Go ahead, Fernando," said Diego de Susa. The boy bent down and opened a trap door. One by one the visitors walked down a dozen stone steps. The basement had no window to give the Jews away. Many small tables were set with brightly burning candles, and in the center was a long table. Everyone took his seat. The master of the house sat in the big armchair at the head of the long table, with Fernando on his right and Mendes on his left.

A deep silence hung over the assembly. Was it as if they were all waiting for another deliverance?

Diego de Susa began the Seder: "Blessed art Thou, O Lord our God, King of the Universe, Creator of the fruit of the vine . . ."

A dish of water passed from guest to guest. Each

357

washed his left hand and passed the dish on. Then they dipped a bit of the lettuce in the tart sauce and twice in the spices. Before the roast lamb was brought in, Diego de Susa raised his voice: "Let us all say Grace," and they all answered, "Blessed be He and blessed be His name."

Only once did Diego de Susa do something unusual. When his son Fernando stood up to ask the question, *"Mah nishtanah*—why is this night different from all other nights of the year?" Diego de Susa smiled and his eyes filled with tears. The entire gathering began to cry and laugh at once.

"Why did they?" asked Fernando to himself. "Why?"

He knew the answer four hours later when the De Susas and a hundred other Jewish families from Seville were on their way to the port of Cadiz. They still wore the same heavy traveling shoes, and these were put to good use. In the port of Cadiz, the full Passover moon shone down upon a Dutch schooner that was ready to sail. She was loaded with spices for the Netherlands, and it was not until it was too late that the Spanish government learned that the ship had been brought by Señor Mendes from Antwerp to carry his fellow Jews to the safety of friendly shores.

The Magician[8]

(age level twelve to fifteen)   ISAAC LOEB PERETZ

One day a magician arrived in a small town in Volynia. And, although this happened at a time just before Passover, a time crowded with all sorts of excitement when every Jew has more cares than hairs on his head, the arrival of the magician nevertheless created a sensation.

An enigmatic fellow, tattered and torn, his head covered by an opera hat (crushed, true enough, but an opera hat just the same), with a Jewish face (his nose alone testified sufficiently to his origin) yet no beard; he carried no passport. Who could tell what sort of man he was? If they asked him, "Where do you come from?" he would say, "From Paris!" If they asked, "Where are you bound for?"—"London!" he would say. "How did you ever happen to land here?"—"Oh, I just wandered over here!" He did his traveling on foot, apparently. And he never showed his face in the House of Prayer—he stayed away even on Sabbath. But if people pestered him or formed a crowd around him, he would vanish, just like that, as though the earth had swallowed him up—and then he would reappear at the other end of the market place.

He hired a hall and began giving exhibitions of his tricks. And what tricks! He swallowed live coals right in front of everybody, just as if they were dumplings; he pulled ribbons out of his mouth, ribbons of all colors—red, green, or whatever color you called out—and each ribbon as long as the suffering of the Jewish folk. Out of his boots he pulled sixteen pairs of turkeys, each one as big as a bear—live turkeys that scattered all over the stage. He would lift his foot, scratch the sole, and there would be a rain of gold coins—until he had scraped up a whole bowl of gold pieces! This evoked much applause, whereupon the magician would whistle, and rolls and Sabbath loaves came flocking through the air just like birds dancing up and down or hopping about in the Quarrel Dance. Then he whistled once more and everything vanished, just as if it had never existed! No loaves, no ribbons, no turkeys—nothing at all.

Oh, well, everybody knows that the Evil Power can also put on a show of miracles! The Egyptian wonderworkers had probably evinced even greater artistry. But the main question was, why was the magician himself so poor?

The man could scrape gold pieces off the soles of his

boots, yet he could not scrape together his rent. He had merely to whistle to bake a batch of rolls and Sabbath loaves, he pulled turkeys out of his boots, yet his face was gaunt—the face of a corpse looked healthier—and hunger was like a flame in his eyes! People made jokes about it; a fifth question had been added to the four traditional ones asked at the Passover supper.

But before talking of the Passover, let us leave the magician and pass on to Hayyim-Jonah and his wife Rivkah-Bailah. Hayyim-Jonah had at one time dealt in timber. On one occasion he had bought a forest for cash but had been denied the right to fell the trees and had lost his shirt on the deal. He had secured a position as clerk to another lumberman but then had lost it, and he had been out of work for several months now. He and his wife had managed to get through the winter somehow —Lord, let no other man experience such a winter! But then, after winter came the Passover. Yet everything had already been pawned, from the candlesticks to the last pillows. And so Rivkah-Bailah said to her husband:

"Go to the Benevolent Society and ask for money to buy *matzot*."

But Hayyim-Jonah's answer was that he placed his trust in God and was not going to humiliate himself before people. Rivkah-Bailah rummaged through all the nooks and crannies in the house and—a miracle from Heaven! —found an old tarnished silver spoon that had been lost for many years. So Hayyim-Jonah went to the market place, sold the spoon, and carried the money he had gotten for it to the fund for the poor.

"They're poor people," he said, "who are in even greater need than we."

Time was passing quickly; there were only two short weeks left till Passover, yet Hayyim-Jonah did not lose hope.

"The Lord," he said, "will not abandon us."

Rivkah-Bailah kept silent; she knew that a woman must defer to her husband. Yet as the days sped by, Rivkah-

33. Seder Plate. China

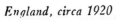
England, circa 1920

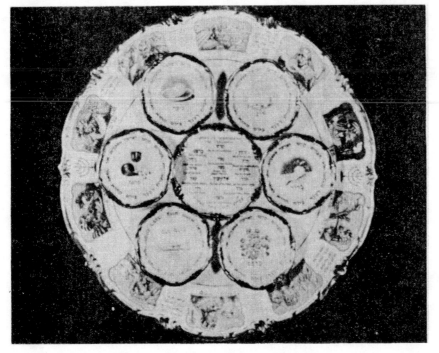

Russia, 18th century

34. The Cup of Elijah. Silver

Bohemia, early 19th century

35. Passover Goblet

36. Candle Holder for the Search for Leaven. Silver

Ilya Scho

The Touro Synagogue, Newport, R. I.

37. Matzah Board

Bailah could not close her eyes all night through, weeping with her face buried in the straw pallet so that Hayyim-Jonah might not hear her. And they still had not as much as a crumb for Passover! In the daytime things were even worse for Rivkah-Bailah than at night, for at night she could at least ease her grief by weeping, whereas in the daytime her cheeks must appear rosy even if she had to pinch them. The neighbors watched her and their pitying glances pierced her like needles. Some questioned her: When was she baking the *matzot?* When was she preparing the beet juice? Those who were on a more intimate footing with her would say: "What's the matter with you, Rivkah-Bailah? If you're in need we'll lend you the money!"

But Hayyim-Jonah wanted no "gifts from the hands of men," and Rivkah-Bailah would not go against his wishes. She tried to decline the offerings gracefully, while her face burned with shame.

The neighbors saw that things were in a bad way and went to the rabbi to find out what was to be done. The rabbi heard them out, sighed, thought, and at last declared that Hayyim-Jonah was a man of learning and a God-fearing one. And if he was not without hope, then there must be hope.

Rivkah-Bailah was left without so much as a candle for the holidays.

And at last it was Passover.

When Hayyim-Jonah came home from the synagogue he saw that all the windows on the square were aglow with the joyousness of the holiday—his house alone stood there like a young widow among the merry guests, like a blind man among those who can see. He did not let his heart sink however; "if the Lord wills it, there will be a holiday in my house as well!"

"A happy holiday!" he said gaily as he entered the house. "A happy holiday to you, Rivkah-Bailah!"

And Rivkah-Bailah's voice, choked with tears, came to him from a dark corner; "Happy holiday! May you

361

have a good year!" And her eyes gleamed like two dying embers.

"Rivkah-Bailah, the holiday is here; it is the eve of the Exodus from Egypt—do you understand? There must be no sorrowing. And besides, what's there to feel sorry about? If the All-Highest did not wish us to have a holiday feast, we must accept that as our due, as a blessing, and share the supper of others. Very well, then—we shall go! They will accept us anywhere. Today all gateways and doors stand wide open. Let everyone that wants to do so come and eat, say the Jews. Let's go. Put on your shawl; we'll walk to the first Jewish house we come to."

And Rivkah-Bailah, who always did as her husband wished, made a supreme effort to restrain the sobs that were straining at her throat, threw a tattered shawl over her shoulders and was ready to go. But at that moment the door opened, and a voice said:

"A happy holiday to you!"

And they answered, although they could not see who had entered.

"I want to be a guest at your supper," said the man who had entered.

"We haven't a supper for ourselves," answered Hayyim-Jonah.

"I have brought the supper with me," said the voice.

"Are we going to hold the service in darkness?" Hayyim-Jonah asked with a sigh.

"There will be light as well!" answered their guest.

He waved his hand—two pairs of silver candlesticks holding lighted candles appeared in the middle of the room and hung in mid-air! The room became light. Hayyim-Jonah and Rivkah-Bailah, amazed, beheld the magician and could not utter a word because of their astonishment and fear. Clutching each other by the hand they stood there gaping and staring. Meanwhile the magician turned toward the table that was standing in a corner and said, "Well, now, my fine fellows, come here and spread a cover over your table!"

362

Immediately a snowy cover fell from the ceiling on the table and covered it, while the table itself moved to the middle of the room and stopped right under the silver candlesticks, which sank onto it.

"Now we need couches to recline on!" said the magician.

Whereupon three benches made their way toward the table and arranged themselves on three sides of it. The magician ordered them to expand their width and thereupon they transformed themselves into easy-chairs.

"Get softer!" the magician bade them—and they became upholstered with red velvet, and at the same instant snow-white pillows plumped down upon them from the ceiling. The couches were ready! Next, a platter with all the ritual ingredients appeared on the table at his bidding, followed by red cups and decanters of wine, *matzot*, and everything else that was needed for a merry feast— even the books of devotion, well bound and with gilt edges.

"And do you have water for the washing of the hands?" asked the magician. "If not, I'll order it—it'll be brought!"

Only at this question did the hosts recover from their astonishment.

"Is this permissible?" Rivkah-Bailah asked Hayyim-Jonah in a whisper—and since Hayyim-Jonah did not know what answer to make to her she counseled him to go to the rabbi and ask.

But he said that he could not leave her alone with the magician—let her go by herself, to which Rivkah-Bailah replied that the rabbi would not believe a simple-minded Jewish woman; he would think that she had gone out of her mind. And so the two of them set out together to see the rabbi, leaving the magician alone with the Passover feast.

And the rabbi's answer was that everything created by enchantment had no real content, inasmuch as all spells were merely for the deception of the eyes. And he ordered them to go home, and if the *matzah* would allow itself to be crumbled, if the wine would let itself be poured into the cups, and the pillows on the couches were actually palpable, why, everything was well. In that case everything was a gift from heaven and they could avail themselves of it. Such was the rabbi's decision.

When Hayyim-Jonah and his wife returned, the magician was no longer there, but the feast stood just as they had left it, and the pillows turned out to be real, the wine flowed freely into the cups, and the *matzot* crumbled without any trouble.

They understood, then, that the prophet Elijah had visited their home. Joyously they celebrated the holiday!

XVIII

A SONG OF SEDER[1]

SARA G. LEVY

Sing a song of Seder,
A table without rye;
Four and twenty visitors,
And not a single pie.
The father is the king tonight,
Filling all the *kosot:*
The mother, though a queen,
Is making the *haroset;*
The children in the parlor
Are planning lots of fun;
They'll hide the *afikoman*
When the Seder is begun.

OUR SEDER[2]

BEN ARONIN

Last night was our Seder.
The table looked fine,

The white and the silver,
The *matzot* and wine.

I asked the Four Questions
As clear as could be.
And this is the story
My father told me.

"We were slaves, once, in Egypt,
But God set us free.
Now who is as happy,
As happy as we?"

SEDER NIGHT[3]

SAMUEL S. GROSSMAN

Why are the hearts of our people so light?
Why is it, home is so wondrously bright?
Happiness, holiness, shining o'er all,
Hear how the men from the synagogue call,
    "*Gut Yom-tov, Gut Yom-tov!*" It's Pesach
    tonight!

The Seder is set, and around in a ring
We Princes are sitting, and father is King,
While heaven is hearing the songs that we sing;
    'Tis *Yom-tov, Gut Yom-tov!* It's Pesach
    tonight!

"Father, four questions: O why do we do
All these strange things?" Then he tells us anew
Beautiful stories of Passover night;
And mother says low, as we hear him recite,
    "Be proud, little fellow, be proud you're a
    Jew!"

366

I hear how the Jews pass across the Red Sea;
God is their leader, and now they are free!
The chosen of God, and His children are we!
 I'm proud, and I'm happy; I'm proud I'm a
 Jew!

WHY MYER LIKES PESACH[4]

ELMA EHRLICH LEVINGER

My, I'm glad the winter's over,
 And that Pesach is so near;
'Cause I think the night of Seder
 Is the best time of the year.

I can stay up long that evening;
 All the silver's polished bright;
And the dishes are all shining,
 And the cloth is clean and white.

And my brothers and big sister,
 Who've moved to some other place,
All are gathered 'round the table,
 When my papa says the grace.

Then I ask him why that evening
 Isn't like another night;
And my mama smiles at grandma
 'Cause I read the Hebrew right.

Afterwards I find the *matzah*—
 Sister says it isn't fair,
'Cause I know that papa hides it
 In the cushions of his chair.

367

'Bout that time I'm kinda sleepy;
But I just hold up my head:
How could they say the *Had Gadya,*
If I had to go to bed?

When I wake up it is morning
And the sun is shining bright;
And I wish that it was next year,
And another Seder night!

THE QUESTIONS[5]
JESSIE E. SAMPTER

I've practiced, practiced day by day
To learn the questions I must say
On Seder night;
Then father, like a king of kings
Now low, now loud the answer sings,
When I have asked aright.

To you and me the story's told
Because 'twas we in days of old
Whom God made free.
To Pharaoh's slave He gave His rod
And made of us a prince of God
And dried for us the sea.

But I would ask one question more:
If we today should crowd the shore
Of every land
With listening mind and daring heart,
Would not the oceans leap apart
Again at God's command?

PASSOVER SONG[6]

JESSIE E. SAMPTER

The birds return through leagues of space,
On barren trees and blossoms burn.
Ye banished birds of Israel's race,
Now call: Return, return!

Two thousand years have Israel's sons
Still prayed: "Next year—Jerusalem."
The swallow flies, the beetle runs,
For wish is deed with them.

But Israel's children pray and sing,
And fast and feast and pray again,
And cry, "O Lord, we wait our king,
To ease our ancient pain!"

Throw off the cloaks in bondage worn
That hide your garments kingly white,
For you must go tomorrow morn,
Since this is Pesach night.

THE SEDER[7]

PHILIP M. RASKIN

Fair is the twilight,
    And fragrant and still;
Little by little
    The synagogues fill.

One by one kindle
    The night's gleaming eyes:
Candles in windows,
    And stars in the skies.

Ended in *Shul* is
    The service divine;
Seder is started
    With legends and wine.

Father is blessing
    The night of all nights;
All who are hungry
    To feast he invites.

"All who are homeless
    Yet masters shall be,
Slaves who are this year—
    The next shall be free!"

Children ask "questions,"
    And father replies;
Playfully sparkle
    The wine and the eyes.

Hymns of Redemption
    All merrily sing,
Queen is each mother,
    Each father, a king.

Midnight. The Seder
    Is come to an end;
Guardian angels
    From heaven descend.

Each one a message
    Of liberty brings,

Scattering blessings
    Of peace from his wings.

PASSOVER[8]

LEVIN KIPNIS

    Passover—the feast of spring,
    Passover—what joy you bring!
    Feast of freedom, feast of light,
    Hence, cold winter, hence, dark night!
        Children, come let us rejoice,
        Let us sing in gladsome voice!

    Passover—the feast of spring,
    Passover—what joy you bring!
    Pretty clothes and wine that's sweet,
    Matzot crisp and nuts to eat.
        Children, come let us rejoice,
        Let us sing in gladsome voice!

BOOK FOUR

Passover Rejoicing

And the children of the captivity kept the Passover upon the fourteenth day of the first month. . . . and kept the feast of unleavened bread seven days with joy; for the Lord had made them joyful . . .

Ezra 6.19-22

NAMES

The festival of Passover is generally known by three names, each with a distinctive significance: *Hag ha-Matzot,* Feast of the Unleavened Bread (Ex. 23.15), the biblical designation in commemoration of the physical exodus; *Hag ha-Pesach,* Festival of the Paschal Offering *(ibid.,* 34.25), with reference to the paschal lamb and the festival which the sages used to stress the spiritual redemption and the religious values of the festival;[1] and *Zeman Herutenu,* Season of Our Freedom, the term found in the liturgy, which marks the establishment of the children of Israel as a free and independent people.

Philo calls Passover the "Crossing-feast" as he traces the name not to the passing over of the Israelites by the destroying angel (Ex. 12.23,27), "but to the crossing of Israel itself from Egypt . . . and no doubt also the crossing of the Red Sea . . ."[2]

In Morocco, the Seder evening is called *Layl al-Rass* (Night of the Heads) as it was customary among Moroccan Jews to eat heads of sheep in commemoration of the paschal offering in the Temple.[3]

THE PASSOVER OF THE CRUSHED

Strange designations were given to Passover in two particular years during the time of the Temple. The Talmud

375

relates that "no man was ever crushed in the Temple Court [in spite of the enormous crowds] except on one Passover in the days of Hillel, when an old man was crushed to death and they called it 'The Passover of the Crushed!' "[4]

The Talmud relates further that "Once King Agrippa, desirous of ascertaining the male population of Israel, ordered the High Priest to pay heed to the paschal lambs. So he took one kidney of each one and there were found sixty myriad couples—double the number of those that came forth from Egypt. . . . and there was not a single paschal lamb on which less than ten people were counted. And it was called 'The Crowded Passover.' "[5]

CALENDRICAL FORMULATIONS

The Jewish calendar is so formulated that the first day of Passover never falls on a Monday, Wednesday or Friday.

The first six days of Passover determine the days of the week when the other festivals will occur. This has been fixed by an ingenious device of combining the first six letters of the Hebrew alphabet with the last six in reverse order; for example, the first letter is joined with the last letter, the second letter with the next-to-the-last and so forth. This results in these combinations:

א"ת, ב"ש, ג"ר, ד"ק, ה"ץ, ו"ף

The days of Passover will always fall as follows:

א	First day on Tishah be-Av	תשעה באב
ב	Second day on Shavuot	שבועות
ג	Third day on Rosh ha-Shanah	ראש השנה
ד	Four day on Simhat Torah	קריאת התורה
		שהיא שמחת תורה
ה	Fifth day on Yom Kippur	צום כפור
ו	Sixth day on the previous Purim[6]	פורים

Recently another combination, ז"ע, consisting of the seventh letter of the alphabet, corresponding to the seventh day of Passover, and the seventh letter from the last, which denotes Independence Day of the State of Israel, has been added:

ז	Seventh day on Israel Independence Day[7]	יום עצמאות

376

FOURS

The number four plays a significant role in the Haggadah and the Seder ceremonials. There are:

Four cups of wine

Four Questions

Four Sons—the wise, the wicked, the simple and the one who does not know how to ask.

Four expressions of redemption—*I will bring you out . . . I will deliver you . . . I will redeem you . . . I will take you* (Ex. 6.6-7).

Four special foods—Pesach (roasted shankbone), *matzah, maror* and *haroset.*

MOSES, THE LEADING MAN

Moses, the leading and inspiring character in the drama of Passover and the greatest prophet of Israel, is mentioned once, and only incidentally in a quoted verse, in the Haggadah. To dramatize the spiritual message of the power of God in the redemption from Egyptian bondage and to avoid the hero-worship of Moses, he who performed the crucial role in the drama is virtually an "extra" in the recorded script. The person was always considered a "messenger of the Lord," a tool in His hands to do His will.

THE PASCHAL SACRIFICE

During the first century of the Common Era, Theudas—the most prominent member of the Jewish community of Rome—well-intentioned though apparently void of Jewish learning, introduced the sacrificing of a lamb on the eve of Passover to fulfill biblical law. This led the rabbinical authorities in Palestine to rebuke him, for this practice was permitted only in the Temple of Jerusalem.[8]

In the nineteenth century both Ashkenazi and Sephardi rabbis were concerned with the possibility of reintroducing the Passover offering in Jerusalem. While the matter

377

was seriously discussed in Responsa, no practical results were achieved.[9]

THE MYSTICAL AFIKOMAN

The *afikoman* is the piece of the middle of the three *matzot* on the Seder table which is eaten at the conclusion of the meal. The Mishnah states that "After the paschal lamb (or Passover meal) one should not disperse in revelry *(afikoman)*."

Afikoman is said to be the Greek *epikomios*, meaning festival procession. The Talmud defines it as "going from one group to another,"[10] as was the custom after a meal, for the purpose of revelry, which the rabbis frowned upon. It is also defined as dessert and dinner music.

Another explanation for *afikoman* is found in the Yemenite Haggadah. There an acrostic interpretation is given as follows:

nuts	אגוזים
fruits	פירות
wine	יין
roasted things	קליות
and meat	ובשר
water	מים
spikenard	נרדים

All of the above and even other foods are forbidden to be tasted after eating the *afikoman*.[11]

The custom developed for the master of the house to secrete the *afikoman* under the pillow upon which he leaned. Children, knowing that the Seder cannot be completed until the *afikoman* is eaten, usually seek to obtain and hold it for "ransom." The "snatching" of the *afikoman* by children was frowned upon by some rabbis who feared that they might develop bad habits.

The search for the hidden *afikoman* might be considered the world's oldest treasure hunt.

The part of the *afikoman* which remains after each celebrant has partaken of a small piece of it has been considered as an antidote to varied evils. Some Jews during the Middle Ages would break off a piece of the *afikoman* and hang it in the house[12] to ward off evil spirits.[13] Jews of Kurdistan keep the remains of the *afikoman* in their rice, flour and salt containers as an augury that these supply receptacles will not be empty throughout the year.[14]

Moroccan Jews believe that, during a voyage, the tossing of the *afikoman* into a stormy sea will ensure a calm and safe journey,[15] for it is written: מכל צרח הצילנו *For he hath delivered me out of all trouble* (Psalms 54.9), and the first letters of each of these words spell *matzah*.

Another approach to the appeasement of a storm has been reported which makes use of an amulet and *matzah shemurah*. A lead plate inscribed with the Hebrew of "I wait for Thy salvation, O Lord" (Gen. 49.18) is hung on the side of a boat and then pieces of *matzah shemurah* are placed in the four corners of the boat and mention is made of אגלא, an acrostic of אתה גבור לעולם אדוני (Thou are mighty forever, O Lord).[16]

WHERE IS ELIJAH?

While the cup of Elijah occupies a place of honor on the Seder table, and during the service the door is opened to welcome the prophet, the harbinger of salvation and consolation, his name appears in the text of the Haggadah only in the Grace After Meals as it is said throughout the year.[17]

LOCAL PASSOVER HYMNS

For many generations, the Jews of Avignon and the Comtat Venaissin were forbidden to leave their own quarters during the period of Easter. They called this period *Yom ha-Hesger*, the "Day of Shutting In," and, as it frequently coincided with Passover, special hymns were intoned in the synagogue. One of these reads, in the translation of Cecil Roth, as follows:

> Like a princess set away
> In her palace on this day:
> Hidden, like a lovely maid
> Thus her prayer 'fore God she laid
> (He Whose spirit, wondrous-wise,
> All that liveth vivifies):
> "Rouse Thee, at this spring-tide feast
> Till our servitude hath ceased!"[18]

The *Mahzor of the Rite of Carpentras for the Three Festivals* (Amsterdam, 1759) contains poems and hymns of thanksgiving for the seventh day of Passover which are unique to this edition. These liturgical additions commemorate the deliverance of the Jews of Carpentras on the seventh day of Passover—the anniversary of the crossing of the Red Sea—in the year 1651, from an attack on the ghetto by a mob of rioting beggars. Called *Yom va-Yosha*, the "Day of *And He saved*" (Ex. 14.30), it is observed with special prayers and the recital of a hymn, by Joseph ben Abraham de Montel, which narrates the story of the deliverance.[19]

LOCAL CUSTOMS

For many centuries Jews lived in the *Ksurs* (forts) of the Sahara desert. One group, known as the "heretics of Wargla," celebrated Passover by leaving their abodes and marching into the desert, as the children of Israel did under the leadership of Moses.[20]

Ancestors of the present Bene Israel of India observed *Anasi Dhakacha San*, "the holiday of the closing of the *Anas*" (an earthen jar containing sour liquid used as a sauce), for eight days from the fourteenth of Nisan. During this period they abstained from the use of leaven, although they had forgotten the origin of the festival.[21]

In some Jewish communities of Hungary, the seventh day of Passover was observed with appropriate dramatization to mark the miraculous dividing of the Red Sea. The Hasidim would assemble in a private home and dine together. After midnight they would take a pitcher of water and dance with it until the water spilled on the floor, or a pan of water would be placed on the floor and the Hasidim would jump over it and dance around it singing, "Then sang Moses."[22]

Some Jews gave expression to their piety and love of performing a *mitzvah* by kissing the *matzot* and bitter herbs on the first two nights of Pesach.[23]

HAGGADAH PARODIES

The format and style of the Passover Haggadah readily lend themselves to imitation through parody. Thus numerous parodies have been written which paraphrase and imitate features of the Haggadah. One of the earliest is the eulogy of Todros Abulafia by Abraham Bedarshi of the thirteenth century. In 1680, Jonah Rapa of Italy authored a caustic satire on Christianity in the style of the Haggadah, which cries out against the Blood Accusation and ridicules Church ceremonials and carnival excesses that are described in minute detail. Probably of the same period is the anonymous parody *The Order of Passover and Its Law,* which satirizes imprudent marriages. A wide variety of topics was utilized to parody the Haggadah and it seems that no subject was immune from sharp sarcasm. Other parodies have been less satirical, sometimes humorous and occasionally homiletical.[24]

One of the most popular parodies is entitled *Order of the Haggadah for Teachers,* by Levi Reuben Simlin, which bemoans the fate of the Jewish teacher. The following translation is an excerpt from this work:

> Why is the teaching profession different from all other professions in the world? Why do all other professions enrich and their practitioners eat, drink and rejoice all the days of the year, but teachers whine and are distressed even on this night? . . .
>
> We were slaves to the householders and to their

children who ruled us with a mighty hand. Even if all the householders were well-versed in Torah, we would have been compelled to reply also to their questions. And if all of us were wise, all of us were intelligent, all of us were authors, and even if all of us were miserable, all of us were poor, it would be our duty to emancipate ourselves from the suffering of teaching, and whosoever hastens to liberate himself before he reaches the gates of death, behold he is praiseworthy . . .

Next year may I be a householder! *(Repeat three times)* [25]

"REBELLION TO TYRANTS IS OBEDIENCE TO GOD"

"If Israel had its Pharaoh, so had the Puritans one in the person of King James I. The Atlantic Ocean was to them the Red Sea. America was the new Canaan and Washington and Adams, their Moses and Joshua!"[26]

This comparison can be substantiated by historical events. On the very day that the Declaration of Independence was adopted, a committee, consisting of John Adams, Benjamin Franklin and Thomas Jefferson, was appointed for the purpose of preparing a design for the seal of the United States of America. The committee report, submitted to the Continental Congress on August 10, 1776, proposed that on one side of the seal there should be "the following device: Pharaoh sitting in an open chariot, a crown on his head and a sword in his hand, passing through the divided waters of the Red Sea in pursuit of the Israelites; rays from a pillow [*sic!*] of fire in the cloud, expressive of the divine Presence and Command beaming on Moses who stands on the shore and extending his hand over the Sea causes it to overwhelm Pharaoh. Motto: Rebellion to Tyrants is Obedience to God."[27]

A WINE SUBSTITUTE

In the YIVO Institute for Jewish Research there is a manuscript announcement, purported to have been issued

382

in Vilna during World War I, which states: "On account of the hard times and the great dearth in which we are living, the rabbis have found it necessary to announce that the poor people who do not have the means to buy wine for the Four Cups can, according to the law, fulfill the duty of the Four Cups with sweet tea."[28]

A PRAYER FOR EATING HAMETZ

The Jewish inmates of the German concentration camp at Bergen-Belsen did not have *matzah* for the observance of Passover in 1944. Although pious Jews in the camp had decided to fast on the festival, the rabbis who were among them decreed that the eating of leaven would be permissible, provided the following prayer be recited before meals:

Before eating leaven, one should say with deep devotion:

Our Father in Heaven, behold it is evident and known to Thee that it is our desire to do Thy will and to celebrate the festival of Passover by eating *matzah* and by observing the prohibition of *hametz*. But our heart is pained that the enslavement prevents us and we are in danger of our lives. Behold, we are prepared and ready to fulfill Thy commandment: "And ye shall live by them and not die by them" . . . Therefore, our prayer to Thee is that Thou mayest keep us alive and preserve us and redeem us speedily so that we may observe Thy statutes and do Thy will and serve Thee with a perfect heart. Amen.[29]

THE SEDER OF THE HUNGER STRIKERS

In the presence of the Chief Rabbis of Palestine, a unique Seder took place in the Holy City of Jerusalem for fifteen leaders of the Jewish community on the first night of Passover in 1946. The celebrants symbolically ate a mere morsel of *matzah,* for they were engaged in the fourth day of a self-imposed hunger strike to protest the detention at La Spezia, Italy, of 1,200 "illegal" refugees bound for Palestine aboard the S. S. "Fede." Burning candles and wreaths of flowers on the white tablecloths lent a festive air to this awe-inspiring occasion. The leader chanted the service from the first printed Haggadah—the only extant copy—that was published in Spain ten years before the expulsion of the Jews from that country in 1492. On the drawn faces of the hunger strikers, among whom was Golda Meir, later Minister for Foreign Affairs of the State of Israel, there were evident signs of eternal hope as they recited, "This year we are slaves; next year may we be free men."[30]

FOR THE SAKE OF RIGHTEOUS WOMEN

A *maggid* in the course of preaching on *Shabbat ha-Gadol,* the Sabbath preceding Passover, said:

"The Talmud states, 'For the sake of the righteous women that were in that generation the children of Israel were redeemed from Egypt.' What did the Talmud mean?

"It is known that the Israelites should have remained in slavery in Egypt four hundred years, as it is written in the book of Genesis: *And they shall afflict them four hundred years.* However, they were enslaved there only two hundred and ten years. The question is, Why was their period of bondage shortened?

"The answer is to be found with the righteous women. They complained to the Almighty that they missed their men folk and beseeched Him to redeem them. God reminded them that the time for redemption had not yet arrived as they were scheduled to be enslaved for nearly two hundred years more.

"Then the righteous women said, 'We are prepared to assume responsibility for our husbands. If You will place them in our hands, we promise You that they will continue to be slaves.'

"The Almighty readily granted their request. That is

385

the reason the Talmud says, 'For the sake of the righteous women . . . the children of Israel were redeemed from Egypt.' "

GIRLS AFTER THE BOYS

The Bible reveals that Pharaoh commanded that every Hebrew male child should be cast into the river. If Pharaoh intended to annihilate the children of Israel, why did he not order the girls as well as the boys to be drowned?

Pharaoh knew that if all the boys were thrown into the river, the girls would jump in after them.

THE ROUTE OF MOSES

Joe, a college freshman, desired to flaunt his newly-acquired wisdom in the face of his pious father. With an air of profundity he remarked:

"My professor told us that Moses did not have any knowledge of geography. If he had, he would have led the children of Israel from Egypt to Palestine in a week instead of forty years."

The father, who lacked the benefits of higher education, shook his head slightly and replied:

"Perhaps Moses did not know geography but I am certain that your professor does not know the Jews. If he had been in the place of Moses, he would not have brought the Jews to the Land of Israel even in forty years. The professor would never have taken them out of Egypt!"

THE CROSSING OF THE RED SEA

One day a lover of art brought home a large canvas in an ornate frame. Displaying it to his wife with deep pride, he said:

"Look at this beautiful Passover painting I bought!"

The wife stared in amazement at the canvas for it was completely blank.

"I do not see anything on this canvas. Did you buy it at the Gallery of Modern Art?" the wife naively inquired. "What is it supposed to be?"

"This is a painting of the Jews crossing the Red Sea," the spouse replied condescendingly.

"But where are the Jews?"

"The Jews already passed through the sea and they are on the shore."

"And where are the Egyptians?"

"The Egyptians are still pursuing the children of Israel and they have not yet reached the sea."

"And where then is the sea itself?"

"The waters of the sea are divided and have receded to the shores so that the Jews should be able to cross."

DIVIDING THE WATERS

A Jew had invited a beggar to his home to partake of a Sabbath meal. The beggar was not at all shy and, as soon as the *Kiddush* was recited, he began to pour for himself drink after drink of his host's best whiskey. He emptied each glassful of schnaps by dunking pieces of the delicious white *hallah* and devouring them.

The host was truly bewildered. He feared greatly that the beggar would finish both the *hallah* and the whiskey and not leave any for his family. Desiring to restrain the beggar without offending him, he said:

"I don't understand why it was necessary for Moses to divide the mighty waters of the Red Sea. If he had given pieces of *hallah* to the children of Israel, they would have been able to dry the sea by dunking the *hallah*."

"That would have been possible," the beggar retorted, momentarily interrupting his drinking and dunking. "Unfortunately, the Red Sea was divided on Passover, when the Jews are not permitted to handle *hallah* and certainly not to eat it."

THE RABBI'S PASSOVER NEEDS

With the arrival of Nisan, a rabbi complained to his wife that he was overwhelmed with problems.

"What are you worried about?" the *rebbetzin* solicitously inquired.

"I have two big worries," the rabbi explained. "First, I need a sermon for the Great Sabbath preceding Passover. Second, I need money so that you can purchase food for the festival."

The *rebbetzin* quickly retorted:

"Don't worry about the sermon. You can use the same one you delivered last year. No one will remember what you preached. On the other hand, you should worry about the money for the Passover food since the storekeepers will surely remember that I still owe them last year's bill."

HALF-READY

Knowing that Hersheleh Ostropoler was very poor, hardly ever having enough food for a meal in his home, Hayyim asked him if he had made the necessary provisions for Passover. Hersheleh replied that he had prepared half the provisions and the other half God would provide.

Amazed to learn of Hersheleh's sudden good fortune, Hayyim inquired how he had succeeded in securing these provisions.

"Don't be so surprised," Hersheleh answered. "You know that there are two major requirements for Passover. First, no leaven shall be seen in a Jew's house and, second, one must eat unleavened bread. The first I have already fulfilled, as leaven has not been seen in my house for a long time. Since I have fulfilled fifty per cent of the requirements, I now rely on the All-Munificent One who will surely provide me with *matzot* and other foods for Passover."

SUPERVISING THE MATZAH-BAKING

Rabbi Israel Lipkin Salanter was most meticulous in the baking of *matzot* for Passover. To make certain that everything was done according to the strictest interpretation of Jewish law, he personally undertook to supervise the baking.

One year the rabbi was bedridden and unable to go to the bakery. He instructed two pupils to go in his stead.

As the pupils were about to depart for their assigned task, they asked their teacher:

"Is there anything special which we should watch?"

"Yes," the rabbi replied. "See that the old woman who does the mixing is paid sufficiently. She is a poor widow."

EARNING THE PASSOVER SUPPLIES

A few days before Passover, Motke Habad of Vilna went to the tailor's shop, seated himself comfortably in a corner and fell asleep.

A customer entered the shop and was surprised to see his friend Motke. Shaking Motke, he awoke him and asked:

"What are you doing here, Motke?"

In a voice loud enough for the tailor to hear, Motke said:

"I'm helping the tailor who is very busy this week. With the approach of Passover he is loaded with work and he doesn't have time to rest. Since I have enough time, I came here to rest for him. I hope that for my helping him the tailor will give me wine and *matzot* for Passover."

MONEY FOR THE POOR

A charity warden went to the home of a rich Jew on the eve of Passover to solicit *Maot Hittim*. He rapped on the door, awaking the affluent one from his afternoon siesta. Angry that his nap was disturbed, the rich Jew opened the door in a sour mood. His mood was translated into action when he saw the warden and he slapped his face. The warden placed one hand on his face to soothe the stinging pain and extended his other hand to the rich man, saying:

"The slap you have given me. Now, what will you give to the poor?"

389

A POOR ORPHAN

The representative of the *Maot Hittim* fund was disappointed with the niggardly donation of the town's wealthiest Jew. He reproached the man in a caustic tone:

"This is too small a contribution for such an important *mitzvah*. Even your son, who is really poor in comparison with you, gave a much larger amount of money."

The rich man was not stirred and retorted:

"How can you compare me with my son? He has a rich father while I am an unfortunate orphan."

MILK AT THE SEDER

A local Jew came to Rabbi Akiba Eger of Posen on the eve of Passover.

"Rabbi, I've a ritual question to ask you," he said. "Is it permissible to use four cups of milk at the Seder instead of four cups of wine?"

"Why would you want to substitute milk for wine? Are you, God forbid, ill?"

"No, rabbi. I am well but I can't afford to buy wine."

The discerning rabbi then said:

"I'm sorry. It is forbidden to use a substitute for wine." Reaching a hand into his pocket, he continued, "Take these twenty rubles and purchase wine."

After the Jew had left, the *rebbetzin* angrily chided her husband:

"Why did you give him twenty rubles for wine? Two or three rubles would have been sufficient."

"Don't be angry," the rabbi asked. "The fact that this poor man was prepared to drink milk at the Seder is evidence that he also didn't have money to buy meat and perhaps not even fish and *matzot*. With the twenty rubles he will be able to observe the Seder properly."

BARON ROTHSCHILD AS MESSENGER

The eve of Passover had arrived and Shmuel and his pious wife Rivkah were bemoaning their dire poverty and especially their lack of earthly goods required for the proper observance of the festival. They considered many ways to cope with their tragic plight but none seemed suitable. Finally, Rivkah prevailed upon her husband to appeal directly to the Almighty and to dispatch a letter to Him explaining their predicament. Shmuel wrote an appropriate missive and cast it to the winds with a prayer on his lips that the message might soar aloft to His Heavenly Abode.

Baron Rothschild happened to be riding in his carriage in the neighborhood and noticed the letter lying on the road. When he read the urgent appeal, his deepest sympathy was aroused. He sent his servant with a hundred rubles for Shmuel.

The servant delivered the money in the name of Baron Rothschild. Without a word of appreciation to the servant or the Baron, Shmuel turned to his wife and said:

"See, Rivkah. God has sent Baron Rothschild as His messenger. I wonder how much Rothschild deducted for his expenses."

A FIFTY PER CENT SUCCESS

When Naphtali Tzvi Horowitz, the Ropshitzer *rebbe,* returned home from the synagogue on the Sabbath before Passover after delivering a *Shabbat ha-Gadol* discourse, his wife noticed that he appeared very tired and depressed. When she asked him why he looked so haggard, Rabbi Naphtali said:

"I exerted myself strenuously in the delivery of my discourse. Anxious to arouse the sympathy of our rich brethren so that they would provide the poor with the requisite Passover provisions, I spoke with much emotion and at great length."

"Were your efforts successful?" the rabbi's wife inquired solicitously.

"I'm certain that I had at least a fifty per cent success," the rabbi sighed. "I'm not certain that the rich Jews will

391

give to the poor but I'm quite certain that the poor are ready to accept if they will only be offered something."

A SIYYUM FOR THE FIRST-BORN

After the morning services on the eve of Passover, the congregants waited impatiently for the rabbi to commence the *Siyyum,* the ceremony of a discourse on Torah, and a festive meal which accompanies the conclusion of the study of a sacred book. By participating in this prescribed meal the congregants would be released from observing the fast incumbent upon first-born sons to recall that God slew the first-born of the Egyptians but spared those of Israel. The rabbi sat at the head of a long table, flanked on both sides by the congregants attentively attuned to the words of Torah they expected to hear. The sage, however, was deeply engrossed in the volume that lay before him and did not utter a word. The Jews, anxious to return home so that they could burn the *hametz* in due time and conclude the Passover preparations, were impatient.

Finally, the rabbi, with a deep sigh, said:

"I am advancing in age and I no longer have the strength to deliver a discourse as has been my practice on this occasion. I will therefore be very brief. This is my message: 'There are many poor Jews in our midst who do not have any money for their Passover needs. I will not make a *Siyyum* until you will give me one hundred rubles for the poor.'"

The short and sharp presentation proved effective.

A PREFERENCE FOR MATZAH

The lord of the manor was in financial straits and borrowed money from a Jew for which he gave a note. When the day came for the note to be redeemed, the creditor appeared at the manor to claim his money. Inasmuch as the situation of the lord had not changed, he informed him that he was unable to fulfill his obligation. When the man indicated that he would appeal to the local authorities, the lord whipped out a revolver, pointed it in the face of the quaking Jew, and said threateningly:

"Either you'll swallow the note or I'll kill you!"

Without the necessity for any further remonstrances, the Jew obediently put the note in his mouth and swallowed it.

Subsequently the baron obtained funds and paid his debt.

Some time later, during the festival of Passover, the lord of the manor summoned the Jew again to negotiate another loan. The latter brought with him a piece of *matzah* and requested the lord to write the note on it.

The confounded lord shouted:

"Are you crazy? What's the meaning of this?"

"I'm afraid that when I return at this time next year for you to redeem the loan I may have to eat the note. As it will again be Passover, I won't want to eat anything that may be leaven. Furthermore, *matzah* is more digestible and tastier than paper."

MATZAH IS MATZAH

Why is *matzah* called *matzah*?

Because it has the shape of *matzah*; it has small holes like *matzah*; it is dry as *matzah*; it tastes like *matzah*. What else can you call it but *matzah*?

LAW-ABIDING JEWS

On the eve of Passover, Rabbi Levi Isaac of Berditchev summoned a group of businessmen who, he suspected, were engaged in smuggling goods across the border. In a harsh tone, he asked them:

"Do you have any smuggled goods?"

"Plenty, rabbi," they readily admitted.

He then inquired:

"Do you have any *hametz* in your homes?"

"God forbid, rabbi," they protested. "We already sold all our *hametz*."

Levi Isaac then lifted his gaze on high and said:

393

"Father in Heaven! See how wonderful the Jews are! The mighty czar of Russia, who has an army, a police force and prisons, has forbidden the people to smuggle; yet, they pay no attention to his law and publicly violate it. But You have forbidden the children of Israel to have *hametz* on Passover and, even though You do not have an army or police force or prisons, they obey Your commandment!"

FOOD FOR SOLDIERS

Rabbi Samuel Mohilever was interested in the welfare of Jews who served in the army, and his congregation had accepted the responsibility for supplying those who were stationed in the town with kosher food.

One year a drought had caused a severe food shortage. The *parnas* of his congregation asked him what could be done to have the necessary kosher provisions for the approaching Passover.

Rabbi Mohilever replied:

"Although it is not usual, I will permit the eating of peas on Passover."

Greatly relieved, the *parnas* said:

"Now we'll be able to feed the soldiers peas."

The rabbi, resenting the easy solution of which the *parnas* was ready to take advantage, quickly replied:

"That I will not permit in our community. You and I, as well as all the congregants, will be permitted to eat peas; however, for the Jewish soldiers we must provide only the most strictly kosher and the best food for the festival."

BEFORE IT IS TOO LATE

Hayyim Nahman Bialik, the late Hebrew poet laureate, came upon several heretics eating bread on the afternoon of the last day of Passover and said to them:

"You had better hurry lest you prolong your meal and Passover may be over before you finish eating. Then you

394

will no longer be committing a sin and it will be permissible for you to eat bread."

A COMMENTARY ON THE HAGGADAH

An author of a commentary on the Passover Haggadah requested a letter of endorsement from a rabbi. The latter carefully examined the manuscript but was unimpressed with its merit.

"I think that there have already been published plenty of commentaries on the Haggadah," the rabbi gently said.

The author indignantly protested:

"You, above all people, should know that from all the other commentaries I can't earn the necessities for Passover."

THANKS ARE NOT ENOUGH

On the eve of Passover, an editor of a new edition of the Haggadah brought his work as a "gift" to a prosperous man. The latter casually perused it and then said:

"I'm glad to have this book. Please accept my thanks for it."

"You are indeed welcome to it," the author rejoined. "Now, I would like to ask you the question 'Why is "A Psalm of Thanks" (Ps. 107) not recited on the eve of Passover?' "

The wealthy Jew said that he did not know the answer and the editor continued:

"On the eve of Passover, when many sacrifices were due, one could not fulfill his duty with mere thanks."

THE HAGGADAH OF HELM

Once upon a time the Haggadah of the Jews of Helm was the same as the Haggadah of the Jews throughout the world and had the following words: "The Torah spoke about Four Sons—one is wise, one is evil, one is simple and one does not know how to ask."

An inspiration came to the Helmites and they realized that it was truly unnecessary for the Haggadah to say

395

"one is wise." It would be clearer to say "one is a Helmite," and all would understand that a wise man was intended. Thereupon they printed a new edition of the Haggadah with the textual emendation so that it now read: "The Torah spoke about Four Sons—one is a Helmite . . ."

After several years, a new inspiration came to the Helmites which made them realize that it was truly unnecessary for the Haggadah to say "one is a Helmite." It would be clearer to say "one is wise" and all would understand that a Helmite was intended. Thereupon they printed new Haggadahs with the textual emendation so that it now read: "The Torah spoke about Four Sons— one is wise . . ."

Since then the Haggadah of the Jews of Helm has been the same as the Haggadah of the Jews throughout the world. However, in a commentary written by a sage of Helm, there will be found this interpretation:

A wise son—a Helmite.

THE RABBIS OF THE HAGGADAH

On the eve of Passover, Hayyim was homeward bound with a new Haggadah that he had promised to buy for his wife. Passing a tavern, he dropped in to quench his thirst. He found, however, that one drink was insufficient for the purpose and ordered a second and a third. When he found that he didn't have enough money to pay for all the whiskey he had drunk, he was forced to leave his new Haggadah as surety.

When Hayim arrived home, his wife asked him for the new Haggadah that he had gone to purchase.

"Listen, I'll tell you what happened," Hayyim began to explain. "I bought a beautiful Haggadah for you and I was tempted to examine it while walking home. I was delighted to find that the Haggadah had great rabbis— Eliezer, Joshua, Elazer ben Azariah, Akiba and Tarfon. So I invited them to join me in a drink that we might all recite a blessing and wish each other *Le-Hayyim* on the eve of Passover. So we entered a tavern and we drank and wished each other *Le-Hayyim*. Unfortunately, the rabbis were weak and became drunk. So they remained in the tavern and I came home alone."

A GRACIOUS HOST

Rabbi Akiba Eger was zealous about offering hospitality and was especially scrupulous about fulfilling the injunction for the Passover Seder: "Let those who are hungry enter and eat with us."

Once at the Seder table a guest accidentally tipped over his goblet of wine. To spare the visitor embarrassment, Rabbi Akiba surreptitiously and quickly moved the table, and knocked over his own cup of wine and remarked apologetically:

"It seems to me that the table is not standing properly."

FOUR CUPS OF WINE

Hayyim the Hasid and Mendel the Mithnagged were disputing the relative merits of their respective sects.

Mendel claimed that Moses the Lawgiver was a Mithnagged for he gave the Torah to the Jews so that they could study.

Naturally, Hayyim could not accept this argument. As evidence that Moses was a Hasid, he pointed out that the Lawgiver did not command the study of four chapters of the Torah on Passover but he did provide for the drinking of four cups of wine.

NEEDED IMPROVEMENTS

A connoisseur of wines once remarked:

"If I had been Moses, I would have improved upon the Passover arrangements. I would have given the Egyptians only four plagues and I would have provided for the Jews ten cups of wine."

HAD GADYA

The rabbi, passing the town's slaughterhouse, observed the *shohet*, who was in a state of intoxication, killing an

397

ox. The infuriated rabbi forthwith forbade the slaughterer to engage in his profession. Friends of the latter besieged the rabbi and pleaded with him to forgive the slaughterer and permit him to resume his work. The rabbi was obdurate and refused to budge from his decision. He explained to them:

"In the song *Had Gadya* that is sung at the conclusion of the Seder, we learn that 'the Angel of Death killed the *shohet* who had slaughtered the ox . . .' Why was the slaughterer slain since he had only performed his duty? The answer is that the *shohet* killed the ox after he had drunk the four cups of wine at the Seder."

A PROPER SEDER CELEBRATION

The Passover Seder was over and Rabbi Levi Isaac of Berditchev had retired for the night. His sleep was interrupted by a startling dream. An angel appeared to him and said:

"Levi Isaac of Berditchev, you should not rest easy! Do you think that you observed the Seder properly? Yankel is the one who is truly observing Passover!"

The following morning at the synagogue Levi Isaac inquired as to the identity of Yankel. When he learned that Yankel was a blacksmith, he approached him and asked:

"Please tell me how you celebrated the Seder last night."

"I'll tell you the truth, rabbi," the blacksmith ashamedly replied. "I don't know how to conduct a Seder. So I filled a large goblet with wine and I said, 'Merciful Lord, You're righteous and kind. I'm a poor, ignorant blacksmith. What can you expect from me?' Then I drank the wine, replenished the goblet and kept drinking till I got drunk."

After hearing this succinct recital, Rabbi Levi Isaac said to the blacksmith:

"You observed the festival according to the Jewish

spirit. Your humility and penitence are more meritorious than a hundred ceremonies."

TELL THY SON

Rabbi Levi Isaac of Berditchev, when reciting the Haggadah, paused as he read the passage concerning the last of the Four Sons, "He who does not know how to ask." Then he ruminated:

"Who does not know how to ask? He is none other than myself, Levi Isaac. Master of the Universe, I do not know how to ask You why Your chosen people, the innocent children of Israel, suffer such a long and dreary exile. However, the Haggadah commands the father of the son who does not know how to ask questions, 'Reveal to him as it is said (in the Torah): *And thou shalt tell to thy son.*' O Lord, surely, I am Your child. Now, therefore, reveal to me why my brethren and I endure such suffering!"

THE REWARD FOR THE AFIKOMAN

Before the start of the Seder, the father secretly told each of his four young sons that he would give a reward to the one who would tell him who had taken the *afikoman.* He also promised that this reward would be even more valuable than that for the one who held the *afikoman.*

As each boy was anxious to receive the better reward, no one took the *afikoman.* And the wise father did not need to give any reward!

TOO MUCH AFIKOMAN

During the Passover week a venerable Jew, who had passed his eightieth birthday, visited a doctor and complained that he felt ill for the first time in his life.

The physician gave him a thorough examination but was unable to find anything wrong with the octogenarian. He realized, however, that if he advised the patient that he was in perfect health, it would be most disappointing to him. He finally gave his "diagnosis":

399

"You are ill because you ate too much *afikoman*."

"How is it possible that I could become sick from eating such a small piece of *matzah?*" the aged Jew inquired.

"I do not know of a more serious cause of illness," the doctor explained. "A person who has eaten eighty pieces of *afikoman* must become ill."

PROPHET OR GUEST

During the Seder service, when Rabbi Menahem Mendel Morgenstern of Kotzk went to open the door to welcome the prophet Elijah, a guest at his table drank the wine from the cup that had been set aside for Elijah. Returning to the table, the rabbi noticed the prophet's empty cup and a look of embarrassment on the face of his guest.

"My dear friend," Rabbi Mendele said, seeking to ease the conscience of the guest, "both you and Elijah are welcome guests in my home. As the prophet did not appear to drink his wine, you are certainly entitled to it."

"AND THE DOG CAME . . ."

A gang of rowdies peered through the window of Reb Yankel's house and watched the observance of the Seder. When the door was opened to welcome the prophet Elijah, one of the rowdies dashed into the house, shouting:

"What were you saying?"

Reb Yankel's quick retort caused the rowdy to flee in shame:

"I was reciting *Had Gadya* and I had just said 'And the dog came.'"

A PRISONER'S COMPLAINT

A Jewish prisoner complained to a visiting rabbi that the warden did not allow the Jewish inmates to observe their religious laws. Naturally, the rabbi was greatly concerned and asked the prisoner for particulars.

"Two weeks ago when we observed Passover," the inmate related, "the warden arranged a Seder for us, but he refused to have it conducted properly. When we were reading the Haggadah and we were supposed to welcome Elijah the Prophet, the warden didn't let us open the door."

A HANDFUL OF NUTS

Joey: Mother, can I have a handful of nuts to play Passover games?
  Mother: Of course. Take a handful from the sack.
  Joey: I would prefer that you give the nuts to me.
  Mother: Why?
  Joey: Your hand is bigger than mine.

OBEDIENT CHILDREN

Mother: Children, I see that you've again eaten the nuts that I gave you for playing Passover games. I told you that no one should eat his nuts.
  Reuben: Mother, no one of us ate his nuts. I gave mine to Simon and he gave me his.

MORE QUESTIONS

Why is Passover like an appointment with a good friend?
  Because you want to keep it.

Why is the Haggadah the same as borsht?
  Because they are both read (red).

When is stealing rewarded and not punished?
  When the *afikoman* is stolen.

Why are hard-boiled eggs eaten on Passover?
  They are a reminder of the Jewish people. The longer eggs are cooked in hot water or roasted on a fire, the harder they become. This is also true of Jews.

Why do we have *haroset* to remind us of the mortar and *maror* to recall the bitter lives of our ancestors in Egypt, but do not have any reminder of the great wealth

401

which the children of Israel took with them when they left the land of bondage?

The Jews still have some of the mortar and bitterness but they no longer have even a faint recollection of the great wealth.

FOLK PROVERBS

Passover is a difficult but a clean festival. (Much labor and money is expended for Passover but it results in a spotlessly clean house.)

He sits like a *matzah*-baker. (One who works only a short time and is idle most of the year.)

He does not mean the Haggadah but the *kneidlach*.

The wise man of the Haggadah!

Even the stingiest miser gladly pours a full cup of wine for Elijah the Prophet.

What good is one *matzah* for a soldier? (This is the complaint of one who receives an insufficient donation.)

The best of the ten plagues are the *kneidlach*.

Give him what is given on Passover. (Plagues.)

If a piece of the *afikoman* is stored in the house, the mice will do no damage. (When the mice eat it, as it is forbidden to eat anything after the *afikoman*, they will be unable to eat anything else.)

XXI

The complex preparations required for the traditional commemoration of Passover have stimulated, on the American scene, the development of a number of programs intended to facilitate an understanding of the festival and to encourage participation in its observance. Some projects are geared to children and others are arranged by adults for their own guidance. This is in accord with the precept of the Talmud which states that "the laws of Passover are expounded and interpreted thirty days before Passover."[1]

Passover Institute

To prepare adults to observe and enjoy the festival, a Passover institute may be conducted. Several weekly sessions may be held, with guest lecturers and demonstrators participating. The following elements may be included in the institute:

> Lecture on the historical background of Passover
> Study of the laws and customs
> Discussion of the modern significance of the festival
> Analysis and interpretation of the Haggadah
> Demonstration of *kashering* and cooking of Passover
> dishes
> Songfest

Exhibit of Haggadahs and books on Passover
Demonstration of Passover games
An institute may be held during the weekend preceding
Passover, commencing immediately following the after-
noon service of *Shabbat ha-Gadol* in the synagogue. This
is the time traditionally reserved for an exposition of
Passover laws by the rabbi and the reading of the first
part of the Haggadah

Model Seder

Religious schools, synagogues and Jewish community cen-
ters may plan a model or demonstration Seder to provide
an experience for children by which they will be prepared
to participate in the family Seder at home.

The children can be stimulated to engage actively in
all of the preliminary arrangements, including the pur-
chasing and preparation of the foods that will be used.
Room decorations, invitations, place-cards, Seder plates
and the other paraphernalia made by the children, will
help to create a festive atmosphere. The children should
be encouraged to come dressed in their best clothing for
the occasion.

Some educators prefer small group Sedarim, while
others see value in a mass Seder. Even in the latter
instance, it is desirable to have family-size tables with one
designated as the head-table. The tables should be set by
the children themselves with all the traditional symbols.
One lad at each table acts as the "head of the family" and
a girl as the "mother." If the children are too young to
conduct the service, adults can play their customary roles.
Though the children may be capable of leading the Seder,
consideration might be given to the involvement of adults
so as to emphasize the family character of the occasion.

Depending on the maturity and background of the
children, selections from the Haggadah are read. Usually
the basic elements of the Seder are presented. Passages
may be read individually, in unison or responsively. Haggadah songs and prayers can be presented through solo,

choral or group singing. The interpolation of explanations and comments will heighten interest in the proceedings. Refreshments, or possibly a light meal, may be served.

The model Seder can be augmented by such educational devices as story-telling, presentation of a short dramatization, showing of a film or film-strip, dancing and games. Care should be taken that the program does not become unduly lengthy.

Community Seder

Although the Passover Seder traditionally belongs in the home, in recent years communal Sedarim have been arranged to meet the needs of homeless people and others who, for one reason or another, do not have the opportunity of enjoying this event with their families and friends. There are other Jews who have not participated in a Seder that is meaningful and inspiring. For them, the communal Seder, conducted in an atmosphere of dignity and sanctity, can be a significant experience as it provides the occasion for an interpretation of much that is sacred in Jewish life. It may also serve to prepare them to conduct a Seder at home.[2]

Careful planning and organization is required to ensure the proper execution of a communal Seder. The creation of a warm and homelike atmosphere will add dignity and inspiration to the occasion. Lighted candles, attractive Seder plates, *matzah* covers, wine cups and decanters, and beautiful flowers should grace the tables. While it may be necessary to have one leader for the entire assemblage, family groupings at small tables may be arranged, each with its own leader.

The use of uniform Haggadahs will facilitate participation in the service.

In the tradition of Passover—"Let all who are hungry enter and eat with us; let all who are forlorn come and celebrate Passover with us"—hospitality should be extended to the homeless, members of the armed services

405

stationed in the vicinity, or college students away from home.

The Third Seder

The "Third Seder" is not a substitute for the observance on the first two nights of Passover. It is a special program of readings, songs and other elements, usually held during the week of the festival. The guests on this occasion may be seated at a long banquet table or smaller tables, attractively set to create a joyous atmosphere. Using the basic pattern of the traditional Haggadah and some of its rich symbolism, the Third Seder may include verse and prose selections from ancient and modern Jewish literature and original writings of participants. Parodies of the Haggadah passages on the Four Questions and the Four Sons and of the song *Dayyenu* may be written to reflect current events and interests. Following the presentation of such parodies, a discussion may be held on one of the following subjects:

> The Ancient Exodus and the Modern Exodus: A Study in Contrasts
>
> Passover's Message to Mankind
>
> Four Questions on the Four Freedoms
>
> The Influence of Passover on the Founding of the American Republic
>
> How Free are the Children of Israel Today?

Creative dramatizations of biblical episodes, unusual observances of Passover, and classical stories will give an added dimension to the program. Skits may be built around the Four Sons, Elijah the prophet of Hope, and similar Haggadah themes.

Quiz programs are often exciting and, at the same time, educational. The guests can be invited to submit questions on aspects of Jewish life that are to be answered by a panel of experts.

A "Seder Sing," featuring Passover hymns, songs of freedom of all peoples, Israeli and Yiddish folksongs, can be conducted.

Refreshments may include wine, Israeli candy, nuts, fruit, macaroons, and other Passover delicacies.

Assignments of readings, solo singing and other roles should be made well in advance. Provision should also be made for rehearsals wherever necessary.

If a Third Seder Haggadah has been prepared, copies should be distributed to each guest to achieve maximum participation. Such a Haggadah will include the passages to be read, the songs to be sung, and instructions for following the order of the Third Seder.

Games for Passover

The custom of distributing nuts to children on the eve of Passover to arouse their curiosity[3] may well account for the origin of playing games with nuts during the festival. Another reason for this traditional and favorite pastime is that the numerical value of the Hebrew for nut (אגוז) is the same as that of the word for good (טוב). Some of the games given below have been played by Jewish children for many generations while others are modern adaptations of popular pastimes.

LEFT OR RIGHT?

One player puts both hands behind his back and places a nut in one hand. He then brings forth both hands and the other player must guess if the nut is in his left or right hand. If he guesses correctly, he takes the nut.

ODDS OR EVENS?

One player holds a number of small nuts in a closed fist. He asks the second player to guess if the nuts in his hand are an even or odd number. If the second player guesses correctly, he takes all the nuts in the hand of the first player. Failing to guess, he forfeits the corresponding number of nuts that the first player held.

NUT-PITCHING

An open box or other receptacle is placed on the floor. Each player is given five nuts and, standing at a fixed line, tries to pitch the nuts into the box. He collects those that did not fall into the box and awaits his next turn. The first player to pitch all his nuts into the box is the winner and he receives all the nuts in the box.

NUT-BOWLING

Place a two-foot board with one end on the floor and the other end leaning on one or more objects so as to form a triangle. Set ten nuts about two feet from the bottom of the board. Each player is given three walnuts which he rolls, one at a time, down the board, aiming to "bowl over" the ten nuts on the floor. He wins all the nuts that his nut hits directly or indirectly. If he fails to hit any nuts, his nut remains on the floor.

NUT RELAY

Two teams of the same number of players stand in parallel lines. The first player in the line of each team is given a twelve-inch ruler with five walnuts placed on it. He walks with it to the end of the room, turns about and brings it to the next player on his team. If a player drops any walnuts he must start from the beginning. When the last player of a team finishes, his team is declared the winner.

NUT-POLO

Slots of different sizes are cut in the bottom of a shoe box or other carton. Each slot is given a numerical value with the highest placed on the narrowest slot. From a given distance each player has a chance to roll five nuts into the slots. The aim is to obtain the highest numerical score.

MOSHEH

Two players are given identical Hebrew books—a Bible, *Festival Prayer Book* or Haggadah. One player is assigned the right-hand pages and the second the left-hand pages. The books are opened simultaneously at random and the pages are turned consecutively. The winner is the one who first finds the Hebrew letters in sequence that spell *Mosheh—Mem, Shin, Heh*—on the last line of a page.

MUSICAL QUIZ

A few bars of a Passover song are played on the piano. The first player who calls out the name of the tune is given a point. The player who has most points is the winner.

CHARADES

The group is divided into two teams. One team is given a few minutes to prepare and present a charade depicting a Passover term or idea. The second team attempts to guess it. The other team then enacts a charade for the first to identify. The following ideas may help to suggest others:

Passover (Pass over)—Objects are placed on the floor and the players pass over them.

Red Sea (red see)—Some of the players enact the crossing of the Red Sea while one of them points to and looks at something red.

Freedom (free dumb)—One player acts as if he is breaking shackles from his body and then another gives an impression of a dumb person.

PANTOMIMES

Among the many subjects for pantomimes related to Passover that may be enacted are these: Slaves in Egypt, Moses on the Nile, Moses at the Red Sea, The Dance of Miriam, The Four Sons and An Only Kid.

QUIZ GAMES

The Haggadah is a good source for developing a set of questions and answers that can be used with different kinds of quiz programs.

FIND THE AFIKOMAN

One of the players leaves the room and an *afikoman*—a piece of *matzah* wrapped in a small napkin—is concealed. As the player re-enters the room, everyone joins in singing a Passover song. If the searcher is distant from the *afikoman*, the singing is done softly and as he comes nearer the volume is increased.

SCAVENGER HUNT

The players can be divided into teams of two or more each. A list of items to be hunted is given to each team. Each item is given a stipulated number of points. Judges may evaluate the items brought in by the players and determine if they are worth the maximum number of points or less. The team with the highest score is the winner. Below is a list of articles that may be requested and the suggested number of points for each. The list distributed to the participants should not include the clues that are given in parentheses.

Passover Haggadah—5
The Story of Passover (an original essay)—10
Afikoman (a piece of *matzah*)—1
Maror (something bitter)—3
The Red Sea (the letter C painted red)—3
Assorted nuts—3
The Days of Passover (a page from a Jewish calendar)—2
Maot Hittim (money for charity)—5
Had Gadyah (picture of a kid)—3

THE STORY OF PASSOVER

All the players are seated in a circle. Each one is given the name of a person or thing connected with the story of Passover—for example: Moses, Aaron, Pharaoh, Red Sea, *matzah*. The leader tells the story of Passover and, as he mentions each name, the player rises in his place, turns around and sits down. When the leader mentions "the children of Israel," all the players rise, turn around and are seated. If a player fails to respond promptly when his name is called, he leaves the game. The leader should prepare and tell the story in such a manner that the names are mentioned frequently.

Arts and Crafts

SEDER PLATE

The special ceremonial plate to contain the six symbolic foods used at the Seder can be made in a variety of ways.

Paper plates can be decorated with water colors, crayons or poster paints. Another method is to cut out designs with different colored papers and paste them to the plate. A coating of shellac over the design and plate will enhance the effect.

Clay is a good medium for making a Seder dish. When the plate is shaped, lines can be scratched on it to mark the compartments or six individual small dishes can be made to hold the foods.

An ordinary porcelain or earthenware platter can be appropriately decorated with enamel paints.

Etching and embossing on metal or wood carving are other techniques that may be employed for the creation of an original Seder dish.

A four-tiered plate (the top tier for the symbolic foods and the others for the three *matzot*) of wood or metal can be an attractive addition to the festival table.

Drawings of the special foods, their Hebrew and English names and short quotations are some of the motifs that may be employed to adorn the plate.

The above media can also be used in the making of a novel plate for *matzot*.

MATZAH COVER

Custom requires the use of a cover with three pockets to contain the three *matzot*—Cohen, Levi and Israel. There

411

are many ways to devise such a cover and one is suggested herewith.

Four pieces of unbleached muslin, linen or cotton, or four white handkerchiefs or napkins may be used. For the top piece, an appropriate design can be drawn on paper and then traced on the material and embroidered. The Hebrew for Cohen, Levi and Israel can be embroidered on each of the other three pieces, centered within one-half inch of one side. The edges of the sides on which the names appear and the bottom edge of the top piece should be hemmed. Cut off one-half inch of the material from the side opposite to that on which Levi is embroidered. Do the same for the Cohen piece but cut off one inch. Cut off one-and-a-half inches of material from the top piece. Lay the four pieces on top of one another so that the embroidered words—Cohen, Levi and Israel—can be seen. Using embroidery stitches, sew all four pieces of material together on the three other sides so that the side on which the names appear will be open for the insertion of the *matzot*.

Instead of embroidery, water colors, or fabric paint that does not spread on cloth, can be substituted.

Crayons may also be used to draw a design and to letter. To impress the colors in the material, it is advisable to turn over the side of the material with the design on a clean piece of wrapping paper, cover it with a slightly damp cloth and then iron until dry.

Covers can be embellished with simple Passover motifs and quotations, such as "Festival of Unleavened Bread," and "Thou shalt eat unleavened bread seven days."

WINE CUPS AND DECANTERS

Wine cups, the cup of Elijah and decanters to adorn the Seder table may be made of clay and then painted appropriately.

Paper cups may be decorated with crayons or paints.

A glass tumbler can be painted with enamel. A design should be first drawn on a sheet of paper that will fit inside the tumbler. The paper can be held in place by pasting it to the rims of the glass, with the design towards the outside. The design is then traced on the outside of the glass with enamel paint. The same procedure can be followed with a decanter, provided its mouth is sufficiently large to allow the paper with the design to fit inside.

Cups and decanters may be decorated with grapes, vines and the blessing for wine. The cup of Elijah may have a characteristic motif.

HAGGADAH JACKETS

A book jacket for a Haggadah is easily made with a sheet of wrapping or heavy, colored paper large enough to cover the book. The jacket can be adorned with Passover symbols, spring motifs, or illustrations of episodes from the Haggadah. A meaningful border design can be effective. The design or illustration can be made with crayons, finger-paints or water colors. Linoleum cutting and potato printing are other good media for this purpose.

A more durable Haggadah jacket can be created by embroidery on cloth or felt and by leather tooling.

OTHER PARAPHERNALIA

Among other useful and creative objects that may be made for the festival are greeting cards, place-cards for the Seder, doilies for the wine cups and an ornamented case for the pillow on which the head of the family leans during the reading of the Haggadah. Both of the last two items can be made of cloth or leather.

Murals and friezes lend themselves for room decorations that can depict sequences related to Passover. The following are some suggested themes: the account of the Exodus; map of the wanderings of the children of Israel; symbols of the twelve tribes; Passover preparations— baking *matzot*, house-cleaning, the search for and the burning of the leaven; the Seder—order of the service; Haggadah scenes—the Four Sons, the ten plagues, opening of door for Elijah, *Had Gadya;* Passover in Israel— spring, a communal Seder, bringing the *Omer*, hora dancing.

413

XXII

DVORA LAPSON

AN ONLY KID (HAD GADYA)

(Dance Game)

The traditional *Had Gadya,* which is sung at the end of the Passover Seder, is the subject for this little dance game.

414

Formation: A group of children arrange themselves in a large circle, one child in the middle representing the kid.

Chorus: Whenever the chorus *Had Gadya* is sung, all clasp hands in a circle while going around counter-clockwise.

The Cat: When the cat is mentioned, the kid chooses a cat from those in the circle. The cat then enters the circle, imitating the movements of a cat, and pursues the kid in and out among the others who still have their hands joined in a circle until the kid escapes, becoming part of the circle. The cat takes the center position.

Chorus: The chorus is then repeated as above.

Other Characters: Action similar to the cat and kid episode occurs each time a new character is mentioned, each child trying to imitate the character he is chosen to be and pursuing the character before him in characteristic manner.

 If this should be presented on the stage, each child may wear a headdress and a costume to suggest the character he is representing.

MIRIAM'S DANCE OF TRIUMPH

The first dance mentioned in the Bible is Miriam's dance, which she and her maidens perform after the successful crossing of the Red Sea.

And Miriam the prophetess, the sister of Aaron, took a timbrel in her hand; and all the women went out after her with timbrels and with dances (Ex. 15.20).

415

Formation: The girls are dressed in long, striped dresses with elbow-length sleeves, and with sashes at the waist. On their heads they wear wide bands with short veils hanging in the back. In their right hands they hold tambourines. Miriam, the soloist, is dressed in the same manner, but a little more elaborately. She may hold cymbals in her hands.

Pantomime: To the beat of drums all run diagonally across the stage, towards the rear, as if fleeing from the Egyptians across the Red Sea. When they reach the rear corner, the drumbeats cease suddenly. They all turn towards the front and walk slowly forward towards the center of the stage, looking curiously down front where the divided waters have come together suddenly. Miriam stands in the middle while the rest separate into groups A and B on each side of her. They then bend low with arms outstretched and make four staccato, joyous gestures gradually upward, tapping the right foot at each gesture.

PART I.

Phrase 1. Miriam takes four skips forward, raising her right hand gradually higher, and four skips backwards, lowering her right hand gradually.

Phrase 2. Miriam repeats the steps of Phrase 1.

Phrase 3. She pivots (turns body in place, accentuating with a knee bend of the leg around which she turns) to the right (with four pivot steps) while holding her right hand over her head, the left hand held down.

Phrase 4. She pivots left with left hand over head.

Phrase 5. She clashes the cymbals four times on her left side, hip height.

During Part I the girls have been tapping or shaking their tambourines in the background.

PART II.

The girls join Miriam in the same dance as Part I, tambourines in their right hands.

PART III.

Phrase 1. Groups A and B move sidewise with eight short sliding steps toward the opposite side of the stage, holding tambourines high.

Phrase 2. Each one now takes eight slides back to place.

Phrase 3. All pivot in place to the right while holding tambourines in their right hands over head.

Phrase 4. All pivot left with tambourines over head in left hands.

Phrase 5. All tap tambourines on left side, hip height. Miriam, in the meantime, improvises in front of the dancers.

PART IV.

All repeat Part II together with Miriam.

Ashirah l'Adonai (2)
Ki Gaoh Gaah (2)
Sus ve-Rokhbo Ramah ba-Yam (2)
I will sing to the Lord (2)
For He hath triumphed gloriously (2)
The horse and the rider hath He thrown into the
sea (2)

(Ex. 15.1)

L'SHANAH HA-BA'AH

(Dance of Hope)

At the conclusion of the Passover Seder it is customary to say "*L'Shanah ha-Ba'ah bi-Yerushalayim*" (Next year may we be in Jerusalem). This dance expresses in folk form the hopeful spirit of the words and the song.

417

Music by
M. Nathanson

© M. Nathanson

Formation: The group stands in a circle, each one facing counter-clockwise with hands at side.

PART I.

Phrase 1. Each one takes three steps forward in the counter-clockwise direction, moving hands gradually forward upwards; then stamps three times in place while hands are held high.

Phrase 2. Repeat Phrase I.

Phrase 3. Continue counter-clockwise with eight running steps while moving hands gradually forward and upwards again.

On the repetition of the music, all make half-turn and, moving in opposite direction (clockwise), repeat all the steps of Phrases 1, 2, 3.

Phrase 4. Partners place right hands on one another's right shoulders and take four steps around clockwise stamping on first count.

Phrase 5. Same as Part I, Phrase 4, continuing clockwise.

Phrase 6. Partners continue with seven running steps, stamping on first count.

On the repetition of the music repeat of Phrases 4, 5, 6, partners place left hands on one another's left shoulders, repeating movements of Phrases 4, 5 and 6 as above, moving in the opposite direction (counter-clockwise).

PART II.

Music starts from the beginning.

Phrases 1 and 2. Partners face each other and snap fingers in four directions (diagonally right upward, diagonally left upward, out to the right side and out to the left side), while moving feet in place.

Phrase 3. Do-si-do. (Partners pass each others' right shoulders, then left shoulders, backwards in eight steps while snapping fingers.)

On repetition of music Phrases 1, 2 and 3, repeat directions of Part II, Phrases 1, 2 and 3.

Phrase 4. All form a circle, while stretching arms to side, palms touching with fingers pointing upward. Turning body slightly to face counter-clockwise all take four steps in counter-clockwise direction, stamping on first count.

Phrase 5. Repeat steps of Phrase 4, continuing counter-clockwise, stamping on first count.

Phrase 6. Take seven running steps, continuing counter-clockwise, stamping on first count.

On repetition of the music, repeat Part II, Phrases 4, 5 and 6, while going in opposite direction (clockwise).

PART III.

Finale.

Phrase 1. Take four steps towards the center of circle gradually lifting hands forward.

Phrase 2. Take four steps back gradually lowering hands, then lifting them upwards in place.

L'Shanah ha-Ba'ah
Bi-Yerushalayim.

XXIII

HANNA GOODMAN

There is a popular saying: "They don't mean the Haggadah but the *kneidlach*." This folk proverb is undoubtedly not intended to deride the story of Passover but to emphasize the role of the special dishes associated with the festival and the added dimension they give to it. These foods, when served during the year, even with Passover ingredients, still lack the *pesachdik* flavor that is tasted only on the holiday.

In past generations Passover preparations went on nearly the year round, starting in the summer months with the harvesting of the wheat for *matzah* and the making of *vishnik* from cherries. When the grapes were ripe in the fall, the Passover wine was made. By Hanukkah, many housewives had fattened the geese and the ducks, and then they rendered the fat from these fowl for use on Passover. On the morning after Purim, it was already *Erev Pesach* in many homes. A corner of a room or a closet was cleaned thoroughly and all leaven removed so that the Passover products which would be bought during the coming weeks could be stored there. Urgent consideration was given to the baking of *matzot*. Beets and water were placed in large earthenware crocks kept for

420

this purpose so that the brew would ferment for *russel borsht,* a favorite Pesach dish.

Dairy products were not used during Passover in many communities as it was impossible to arrange for their supervision. The prohibition to refrain from eating leaven eliminated the use of many foods. This resulted in the creation of special foods for Passover. *Matzah* is not only a staple in place of bread but, as meal, it is an ingredient of many Pesach dishes.

In this modern age the task of the Jewish homemaker has been simplified. She can purchase machine-made *matzot,* borsht in jars, a wide variety of packaged foods, and even chocolate, ice cream and other Kosher l' Pesach delicacies, all manufactured under rabbinical supervision.

A SEDER MENU

Wine   Matzot

Hors D'oeuvres
Karpas in Salt Water   Bitter Herb and Haroset
Hillel Sandwich

Entrees
Hard-boiled Egg in Salt Water
Stuffed Fish on Lettuce
Soup with Kneidlach

Main Course
Turkey with Matzah Dressing
Honeyed Sweet Potatoes   Green Salad

Dessert
Assorted Nuts   Fresh Fruit
Sponge Cake   Macaroons
Tea

421

HAROSET

2 apples
¼ cup shelled almonds
¼ cup shelled walnuts
1 teaspoon ginger
1 teaspoon cinnamon
¼ cup sweet wine
½ cup raisins

Quarter and core the apples. Grind the apples, raisins and nuts, and then add the ginger and cinnamon. Blend in the wine. The above quantities allow enough for twelve portions. The finished *haroset* will keep in the refrigerator for a couple of weeks.

KNEIDLACH (MATZAH-BALLS)

4 eggs
1 teaspoon salt
½ teaspoon white pepper
½ cup soup stock or water
6 tablespoons chicken fat
½ teaspoon cinnamon
(optional)
1 cup *matzah* meal

Beat the eggs with the salt, cinnamon, pepper and chicken fat. Add the *matzah* meal and the soup or water. Mix thoroughly. Cover and allow the mixture to stand in the refrigerator for one hour or more. Bring four quarts of water to a boil. Shape the mixture into *matzah*-balls and drop in boiling water. Cook covered for half an hour. Balls are then ready to be added to soup. Twelve large *matzah*-balls can be made with these ingredients.

SPONGE CAKE

6 eggs, separated
¾ cup sugar
½ cup cake meal
¼ cup orange juice
grated peel of 1 lemon
2 tablespoons potato flour

Beat the egg yolks; add sugar and beat until lemon-colored. Add the lemon peel and orange juice, and the cake meal and potato flour which have been sifted together. Beat the egg whites until stiff, and add to the egg yolk mixture, folding gently. Pour in a round ungreased cake pan. Bake for 45 minutes in a 350° oven.

BORSHT (BEET SOUP)

4 medium-size beets	8 cups of water
2 teaspoons salt	¼ cup sugar
6 tablespoons lemon juice	2 eggs

Cook the beets in water until they are soft. Peel the beets and then grate or shred them. Put the beets into eight cups of water and add the salt. Bring to a boil and cook for 20 minutes. Add the sugar and lemon juice. Taste the soup and add more sugar or lemon to correct seasoning. Beat the eggs with a little water. Add the soup very slowly to the beaten eggs, being careful that it does not curdle. This recipe provides ten portions. If the meal is a dairy one, sour cream may be added before serving.

BEET PRESERVES

4 cups cooked beets	1 cup sugar
1 lb. honey	juice of 1 lemon
½ cup walnuts	2 teaspoons powdered ginger

Bring the honey and sugar to a boil in a deep pot. Cook slowly for 15 minutes. Cut the beets into julienne pieces and add to the mixture of honey and sugar. Cook for half an hour. Add the ginger, nuts and lemon juice and then cook for 15 minutes longer.

BAGELS

1 cup boiling water	1 tablespoon sugar
½ cup shortening (or oil)	1½ teaspoons salt
2 cups *matzah* meal	6 eggs

Place the boiling water in a pot and add the shortening. When the shortening is melted, add the dry ingredients (meal, sugar and salt) all at once and beat rapidly, with the pot still on the fire, until the mixture forms a ball and leaves the side of the pot. Remove the pot from heat. Add the eggs one at a time, mixing hard until the mixture is thick and smooth. Shape into bagels. Place on a greased baking sheet. Bake in a 375° oven for one hour or until nicely browned. The above ingredients should yield twelve bagels.

MATZAH BREI

4 *matzot*	1½ teaspoons salt
4 eggs	butter or shortening

Soak the *matzot* just enough to soften them. Break the eggs in a bowl and beat with the salt. Add the soaked *matzot*. Heat the butter or shortening in a frying pan over a moderate flame. Pour the mixture and fry until golden on underside, turn over with a spatula and fry on the other side. Serve with sugar and cinnamon. Four servings.

MATZAH-MEAL PANCAKES

4 eggs	1 cup *matzah* meal
¾ cup milk or water	1 tablespoon sugar
1½ teaspoons salt	

Beat the eggs with milk or water. Add salt, sugar and *matzah* meal. Beat well. Drop with a spoon into hot shortening and fry until brown. Turn and brown on other side. Serve with sugar or jam.

ALMOND MACAROONS

4 egg yolks	2 cups ground almonds
1 cup sugar	

Beat the egg yolks well; add the sugar and beat until lemon-colored. Add the ground almonds and mix thoroughly. Chill for easy handling. Take small pieces of the mixture and shape into small balls. Place the macaroons on a greased baking sheet. Top with half an almond, if desired. Bake in 350° oven for ten minutes. Fifty macaroons.

COCOANUT MACAROONS

4 egg whites	1 cup sugar
1 cup freshly-grated cocoanut	½ cup broken walnuts

Beat the egg whites until frothy. Add the sugar and beat until stiff. Fold in the cocoanut and walnuts. Drop by teaspoon on baking sheet which is covered with wax paper. Bake for 30 minutes in a 300° oven. Remove from oven. Let stand a few minutes before removing from baking sheet. Sixty macaroons.

BOOK FIVE

Commemoration of Passover

The feast of unleavened bread shalt thou keep; seven days thou shalt eat unleavened bread, as I commanded thee . . .

Exodus 23.15

The observance and laws of Passover are enjoined in numerous biblical passages; for example: *And this day shall be unto you for a memorial, and ye shall keep it a feast to the Lord; throughout your generations* ... (Ex. 12.14) and *The feast of unleavened bread shalt thou keep* ... (*ibid.*, 23.15). The purpose of the annual commemoration is to recapture the spirit of the historical mission of ancient Israel for which they were freed from the bondage of Egypt. In all generations Passover signified the eternal hope of ultimate Redemption for all mankind. Its buoyant message of universal freedom was a clarion call to the oppressed of all nations and especially to the Jewish people.

As winter turns into spring, heralding the approach of Passover, the Jewish people eagerly anticipate and prepare for its observance with tender and yet exacting care. The advent of the festival excites the imagination and the preparations are made with deep devotion and quiet joy. The festivity attendant on Passover is a natural expression of gratitude to God for deliverance as every Jew "in every generation must regard himself as having been personally freed from Egypt."

The laws of Passover, rooted in numerous passages of

429

the Holy Scriptures, have been elaborated and detailed by Jewish sages during the course of centuries to insure the fulfillment of the biblical commandments. The sturdy pillars of Jewish Law created a fence that encompassed the duties stated in the Bible as well as other practices and customs which also served to emphasize the historicity of the festival and the spiritual yearnings of the people. The time-honored embellishments have become beloved traditions that enhance the beauty of the festival.

The rich symbolism of Passover is an assurance that its story and message will be fully understood. The laws and customs, linked as they are with the past, provide one with an opportunity to experience the realities of Jewish history.

Despite the numerous and unusual provisions involved in the observance of Passover, which incidentally have been considerably eased in this modern and mechanized age, the joyous festival of freedom and faith is warmly welcomed in Jewish homes. Like all other Jewish festivals, Passover is observed both in the synagogue and in the home. However, it is in the latter place that the festival assumes its unique role. The entire atmosphere is transformed and permeated with a picturesque charm and a festive spirit.

Special attention is paid to the children of the family, for the Bible states: *And thou shalt tell thy son in that day, saying: It is because of that which the Lord did for me when I came forth out of Egypt (ibid.,* 13.8). Thus, Passover has always had a family character that further endeared the festival to the hearts of the Jewish people.

The Month of Nisan

Nisan, the month in which Passover falls, has a special status. With the exception of the day preceding Passover, fasting is not permitted during the entire month. According to the Talmud, the Tabernacle was erected on the

430

first of Nisan and one representative of each of the twelve tribes offered a sacrifice on one of the first twelve days of the month. Each of these days was deemed a festival.[1] Then Passover is observed for eight days starting on the fifteenth of Nisan. Thus, since most of Nisan is festive, the entire month is so regarded. *Tahanunim*, supplications and penitential prayers, are not recited.[2]

Shabbat ha-Gadol

The Saturday preceding Passover is known as *Shabbat ha-Gadol*, the Great Sabbath. A number of reasons have been given to account for this significant designation. According to our sages, the Exodus, on the fifteenth of Nisan, took place on a Thursday and therefore the preceding Sabbath was the day about which God said to Moses: *In the tenth day of this month they shall take to them every man a lamb* (Ex. 12.3). By taking, for the paschal offering, lambs, which the Egyptians considered sacred animals, they demonstrated the ineffectiveness of the Egyptian gods; nevertheless, the Egyptians did not interfere with them, as Moses feared, for he said, *If we sacrifice the abomination of the Egyptians before their eyes, will they not stone us?* (ibid., 8.22). This miracle gave rise to naming the day on which it occurred as the Great Sabbath.[3] The name may also be derived from the *Haftarah* (Mal. 3.4-24) that is read on *Shabbat ha-Gadol* which speaks of the "great day": *Behold, I will send you Elijah the Prophet before the coming of the great and awe-inspiring day of the Lord (ibid.,* 23).[4]

As the Talmud states that thirty days before Passover one should inquire about and expound its laws,[5] it became the practice that on the preceding Sabbath, after the afternoon service, Jews assembled to hear a discourse on the regulations concerning the festival,[6] delivered by the one considered the *greatest* authority; hence, this day was called the Great Sabbath. Others, perhaps maliciously,

431

have claimed that the undue length of the discourse which went on until long past the Sabbath accounts for the name.

In the morning service of this Sabbath, special *Piyyutim* are read including "And It Was in the Midst of the Night" and "The Order of the Passover is Concluded" which are part of the Haggadah. After the Sabbath afternoon service, the first part of the Haggadah is reviewed to get accustomed to its reading.[7]

Maot Hittim

Especially for Passover, the festival of freedom, care must be taken to provide for the poor, as the costs for its observance are greater than usual, and they—as all other Jews—should be able to celebrate free of worry. The practice of distributing *Maot Hittim,* wheat money, or *Kimha de-Pisha,* flour for Passover, was instituted so that the needs of the indigent might be met.[8] This custom has given rise to the creation of special Passover funds in local communities.

Prohibition of Leaven

The prohibition of leaven, *hametz,* is stated in the Bible: *Seven days shall ye eat unleavened bread; howbeit the first day ye shall put away leaven out of your houses* (Ex. 12.15). Biblical injunctions specify that *hametz* must not be seen nor found in one's possessions.[9] In accordance with these laws it is necessary to make a thorough search for *hametz* and to remove it the day before Passover.[10] This usually becomes the occasion for a thorough spring cleaning.

The Bible states that the children of Israel *baked unleavened cakes of the dough which they brought out of Egypt, for it was not leavened; because they were thrust out of Egypt, and could not tarry . . .* (*ibid.,* 39). Thus,

432

the prohibition of eating *hametz* became a memorial of the Exodus: *"Remember this day, in which ye came out from Egypt . . . there shall no leavened bread be eaten"* (*ibid.*, 13.3).

The prohibition of *hametz* applies to the fermented products of five kinds of grain: wheat, barley, oats, rye and spelt. It is likewise forbidden to use any foods that contained *hametz*.

Rabbinic practice throughout the centuries was to permit the use of most vegetables, with the exception of those in the family of peas as they are liable to fermentation. Nowadays the (Ashkenazi) practice is to prohibit use of rice, peas and all types of beans.

Generally speaking, in order to refrain from *hametz* during Passover, observant Jews do not use those processed foods and food products which do not have a proper rabbinical endorsement.

Kashering

The removal of *hametz* also implies the changing of all dishes, silverware and other kitchen utensils, since they usually absorb leaven. Separate sets of dishes and utensils are generally provided for Passover, although it is possible for some items to be made fit for use by the process of *kashering*. This procedure is based on the principle that a utensil which absorbs *hametz* also exudes it and, therefore, the *kashering* must be done in the same manner in which the object is used.[11] Because of the complexity and variety of ways that are involved, it is advisable to consult a rabbi for specific instructions.

Following are some examples of methods of *kashering*. Pots and pans that are used on a fire must be glowed, that is, heated to such an extent that they become red hot and emit sparks.

Silverware made entirely of metal can be made usable

433

for Passover by thorough cleansing and then by complete immersion in boiling water. A hot iron or stone is placed in the purging vessel to facilitate the process.

Glassware must be cleaned well and then completely immersed in cold water for three days. The water should be changed daily.

There are many items that cannot be made fit for Passover use. Among them are baking dishes and other baking utensils, woodenware, earthenware, enamel, crockery and porcelain objects. A rabbi should be consulted regarding utensils that are dented or have handles, and sieves and graters, which are difficult to *kasher*.

Special care must be taken with the oven and stove. They should be cleaned and scraped thoroughly and then heated to a glow. Metal or asbestos sheets are placed on top of the range so that the Passover pots and pans do not come into direct contact with the stove.

The Search for Leaven

To be certain that no leaven will be seen or found in the house during Passover and that no one will inadvertently eat thereof, a search for leaven, *Bedikat Hametz,* is made at the beginning of the evening of the fourteenth of Nisan.[12] As the home has usually been thoroughly cleaned and rid of all *hametz* by this time, it is customary to place pieces of bread in several parts of the house which then become the object of the search as otherwise *hametz* might not be found and the benediction that is recited prior to the search would be pronounced in vain.[13] However, as the head of the family does not know where the bread pieces were placed, he must make a thorough search.

The following benediction, which also applies to the burning of the *hametz* on the following morning, is recited:

434

ברוך אתה ה' אלהינו מלך העולם אשר קדשנו במצותיו
וצונו על ביעור חמץ.

Blessed art Thou, O Lord our God, King of the
Universe, who has sanctified us by His commandments, and has commanded us to remove the leaven.[14]

Then the family head makes the search by the light of
a candle. The bread morsels and all other leaven that are
found are swept with a feather into a wooden spoon and
wrapped in a cloth. On the conclusion of the search, the
following is said:
> Any kind of leaven which remains in my possession
> that I have not seen nor removed or about which I
> do not know shall be regarded as non-existent and
> considered as the dust of the earth.[15]

Burning the Hametz

On the morning of the fourteenth day of Nisan, before
ten o'clock, the *hametz* that remains is burned and the
following statement is made:
> Any kind of leaven which remains in my possession
> whether or not I have seen it, whether or not I have
> removed it, shall be regarded as non-existent and
> considered as the dust of the earth.

Hametz is generally not eaten after 9:00 A.M. on the
day before Passover.[16]

The Sale of Hametz

The rabbis recognized the difficulties and hardships of
those who possessed leaven in large quantities and would
suffer substantial losses if they destroyed all of their
hametz. To obviate this situation, they instituted *Mekirat*

435

Hametz, the transfer of leaven to a non-Jew by a legal bill of sale. Because of the intricacies of the legal formulation, a rabbi is usually designated by his congregants as their agent to execute the transaction. While the physical transfer of the leaven is not made, the non-Jew has the legal right to take possession of it.

All *hametz* that is sold, as well as the non-Passover dishes and utensils after having been thoroughly cleaned, should be placed in a separate locked closet or spare room so that it is out of sight.[17]

After Passover, the rabbi buys back the leaven from the non-Jew and thus restores it to the possession of the original owners.[18]

Matzah

While the law is that it is forbidden to eat *matzah* on the day before Passover,[19] the custom is to avoid doing so for a longer period prior to the festival so that the unleavened bread will be eaten at the Seder with a hearty appetite, thus expressing a love for the fulfillment of a commandment.[20]

The duty to eat *matzah* is binding only on the first night of Passover,[21] although the partaking of leaven is forbidden throughout the festival. This accounts for the fact that the special benediction "on eating unleavened bread" is said only at the Seder and *matzah shemurah* (unleavened bread that is watched) is used then.

The biblical commandment *And ye shall observe the feast of unleavened bread* (Ex. 12.17) implies that one must be careful to watch that the dough for the *matzah* should not become leavened.[22] In the preparation of *matzah,* the bakers must take precautions, in the kneading and baking processes, that the dough should not ferment and thus become leavened. A further precaution is taken through the careful watching of the wheat for the *matzah,* during its harvesting and milling, to assure that rain or dampness will not cause fermentation. The unleavened bread that is made with this extra care is known as *matzah shemurah* and is eaten by the more pious throughout the entire festival. It is also known as *matzot mitzvah*, unleavened bread of the precept.[23]

The Fast of the First-Born

As a reminder that the Lord *passed over the houses of the children of Israel* (Ex. 12.27) and spared their eldest sons on the eve of Passover when the first-born of the Egyptians were slain, the fourteenth day of Nisan is observed as *Ta'anit Bekhorim,* a fast day for the first-born son of every Jewish family.[24]

The custom prevails today that the first-born participate in a *Seudat Mitzvah,* a religious meal following a *Siyyum,* the completion of the study of a tractate of the Talmud. Participation in this study and meal exempts one from the duty of fasting.

Erub Tabshilin

On the first two and the last two days of Passover it is permissible to prepare only the food that is required for those days. However, the preparation of food on those days for the Sabbath that immediately follows is forbidden unless it was started before the festival. Hence, a symbolic mixture of cooked or roasted foods, *Erub tabshilin,* consisting of meat, fish, or egg with *matzah,* is made on the eve of the festival, which is to be eaten on the following Sabbath.

The following benediction is said:

ברוך אתה ה' אלהינו מלך העולם אשר קדשנו במצותיו וצונו על מצות ערוב.

437

Blessed art Thou, O Lord our God, who has sanctified us by His commandments, and has commanded us to observe the *erub*.

The Table Setting

The table for the *Seder* is set before nightfall with a white cloth, beautiful vessels and the necessary appurtenances,[25] including the *ke'arah*, the three *matzot* in a special three-part cover, wine cups, and the cup for Elijah.

KE'ARAH

The *ke'arah*, a large platter, contains these unique foods used at the Seder:

Betzah, roasted egg, representing the *Hagigah* or festival offering.

Zeroa, roasted bone, a memorial of the paschal lamb offered on the night of Passover in the Temple.

Maror, bitter herb.

Karpas, green vegetable.

Haroset, a sweet pap mixture.

Salt water.[26]

While there are varying ways of arranging the foods on the *ke'arah*, the following method may be used: the *betzah, maror* and *zeroa* are placed, from left to right, in one row and the *karpas*, salt water and *haroset*, in the same order in a second line.

THE THREE MATZOT

On Sabbaths and festivals, with the exception of the first two nights of Passover, one is obligated to break bread and say the blessing over two whole loaves of bread, for it is written that . . . *on the sixth day they gathered twice as much bread* (Ex. 16.22),[27] referring to the double portion of manna that fell on Fridays when the Israelites were in the wilderness. On these two nights, a third loaf or cake of unleavened bread is added to fulfill the commandment of eating *the bread of affliction* (Deut. 16.3),

438

for the Jewish sages did not want the two loaves used every Sabbath and festival to recall the bread of affliction.

The cabalists called these three *matzot* by the names of the three divisions of Israel—Cohen, Levi and Israel—to symbolize the unity of the Jewish people.

THE FOUR CUPS OF WINE

Each celebrant has a goblet from which he drinks four times during the Seder: when the *Kiddush* is recited, as on every Sabbath and festival; following the benediction of redemption; at the end of the grace after meals; and before the conclusion of the Seder.[28]

It is generally stated that the drinking of the four cups of wine recalls the four expressions of redemption in Exodus 6.6-7, the biblical verses wherein God promised to liberate the Israelites from Egypt.[29]

CUP OF ELIJAH

A controversy arose among the gaonim in the Middle Ages and among the later rabbis about the necessity of drinking four or five cups of wine, as there is a fifth expression related to redemption: *And I will bring you in unto the land* . . . (Ex. 6.8). Since they did not reach an agreement, they decided that a fifth cup of wine should be placed on the table but not be used. The talmudic expression for the settlement of a doubt was ". . . until Elijah arrives." As it was hoped that the problem of the controversial fifth cup would likewise be settled by Elijah, this goblet was named for him.[30]

The use of the cup of Elijah, a comparatively late custom dating probably from the eighteenth century, has become a symbol of the eternal hope for freedom and salvation that will be realized with the coming of the prophet.

The opening of the door following the Grace After Meals is also a reminder to trust in divine Providence on the "night of watching" and thus express one's belief in the promise of salvation from enemies and of the messianic era that will be fulfilled with the coming of the

439

prophet on Passover.[31] This tradition, a much earlier one, is based on the talmudic statement that "in Nisan they were redeemed and in Nisan they are destined to be redeemed."[32]

WEARING OF THE KITTEL

A kittel, or white robe, is worn by the leader of the Seder. Among the various reasons for this custom is the explanation that white is symbolic of joy and that, according to the Talmud, white clothes are worn on festive occasions.[33] "The children of Israel wear white, eat and drink and rejoice for they know that the Holy One, Blessed be He, performs miracles for them."[34]

THE PRACTICE OF RECLINING

One is obliged to recline at the Seder table as a sign of freedom, for that was the manner of free men in ancient days.[35] Even the poor of Israel are expected to recline while they eat at the Seder as an expression of their independence,[36] even though they may be subject to hardships throughout the year.

The practice of reclining while eating was a general one at the time that the Passover observances were instituted. Accordingly, in the series of questions to be asked at the Seder that is found in the Babylonian Mishnah, there is no reference to leaning.[37] After the destruction of the Temple and when this custom was no longer in vogue, the Seder night was the only time during the year when Jews reclined while dining. Hence, the question relevant to this practice was included in the Four Questions.

Order of the Home Service

KADDESH (SANCTIFYING THE FESTIVAL)

The Seder starts with the chanting by the leader of the *Kiddush*, a proclamation of the sanctity of the festival, over a cup of wine. While on Sabbaths and other festivals, everyone drinks the wine of the *Kiddush* from the cup of the leader, at the Seder each one has his own cup of wine. The wine is drunk in a reclining position.[38]

U-REHATZ (WASHING THE HANDS)

Before one dips food into a liquid, one is required to wash his hands;[39] therefore, before partaking of the *karpas*, the hands are washed without reciting the blessing.[40]

KARPAS (DIPPING THE GREENS)

A small piece of celery or other green vegetable, *karpas*, is dipped in salt water and the benediction for vegetables is said. This unusual practice is for the purpose of arousing the interest of the children.[41] Many people have associated the vegetable, symbolically, with the joyous festival of spring and the salt water with the tears shed by the Israelites during their years of enslavement in Egypt.[42]

YAHATZ (DIVIDING THE MIDDLE MATZAH)

The middle of the three *matzot* is divided into two. The larger piece, called the *afikoman*, is then wrapped in a napkin and hidden under the pillow on which the leader reclines. The smaller piece is returned to its place.[43] The purpose of this procedure is to retain the interest of the children throughout the Haggadah ceremony.

MAGGID (NARRATING THE PASSOVER STORY)

See above, Chapter V, "The Development of the Passover Haggadah."

REHATZ (WASHING THE HANDS)

The hands are washed and the appropriate blessing is said, in accord with usage prior to eating bread.

MOTZI (BLESSING THE BREAD)

The blessing on bread is recited.

441

MATZAH (BLESSING THE UNLEAVENED BREAD)

The blessing on unleavened bread is recited.[44]

MAROR (EATING THE BITTER HERB)

As a reminder that *the Egyptians made the children of Israel to serve with rigor. And they made their lives bitter with hard service, in mortar and in brick* (Ex. 1.13-14), it has been ordained that bitter herbs shall be eaten *(ibid., 12.8).*

The bitter herb is dipped into *haroset* and the blessing recited.

Haroset, a mixture of apples, nuts, almonds, cinnamon and wine, is symbolic of the mortar out of which the children of Israel made bricks in Egypt.[45]

While one may eat different kinds of herbs to fulfill one's obligation,[46] it is customary to use horseradish.

KOREK (WRAPPING THE MAROR WITH MATZAH)

A piece of the third *matzah* is taken and the bitter herb combined with it to make a sandwich to fulfill the commandment . . . *they shall eat it with unleavened bread and bitter herbs* (Nu. 9.11).

The Talmud tells us that this practice was introduced by Hillel[47] during the days of the second Temple.

SHULHAN OREKH (SERVING THE MEAL)

It is customary to start the meal with an entrée of hard-boiled eggs in salt water, symbolic of mourning.[48] The egg, also eaten at the mourner's first meal,[49] is said to represent the idea of resurrection. Jewish sages have felt that even joyous occasions, such as the festive meal of the Seder, should have a symbol of sadness in memory of the destruction of the Temple.

TZAFUN (EATING THE CONCEALED AFIKOMAN)

At the conclusion of the meal, a piece of the *afikoman* is distributed to all the celebrants so that each may partake of it.[50] The custom has arisen that the children obtain

442

possession of the *afikoman* during the course of the Seder and hold it until it is redeemed with a gift. This may be based on the talmudic statement "they hasten [the eating of] the *matzot* on the nights of Passover so that the children should not sleep,"[51] which has been interpreted to mean "they snatch the *matzot.*"

BAREKH (RECITING THE GRACE AFTER MEALS)

The grace after meals is recited.

HALLEL (PRAISING THE LORD)

The reading of *Hallel* (Ps. 115-118) is completed, the first part having been read before the meal. This is followed by a "benediction over song"[52] and the Great *Hallel* (Ps. 136), so called because it is composed of twenty-six lines of praise to God for His enduring mercy, corresponding to the twenty-six generations of man, from creation until the giving of the Torah, to whom the Lord showed kindness.[53] Furthermore, twenty-six is the numerical equivalent of the Hebrew Tetragrammaton.

NIRTZAH (CONCLUDING THE SERVICE)

The Seder having been performed according to its law and statute, a closing poem is chanted and the hope expressed that the children of Israel will be "next year in Jerusalem."

This is followed by a number of supplementary hymns. See above, Chapter XV, "Passover in Music."

The Passover Liturgy

The liturgy of the first and last two days of Passover is largely similar to the Sabbath service, with the addition of *Hallel* and *piyyutim*, poetical insertions. Some of the *piyyutim* for the first evening, called *ma'arabiyyot*, using the theme of the "night of watching" (Ex. 12.42), describe the wonders effected by God on this night of

Passover. Others recall the bondage in Egypt and express the hope for future manifestations of God's providence. While the *ma'arabiyyot* for the second night largely express the same thoughts, one of them recounts events in the Bible when the children of Israel were spared from enemies.

The additions to the morning service, *yotzerot*, of the first two days of Passover and the Sabbath of *Hol ha-Moed* are based on the Song of Songs, the scroll read on the above Sabbath.

The morning services of the intermediate days, largely the same as those of weekdays, are followed by half *Hallel*, the reading of the Torah and the additional service.

The dominant theme of the *piyyutim* on the seventh and eighth days of Passover is the Song of Moses sung at the Red Sea. A hymn, "A New Song Sang the Redeemed," by Judah Halevi, is found in the morning service of the seventh day.

The *Amidah* includes this insertion:

> Thou, O Lord our God, hast lovingly given us festivals for gladness, feasts and seasons for rejoicing: this Feast of Unleavened Bread, Festival of our Freedom, a holy convocation in remembrance of the Exodus from Egypt.

HALLEL

Hallel, psalms of praise, sung by the Levites during the slaughter of the Passover offering,[54] is recited on the first two days of Passover. On the intermediate and last two days of the festival an abbreviated *Hallel* is said[55] for it was on the seventh day of Passover that the Egyptians were drowned in the Red Sea. "And the angels wanted to chant their hymns, but the Holy One blessed be He said, 'My creatures are drowning in the sea and shall you chant hymns?' "[56] This may also be attributed to the injunction: *Rejoice not when thine enemy falleth* (Prov. 24.17). As *Hol ha-Moed* could not be more important than the last

444

days of Passover, the half *Hallel* is also said on these intermediate days.

PRAYER FOR DEW

Tal, a prayer for dew in the land of Israel, is chanted on the first day of Passover during the additional service.[57] Composed during the eighth century by Elazar ha-Kalir, this prayer, a reversed alphabetical acrostic, expresses the hope that the earth will be fertilized by dew during the dry season and that the land of Israel will be restored.

MEMORIAL SERVICES

Yizkor, a memorial service for the souls of deceased parents and other relatives, is held on the last day of Passover. While the recital of prayers accompanied by charity for the dead was in vogue during the talmudic period,[58] it was not introduced into the festival liturgy until very much later.

Scriptural Readings

The portions of the Torah read on Passover deal with the account of the Exodus, the crossing of the Red Sea and the laws of the festival.

Two scrolls are used on each day of Passover, *Maftir* being read in the second one.

Following is the order of the scriptural readings, and some of their subjects which make these passages relevant to Passover:

First Day:

Exodus 12.21-51

The last of the ten plagues, the events leading to the Exodus, and the laws of the first Passover.

Numbers 28.16-25 *(Maftir)*

The paschal offerings.

Joshua 5.2-6.1,27 *(Haftarah)*

The Passover celebration at Gilgal.

Second Day:
> Leviticus 22.26-23.44
>> Laws concerning the major festivals and reference to the *Omer*.
>
> Numbers 28.16-25 *(Maftir)*
>> The paschal offerings.
>
> II Kings 23.1-9,21-25 *(Haftarah)*
>> The Passover celebration of King Josiah.

First Intermediate Day:
> Exodus 13.1-16
>> Unleavened bread and the first-born, recalling the first-born Israelites who were spared in Egypt.
>
> Numbers 28.19-25 *(Maftir)*

Second Intermediate Day:
> Exodus 22.24-23.19
>> The Feast of Unleavened Bread.
>
> Numbers 28.19-25 *(Maftir)*

Third Intermediate Day:
> Exodus 34.1-26
>> The pilgrimage festivals and *matzah*.
>
> Numbers 28.19-25 *(Maftir)*

Fourth Intermediate Day:
> Numbers 9.1-14
>> Laws of Passover.
>
> Numbers 28.19-25 *(Maftir)*

Shabbat Hol ha-Moed:
> Song of Songs
>> An allegory attesting to the love of God for Israel which was exemplified in the redemption from Egyptian bondage. The appropriateness and timeliness of reading this scroll are also based on the reference to the Exodus (1.9) and to the hailing of spring which generally coincides with Passover:
>>> For, lo, the winter is past,
>>> The rain is over and gone;
>>> The flowers appear on the earth;

> The time of singing is come,
> And the voice of the turtle dove is
> heard in our land (2.11-12).

(If the seventh or eighth day falls on a Sabbath, the Song of Songs is read then. Some also read it at the conclusion of the Haggadah.)

Exodus 33.12-34.26
> The pilgrimage festivals and *matzah.*

Numbers 28.19-25 *(Maftir)*

Ezekiel 27.1-14 *(Haftarah)*
> Ezekiel's vision of the valley of dry bones is associated with resurrection and Redemption. The dry bones seen by the prophet were said to be the skeletons of sons of Ephraim who hastened to escape from Egypt before the general Exodus and were killed in the wilderness.[59]

Seventh Day:
> Exodus 13.17-15.26
>> The crossing of the Red Sea and the Song of Moses.
>
> Numbers 28.19-25 *(Maftir)*
>
> II Samuel 22.1-51 *(Haftarah)*
>> A song of deliverance of David, paralleling the Song of Moses.

Eighth Day:
> Deuteronomy 14.22-16.17 (on the Sabbath)
>
> Deuteronomy 15.19-16.17 (on a weekday)
>> Passover and the pilgrimages.
>
> Numbers 28.19-25 *(Maftir)*
>
> Isaiah 10.32-12.6 *(Haftarah)*
>> Isaiah's portrayal of the messianic era; reference to Egypt.

Counting of the Omer

And ye shall count unto you from the morrow after the day of rest,[60] *from the day that ye brought the sheaf (Omer) of the waving; seven weeks shall there be com-*

plete; even unto the morrow after the seventh week shall ye number fifty days . . . (Lev. 23.15-16).

Sefirat ha-Omer, the counting of the *Omer,* a sheaf or a dry measure of barley from the new spring harvest that was brought to the Temple on the second day of Passover, is observed to this day.

The purpose of the counting, according to cabalists, is to join Passover, the festival of physical redemption and emancipation, with Shavuot, the festival when the children of Israel received the Law which made them spiritually free. As the object of the Exodus of the children of Israel from Egypt was the receiving of the Torah, the days between the two festivals are anxiously and expectantly counted, just as one awaits a close friend by counting the days until his arrival.[61]

Starting on the second night of Passover until the eve of Shavuot, a special benediction "concerning the counting of the *Omer"* is recited and then the number of the day and of the week is stated.

Reform Service

Reform Jews observe the first and the seventh days of Passover and consequently they hold a Seder only the first night.

The Passover liturgy of Reform Jews, part of the *Union Prayer Book,* follows that of the Sabbath with a number of additions. Special prayers are said by the reader at all services. In the morning service there are also responsive readings and Psalms 113, 114 and 118 of the *Hallel* are read.

A prayer for dew is recited on the first morning of Passover and a special prayer is added on the Sabbath during Passover. On the seventh day a memorial service is included.

The following scriptural portions are read:

Shabbat ha-Gadol:
    Weekly portion
    Malachi 3.4-24 *(Haftarah)*
        The day of judgment and the promise of the coming of Elijah.
First Day:
    Exodus 12.37-42,13.3-10
        Unleavened bread and the night of watching.
    Isaiah 43.1-15 *(Haftarah)*
        A prophecy of Israel's salvation.
Shabbat Hol ha-Moed:
    Exodus 33.12-34.26
        The pilgrimage festivals and *matzah.*
    Song of Songs 2.7-17 *(Haftarah)*
    or Ezekiel 37.1-15 *(Haftarah)*
Seventh Day:
    Exodus 14.30-15.18
        The Song of Moses at the Red Sea.
    Isaiah 11.1-6,9; 12.1-6 *(Haftarah)*
        The prophecy of the messianic era and two hymns.

Glossary of Passover Terms

ADDIR HU (Mighty is He)—A hymn sung at the Seder.

AFIKOMAN (Dessert)—A broken piece of *matzah* put aside at the beginning of the Passover Seder which is eaten at the end of the meal; also, post-prandial revelry, celebrated by going from home to home. See *Yahatz* and *Tzafun*.

BEDIKAT HAMETZ (Searching for leaven)—The search for leaven on the eve before Passover. See *Hametz*.

BIUR HAMETZ (Burning of leaven)—The burning of the *hametz* on the morning before Passover. See *Hametz*.

CUP OF ELIJAH—A cup of wine placed on the Passover table to express the wish for the coming of Elijah, the prophet of hope and faith.

EGG—An egg placed on the Seder plate, symbolic of the festival offering brought to the Temple on Passover; also, symbolic of mourning for the destruction of the Temple.

EHAD MI YODE'A (Who knows One?)—A song sung at the Seder.

ELIJAH—See Cup of Elijah.

EREV PESACH (Eve of Passover)—The day preceding the festival.

FOUR QUESTIONS—Questions related to the distinctive character of Passover which are asked by the youngest child at the Seder.

FOUR SONS—The Haggadah expounds on four types of sons, representing different religious attitudes.

HAD GADYA (One Kid)—An Aramaic song sung at the Passover Seder.

HAGGADAH (Narration)—The special book read at the Passover Seder.

HAG HA-MATZOT (Festival of Unleavened Bread)—One of the names for Passover.

HAG HA-PESACH (Festival of the Paschal Lamb Offering)—Another name for Passover.

451

Glossary of Passover Terms

HAG HE-ABIB (Festival of Spring or of the ripening of barley)—Another designation for Passover.

HAMETZ (Leaven)—Leavened bread and food, as well as all dishes and cooking utensils used throughout the year, whose use is forbidden on Passover.

HAROSET—A mixture of nuts, apples, cinnamon and wine eaten at the Passover Seder, associated with the brick and mortar used by the enslaved Israelites.

HOL HA-MOED (Semi-festive days)—The four intermediary days between the first and the last two days of Passover.

KARPAS (Parsley or other green vegetable)—One of the items used during the Seder, associated with the spring festival.

KE'ARAH (Platter)—The special platter used at the Seder to contain the symbolic foods.

KIDDUSH (Sanctification)—A prayer sanctifying the Sabbaths and festivals, usually chanted over wine, both evening and morning.

KITTEL (Robe)—A white robe worn at the Seder by the head of the family.

KNEIDLACH—Dumplings eaten on Passover.

KOSHER—Ritually fit for use.

KOSHER L' PESACH (Fit for Passover)—Food that is ritually fit for use during Passover.

MAH NISHTANNAH (Why is this different?)—The opening words of the Four Questions recited during the Passover Seder.

MAHZOR—A *Festival Prayer Book.*

MAOT HITTIM (Money for wheat)—Funds to meet the Passover needs of the poor.

MAROR (Bitter)—Bitter herbs, usually horseradish, eaten at the Seder to recall the bitterness suffered by the children of Israel in Egypt.

MATZAH—Unleavened bread eaten during Passover.

MATZOT—Plural of *matzah.*

MEKIRAT HAMETZ (Selling of leaven)—The bailment sale to a non-Jew of any *hametz* that has not been discarded or burnt prior to Passover. See *hametz.*

PASSOVER—See Pesach.

PESACH (Passover)—Festival of Passover, commemorating the Exodus from Egypt; the paschal sacrifice.

SEDER (Order)—The order of service in the home on the first two nights of Passover.

SEFIRAH (Counting)—The seven week period from the second day of Passover to Shavuot.

SHABBAT HA-GADOL (The Great Sabbath)—The Sabbath which falls before Passover.

SHULHAN OREKH (Prepared table)—The meal served at the Passover Seder.

SIYYUM BEKHORIM (Completion by the first-born)—Participation in the completion of the study of a tractate of the Talmud followed by a feast on

452

the eve of Passover exempts first-born males from fasting on this day. See *Ta'anit Bekhorim.*

TA'ANIT BEKHORIM (Fast of the first-born)—The day before Passover is a day of fasting for the first-born males in gratitude for God's sparing of the first-born Israelites in Egypt.

TAL (Dew)—Prayer for dew recited during the synagogue services on the first day of Passover.

TZAFUN (Hidden)—After the meal, the piece of *matzah* hidden for *afikoman* is eaten. See *Yahatz.*

YAHATZ (Break in two)—The breaking of the middle of the three *matzot* of which one piece is put away for the *afikoman.*

ZEMAN HERUTENU (Season of Our Freedom)—Another name for the Passover festival.

ZEROA (Shankbone)—Roasted shankbone placed on the Seder platter as a reminder of the paschal lamb sacrificed by the children of Israel.

Bibliography

GENERAL

ABRAHAMS, ISRAEL, *Festival Studies: Being Thoughts on the Jewish Year*, Julius H. Greenstone, Philadelphia, 1906, pp. 1-4, 40-55, 103-110, 167-173.

ADLERBLUM, NIMA H., *A Perspective of Jewish Life Through its Festivals*, Jewish Forum Publishing Co., New York, 1930, pp. 20-29.

AGUILAR, GRACE, *The Women of Israel*, Groombridge and Sons, London, 1872, pp. 124-135.

AHAD HA-AM, *Essays: Letters: Memoirs*, trans. and ed. by Leon Simon, East and West Library, Oxford, 1946, pp. 102-115.

ALEXANDER, W. A., *A Book for Passover and Other Holidays*, Lakeside Press, Chicago, 1937, pp. 11-29.

AYYALI, MEIR (ed.), *Hagim u-Zemanim*, Gazit, Tel Aviv, 5709, I, 91-282.

BARUCH, Y. L. and LEVINSKI, YOM-TOV (eds.), *Sefer ha-Moadim: Shalosh Regalim:Pesach*, Oneg-Shabbat Society and Dvir, Tel Aviv, 1948.

BERNSTEIN, PHILIP S., *What the Jews Believe*, Farrar, Straus and Young, New York, 1950, pp. 55-74.

BLUMENFELD, ISRAEL, *Pessach-Buch: 5706-1946*, Judische Rundschau, Marburg, Germany, 1946.

The Book of Passover, Jewish Pocket Books, New York, 1947.

BROIDA, EPHRAIM, *The Call to Freedom: A Jewish Anthology*, Hechaluz Organizations of Great Britain, London, 1941.

BUBER, MARTIN, *Moses*, East and West Library, Oxford and London, 1946.

BUGATCH, SIMON; ESTERSON, SIDNEY I.; and KAPLAN, LOUIS L.; *Spotlight on Passover*, Board of Jewish Education, Baltimore, 1951.

COHEN, BERYL D., *Judaism in Theory and Practice*, Bloch Publishing Co., New York, 1948, pp. 192-197.

COHEN, YEHUDAH PINHAS (ed.), *Mi-Shibud le-Geulah*, Mosad ha-Rab Kook, Jerusalem, 5703.

DE HAAS, JACOB, *Encyclopedia of Jewish Knowledge*, Behrman House, New York, 1938.

EDIDIN, BEN M., *Jewish Holidays and Festivals*, Hebrew Publishing Co., New York, 1940, pp. 131-153.

———, *Jewish Life and Customs: Unit Six: Passover*, Jewish Education Committee of New York, 1944.

EHRMANN, ELIESER L., *Arbeitsplan fur Pessach*, Reichsvertretung der Juden in Deutschland, Berlin, 1938.

———, *Pessach: Ein Quellenheft*, Schocken Verlag, Berlin, 1938.

EISENSTEIN, IRA, *What We Mean By Religion*, Behrman House, New York, 1938, pp. 99-110.

EPSTEIN, MORRIS, *A Pictorial Treasury of Jewish Holidays and Customs*, Ktav Publishing Co., New York, 1959, pp. 84-99.

The Festivals: Pesach, Rosh Hashana, Sukkot (Mayanot), World Zionist Organization, Jerusalem, 1956, pp. 9-75.

FINKELSTEIN, LOUIS, *The Beliefs and Practices of Judaism*, Devin-Adair Co., New York, 1952, pp. 56-61.

454

Bibliography

FISHMAN, JUDAH LEB HA-KOHEN, *Hagim u-Moadim,* Mosad ha-Rab Kook, Jerusalem, 1944, pp. 169-242.

GASTER, THEODOR H., *Festivals of the Jewish Year: A Modern Interpretation and Guide,* William Sloane Associates, New York, 1953, pp. 31-58.

———, *Passover: Its History and Traditions,* Henry Schuman, New York, 1949.

GOLDIN, HYMAN E., *The Jewish Woman and Her Home,* Jewish Culture Publishing Co., Brooklyn, N. Y., 1941, pp. 147-167.

———, *The Story of Passover and Its Celebration,* Bloch Publishing Co., New York, 1930.

———, *A Treasury of Jewish Holidays,* Twayne Publishers, New York, 1952, pp. 128-187.

GOLDMAN, ALEX J., *A Handbook for the Jewish Family,* Bloch Publishing Co., New York, 1958, pp. 167-262.

GOLUB, JACOB S., *The Zionist Pesach Book,* Zionist Organization of America, New York, 1937.

——— (ed.), *Library Bulletin,* II, no. 6 (March, 1941), Jewish Education Committee of New York.

GOODMAN, PHILIP, *Passover Program Material for Youth and Adults,* National Jewish Welfare Board, New York, 1946.

———, *Habanoth Manual,* Women's Branch, Union of Orthodox Jewish Congregations, New York, 1937, pp. 61-71.

GORDON, ALBERT I., *How to Celebrate Passover at Home,* United Synagogue of America, New York, 1947.

GREENBERG, BETTY D. and SILVERMAN, ALTHEA O., *The Jewish Home Beautiful,* National Women's League of the United Synagogue of America, New York, 1941, pp. 28-31, 58-60, 71-72, 80, 109-117.

GREENSTEIN, JOSEPH, *Let My People Go,* Zionist Organization of America, New York, 1946.

GREENSTONE, JULIUS H., *Jewish Feasts and Fasts,* Philadelphia, 1945, pp. 171-218.

———, *The Jewish Religion,* Jewish Chautauqua Society, Philadelphia, 1915, pp. 29-49.

HAMIEL, HAYYIM (ed.), *Mayanot:Pesah,* Department of Torah Education and Culture in the Diaspora, World Zionist Organization, Jerusalem, 1953.

HERRMANN, HUGO, *Chad Gadya: Das Pessachbuch,* Jüdischer Verlag, Berlin, 1914.

Herut: Yalkut Shel Pesah, Histadrut ha-Obdim be-Eretz Yisrael, Tel Aviv, 5695.

HOENIG, SIDNEY B., "The Duration of the Festival of Matzot," *Jewish Quarterly Review,* II, no. 4 (April, 1959), pp. 271-277.

ISAACS, MIRIAM and WEISS-ROSMARIN, TRUDE, *What Every Jewish Woman Should Know,* Jewish Book Club, New York, 1941, pp. 55-58, 89-90.

JACOBSON, BERNHARD S., *Pesah: Arbeitsplan und Stoffsammlung,* Tenuat Tora Wa'awoda in Deutschland, Hamburg, 5696.

The Jewish Encyclopedia, 12 vols., Funk and Wagnalls, New York, 1901-1905. See *Afikoman,* Egypt, Exodus, *Had Gadya,* Haggadah, Leaven, *Mazzah,* Moses, Passover, Plague, Seder.

455

Bibliography

JOSEPH, MORRIS, *Judaism as Creed and Life,* London and New York, 1925, pp. 212-223.

KAPLAN, MORDECAI M., *The Meaning of God in Modern Jewish Religion,* Behrman House, New York, 1937, pp. 265-296.

KASOVICH, ISRAEL, *The Eternal People,* Jordan Publishing Co., New York, 1927, pp. 23-46.

LEHRMAN, S. M., *The Jewish Festivals,* Shapiro, Vallentine and Co., London, 1938, pp. 38-58.

LEVI, SHONIE B. and KAPLAN, SYLVIA R., *Across the Threshold,* Farrar, Straus & Cudahy, New York, 1959, pp. 105-114.

LEVINGER, ELMA E., *Jewish Festivals in the Religious School,* Union of American Hebrew Congregations, Cincinnati, 1923, pp. 159-206, 449-502.

———, *Passover Entertainments,* Union of American Hebrew Congregations, Cincinnati, 1924.

LEVY, ISAAC, *A Guide to Passover,* Jewish Chronicle Publications, London, 1958.

LEWITTES, MENDEL, *Passover,* Union of Orthodox Jewish Congregations of America, New York.

LIPSON, M. (ed.), *Moadim: Sefer Pesah,* Jewish National Fund and Omanut, Tel Aviv, 1946.

MARKOWITZ, S. H., *Leading a Jewish Life in the Modern World,* Union of American Hebrew Congregations, Cincinnati, 1942, pp. 250-277.

———, *Passover: Adjusting the Jewish Child to His World,* part VI, National Federation of Temple Sisterhoods, Cincinnati.

MELAMED, DEBORAH M., *The Three Pillars,* Women's League of the United Synagogue of America, New York, 1927, pp. 95-105.

MORGENSTERN, JULIAN, "The Origin of Massoth and the Massoth-Festival," *American Journal of Theology,* XXI, no. 2 (April, 1917), pp. 275-293.

NECHES, SOLOMON M., *As At This Day,* Bloch Publishing Co., New York, 1930, pp. 18-24.

NEHER, ANDRÉ, *Moses and the Vocation of the Jewish People,* Harper Torchbooks, New York, 1959.

ORLINSKY, HARRY M., "Moses," *Great Jewish Personalities in Ancient and Medieval Times,* ed. by Simon Noveck, Farrar, Straus & Cudahy, New York, 1959, pp. 9-39.

Pesach: A Manual, Union of Orthodox Jewish Congregations of America, New York, 1959.

Pessah: Ses Origines—Sa Signification—Comment on le Célèbre, Editions O.P.E.J., Paris, 1949.

RABINOWITZ, ESTHER (ed.), *Hagim u-Moadim be-Hinuk,* Urim, Tel Aviv, 5714, pp. 223-252.

RIVKIN, B., *Yidishe Yom-Tovim,* Morris S. Sklarsky, New York, 1950, pp. 101-141.

ROTH, CECIL (ed.), *The Standard Jewish Encyclopedia,* Doubleday & Co., Garden City, N.Y., 1959.

SCHAUSS, HAYYIM, *The Jewish Festivals,* Union Of American Hebrew Congregations, Cincinnati, 1938, pp. 38-85.

SOLTES, MORDECAI, *The Jewish Holidays: 250 Questions and Answers on Their Origin, Significance, and Observance,* National Jewish Welfare Board, New York, 1931, pp. 26-31, 61-64.

The Story of Pesach, B. Manischewitz Co., Cincinnati, 1947.

STRACK, HERMANN L., *The Jew and Human Sacrifice* [Human Blood and Jewish Ritual], Bloch Publishing Co., New York, 1909.

SUSSMAN, SAMUEL and SEGAL, ABRAHAM, *50 Assembly Programs for the Jewish School,* United Synagogue Commission on Jewish Education, New York, 1948, pp. 105-112.

THIEBERGER, FRIEDRICH (ed.), *Jüdisches Fest: Jüdischer Brauch,* Jüdischer Verlag, Berlin, 1936, pp. 198-279.

UNGER, MENASHE, *Chassidus un Yom-Tov,* New York, 1958, pp. 229-287.

The Universal Jewish Encyclopedia, 10 vols. New York, 1939-1943. See Egypt, Exodus, Haggadah, Leaven, *Mazzah,* Moses, Passover, Plague, Seder.

UNTERMAN, ISAAC, *The Jewish Holidays,* Bloch Publishing Co., New York, 1950, pp. 175-228.

VAINSTEIN, YAACOV, *The Cycle of the Jewish Year,* World Zionist Organization, Jerusalem, n.d., pp. 118-129.

WAHRMANN, NAHUM, *Moadim,* Kiryat Sefer, Jerusalem, 1957, pp. 108-128.

———, *Hage Yisrael u-Moadav,* Ahiasaf, Jerusalem, 1959, pp. 139-162.

WAXMAN, MEYER, *A Handbook of Judaism,* Bloch Publishing Co., New York, 1947, pp. 60-69.

I. THE ORIGINS OF PASSOVER

BESPROSVANY, H., *Der Urshprung Fun Pesah,* Yidishen Historishen Seminar, New York, 1926.

GREEN, WILLIAM HENRY, *The Hebrew Feasts in Their Relation to Recent Critical Hypotheses,* London, 1886, pp. 83-239.

HERTZ, JOSEPH H. (ed.), *The Pentateuch and Haftorahs,* Soncino Press, London, 1960, I, 205-274, 394-400.

ORLINSKY, HARRY M., *Ancient Israel,* Cornell University Press, Ithaca, N.Y., 1954, pp. 31-36.

WIENER, HAROLD M., "The Date of the Exodus," *Bibliotheca Sacra,* July, 1916, pp. 454-480.

———, "The Religion of Moses," *Bibliotheca Sacra,* July, 1919, pp. 323-358.

WRIGHT, GEORGE ERNEST and FILSON, FLOYD VIVIAN (eds.), *The Westminster Atlas to the Bible,* Westminster Press, Philadelphia, 1945, pp. 37-41.

YAHUDA, A. S., "Pa'rashat Shibud Yisrael be-Mizraim" (Portion of the Slavery of Israel in Egypt), *Sefer ha-Shanah,* ed. by Menachem Ribalow, Histadruth Ivrith of America, New York, 1942, VI, 73-83.

———, "Shenat Yeziat Mizraim" (Year of Exodus from Egypt), *Sefer ha-Shanah,* ed. by Menachem Ribalow, Histadruth Ivrith of America, New York, 1944, VII, 126-135.

Bibliography

IV. PASSOVER IN MANY LANDS

CHAGALL, BELLA, *Burning Lights,* Schocken Books, New York, 1946, pp. 202-243.

JEREMIAS, JOACHIM, *Die Passahfeier der Samaritaner,* Alfred Topelmann, Giessen, 1932.

LEVIN, SHMARYA, *Childhood in Exile,* Harcourt, Brace and Co., New York, 1929, pp. 165-178.

SACHS, A. S., *Worlds That Passed,* Jewish Publication Society of America, Philadelphia, 1928, pp. 99-107.

WEINREICH, BEATRICE S., "The Americanization of Passover," *Studies in Biblical and Jewish Folklore,* Indiana University Press, Bloomington, 1960, pp. 327-366.

WHITING, JOHN D., *Samaritanernas Paskfest: I Ord Och Bild,* Albert Bonniers Farlag, Stockholm, 1917.

———, "The Last Israelitish Blood Sacrifice: How the Vanishing Samaritans Celebrate the Passover on Sacred Mount Gerizim," *National Geographic Magazine,* XXXVII, no. 1 (January, 1920), pp. 1-46.

WILSON, EDMOND, "Samaritan Passover," *Red, Black, Blond, and Olive Studies in Four Civilizations: Zuni, Haiti, Soviet Russia, Israel,* Oxford University Press, New York, 1956, pp. 427-435.

ZEDEKAH, ABRAHAM (ed.), *Zebah Korban ha-Pesah: Haggadah Shel Pesah: Nusah Shomron (Samaritan Haggadah & Pessah Passover),* Tel Aviv, 1958, Samaritan 5596.

V. THE DEVELOPMENT OF THE PASSOVER HAGGADAH
(available editions)

From Twilight to Dawn: The Traditional Pessach Haggadah, arranged by Shlomo Kahn, Scribe Publications, New York, 1960. English trans. and commentaries.

The Haggadah, ed. and trans. by Cecil Roth, Soncino Press, London, 1934. Introduction and notes.

The Haggadah, illus. by Allweil, trans. and notes by Joseph Loewy and Joseph Guens, Sinai, Tel Aviv.

The Haggadah, written and illuminated by Arthur Szyk, ed. by Cecil Roth, Massadah and Magen, Jerusalem and Tel Aviv, 1956. English trans.

Haggadah for Passover, illus. by Saul Raskin, New York, 1941. English trans.

The Haggadah Of Passover, trans. by Abraham Regelson, illus. by Siegmund Forst, introductory notes and supplement by Sidney B. Hoenig, music by Joshua S. Weisser, Shulsinger Brothers, New York, 1949.

The Haggadah of Passover, trans. by Abraham Regelson, illus. by Siegmund Forst, supplement by Charles B. Chavel, Shulsinger Brothers, New York, 1956.

Haggadah of Passover, introduction by Louis Finkelstein, trans. by Maurice Samuel, music by Moshe Nathanson, Hebrew Publishing Co., New York, 1942.

The Haggadah Of Passover, ed. by David and Tamar De Sola Pool, Bloch Publishing Co., New York, 1952. English trans.

Haggadah Shlemah, ed. by Menahem M. Kasher, Torah Shlemah, Jerusalem, 5715. Introduction and commentaries.

The Kaufmann Haggadah: Facsimile edition of manuscript 422, introduction by Alexander Scheiber, Hungarian Academy of Sciences, Budapest, 1957.

The New Haggadah for the Pesah Seder, ed. by Mordecai M. Kaplan, Eugene Kohn and Ira Eisenstein, illus. by Leonard Weisgard, Behrman House, New York, 1942. English trans.

Ozar Perushim Ve-Ziyurim El Haggadah Shel Pesah, ed. by J. D. Eisenstein, illus. by Lola, Wolf Sales, New York, 1947.

Passover Haggadah, ed. by S. Skolsky, trans. by E. M. Lask, illus. by Z. Livni, Yavneh, Tel Aviv.

Passover Haggadah, illus. by Abraham Israel, trans. by Sidney B. Hoenig, Hebrew Publishing Co., New York, 1959.

The Passover Haggadah, trans. by Philip Birnbaum, Hebrew Publishing Co., New York, 1953. Notes.

The Passover Haggadah, ed. by Nahum N. Glatzer, Schocken Books and Farrar, Straus and Young, 1953. English trans. and commentary.

The Passover Haggadah, ed. by Menahem M. Kasher, New York, 1950. English trans. and commentaries.

Passover Haggadah With Explanatory Notes and Original Readings, ed. by Morris Silverman, illus. by Ezekiel Schloss, Prayer Book Press, Hartford, Conn., 1959. English trans.

The Pessach Haggadah, illuminated by Kafra, trans. by I. Edward Kiev, Feldheim, New York, 1949.

Seder Haggadah Shel Pesah, ed. and explained by Daniel Goldschmidt, Schocken, Tel Aviv, 1947.

Standard Haggadah, trans. by Hyman E. Goldin, illus. by Reuben Leaf, Bloch Publishing Co., New York.

The Union Haggadah, Central Conference of American Rabbis, 1923. Literary supplement, music.

VII. PASSOVER IN THE BIBLE

COHEN, A. (ed.), *The Soncino Chumash,* Soncino Press, London, 1956.

COHEN, MORTIMER J., *Pathways Through the Bible,* Jewish Publication Society of America, Philadelphia, 1946, pp. 65-81.

GOLDMAN, SOLOMON, *The Book of Human Destiny: From Slavery to Freedom,* Abelard-Schuman, New York, 1958.

HERTZ, J. H. (ed.), *The Pentateuch and Haftorahs,* Soncino Press, London, 1960, I, 205-274, 394-400.

VIII. PASSOVER IN POST-BIBLICAL WRITINGS

CHARLES, R. H. (ed.), *The Book of Jubilees,* London, 1902.

Josephus, with an English trans. by H. St. J. Thackeray and Ralph Marcus

Bibliography

(Loeb Classical Library), Harvard University Press, Cambridge, Mass., 1926-1943.

Philo, with an English trans. by F. H. Colson (Loeb Classical Library), Harvard University Press, Cambridge, Mass., VI (1935); VII (1937).

Philo Supplement II: Questions and Answers on Exodus, trans. by Ralph Marcus (Loeb Classical Library), Harvard University Press, Cambridge, Mass., 1953.

IX. PASSOVER IN TALMUD AND MIDRASH

Babylonian Talmud, trans. into English with notes, under the editorship of Isidore Epstein, Soncino Press, London, 1935-1950.

BIALIK, HAYYIM NAHMAN and RAVNITZKI, Y. H., *Sefer ha-Agadah,* Dvir, Tel Aviv, 1947, pp. 43-56.

EISENSTEIN, J. D., *Otzar Midrashim,* 2 vols., J. D. Eisenstein, New York, 1915.

"Exodus," trans. by S. M. Lehman, *Midrash Rabbah,* ed. by H. Freedman and Maurice Simon, Soncino Press, London, 1939.

FLEG, EDMOND, *The Life of Moses,* trans. by S. H. Guest, E. P. Dutton & Co., New York, 1928.

GAER, JOSEPH, *The Lore of the Old Testament,* Little, Brown and Co., Boston, 1951, pp. 139-157.

GINZBERG, LOUIS, *The Legends of the Jews,* Jewish Publication Society of America, Philadelphia, 1910; II, 243-375; III, 5-36; V, 391-439; VI, 1-13.

GOLDIN, HYMAN E., *The Book of Legends,* Jordan Publishing Co., New York, 1929.

LAUTERBACH, JACOB Z. (ed.), *Mekilta de-Rabbi Ishmael,* 2 vols., Jewish Publication Society of America, Philadelphia, 1933.

LEVNER, J. B., *Kol Aggadot Yisroel,* Toshia Press, Warsaw, 1902.

————, *The Legends of Israel: From the Birth to the Death of Moses,* trans. by Joel Snowman, James Clarke and Co., London, 1956.

Midrash on Psalms (Midrash Tehillim), 2 vols., trans. from the Hebrew and Aramaic by William G. Braude, Yale University Press, New Haven, 1959.

Pirke de-Rabbi Eliezer, trans. and annotated with introduction and indices, by Gerald Friedlander, Kegan Paul, Trench, Trubner and Co., London; Bloch Publishing Co., New York, 1916.

SEGAL, SAMUEL M., *Elijah,* Behrman's Jewish Book House, New York, 1935.

Talmud (Bab.), Pesahim, Vilna, 1895.

XI. PASSOVER IN JEWISH LAW

ABRAHAM HE-YARHI, *Sefer ha-Manhig,* Lemberg, 1858, "Hilkot Pesah."

CARO, JOSEPH, *Orah Hayyim,* "Hilkot Pesah."

EISENSTEIN, J. D., *Otzar Dinim u-Minhagim*, Hebrew Publishing Co., New York, 1917, pp. 91, 125, 135, 247, 281, 340.

GANZFRIED, SOLOMON, *Code of Jewish Law*, trans. by Hyman E. Goldin, Hebrew Publishing Co., New York, 1927, III, 23-52.

HIGGER, M., *"Sefer Amarkol:* The Halakhoth of Passover," *Alexander Marx Jubilee Volume*, Hebrew Section, Jewish Theological Seminary of America, New York, 1950, pp. 143-173.

Laws and Customs of Israel, trans. by Gerald Friedlander, Shapiro, Vallentine and Co., London, 1934, pp. 307-333.

The Mishnah, trans. from the Hebrew by Herbert Danby, Clarendon Press, Oxford, 1933, pp. 136-151.

MOSES BEN MAIMON, *The Code of Maimonides: Book Nine: The Book of Offerings*, trans. by Herbert Danby, Yale University Press, New Haven, 1950, pp. 1-45.

MOSES BEN MAIMON, "Hilkot Hametz u-Matzah," *Mishneh Torah*, Amsterdam, 1702.

SAMUEL BEN MOSES AL-MAGRIBI, "The Karaite Holidays," *Karaite Anthology: Excerpts from the Early Literature*, trans. with notes by Leon Nemoy, Yale University Press, New Haven, 1952, pp. 196-214.

ZEVIN, SHLOMOH YOSEF, *Ha-Moadim be-Halakah*, Betan ha-Sefer, Tel Aviv, 5709, pp. 215-291.

XIII. PASSOVER IN THE SHORT STORY AND NOVEL

ABRAMOWITZ, S. J. (Mendele Mocher Soferim, pseud.), "The Exchange," *Yisroel: The Jewish Omnibus*, ed. by Joseph Leftwich, James Clarke, London, 1933, pp. 442-448.

Anonymous, "The Clever Rabbi," *Yiddish Tales*, by Helena Frank, Jewish Publication Society of America, Philadelphia, 1912, pp. 581-587.

ASCH, SHOLEM, *Moses*, trans. by Maurice Samuel, G. P. Putnam's Sons, New York, 1951.

AUSUBEL, NATHAN, "The Hidden Saint" and "Golem of Prague," *A Treasury of Jewish Folklore*, Crown Publishers, New York, 1948, pp. 204-205, 605-612.

BLOCH, CHAIM, "The Birth of Judah Loew," "A Passover Miracle" and "Caught in His Own Net," *The Golem*, Behrman House, New York, 1924, pp. 38-44, 96-105, 125-133.

BRUGGEN, CARRY VAN, "Seder Night," trans. by A. Von Son, *Yisroel: The Jewish Omnibus*, ed. by Joseph Leftwich, James Clarke, London, 1933, pp. 702-706.

BUBER, MARTIN, "A Seder That Went Wrong," *For the Sake of Heaven*, trans. by Ludwig Lewisohn, Jewish Publication Society of America, Philadelphia, 1945, pp. 270-276.

FAST, HOWARD, *Moses: Prince of Egypt* (a novel), Crown Publishers, New York, 1958.

FIEDLER, LESLIE A., "The Dancing of Reb Hershl with the Withered Hand," *The Chosen*, ed. by Harold U. Ribalow, Abelard-Schuman, New York, 1959, pp. 61-73.

FRISHMAN, DAVID, "Sinai," *Yisroel: The Jewish Omnibus*, ed. by Joseph Leftwich, James Clarke, London, 1933, pp. 582-588.

Bibliography

———, "The Story of a Slave," trans. by Ben Halpern, *Pesach*, Habonim, New York, pp. 18-20.

GOLDSMITH, MILTON, "A Happy Passover," *Rabbi and Priest*, Jewish Publication Society of America, Philadelphia, 1891, pp. 133-137.

HALLSTROM, PER, "Arsareth," *Candles in the Night: Jewish Tales by Gentile Authors*, ed. by Joseph L. Baron, Jewish Publication Society of America, Philadelphia, 1940, pp. 103-129.

HALPER, ALBERT, "Warm Matzos," *The Golden Watch*, Henry Holt and Co., New York, 1953, pp. 89-111.

HEINE, HEINRICH, "Passover Eve," *A Golden Treasury of Jewish Literature*, by Leo W. Schwarz, Farrar & Rinehart, New York, 1937, pp. 233-237.

———, "A Seder Night," trans. by Elkan N. Adler, *Yisroel: The Jewish Omnibus*, ed. by Joseph Leftwich, James Clarke, London, 1933, pp. 242-244.

KOLB, LEON, *Moses: The Near Easterner* (a novel), Genuart Co., San Francisco, 1956.

LEIBERT, JULIUS A., *The Lawgiver* (a novel about Moses), Exposition Press, New York, 1953.

LERNER, ISAIAH, "Bertzi Waserfuhrer," *Yiddish Tales*, by Helena Frank, Jewish Publication Society of America, Philadelphia, 1912, pp. 212-218.

LEVINGER, E. E., "A Son of Pharaoh" and "Dawn Through the Darkness," *Tower of David*, Bloch Publishing Co., New York, 1924, pp. 132-138, 139-148.

MANN, THOMAS, *The Tables of The Law*, Alfred A. Knopf, New York, 1945.

PERETZ, ISAAC LOEB, "A Chat," *Yiddish Tales*, by Helena Frank, Jewish Publication Society of America, Philadelphia, 1912, pp. 313-318.

———, "The Seder of the Dogs," *Brooklyn Jewish Center Review*, New York, XXXVII, no. 3 (March, 1959).

RABINOWITZ, S. J. (Sholom Aleichem), "Passover Fugue," *A Golden Treasury of Jewish Literature*, by Leo W. Schwarz, Farrar & Rinehart, New York, 1937, pp. 342-349.

———, "A Page from The Song of Songs," "Passover in a Village," "Elijah The Prophet," and "This Night," *Jewish Children*, trans. by Hannah Berman, Bloch Publishing Co., New York, 1926, pp. 9-19, 20-32, 33-37, 241-268.

———, "The Passover Guest" and "Fishel the Teacher," *Yiddish Tales*, by Helena Frank, Jewish Publication Society of America, Philadelphia, 1912, pp. 153-161, 125-142.

———, "Passover in a Village," trans. by Hannah Berman, *Yisroel: the Jewish Omnibus*, ed. by Joseph Leftwich, James Clarke, London, 1933, pp. 455-461.

———, "A Page from the Song of Songs," "Home for Passover," "In Haste," and "A Country Passover," *The Old Country*, trans. by Julius and Frances Butwin, Crown Publishers, New York, 1946, pp. 42-50, 75-92, 146-157, 336-346.

———, "On Account of a Hat," "The Pair," "A Page from the Song of Songs," "Home for Passover," "In Haste" and "A Country Passover," *Selected Stories of Sholom Aleichem*, introduction by Alfred Kazin. Modern Library, New York, 1956, pp. 3-11, 12-27, 66-73, 97-113, 163-172, 339-349.

——, "On Account of a Hat," "The Pair," and "A Page from the Song of Songs," *A Treasury of Yiddish Stories*, by Eliezer Greenberg and Irving Howe, Viking Press, New York, 1954, pp. 111-118, 193-205, 421-427.

——, "The Littlest of Kings" and "The Passover Expropriation," *Tevye's Daughters*, trans. by Frances Butwin, Crown Publishers, New York, 1949, pp. 114-127, 273-280.

——, "A Premature Passover," *Sholom Aleichem Panorama*, ed. by Melech Grafstein, *Jewish Observer*, London, Ontario, 1948, pp. 109-112.

——, "The Passover Eve Vagabonds" and "The Ruined Passover," *Stories and Pictures*, trans. by Curt Leviant, Thomas Yoseloff, New York, 1959, pp. 214-221, 287-302.

RAKOUS, V., "How Rezi Baked Matzos," trans. by Paul Selver, *Yisroel: The Jewish Omnibus*, ed. by Joseph Leftwich, James Clarke, London, 1933, pp. 714-721.

REISEN, ABRAHAM, "The Rich Poor Man," *Yisroel: The Jewish Omnibus*, ed. by Joseph Leftwich, James Clarke, London, 1933, pp. 467-473.

SAMUEL, MAURICE, "Expropriation," *The World of Sholom Aleichem*, Alfred A. Knopf, New York, 1943, pp. 119-122.

SCHAPIRO, LOB, "If It Was a Dream," *Yiddish Tales*, by Helena Frank, Jewish Publication Society of America, Philadelphia, 1912, pp. 481-490.

SHOLOM ALEICHEM. See S. J. Rabinowitz.

SINCLAIR, JO, *Wasteland* (a novel), Harper & Bros., New York, 1946.

SINGER, JEANNE, *This Festive Season*, Harcourt, Brace and Co., New York, 1943.

STEINBERG, JUDAH, "At The Matzes," *Yiddish Tales*, by Helena Frank, Jewish Publication Society of America, Philadelphia, 1912, pp. 259-265.

STRINDBERG, JOHAN AUGUST, "Peter the Hermit," *Candles in the Night: Jewish Tales by Gentile Authors*, ed. by Joseph L. Baron, Jewish Publication Society of America, Philadelphia, 1940, pp. 97-99.

UNTERMEYER, LOUIS, *Moses* (a novel), New York, Harcourt, Brace & Co., 1928.

VON SACHER MASOCH, LEOPOLD, "Schalem Alechem," *Jewish Tales*, A. C. McClurg & Co., Chicago, 1894, pp. 162-171.

WALTARI, MIKA, *The Egyptian* (a novel), G. P. Putnam's Sons, New York, 1949.

WENDROFF, Z., "Two Pleasures: Told by Yoina the Shadchan," *A Treasury of Jewish Humor*, ed. by Nathan Ausubel, Doubleday & Co., Garden City, N.Y., 1951, pp. 277-283.

WILSON, DOROTHY CLARKE, *Prince of Egypt* (a novel), Westminster Press, Philadelphia, 1949.

WILSON, EDMUND, "The Messiah at the Seder," *A Piece of My Mind*, Farrar, Straus and Cudahy, New York, 1956, pp. 108-135.

ZANGWILL, ISRAEL, "For Auld Lang Syne, My Dear," "The Dead Monkey," "The Shadow of Religion" and "Seder Night," *Children of The Ghetto*, Jewish Publication Society of America, Philadelphia, 1892, pp. 226-318.

——, "Elijah's Goblet," *Ghetto Comedies*, Jewish Publication Society of America, Philadelphia, 1907, pp. 383-387.

Bibliography

———, "Chad Gadya," *Dreamers of the Ghetto,* Harper & Brothers, New York, 1898, pp. 493-513.

XIV. PASSOVER IN POETRY

AUSUBEL, NATHAN and MARYNN, *A Treasury of Jewish Poetry,* Crown Publishers, New York, 1957, pp. 3-4, 83, 93, 204-210, 273, 286, 300, 422.
FRIEDLANDER, JOSEPH, *The Standard Book of Jewish Verse,* Dodd, Mead and Co., New York, 1917, pp. 40-65, 349-360.
KOHUT, GEORGE, ALEXANDER, *A Hebrew Anthology,* Bloch Publishing Co., New York, 1912, I, pp. 80-100.

XV. MUSIC OF PASSOVER
General Books on Jewish Music

GRADENWITZ, PETER, *The Music of Israel,* W. W. Norton & Co., New York, 1949.
IDELSOHN, ABRAHAM ZVI, *Jewish Music in Its Historical Development,* Henry Holt & Co., New York, 1929.
RABINOVITCH, ISRAEL, *Of Jewish Music,* The Book Center, Montreal, 1952.
ROTHMULLER, ARON MARKO, *The Music of the Jews,* Beechhurst Press, New York, 1954.
SAMINSKY, LAZARE, *Music of the Ghetto and the Bible,* Bloch Publishing Co., New York, 1934.
WEISSER, ALBERT, *The Modern Renaissance of Jewish Music,* Bloch Publishing Co., New York, 1954.

Collections Containing Passover Songs

ALGAZI, LÉON, *Chants Sephardis,* World Sephardi Federation, London, 1958.
COOPERSMITH, HARRY, *The Songs We Sing,* United Synagogue Commission on Jewish Education, New York, 1950.
EISENSTEIN, JUDITH K., *The Gateway to Jewish Song,* Behrman House, New York, 1939.
———, *Festival Songs,* Bloch Publishing Co., New York, 1943.
EISENSTEIN, JUDITH K., and PRENSKY, FRIEDA, *Songs of Childhood,* United Synagogue Commission on Jewish Education, New York, 1955.
Shire Pesah, Part 2, Mercaz Latarbut of Histadrut, Tel Aviv.
Union Songster, Central Conference of American Rabbis, New York, 1960.

Choral Music

EPHROS, GERSHON, *Cantorial Anthology,* III, Bloch Publishing Co., New York, 1948.

JOCHSBERGER, TZIPORAH, *Hallel Service,* Jewish Reconstructionist Foundation, New York.
SHARETT, YEHUDAH, *Seder Shel Pesah: Nusah Yagur,* Mercaz Latarbut of Histadrut with Kibbutz Meuhad, Tel Aviv, 1951.

XVI. PASSOVER IN ART

FOONER, MICHAEL, "Joel ben Simeon, Illuminator of Hebrew Manuscripts in the 15th century," *Jewish Quarterly Review,* XXVII, no. 3 (January, 1937), pp. 217-232.
GOLDSCHMIDT, LAZARUS, *The Earliest Illustrated Haggadah Printed by Gershom Cohen at Prague,* London, 1940.
ITALIENER, BRUNO (ed.), *Die Darmstaedter Pessach-Haggadah,* Leipzig, 1927.
KATZ, B., and LOEWE, H., *Die Pessach Haggadah des Gerschom Kohen, gedruckt zu Prag 5287-1527,* Berlin, 1925.
LANDSBERGER, FRANZ, "The Cincinnati Haggadah and its Decorator," *Hebrew Union College Annual,* XV (1940), pp. 529-558; "Jewish Artists before the Period of Emancipation," *ibid.,* XVI (1941), pp. 321-414; "New Studies in Early Jewish Artists," *ibid.,* XVIII (1944), pp. 279-318; "The Second Cincinnati Haggadah," *ibid.,* XXIII, part 2 (1950-1951), pp. 503-521; "The Washington Haggadah and its Illuminator," *ibid.,* XXI (1948), pp. 73-103.
LEVEEN, JACOB, *The Hebrew Bible in Art,* London, 1944.
MARX, ALEXANDER, "The Darmstadt Haggadah," *Jewish Quarterly Review,* XIX, no. 1 (July, 1928), pp. 1-16; "Illustrated Haggadahs," *ibid.,* XIII (1923), pp. 513-519 (both articles are reprinted in Marx's *Studies in Jewish History and Booklore,* New York, 1944, pp. 256-270; 271-276); "Two Illustrated Haggadahs," *Jewish Quarterly Review,* XVI, no. 4 (April, 1926), pp. 471-474.
Milgrom: Magazine for Art and Letters, Berlin-London, no. 1 (1922) and no. 4 (1924), mostly for plates, some in color.
MUELLER, HEINRICH, and SCHLOSSER, JULIUS VON, *Die Haggadah von Sarajevo,* Vienna, 1898.
NAMENYI, ERNEST, "La Miniature Juive au 17e et au 18e siècle," *Revue des Etudes Juives,* CXVI (Jan.-Dec., 1957), pp. 27-71.
RADOJCIC, SVETOZAR, *Haggadah of Sarajevo,* Belgrad, 1953. Plates.
Rimon: Magazine for Art and Letters, Berlin-London, no. 1 (1922) and no. 4 (1924), mostly for plates, some in color.
SCHEIBER, ALEXANDER, *The Kaufmann Haggadah,* Budapest, 1957.
WISCHNITZER, RACHEL, "Autour du mystère de la Haggada de Venise," *Revue des Etudes Juives,* XCIV, 188 (April-June, 1933), pp. 184-192.
———, "Haggadah-Illustration," *Encyclopaedia Judaica,* VII (1931), cols. 794-813.
———, "Von der Holbeinbibel zur Amsterdamer Haggadah," *Monatsschrift fuer Geschichte und Wissenschaft des Judentums,* n.s., XXXIX, nos. 7-8 (July-Aug., 1931), pp. 269-286.
———, "Illuminated Haggadahs," *Jewish Quarterly Review,* XIII, no. 2

(1922), pp. 193-218; "Studies in Jewish Art," *ibid.*, XXXVI, no. 1 (July, 1945), pp. 47-59.

——, *Symbole und Gestalten der Juedischen Kunst,* Berlin, 1935 (with 15 illustrations from Haggadahs).

——, "Haggadah, Passover: Illustration," *Universal Jewish Encyclopedia,* V (1941), pp. 157-164.

XVII. STORIES FOR PASSOVER

ABRAMSON, LILLIAN S., "Passover in Poland," *Join Us For the Holidays,* National Women's League, New York, 1958, pp. 41-42.

ALOFSIN, DOROTHY, "The Cup of Elijah," *Happiness for Sale,* Bloch Publishing Co., New York, 1946, pp. 11-23.

ARONIN, BEN, "The Magic Wine Cup," *The World Over Story Book,* ed. by Norton Belth, Bloch Publishing Co., New York, 1952, pp. 289-292.

BEARMAN, JANE, and WEIL, MILDRED, *Shalom!,* Jonathan David Co., New York, 1958, pp. 40-43.

BIAL, MORRISON DAVID, *The Passover Story,* pictures by Stephen Kraft, Behrman House, New York, 1952.

BIALIK, HAYYIM NAHMAN, "The Shamed Trumpet," *Aftergrowth and Other Stories,* Jewish Publication Society of America, Philadelphia, 1939, pp. 141-188.

——, "The Trumpet Was Ashamed," *The World Over Story Book,* ed. by Norton Belth, Bloch Publishing Co., New York, 1952, pp. 93-98.

BRAVERMAN, LIBBIE L., *Children of the Emek,* Furrow Press, Brooklyn, New York, 1937, pp. 85-89.

BRONSTEIN, CHARLOTTE, "Passover," *Tales of the Jewish Holidays,* Behrman House, New York, 1959.

BURSTEIN, ABRAHAM, "A New Way of Getting Matzoth" and "Abie Impersonates Elijah," *The Ghetto Messenger,* Bloch Publishing Co., New York, 1928, pp. 61-65, 178-182.

CANFIELD, WILLIAM W., *The Sign Above the Door,* Jewish Publication Society of America, Philadelphia, 1912.

CHANOVER, HYMAN and ALICE, *Pesah is Coming!* and *Pesah is Here!* illus. by Leonard Kessler, United Synagogue Commission on Jewish Education, New York, 1956.

COHEN, LENORE, *Bible Tales for Very Young Children,* Union of American Hebrew Congregations, Cincinnati, 1934, pp. 96-137.

EINHORN, DAVID, "A Passover Dream," *The World Over Story Book,* ed. by Norton Belth, Bloch Publishing Co., New York, 1952, pp. 317-322.

EPSTEIN, MORRIS, "Just Reward," *My Holiday Story Book,* Ktav Publishing House, New York, 1958, pp. 38-43.

FAST, HOWARD, "Moses and the Escape from Bondage," *The Romance of a People,* Hebrew Publishing Co., New York, 1941, pp. 52-77.

FINE, HELEN, "Out, Chomets!" and "I'm a Free Goat, Too," *G'dee,* Union of American Hebrew Congregations, New York, 1958, pp. 110-126.

GAER, JOSEPH, "When Thermutis Was Princess" and "The Dream of a Great Prophet," *The Burning Bush,* Union of American Hebrew Congregations, Cincinnati, 1929, pp. 91-149.

——, "Prince Tothan and Tamarah" and "The First Plague," *The Magic Flight*, Frank Maurice, Inc., New York, 1926, pp. 61-79.

GAMORAN, MAMIE G., "Four Questions," "The Samaritans," "Detectives," "At the Seder," and "The Wish," *Hillel's Happy Holidays*, Union of American Hebrew Congregations, Cincinnati, 1939, pp. 144-175.

——, "Proclaim Liberty Throughout the Land," *Days and Ways*, Union of American Hebrew Congregations, 1941, pp. 115-137.

GARVEY, ROBERT, "The Matzoh Man," *Happy Holiday!*, Ktav Publishing House, New York, 1953, pp. 55-63.

——, "The Matzoh Man," *The World Over Story Book*, ed. by Norton Belth, Bloch Publishing Co., New York, 1952, pp. 292-297.

——, "When It's Passover," *Now It's Passover; Now It's Purim*, Ktav Publishing Co., New York, 1954.

——, *Passover Activity Book*, pictures by Gabe Josephson, Ktav Publishing Co., New York, 1956.

GASTER, MOSES, *The Story of Passover*, M. L. Cailingold, London, 1939.

GERSON, EMILY GOLDSMITH, "The Luck of the Cohens" and "Home Again," *A Modern Esther and Other Stories*, Julius H. Greenstone, Philadelphia, 1906, pp. 25-30, 125-131.

GOLDIN, HYMAN E., *The Book of Legends*, Hebrew Publishing Co., New York, 1937, I, pp. 275-345.

——, "Passover," *Holidays Tales; Jewish Holidays and Their Legends*, Hebrew Publishing Co., New York, 1929, pp. 14-90.

GOLDMAN, EDITH B., "One Happy Passover," *A Handbook for the Jewish Family*, by Alex J. Goldman, Bloch Publishing Co., New York, 1958, pp. 259-262.

GOLUB, ROSE W., "A Brotherhood Seder," *Down Holiday Lane*, Union of American Hebrew Congregations, New York, 1947, pp. 124-133.

ISAACS, ABRAM S., "A Voice for Freedom," *Under the Sabbath Lamp*, Jewish Publication Society of America, Philadelphia, 1919, pp. 124-138.

ISH-KISHOR, SULAMITH, "The Chometz-Finder," *The Palace of Eagles And Other Stories*, Shoulson Press, New York, 1948, pp. 143-152.

——, *The Bible Story, Part I*, United Synagogue of America, New York, 1921, pp. 85-113.

——, "A Legend of Moses" and "The Rabbi of Tortosa," *The Heaven on the Sea and Other Stories*, Bloch Publishing Co., New York, 1924, pp. 140-143, 153-163.

LANDA, GERTRUDE (Aunt Naomi), "The Water-Babe," *Jewish Fairy Tales and Legends*, Bloch Publishing Co., New York, 1919, pp. 127-132.

LEARSI, RUFUS, "Two Elijahs," *Kasriel the Watchman*, Jewish Publication Society of America, Philadelphia, 1925, pp. 129-144.

LEVINGER, ELMA EHRLICH, "Moses," *Wonder Tales of Bible Days*, Jewish Publication Society of America, Philadelphia, 1929, pp. 103-140.

——, "The Unwelcome Guest," *In Many Lands*, Bloch Publishing Co., New York, 1923, pp. 83-90.

——, "A Real Passover," *Jewish Holyday Stories*, Bloch Publishing Co., New York, 1918, pp. 121-145.

——, "Playmates in Egypt," *Playmates in Egypt*, Jewish Publication Society of America, Philadelphia, 1920, pp. 13-21.

——, "A Spring Song," "The Best Ever Seder," "A Son of Egypt," "The

467

Lamb of Sacrifice," and "The Passover Stranger," *Tales Old and New,* Bloch Publishing Co., New York, 1926, pp. 129-165.

LONG, LAURA, *The Chosen Boy: A Story of Moses, Who Led His People from Slavery to the Promised Land,* Bobbs-Merrill Co., New York, 1952.

LUBINSKI, CURTIS, "A Passover in Spain," *The World Over Story Book,* ed. by Norton Belth, Bloch Publishing Co., New York, 1952, pp. 227-232.

LURIE, ROSE G., "Adventures in the Desert," *The Great March: Post-Biblical Jewish Stories,* Book II, Union of American Hebrew Congregations, Cincinnati, 1939, pp. 241-254.

MARENOF, MARTHA, "Pesach," *Stories Round the Year,* Dot Publications, Detroit, 1960, pp. 119-136.

PERETZ, I. L., "The Conjuror," *As Once We Were,* by I. L. Peretz, trans. by Elly T. Margolis, Los Angeles, 1951, pp. 250-255.

PESSIN, DEBORAH, "Joel's Seder," *Jewish Life and Customs,* Unit Six: "Passover," Jewish Education Committee of New York, 1944, pp. 10-17.

———, "How Vav's Cousin Saved the Jews," *Aleph Bet Story Book,* Jewish Publication Society of America, Philadelphia, 1946, pp. 35-40.

POSY, ARNOLD, *Holiday Night Dreams,* Bloch Publishing Co., New York, 1953.

ROSS, SHARON L., *The Happy Matzo Family,* Bloch Publishing Co., New York, 1952.

SCHARFSTEIN, EDYTHE and SOL, *The Book of Passover,* Ktav Publishing House, New York, 1950.

SCHWAB, HERMANN, "A Seder Night," *Dreams of Childhood,* Anscombe, London, 5709, pp. 3-4.

SHIPPEN, KATHERINE B., *Moses,* Harper & Bros., New York, 1949.

SILBER, MENDEL, *Scripture Stories,* Behrman House, New York, 1918, I, pp. 115-136.

SILVERMAN, ALTHEA O., "Habibi and Yow Go to Grandfather's for Seder," *Habibi and Yow: A Little Boy and His Dog,* Bloch Publishing Co., New York, 1946, pp. 83-92.

SMITH, HAROLD P., *A Treasure Hunt in Judaism,* Hebrew Publishing Co., New York, 1942, pp. 105-119.

SOFER, D. P., "Passover Speaks to Dan," *Spotlight on Passover,* by Simon Bugatch, Sidney I. Esterson and Louis L. Kaplan, Board of Jewish Education, Baltimore, 1951, pp. 11-17.

SOLOFF, MORDECAI I., *When the Jewish People Was Young,* Union of American Hebrew Congregations, Cincinnati, 1934, pp. 56-79.

SPITZ, LEON, "It Happened on Pesah Night," *What the Liberty Bell Proclaimed,* National Women's League of United Synagogue of America, 1951, pp. 102-110.

STEINBERG, JUDAH, "The Breakfast of the Birds," *The Breakfast of the Birds and Other Stories,* trans. by Emily Solis Cohen, Jr., Jewish Publication Society of America, Philadelphia, 1936, pp. 13-19.

SUPER, ARTHUR SAUL, and HALPERN, JOSEPH, "At the Seder Table," *Storytime,* Edward Goldston, London, 1946, pp. 209-214.

TAYLOR, SYDNEY, "Mama Has Her Hands Full," *All-of-a-kind Family,* Wilcox and Follett Co., New York, 1951, pp. 112-131.

TRAGER, HANNAH, "A Tale of the Passover," *Festival Stories of Child*

Life in a Jewish Colony in Palestine, E. P. Dutton and Co., New York, 1920, pp. 1-23.
WEILERSTEIN, SADIE ROSE, "Helping for Pesah" and "The Adventure of the Pesah Dishes," *What the Moon Brought,* Jewish Publication Society of America, Philadelphia, 1942, pp. 107-114, 115-136.
——, *The Adventures of K'tonton; A Little Jewish Tom Thumb,* National Women's League of United Synagogue of America, New York, 1935.
——, "The Train That Knew About Pesach," *What Danny Did: Stories for the Wee Jewish Child,* Bloch Publishing Co., New York, 1944, pp. 80-84.
——, "A Seder on Lincoln's Birthday," *Little New Angel,* Jewish Publication Society of America, Philadelphia, 1947, pp. 91-102.
WENGROV, CHARLES, *Passover in Song and Story,* Shulsinger Bros., New York, 1960.
WOLFENSTEIN, MARTHA, "A Renegade," *A Renegade and Other Tales,* Jewish Publication Society of America, Philadelphia, 1905, pp. 11-44.
——, "How Shimmele Became a Sceptic," *Idylls of the Gass,* Jewish Publication Society of America, Philadelphia, 1901, pp. 51-65.
ZELIGS, DOROTHY F., *The Story Bible: Together with Tales From the Midrash,* Behrman House, New York, 1949, pp. 124-154.
——, "The Passover Guest," *Holiday Storybook,* compiled by the Child Study Association of America, Thomas Y. Crowell Co., New York, 1952, pp. 101-111.
——, "Passover," *The Story of Jewish Holidays and Customs For Young People,* Bloch Publishing Co., New York, 1942, pp. 149-172.

Most Passover issues of the following periodicals have appropriate stories: *Habonim, The Jewish Child, Our World, World Over, Young Israel,* and *Young Judaean.*

XX. PASSOVER FOLKLORE

BERNSTEIN, IGNATZ, *Yiddishe Sprichworter un Redensarten,* Warsaw, 1908.
DAVIDSON, EFRAIM, *Sehok Penu,* Matmonim, Tel Aviv, 1951.
DRUYANOV, A., *Sefer ha-Bedihah veha-Hidud,* Dvir, Tel Aviv, 1935.
GOODMAN, PHILIP, *Rejoice in Thy Festival: A Treasury of Wisdom, Wit and Humor for the Sabbath and Jewish Holidays,* Bloch Publishing Co., New York, 1956, pp. 175-221.
LIPSON, M., *Midor Dor,* Dorot, Tel Aviv and New York, 1938, III, pp. 115-128.
——, *Moed,* Omanut, Tel Aviv, 1945.
LITWIN, A., *Likbod Pesah,* New York, 1938.
NEWMAN, LOUIS I., *The Hasidic Anthology,* Bloch Publishing Co., New York, 1944, pp. 307-310, 416-419.
OLSVANGER, IMMANUEL, *L'Chayim,* Schocken Books, New York, 1949.
——, *Royte Pomerantsen,* Schocken Books, New York, 1947.

Bibliography

PERSKY, DANIEL, "Likbod Pesah," *Zemanim Tobim,* Pardes, New York, 5704, pp. 175-205.

———, "Pesah," *Matamim le-Hag,* Pardes, New York, 1939, pp. 155-178.

———, "Le-Pesah," *Likbod ha-Regel,* the author, New York, 5707, pp. 212-303.

SEDAN, DOV, *Kaarat Egozim,* M. Newman Publishing House, Tel Aviv, 5713.

———, *Kaarat Tzimukim,* M. Newman Publishing House, Tel Aviv, 5710.

TENDLAU, ABRAHAM, *Sprichworter Und Redensarten,* Schocken Verlag, Berlin, 1934.

ZEVIN, SHLOMOH YOSEF, *Sipure Hasidim . . . le-Moade ha-Shanah,* Avraham Zioni, Tel Aviv, 1958, pp. 253-315.

XXI. PASSOVER PROGRAMS AND PROJECTS

BONDER, DAVID, *A Modern Haggadah compiled for the Third Seder of a Jewish Community Center,* YM&YWHA, Newark.

EISENBERG, AZRIEL, *A Modern Haggadah,* Bureau of Jewish Education, Cincinnati.

GOODMAN, HANNAH GRAD, *A Modern Haggadah for B.B.Y.O. Third Seder,* B'nai B'rith Youth Commission, Washington, D.C.

GOODMAN, PHILIP, *A Passover Program for Youth and Adult Groups,* Institutional Synagogue, New York.

GORDON, IRWIN, *Passover Program,* Joint Commission for Coordinated Community Service, New York.

Haggadah for the Third Seder, Labor Zionist Organization of Greater Boston, 1947.

JAHR, BERT, *Annual Third Passover Seder Ceremony,* YM&YWHA, Newark, 1946.

Passover Seder for Young Judaea Groups, National Young Judaea, New York, 1949.

School Seder Manual, Jewish Education Committee, New York, 1949.

Children's Haggadahs

The Children's Haggadah, ed. by A. M. Silberman, illus. by Erwin Singer, trans. by Isidore Wartski and Arthur Saul Super, Shapiro, Vallentine & Co., London, 1954.

Children's Passover Haggadah, trans. by Ben-Ami Scharfstein, illus. by Siegmund Forst, Shilo Publishing House, New York, 1945.

Haggadah For Children, ed. by Martha Marenoff, Newton Center, Mass.

Haggadah For Children, prepared by Jacob P. Rudin, Bloch Publishing Co., New York.

Haggadah Service For American Jewish Children, ed. by Margaret M. Soifer, Furrow Press, Brooklyn, N.Y.

Haggadah For Young American Jews, prepared by Isidore E. Krakower, Malerman, Philadelphia, 1951.

The School Haggadah, trans. by Saadyah Maximon, illus. by Siegmund Forst, Shulsinger Brothers, 1958.

School Seder Manual, Jewish Education Committee, New York, 1949.

Kindergarten and Crafts Material

BEARMAN, JANE, *Passover Party*, Union of American Hebrew Congregations, Cincinnati, 1947.

BERNSTEIN, LEAH, *Passover Pictures to Color*, Minneapolis, 1945.

BLOCH, JOSEPH, *Passover Coloring Book*, Ktav Publishing House, New York.

COMINS, HARRY L., and LEAF, REUBEN, *Arts-Crafts for the Jewish Club*, Union of American Hebrew Congregations, Cincinnati, 1934, pp. 44-47, 152-155, 176-179, 217-224.

COVICH, EDITH S., *The Jewish Child Every Day*, Union of American Hebrew Congregations, Cincinnati, 1947, pp. 37-43.

EGELSON, GUSSIE E., "Passover Handwork," *Kindergarten Handwork for the Holidays*, Union of American Hebrew Congregations, Cincinnati.

EISENBERG, AZRIEL, and ROBINSON, JESSIE B., *My Jewish Holidays*, United Synagogue Commission on Jewish Education, New York, 1958, pp. 130-146.

GEZARI, TEMIMA N., *Jewish Festival Crafts*, National Jewish Welfare Board, New York, 1946, pp. 27-30.

GOLUB, ROSE W., "Passover," *Festival Course for Primary Grades*, Bureau of Jewish Education, Cincinnati.

GOODMAN, HANNAH GRAD, *Pupil's Activity Book for Days and Ways*, Union of American Hebrew Congregations, Cincinnati, 1942, pp. 57-65.

HARRIS, HANNAH; LEIDERMAN, LILLIAN T.; and PEIKES, ANNETTE; *Hebrew Kindergarten Manual*, Mizrachi National Education Committee, New York, 1946, pp. 85-87.

HONOR, JENNIE G., *Kindergarten Manual for Jewish Religious Schools*, United Synagogue Commission on Jewish Education, New York, 1949, pp. 50-54.

LANDMAN, EVA, *Kindergarten Manual*, Union of American Hebrew Congregations, Cincinnati, 1918, pp. 156-170.

LEIDERMAN, LILLIAN T. and ABRAMSON, LILLIAN S., *Jewish Holiday Party Book*, Bloch Publishing Co., New York, 1954, pp. 41-45.

PESSIN, DEBORAH and GEZARI, TEMIMA N., *The Jewish Kindergarten*, Union of American Hebrew Congregations, Cincinnati, 1944, pp. 249-277.

ROBINSON, JESSIE B., *Holidays are Fun*, Bloch Publishing Co., New York, 1950, pp. 43-48.

ROSENZWEIG, EFRAIM and MARION J., *Now We Begin*, Union of American Hebrew Congregations, Cincinnati, 1937, pp. 83-115.

Passover, Jewish Home Institute Series, Bureau of Jewish Education, New York, 1927-28.

Films

Freedom Rings. Distributed by Jewish Chautauqua Society. Black and white. 13½ minutes. 16mm. $35.00. Rental free. A Christian boy attending a Seder learns about Passover.

471

Bibliography

Home for Passover. Script by James Yaffe. Kinescope produced by NBC and Jewish Theological Seminary of America. Distributed by National Academy for Adult Jewish Studies. Black and white. 30 minutes. 16mm. Rental $8.50. Based on a story by Sholom Aleichem.

Moses Series: "Moses in Egypt," "Moses and His People," "Moses and the Ten Commandments." Produced by National Council of Churches of Christ. Distributed by Jewish Educational Film Library. Color. 15 minutes each. 16mm. Rental $7.50.

The Omer Festival. Distributed by Jewish National Fund. Color. 10 minutes. 16mm. Rental free. A modern Israeli version.

The Passover of Rembrandt van Rijn. Script by Morton Wishengrad. Kinescope produced by NBC and Jewish Theological Seminary of America. Distributed by National Academy for Adult Jewish Studies. Black and white. 30 minutes. 16mm. Rental $8.50. The artist's search for a model for Moses and his participation in a Seder.

Visitor from America. Kinescope produced by NBC and Jewish Theological Seminary of America. Distributed by National Academy for Adult Jewish Studies. Black and white. 30 minutes. 16mm. Rental $8.50. An American Jew returns to the old country on Passover.

Filmstrips

Baby Moses. Produced and distributed by Society for Visual Education. Color. 62 frames. $5.00. The early life of Moses.

Life of Moses. Produced and distributed by Cathedral Films. Color. Series of 7 filmstrips, from 23 to 36 frames each. $5.00 each.

The Life of Moses. Produced by Victor Kayfetz. Distributed by Jewish Education Committee of New York. Black and white. Three parts: 28, 29 and 32 frames. $7.50.

Miriam and Moses. Produced and distributed by Society for Visual Education. Color. 22 frames. $4.00. The early life of Moses.

Moses. Produced and distributed by Alexark and Norsim. Color. Two parts: 34 and 35 frames. $7.50 each.

Moses. Produced and distributed by Society for Visual Education. Color. Two parts: 41 and 42 frames. $6.50 each.

Our Festival of Passover. Produced and distributed by Alexark and Norsim. Color. 39 frames. $7.50. The story of the Exodus.

The Seder. Produced by Alexander Arkatov. Distributed by Bureau of Jewish Education, Los Angeles. Black and white. Two parts: 28 and 36 frames. $3.00 each.

The Story of Passover. Produced by Victor Kayfetz. Distributed by Jewish Education Committee of New York. Black and white. 52 frames. $3.50. The historical and religious background of the Seder.

For additional films and filmstrips, see *Audio-Visual Program Aids for the Jewish Festivals,* prepared by Zalmen Slesinger, American Association for Jewish Education, New York, 1957.

Recordings

The Adventures of an Afikoman. Story by Heidy. Music by Ivan Lane. Reena Record Co. 1-10" record.

Hagadah. Recorded by Sam Eskin. Notes by Theodor Gaster. Folkways Records and Service Co. 8921. 1-12" L.P. 33⅓ RPM. A Seder in a Yemenite home.

Israel in Egypt. By George Frederick Handel. Performed by the University of Utah Chorus and the Utah Symphony Orchestra under Maurice Abravanel. Westminster 2224.

Mother Goose Rhymes for Passover. Sung by Habibi. Told by Fred Vogel. Ktav Publishing House. 1-7" record. Six songs.

Opus Americanum No. 2. French National Radio Diffusion Orchestra conducted by Darius Milhaud. Capital Recordings, P-8114 L.P. The life of Moses.

Passover. Sung by Emanuel Rosenberg. Directed by Judith K. Eisenstein. Allegro Records. Holiday 107. 2-10" records. Selections from the Haggadah.

Passover Music Box. Sung by Shirley R. Cohen. Narrated by Eli Gamliel. Kinor Records. 1-10" record. Eight children's songs.

Passover Seder. Sung by Jan Peerce. Choir directed by Abraham Ellstein. Arranged by Ario S. Hyams. Directed by Barry Hyams. RCA Victor LM-1971 Red Seal.

The Passover Story. Written by Maurice Barrett. Narrated by Sam Jaffe. Union of American Hebrew Congregations. 2-10" records. The Exodus story and selections from the Haggadah.

Pesach Holiday Songs. Performed by Seymour Silbermintz and ensemble. Produced by Ben David. Torah Umesorah. TU-1.

Pesach Melodies. Performed by Samuel Kligfeld. Reena Record. 114-115. 1-12" L.P. or 3-10" records (78 RPM).

Seder Melodies. Sung by Robert H. Segal and choir. National Women's League of the United Synagogue of America. 3-10" records.

S'firo. Sung by Pierre Pinchik. Victor 38-1013.

Sh'ma Yisroel and Tal. Sung by Leib Glantz. Victor 38-1003.

Song of Songs. Performed by Naomi Zuri. Orchestrated and conducted by Shabatai Petrushka. Accompanied by Kol Israel Symphony Orchestra. Arzi Records. D-102. 1-10" L.P., 33⅓ RPM. Same in 3-10" records. Selections from Song of Songs.

Song of Songs. Reading by Morris Carnovsky, Carol Veazie, Anne Meachem, Henry Bate. Produced and directed by Beverly Merill. 1-12" L.P., 33⅓ RPM. A chorale reading in Hebrew and English.

The Time of Singing. Text by Harriet Herbert. Sung by Michael Alexander. Book Records. 1-10" L.P., 33⅓ RPM. The story and songs of Passover.

For further information, see *Reviews of Selected Recordings of Jewish Music,* ed. by Eric Werner, National Jewish Music Council, New York, 1953.

Bibliography

Passover Plays

(Based on *Passover Dramatics Resources for the Group Leader,* by Leah M. Jaffa, National Jewish Welfare Board, New York).

min—minutes; m—male; f—female

BECKER, CHARLES and FINKELSTEIN, PHILIP, *The Quest for Freedom,* Union of American Hebrew Congregations, New York. 4 scenes, prologue and epilogue, 25 min. Youth and young adults. 53 m, 1 f, extras. A series of episodes of Israel's struggles for freedom: the Exodus, Bar Kokhba rebellion, the marranos, and others.

BRILLIANT, NATHAN and BRAVERMAN, LIBBIE, "A Passover Seder in Action and Pictures," *Religious Pageants for the Jewish School,* Union of American Hebrew Congregations, New York. 15 min. Children and teen-agers. 1 m, 1 f, 4 extras. Seder program with use of slides and audience participation.

————, "They Who Dreamed of Freedom," *Religious Pageants for the Jewish School,* Union of American Hebrew Congregations, New York. 17 min. Children. 5 m, 2 f, 2 extras, 3 mass groups. A pageant on the Exodus from Egypt and the modern exodus to Israel.

FREEHOF, LILLIAN S., *In Pesach Land,* Union of American Hebrew Congregations, New York. 2 acts, 15 min. Children. 9 m, 3 f. A little girl dreams she is in Pesach land and travels with her newly made friends: *Matzot,* Wine, *Haroset,* and other symbols of the holiday.

GAMORAN, MAMIE G., *Men of Freedom,* National Jewish Welfare Board, New York. 15 min. Adults. 20 m, 4 extras. A pageant-like narration which presents, as part of a Seder ceremony, great men of many nations who have led their own peoples in their struggle for freedom.

GARVEY, ROBERT, *A Passover Story,* adapted for radio by Marian Gordon, Jewish Education Committee of New York. 15 min. Children and teen-agers. 5 m, 3 f, 10 extras. An *afikoman* is the hero of this script and his experiences are told with imagination.

GROSSMAN, SAMUEL S. and GOLDFARB, SAMUEL E., *Jews in Egypt*: An operetta, Jewish Songster Publishing Society; available from Bloch Publishing Company, New York. 6 scenes, 2 sets, 25 min. All ages. 5 m, 5 f, chorus. An operetta built around the story of Passover.

KLAPERMAN, LIBBY M., "The Passover Melody," *Hachodesh,* April 1953, Women's Branch, Union of Orthodox Jewish Congregations of America, New York. 1 act, 12 min. Adults. 2 f, 2 m or f, 1 child. A dramatic narrative which captures the spirit of Passover.

————, "Pesach Patter," *Hachodesh,* April, 1957, Women's Branch, Union of Orthodox Jewish Congregations of America, New York. 1 act, 20 min. Adults. 4 f. A group of ladies reminisce about Passover of their youth and discuss preparations for the Seder.

LEVINGER, ELMA EHRLICH, *The Silver Cup,* Union of American Hebrew Congregations, New York. 1 act, 30 min. Children. 4 m, 1 f. A folk play set in Europe of the past century.

474

———, *Out of Egypt,* Union of American Hebrew Congregations, New York. 3 acts, 60 min. Children. 6 m, 1 f, extras. A dramatic portrayal of the delivery of the Jews from the bondage of Pharaoh. Related in biblical style prose.

MILLER, SIGMUND, *The Slave,* Eternal Light radio script, April 10, 1949, Jewish Theological Seminary of America, New York. 25 min. Youth and adults. 4 m, 1 f, 3 m or f. The story of a slave who preferred the security of slavery to the uncertainties of freedom.

MINDEL, JOSEPH, *A Journey with Elijah,* Eternal Light radio script, November 8, 1953, Jewish Theological Seminary of America, New York. 25 min. Youth and adults. 8 m, 1 f. A shoemaker takes a trip with Elijah and notes reactions of people to the deeds of the wonder working patron.

ROSTEN, HEDDA, *Out of Their Bondage,* Eternal Light radio script, April 13, 1947, Jewish Theological Seminary of America, New York. 25 min. Youth and adults. 8 m, 1 extra. The story of the emissaries who, at the time that the Nazis were losing the war, went to Himmler and asked him to evacuate the Jews, unharmed, from concentration camps.

SOIFER, MARGARET K., *Let My People Go,* Furrow Press, Brooklyn, N.Y. 30 min. Youth and adults. 7 m, 4 f. A picture of an Israelite family in Egypt just before the Exodus.

WISHENGRAD, MORTON, *Tender Grass,* Eternal Light radio script, March 30, 1947, Jewish Theological Seminary of America, New York. 25 min. Adults. 5 m, 6 f, 1 singer. A fantasy for the festival of Passover, built around birds, children, Elijah, love and song.

———, *The Exodus of Asher Levy,* Eternal Light radio script, April 6, 1952, Jewish Theological Seminary of America, New York. 25 min. Teen-agers and adults. 8 m, 1 f, 3 extras. Levy and his wife are among the first Jewish settlers in New Amsterdam. The climax of their struggle to remain in this country comes during their first Passover here.

WYENN, THAN R., *In The Wilderness,* Bureau of Jewish Education, Los Angeles. 2 scenes, 10 min. Children. 3 m, 1 f. A nine-year old boy has a day-dream about a group of children who, having been in the desert and very hungry for a long time, find the manna which saves the Israelites from starvation.

CITRON, SAMUEL, *Authentic Costumes for Jewish School Plays: Passover,* Jewish Education Committee of New York. Thirteen plates of costumes for characters prominent in the Passover story, together with drawings of miniature patterns.

XXII. DANCES FOR PASSOVER

CHOCHEM, CORINNE, *Jewish Holiday Dances,* Behrman House, New York, 1948, pp. 59-63.

LAPSON, DVORA, *Jewish Dances the Year Round,* Jewish Education Committee of New York, 1952, pp. 54-67.

Bibliography

XXIII. PASSOVER DISHES

BELLIN, MILDRED GROSBERG, *The Jewish Cook Book,* Bloch Publishing Co., New York, 1958, pp. 391-409.

BERG, GERTRUDE, and WALDO, MYRA, *The Molly Goldberg Jewish Cookbook,* Doubleday & Co., Garden City, N. Y., 1959, pp. 262-278.

GREENBAUM, FLORENCE KREISLER, *Jewish Cook Book,* Bloch Publishing Co., New York, 1931, pp. 379-397.

GREENBERG, BETTY D. and SILVERMAN, ALTHEA O., *The Jewish Home Beautiful,* Women's League of the United Synagogue of America, New York, 1941, pp. 109-117.

LEONARD, LEAH W., *The Jewish Holiday Cook Book,* Crown Publishers, New York, 1955, pp. 78-116.

LONDON, ANNE and BISHOV, BERTHA KAHN, *The Complete American-Jewish Cookbook,* World Publishing Co., Cleveland, 1952, pp. 3-23.

XXIV. THE OBSERVANCE OF PASSOVER

BIRNBAUM, PHILIP, *Daily Prayer Book,* Hebrew Publishing Co., New York, 1949, pp. 586-646.

Ceremonial for Opening the Door for Elijah, Central Conference of American Rabbis, Cincinnati, 1942.

DEMBITZ, LEWIS N., *Jewish Services in Synagogue and Home,* Jewish Publication Society of America, Philadelphia, 1898, pp. 356-367.

HERTZ, JOSEPH H., *The Authorised Daily Prayer Book,* Bloch Publishing Co., New York, 1952, pp. 788-837.

IDELSOHN, A. Z., *Jewish Liturgy,* Henry Holt and Co., 1932, pp. 188-204.

LEVI, ELIEZER, *Yesodot ha-Tefilah,* Betan ha-Sefer, Tel Aviv, 5712, pp. 216-229.

Union Hymnal, 3rd ed., Central Conference of American Rabbis, Cincinnati, 1940, pp. 124-140, 475-487.

Union Prayer Book, I, Central Conference of American Rabbis, Cincinnati, 1940, pp. 181-277.

Notes

Chapter I

THE ORIGINS OF PASSOVER

[1] Orlinsky, Harry M., *Ancient Israel*, Cornell University Press, Ithaca, N.Y., 1954, pp. 31-36.

[2] *Against Apion*, I, 14, ed. H. St. J. Thackeray (Loeb Classical Library), New York, 1926.

[3] Steindorff, G. and Seele, K. C., *When Egypt Ruled the East*, Chicago, 1942.

[4] Wilson, J. A., *The Burden of Egypt*, Chicago, 1951, p. 256.

[5] Hertz, Joseph H. (ed.), *The Pentateuch and Haftorahs*, Soncino Press, London, 1960, I, 394-396.

[6] Griffith, Francis L., "Egypt," *Encyclopedia Britannica*, 11th ed.

Chapter II

PASSOVER AND THE LAST SUPPER

[1] Zeitlin, Solomon, "The Liturgy of the First Night of Passover," *Jewish Quarterly* Review, XXXVIII, no. 4 (April, 1948), pp. 444-449.

[2] *Dialogue With Trypho*, 111.

[3] See S. Zeitlin, "The Date of the Crucifixion according to the Fourth Gospel" (and the literature there quoted), *Journal of Biblical Literature*, 1932.

[4] Augustine, *De Civitate Dei*, X, 6.

[5] *Epist*. XV, 1 *Corpus Scriptorum et Ecclesiasticorum Latinorum*, 111, 2.

[6] *II Maccabees* 1.2.; *III Maccabees* 7.16; *Sirach* 37.11; *Wisdom of Solomon* 18.2. Compare also Josephus, *Antiquities* IV.13.

[7] *De Specialibus Legibus Lib. I (De Victimus)*.

[8] *Ibid.*, 6.

[9] Comp. Irenaeus, *Contra Haerses*, IV, 18. ". . . but the Eucharist, consisting of two realities, earthly and heavenly so also our bodies, when they receive the Eucharist, are no longer corruptible, having the hope of the resurrection to eternity." See also Ignatius to the *Smyrnaeans*, 7.

[10] This name is used in all the Romance languages (French-*Pâques;* Italian-*Pasqua*).

[11] *Panarion Haer.* 70.10.

[12] Eusebius refers to these epistles which were called Festals Epistles.

Chapter III

PASSOVER AND THE RITUAL MURDER LIBEL

[1] From the Prologue to *The Rabbi of Bacharach*, trans. by Aaron Kramer, *The Poetry and Prose of Heinrich Heine*, ed. by Frederick Ewen, Citadel Press, New York, 1948, p. 268.

Notes

[2] Bloch, Joseph S., *Israel and the Nations*, English trans., Berlin-Vienna, 1927, devotes its last chapter to the Ritual Murder accusation and begins by citing the defense against this charge made by Christians during the first three centuries of the Christian Era.

[3] Tcherikover, Victor, *Hellenistic Civilization and the Jews*, Jewish Publication Society of America, Philadelphia, 1959, pp. 366 f. Cf. Parkes, James, *The Conflict of the Church and the Synagogue*, Soncino Press, London, 1934, p. 16.

[4] The Purim riots referred to by Theodosium II in the 5th century are in an entirely different case: cf. Parkes, *ibid.*, p. 234.

[5] Roth, Cecil, *History of the Jews in England*, Oxford University Press, Oxford, 1941, p. 13; Adler, Michael, *The Jews of Medieval England*, London, 1939, p. 185.

[6] Trachtenberg, Joshua, *The Devil and the Jews*, Yale University Press, New Haven, 1943, ch. 10, esp. pp. 148-9.

[7] Grayzel, Solomon, *The Church and the Jews in the XIIIth Century*, Dropsie College, Philadelphia, 1933, pp. 263, 265.

[8] *Ibid.*, pp. 269-71.

[9] *Ibid.*, p. 275. Stern, Moritz, *Päpstliche Bullen uber die Blutbeschuldigung*, Munich, 1900, pp. 18-23.

[10] *Idem, Urkundliche Beiträge uber die Stellung der Papste zu den Juden*, Kiel.

[11] Stern, *Päpstliche Bullen. . .*, pp. 31 ff.

[12] Roth, Cecil, *The Ritual Murder Libel and the Jews: The Report of Cardinal Lorenzo Ganganelli*, London, 1935. The report is here given in full.

[13] Posener, S., *Adolphe Crémieux: a Biography*, Jewish Publication Society of America, Philadelphia, 1940, pp. 89 ff.

[14] Elbogen, Ismar, *A Century of Jewish Life*, Jewish Publication Society of America, Philadelphia, 1944, pp. 155-9 *et passim*.

[15] Dubnow, Simon, *A History of the Jews in Russia and Poland*, Jewish Publication Society of America, Philadelphia, 1920, III, 164 ff. Cf. Tager, Alexander S., *The Decay of Czarism*, Jewish Publication Society of America, Philadelphia, 1935.

[16] Weinreich, Max, *Hitler's Professors*, Yiddish Scientific Institute (YIVO), New York, 1946, p. 207.

[17] Reported by the Jewish Telegraphic Agency, December 24, 1952.

Chapter IV

PASSOVER IN MANY LANDS

[1] This account, consisting of fact and fancy based on talmudic and other sources, is taken from *Shebet Yehudah*, by Solomon ibn Verga (Hanover, 1855), pp. 105-106. The author lived in the 15th and 16th centuries. The English translation is from the *Babylonian Talmud*, ed. and trans. by Michael L. Rodkinson, Boston, 1918, III, 142-145.

[2] Gaster, Theodor Herzl, *Passover: Its History and Traditions*, Henry Schuman, New York, 1949, pp. 77-83.

[3] Schauss, Hayyim, *The Jewish Festivals,* Union of American Hebrew Congregations, Cincinnati, 1938, pp. 58-60.
[4] Faitlovitch, Jacques, "The Falashas," *American Jewish Year Book, 5681,* XXII (1920), p. 89.
[5] *Hamelitz,* no. 75 (1903). Trans. by Hyman E. Goldin, in his *The Story of Passover and Its Celebration,* Bloch Publishing Co., New York, 1930, pp. 82-87.
[6] Levin, Shmarya, *Childhood in Exile,* trans. by Maurice Samuel, Harcourt, Brace & World, Inc., New York, 1929, pp. 165-178.
[7] Morgenstern, Soma, *The Third Pillar,* trans. by Ludwig Lewisohn, Farrar, Straus & Cudahy, New York, 1955, pp. 57-60.
[8] *The Jewish Messenger,* XIX, no. 13 (March 30, 1866), p. 2; reprinted, in part, in *American Jewry and the Civil War,* by Bertram W. Korn, Jewish Publication Society of America, Philadelphia, 1951, pp. 90-92.
[9] *Poland of Today,* III, no. 4 (April, 1948), pp. 3-4, 19.
[10] *G.I. Holy Days,* National Jewish Welfare Board, New York, 1944.
[11] Mosenson, Moshe, *Letters from the Desert,* Sharon Books, New York, 1945, pp. 105-112.
[12] *Israel Speaks,* IX, no. 7 (1955), p. 8.

Chapter V

THE DEVELOPMENT OF THE PASSOVER HAGGADAH

[1] Reform Jews and Jews in Israel read it only the first evening.
[2] The word Haggadah is first mentioned in the Talmud, Pesahim 115b.
[3] Zeitlin, Solomon, "The Liturgy of the First Night of Passover," *Jewish Quarterly Review,* n.s., XXXVIII, no. 4 (April, 1948), pp. 431-432.
[4] Exodus 12.26, 13.8, 14, Deuteronomy 6.20.
[5] Moses ben Maimon, *Mishneh Torah, Hilkot Hametz u-Matzah* 7.1.
[6] Finkelstein, Louis, "The Origin of the Hallel," *Hebrew Union College Annual,* XXIII, part II (1950-1951), pp. 319-337.
[7] Finkelstein, Louis, "Pre-Maccabean Documents in the Passover Haggadah," *Harvard Theological Review,* XXXV, no. 4 (1942), pp. 291-332.
[8] *Ibid.,* XXXVI, no. 1 (1943), pp. 1-38.
[9] Finkelstein, Louis, "The Oldest Midrash: Pre-Rabbinic Ideals and Teachings in the Passover Haggadah," *Harvard Theological Review,* XXXI, no. 4 (1938), pp. 291-317. See E. D. Goldschmidt, in *Seder Haggadah Shel Pesah* (Schocken, Tel Aviv, 1947), p. 16, and *Haggadah Shel Pesah* (Bialik Institute, Jerusalem, 1960), pp. 30-47, who disagrees with Finkelstein's deductions.
[10] Pesahim 10.
[11] Goldschmidt, *Haggadah Shel Pesah, supra,* p. 12, quotes authorities who claim that the roast was eaten even after the destruction of the Temple as a reminder.
[12] *Ibid.,* pp. 12-13.
[13] Pesahim 10.5.
[14] Goldschmidt, *supra,* p. 52, suggests that the reasons for the "three

Notes

things" are given to controvert those who ate them in remembrance of
the Last Supper.

[15] Pesahim 10.5.

[16] Pesahim 10.2, 4, 7.

[17] Pesahim 10.4.

[18] Pesahim 116a.

[19] Pesahim 34b.

[20] *Mekilta de Rabbi Ishmael* . . . Jacob Z. Lauterbach, Jewish Publication
Society of America, Philadelphia, 1933, I, 166-167.

[21] For a discussion of the sources, see Finkelstein, Louis, "Pre-Maccabean
Documents in the Passover Haggadah," *Harvard Theological Review*,
XXXVI, no. 1 (1943), pp. 1-38, and Goldschmidt, *Haggadah Shel
Pesah, supra*, pp. 22-29.

[22] Pesahim 10.4.

[23] A similar story is found in Tosefta Pesahim 10.12.

[24] Psalms 79.6-7, 69.25, Lamentations 3.66.

[25] Kasher, Menahem M., *Haggadah Shlemah,* Jerusalem, 5715, p. 179-180,
cites numerous other reasons.

[26] Numbers Rabbah 20.12.

[27] *Haggadot: Passover Exhibition,* Schocken Library, Jerusalem, 1955.

[28] Wiener, S., *Bibliographie der Oster Haggadah,* St. Petersburg, 1901
[or 1902].

[29] Yaari, Abraham, "Additions to Wiener," *Kiryat Sefer,* VI (1929-30),
pp. 531-562; VIII (1931-32), pp. 122-126; Duker, Abraham G., *ibid.,*
VII (1930-31), pp. 574-584; VIII (1931-32), pp. 100-121 [reprinted
under the title *Eged-Hagadot,* Jerusalem, 1931]; Rivkind, Isaac, *ibid.,*
XII (1935-36), pp. 230 ff, 360 ff.; Simches, B., *ibid.,* XIII (1936-37),
p. 138; Liberman, Hayyim, *ibid.,* XV (1938-39), pp. 258-268.

[30] Tauber, Maurice F., *A Report on the Library of the Jewish Theological
Seminary of America,* New York, 1959, p. 81.

[31] Yaari, Abraham, *Bibliografiah Shel Haggadot Pesah,* Bamberger &
Wahrman, Jerusalem, 1960.

[32] *Haggadot: Passover Exhibition,* Schocken Library, Jerusalem, 1955;
Yaari, *supra,* nos. 1, 2, 3, 5, 6.

[33] Rosenbach, A.S.W., *An American Jewish Bibliography,* American Jewish Historical Society, New York, 1926, p. 318; Bloch, Joshua, *The People and the Book,* New York Public Library, 1954, p. 111.

[34] *Orah Hayyim. Rama* 473.

[35] *Union Haggadah: Revised,* Central Conference of American Rabbis,
1923, pp. 157-159; Idelsohn, A. Z., *Jewish Liturgy and Its Development,* Henry Holt & Co., New York, 1932, pp. 294-295.

[36] *The Union Haggadah,* Cincinnati, 1907, p. vi.

[37] Behrman House, New York, 1941.

[38] Learsi, Rufus, "We Want to Remember—But How?," *Congress Weekly,*
XXII, no. 13 (March 28, 1955), pp. 5-7.

[39] Ben-Mordecai, Isaac, "Israel Remembers—Shall We Forget?," *American
Zionist,* March, 1955, pp. 7, 9; Pearl, Chaim, "Need for a New Ritual,"
London *Jewish Chronicle,* April 11, 1958, pp. 17, 19.

[40] *Passover Haggadah* . . . edited by Morris Silverman, Prayer Book
Press, Hartford, Conn., 1959, pp. 44-46.

480

⁴¹ *The Passover Haggadah,* edited by Menachem M. Kasher, New York, 1950, pp. 4, 19.

⁴² Jerusalem Pesahim 37b.

⁴³ *Passover Haggadah* . . . edited by Morris Silverman, *ibid.,* p. 66.

⁴⁴ Greenburg, William H., *The Haggadah according to the Rite of Yemen,* London, 1896, p. 6.

⁴⁵ *Haggadah Shel Pesah Le-Hayyale Zeva Hagannah le-Yisrael: Nusah Ahid,* Tel Aviv, 5716.

⁴⁶ *The Passover Haggadah for Jewish Personnel in the Armed Forces of the United States,* National Jewish Welfare Board, New York, 1952.

⁴⁷ Korea, 1952; Cherry Point, N.C., 1953; Fort Belvoir, 1956.

⁴⁸ Davidson, Efraim, *Sehok Pinu,* Matmonim, Tel Aviv, 1951, p. 491.

⁴⁹ Heinemann, Joseph, "Kibbutz Passover," *Israel Speaks,* VII, no. 6 (March 20, 1953), pp. 1, 5.

⁵⁰ Peli, Pinhas H., *"Ha-Hityashbut ha-Obedet Mehapeset Nusah Haggadah,"* Jerusalem *Sheluhot,* no. 51 (Nisan, 5717), pp. 5-9.

⁵¹ *Haggadah Shel Pesah, Ha-Kibbuz ha-Meuhad "Ha-Bahrut,"* Shekunat Borokov, 5688; Davidson, *supra.*

Chapter VI

THE BAKING OF MATZOT

¹ Pesahim 37a, Rashi The figured *matzot* are called סריקין מצוויירין which may indicate that the perforations and designs were done with a comblike implement, as סריקין indicates.

² *Hilkot Hametz u-Matzah* 5.15.

³ *Magid Mishnah* on *Hametz u-Matzah* 5.15.

⁴ *Orah Hayyim* 460.4.

⁵ *Eshel Abraham, Orah Hayyim* 460.4.

⁶ Abrahams, Israel, "The Shape of Matzoth," *The Book of Delight and Other Papers,* Jewish Publication Society of America, Philadelphia, 1912, pp. 290-300.

⁷ *Bet Hillel, Yoreh Deah* 96.

⁸ Rashi, *Moed Katan* 4 b.

⁹ Pesahim 3.4

¹⁰ Moellin, Jacob, *Minhage Maharil, Pesah.*

¹¹ *Orah Hayyim* 458.1.

¹² Szpetman, S. Z., *Bagilufin: Fargangene Velten,* London, 1951, pp. 8-12.

¹³ Peli, Pinchas H., "Jerusalem Celebrates Passover," *Congress Weekly,* XXIV, no. 14 (April 18, 1957), p. 10; *"Afiat Matzot b-Yerushalayim," Shluhot,* no. 51 (Nisan, 5717), p. 3.

¹⁴ Gordon, Nisan, *"M'bakt Matzah in New York Vi in Der Alter Heim," Day-Jewish Journal,* May 22, 1956, p. 7.

¹⁵ Eisenstein, Judah D., *Otzar Dinim u-Minhagim,* New York, 1917, p. 248; Freehof, Solomon B., *The Responsa Literature,* Jewish Publication Society of America, Philadelphia, 1955, pp. 181-189.

¹⁶ Zarchin, Michael M., *Jews in the Province of Posen,* Dropsie College

for Hebrew and Cognate Learning, Philadelphia, 1939, pp. 23, 73.

[17] Roth, Cecil, *The Great Synagogue:London: 1690-1940,* Edward Goldston & Son, London, 1950, p. 225.

[18] Lucas, Nathaniel S., *"Matza* Meanderings," *The Jewish Monthly,* London, II, no. 1 (April, 1948), pp. 12-18.

[19] Persky, Daniel, *Likbod ha-Regel,* New York, 5707, pp. 259-264.

[20] During the Reign of Terror, the leaders of the Jewish community of Carpentras were compelled to give two large pans used for mixing the dough for *matzot* to the munitions agency. See Szajkowski, Z., "Jewish Religious Observance During the French Revolution of 1789," *YIVO Annual of Jewish Social Science,* XII (1959), p. 216.

[21] Lowenthal, Marvin, *A World Passed By,* Behrman House, New York, 1938, p. 109.

[22] de Sola Pool, David and Tamar, *An Old Faith in the New World: Portrait of Shearith Israel: 1654-1954,* Columbia University Press, New York, 1955, pp. 238-239.

[23] Kohler, Max J., "Phases of Jewish Life in New York Before 1800," *Publications of the American Jewish Historical Society,* no. 2 (1894), pp. 77-106.

[24] "Items relating to Congregation Shearith Israel, New York, Lyons Collection Volume II," *Publications of the American Jewish Historical Society,* no. 27 (1920), p. 104.

[25] Grinstein, Hyman B., *The Rise of the Jewish Community of New York, 1654-1860,* Jewish Publication Society of America, Philadelphia, 1945, pp. 306-310, 575-576.

[26] Korn, Bertram W., *Eventful Years and Experiences: Studies in Nineteenth Century American Jewish History,* American Jewish Archives, Cincinnati, 1954, p. 28; *Occident and American Jewish Advocate,* Philadelphia, VII, no. 1 (April, 1849), p. 59.

[27] Grinstein, *supra,* p. 471.

[28] *Jewish Encyclopedia,* VIII, 395.

[29] P. 307.

Chapter VII

PASSOVER IN THE BIBLE

[1] *The Holy Scriptures,* Jewish Publication Society of America, Philadelphia, 1917.

Chapter VIII

PASSOVER IN POST-BIBLICAL WRITINGS

[1] Finkelstein, Louis, "Pre-Maccabean Documents in the Passover Haggadah," *Harvard Theological Review,* XXXVI, no. 1 (Jan., 1934), p. 27.

[2] Cowley, A. (ed.), *Aramaic Papyri of the Fifth Century, B.C.,* Clarendon Press, Oxford, 1923, no. 21, pp. 60-65.

³ "The Wisdom of Solomon," *The Apocrypha: An American Translation,* by Edgar J. Goodspeed, University of Chicago Press, Chicago, 1938, pp. 212-215.

⁴ Eusebius, *Preparation for the Gospel,* trans. from a revised text by Edwin Hamilton Gifford, Oxford, 1903, part I, pp. 467-475.

⁵ *Philo,* with an English translation by F. H. Colson (Loeb Classical Library), Harvard University Press, Cambridge, Mass., 1937, vol. 7, pp. 269-271, 403-405.

⁶ *Philo* Supplement II, *Questions and Answers on Exodus,* trans. by Ralph Marcus (Loeb Classical Library), Harvard University Press, Cambridge, Mass., 1953, pp. 24-25.

⁷ *Philo,* with an English translation by F. H. Colson (Loeb Classical Library), Harvard University Press, Cambridge, Mass., 1953, VI, 311-313.

⁸ *Josephus,* with an English translation by H. St. J. Thackeray (Loeb Classical Library), *Jewish War,* VI, 9.3-4, Harvard University Press, Cambridge, Mass., 1930, III, 497-499.

⁹ *The Works of Flavius Josephus,* trans. by William Whiston, *Against Apion,* I. 25-26, London, 1806, IV, 308-309.

¹⁰ *Josephus,* with an English translation by H. St. J. Thackeray (Loeb Classical Library), *Jewish antiquities,* II, 311-317, Harvard University Press, Cambridge, Mass., 1930, IV, 301-303.

¹¹ *Ibid.,* II, 333-337, 311-313.

Chapter IX

PASSOVER IN TALMUD AND MIDRASH

The citations in the text are those of the original sources; these do not always correspond with the sources of the translations.

The translations, in some cases abbreviated and occasionally adapted, have been taken from the following works:

Sefer Ha-Yashar and *Midrash Tanhuma Ha-Kadom veha-Yashan* in *The Legends of the Jews,* by Louis Ginzberg, Jewish Publication Society of America, Philadelphia, 1913.

Pirke de-Rabbi Eliezer, trans. and annotated with introduction and indices, by Gerald Friedlander, Kegan Paul; Trench, Trubner and Co., London, and Bloch Publishing Co., New York, 1916.

Shir Ha-Shirim, trans. by Maurice Simon, and *Exodus,* trans. by S. M. Lehrman, in *Midrash Rabbah,* trans. under the editorship of H. Freedman and Maurice Simon, Soncino Press, London, 1939.

Megillah and *Berakot,* trans. by Maurice Simon, *Sotah,* trans. by A. Cohen, and *Pesahim,* trans. by H. Freedman, in *The Babylonian Talmud,* trans. into English with notes, under I. Epstein (ed.), Soncino Press, London, 1935-1950.

Mekilta de-Rabbi Ishmael, edited and trans. by Jacob Z. Lauterbach, Jewish Publication Society of America, Philadelphia, 1933.

The Midrash on Psalms (Midrash Tehillim), trans. from the Hebrew and Aramaic by William G. Braude, Yale University Press, New Haven, 1959.

Notes

Chapter X

PASSOVER IN MEDIEVAL JEWISH LITERATURE

[1] *Kitab al Khazari,* by Judah Halevi, translated by Hartwig Hirschfeld, Bernard G. Richards Co., New York, 1927, pp. 58-59.

[2] *Ibid.,* p. 114.

[3] *The Guide for the Perplexed,* by Moses Maimonides, trans. by M. Friedlander, London, 1881, pp. 352-353.

[4] *The Book of Doctrines and Beliefs,* by Saadya Gaon, trans. by Alexander Altmann, East and West Library, Oxford, 1946, pp. 168-169.

[5] *Zohar,* trans. by Harry Sperling and Maurice Simon, Soncino Press, London, 1931-34, III, 126-127.

Chapter XI

PASSOVER IN JEWISH LAW

[1] *The Mishnah,* trans. by Herbert Danby, Clarendon Press, Oxford, 1933, pp. 201-206.

[2] *Introductory Notes and Supplement . . . to the Haggadah,* compiled by Sidney B. Hoenig, Shulsinger Bros., New York, 1949, p. 35.

[3] Moses ben Maimon, *Mishneh Torah, Hilkot Hametz u-Matzah.*

[4] *The Guide,* X, 10-11, in *Karaite Anthology: Excerpts from the Early Literature,* trans. . . . with notes by Leon Nemoy, Yale University Press, New Haven, 1952, pp. 207, 213-214.

[5] Ganzfried, Solomon, *Code of Jewish Law,* trans. by Hyman E. Goldin, Hebrew Publishing Co., New York, 1927, III, 23-47.

Chapter XII

PASSOVER IN MODERN PROSE

[1] Rosenzweig, Franz, *Der Stern der Erlosung,* Frankfort-on-the-Main, 1921. Trans. by Nahum N. Glatzer in his *Franz Rosenzweig: His Life and Thought,* Schocken, and Farrar, Straus and Young, New York, 1953, pp. 319-321.

[2] Kohler, Kaufman, *Jewish Theology,* Macmillan, New York, 1918, p. 462.

[3] Lazarus, Moritz, *The Ethics of Judaism,* Jewish Publication Society of America, Philadelphia, 1900, part I, pp. 231-232, 28-29.

[4] Churchill, Winston S., *Thoughts and Adventures,* Thorton Butterworth, London; Charles Scribner's Sons, New York, 1932, pp. 283-294.

[5] Katzenelson, Berl, *Revolutionary Constructivism,* Young Poale Zion Alliance, New York, 1937, p. 19.

[6] Joseph, Morris, *Judaism As Creed and Life,* George Routledge and Sons, London, 1903, pp. 213-215.

484

[7] Gottheil, Gustav, *Sun and Shield*, Brentano's, New York, 1896, pp. 77-78.

[8] "Moses: A Lecture (1878)," *The Writings of Henry George*, Doubleday and McClure Co., New York, 1898, VIII, 21.

[9] *Ahad Ha-Am: Essays, Letters, Memoirs*, trans. and edited by Leon Simon, East and West Library, Oxford, 1946, pp. 103-108.

[10] Herzl, Theodor, *Old-New Land*, trans. by *Lotta Levensohn*, Bloch Publishing Co., New York, 1941, p. 187.

[11] Samuel, Maurice, *Prince of the Ghetto*, Alfred A. Knopf, New York, 1948, pp. 128-131.

[12] Neher, André, *Moses and the Vocation of the Jewish People*, trans. by Irene Marinoff, Harper Torchbooks, New York, 1959, pp. 126-138.

Chapter XIII

PASSOVER IN THE SHORT STORY

[1] Heine, Heinrich, *The Rabbi of Bacharach*, trans. by E. B. Ashton, Schocken Books, New York, 1947, pp. 10-17.

[2] Zangwill, Israel, *Ghetto Comedies*, Jewish Publication Society of America, Philadelphia, 1938, pp. 383-397.

[3] Sholom Aleichem, *Jewish Children*, trans. from the Yiddish by Hannah Berman, Alfred A. Knopf, New York, 1926, pp. 33-37.

[4] Buber, Martin, *For The Sake of Heaven*, trans. by Ludwig Lewisohn, Jewish Publication Society of America, Philadelphia, 1945, pp. 270-276.

[5] Agnon, S. J., *The Bridal Canopy*, trans. by I. M. Lask, Doubleday, Doran & Co., New York, 1937, pp. 200-206.

[6] Halper, Albert, *The Golden Watch*, Henry Holt & Co., New York, 1953, pp. 89-111.

Chapter XIV

PASSOVER IN POETRY

[1] Ibn Gabirol, Solomon, *Selected Religious Poems*, trans. by Israel Zangwill, Jewish Publication Society of America, Philadelphia, 1923, pp. 76-77.

[2] *The Jewish Year*, trans. and composed by Alice Lucas, Macmillan Co., New York, 1898, pp. 125-127.

[3] Zangwill, Israel, *Blind Children*, Funk & Wagnalls Co., New York, 1903, p. 116.

[4] *Poems for Young Judaeans*, Young Judaea, New York, 1925, pp. 163-164.

[5] Johnson, James Weldon, *God's Trombones: Some Negro Sermons in Verse*, Viking Press, New York; George Allen and Unwin, London, 1927, pp. 47-54.

[6] *Selected Poems of Hayyim Nahman Bialik*, trans. from the Hebrew by Maurice Samuel, The New Palestine, New York, 1926, pp. 27-38.

[7] Trans. from the Yiddish by Max Rosenfeld in *"Jewish Life" Anthology, 1946-1956*, Jewish Life, New York, 1956, pp. 146-147.

Notes

[8] *Contemporary Poetry,* Winter 1946; and Kruger, Fania, *The Tenth Jew,* Kaleidograph Press, Dallas, 1949, pp. 21-22.

[9] Trans. by Ruth Finer Mintz, in *Poetry,* XCII, no. 4 (July, 1958), p. 213.

[10] Schwarz, Leo W., editor, *A Golden Treasury of Jewish Literature,* Farrar & Rinehart, New York, 1937, pp. 649-651.

Chapter XV

MUSIC OF PASSOVER

[1] Rabinovitch, Israel, *Of Jewish Music: Ancient and Modern,* The Book Center, Montreal, 1952, pp. 105-110.

[2] Saminsky, Lazare, *Music of the Ghetto and the Bible,* Bloch Publishing Co., New York, 1934, p. 15. This is sung with orchestral accompaniment (Saminsky-Lavry), by Emma Schaver, in her record, "From the Heart of the People." Mercury MG20052.

[3] Ephros, Gershon, *Cantorial Anthology, III,* Bloch Publishing Company, New York, 1948. Traditional, from the Baer Collection, *Boruch,* no. 2, p. 176.

[4] *Ibid.,* from *L'dor Va-Dor,* no. 2, p. 168.

[5] *Ibid.,* p. 353. From the Leo Lange Collection.

[6] Idelsohn, Abraham Z., *Thesaurus of Oriental Jewish Melody,* I (Yemenites), Breitkopf and Hartel, Leipzig, 1914.

[7] Ephros, *supra,* p. 89. From the Sherman Collection.

[8] A good example of oriental Seder music may be heard on the record, "Haggadah," recorded in Israel in a Yemenite home, Passover, 1953, by Sam Eskin, with notes by Theodor Gaster. Folkways 8921.

[9] Idelsohn, *supra,* II (Babylonian Jews), B. Harz, Vienna, 1922.

[10] Algazi, Léon, *Chants Sephardis,* World Sephardi Federation, London, 1958, p. 20.

[11] *Yeda Am,* II, no. 2-3, p. 173. Notated by Yosef Ben Israel.

[12] This may be heard in the record, *Theodore Bikel Sings Yiddish Songs.* Electra 141.

[13] Rabinovitch, *supra,* pp. 100-104.

[14] *Yeda Am, supra,* p. 174. Notated by Avraham Poliava, from his father, Reb Aaron.

[15] Brod, Max, "The Haggadah of Paul Dessau," *Musica Hebraica,* Jerusalem, 1938, I-II, pp. 21 ff.

[16] Schoenberg, Arnold, *Moses and Aaron.* Columbia K3L-241.

[17] Milhaud, Darius, *Opus Americanum No. 2.* Capitol P-8114.

Chapter XVI

PASSOVER IN ART

[1] Relief from Kuyunjik, British Museum.

[2] Sarcophagus of the Satraps, Istanbul Museum.

[2] Morey, C. R., "Notes on East Christian Miniatures," *The Art Bulletin,* XI. 1 (March, 1929), fig. 99.

[4] Italiener, Bruno (ed.), *Die Darmstaedter Pessach-Haggadah,* Leipzig, 1927, text vol., p. 235.

[5] Schwab, M., "Haggadahhandschriftillustrationen aus Ms. Hebr. No. 1388 der Pariser Nationalbibliothek," *Mitteilungen zur Juedischen Volkskunde,* VIII. 15, n.s. I (1905), fig. 6, p. 77; idem., "Une Haggadah Illustrée, No. 1388," *Revue des Etudes Juives,* XLV. 89 (July-September, 1902), p. 118.

[6] Schramm, A., *Der Bilderschmuck der Fruehdrucke,* Leipzig, 1934, fig. 458.

[7] Mayer, August L., "Die Kunsthistorische Wuerdigung der Handschrift," *Die Darmstaedter Pessach-Haggadah, supra,* p. 59.

[8] Mueller, D. H. und Schlosser, J. von, *Die Haggadah von Sarajevo,* Vienna, 1898, plates vol., fol. 25. The illustrations in this volume are designated by folio numbers of the Sarajevo Haggadah manuscript.

[9] I owe this quotation to Dr. Boaz Cohen.

[10] Radojcic, S., *Haggadah of Sarajevo,* Belgrad, 1953, pl. 7.

[11] Mueller and Schlosser, *op. cit.,* text vol., p. 100 and pl. II.

[12] *Ibid.,* p. 101.

[13] Landsberger, Franz, "The Washington Haggadah and its Illuminator," *Hebrew Union College Annual* [*HUCA*], XXI (1948), fig. 2.

[14] Mueller and Schlosser, *op. cit.,* text vol., p. 140.

[15] Leveen, Jacob, *The Hebrew Bible in Art,* London, 1944, pl. XXXII. 2.

[16] Scheiber, Alexander, *The Kaufmann Haggadah,* Budapest, 1957, p. 3.

[17] Leveen, *op. cit.,* p. 102, pl. XXXI. 1.

[18] Mueller and Schlosser, *op. cit.,* text vol., p. 212, n. 1.

[19] Italiener, *op. cit.,* p. 22.

[20] Ginzberg, Louis, *The Legends of the Jews,* Philadelphia, 1942, V, p. 190, n. 58.

[21] Mueller and Schlosser, *op. cit.,* text vol., p. 204.

[22] Landsberger, *op. cit.,* p. 77, n. 8.

[23] Mueller and Schlosser, *op. cit.,* text vol., p. 186 and pl. XXX. 2.

[24] Landsberger, "The Cincinnati Haggadah and its Decorator," *HUCA,* XV (1940), fig. 5.

[25] Mueller and Schlosser, *op. cit.,* text vol., pp. 104-105.

[26] Pesahim 5.7; 10.6.

[27] Wischnitzer, Rachel, "Ein Juedischer Buchmaler des 15. Jahrhunderts," *Jahrbuch fuer Juedische Geschichte und Literatur,* XXX (1937), pp. 1-11; idem., "Une Bible enluminée par Joseph ibn Hayyim," *Revue des Etudes Juives,* LXXIII. 146 (Oct.-Dec., 1921), pp. 161-172.; Roth, Cecil, "A Masterpiece of Medieval Spanish-Jewish Art: The Kennicott Bible," *Sefarad,* 1952, pp. 351-368.

[28] Fooner, M., "Joel ben Simeon, Illuminator of Hebrew Manuscripts in the 15th century," *Jewish Quarterly Review,* n.s., XXVII, no. 3 (January, 1937), pp. 217-232. Landsberger has discussed the Joel ben Simeon problem in *HUCA,* 1940, 1941, 1944 and more in detail in "The Washington Haggadah and its Illuminator," *HUCA,* XXI (1948), pp. 73-103.

[29] *Die Pessach Haggadah des Gerschom Kohen,* 1527. Facsimile ed. by B. Katz and H. Loewe, Berlin, 1925. It actually appeared in Dec. 1926.

[30] Italiener, *op. cit.,* p. 28.

[31] Mueller and Schlosser, *op. cit.,* text vol., p. 225. Schlosser mentions

Michelangelo's Moses by an oversight. He had in mind the Jeremiah.

[32] Wischnitzer, Rachel, *Symbole und Gestalten der Juedischen Kunst,* Berlin, 1935, p. 97 and fig. 57.

[33] Landsberger, Franz, "Jewish Artists before the Period of Emancipation," *HUCA,* XVI (1941), p. 360. A selection of illustrations from the Mantua Haggadah, edition of 1568, has appeared in a small pamphlet *Bilder aus der Mantuaner Hagada,* by K. Schwarz, Berlin, 1920.

[34] Wischnitzer, Rachel, "Passover Art and the Italian Renaissance," *The Reconstructionist* (April 4, 1958), p. 8 ff.

[35] Italiener, *op. cit.,* p. 22.

[36] Wischnitzer, Rachel, "Von der Holbeinbibel zur Amsterdamer Haggadah," *Monatschrift fuer Geschichte und Wissenschaft des Judentums,* n.s., XXXIX, nos. 7-8 (July-August, 1931), pp. 269-286.

[37] Landsberger, Franz, "The Second Cincinnati Haggadah," *HUCA,* XXIII, part 2 (1950-1951), p. 509.

[38] Moses, Elisabeth, "Juedische Kult-und Kunstdenkmaeler in den Rheinlanden," Publication of *Rheinischer Verein fuer Denkmalpflege und Heimatschutz,* 1931, heft 1, p. 189, n. 1.

[39] *Ibid.,* pp. 187-189, with illustrations.

[40] Landsberger, *op. cit.,* p. 503 ff.

[41] Wischnitzer, Rachel, *Symbole und Gestalten der Juedischen Kunst, supra,* figs. 59 and 60, pp. 98-100.

[42] *Idem,* "Studies in Jewish Art," *Jewish Quarterly Review,* XXXVI, no. 1 (July, 1945), p. 58 ff.; "Passover Art and the Italian Renaissance," *supra,* p. 10.

[43] "Studies in Jewish Art," *supra,* p. 54 ff.

[44] Hallo, R., *Juedische Kult-und Kunstdenkmaeler im Hessischen Landes-Museum zu Kassel,* Kassel, 1928, p. 24 and pl. VII.

[45] *Rare Judaica: Parke-Bernet Auction Catalogue,* New York, 1956, p. 19, nos. 93 and 91.

[46] Hallo, R., "Judaica," *Religioese Kunst aus Hessen und Nassau: Exhibition Catalogue,* Marburg, 1932, p. 30, nos. 91 and 92.

[47] *Rare Judaica, supra,* p. 48, no. 221.

[48] Hallo, R., "Judaica," *supra,* p. 29, nos. 89 and 90.

Chapter XVII

STORIES FOR PASSOVER

[1] Weilerstein, Sadie Rose, *What Danny Did: Stories for the Wee Jewish Child,* Bloch Publishing Co., New York, 1944, pp. 80-84.

[2] Weilerstein, Sadie Rose, *The Adventures of K'tonton: A Little Jewish Tom Thumb,* National Women's League of the United Synagogue, New York, 1935, pp. 49-54.

[3] Edidin, Ben M. (ed.), *Jewish Life and Customs: Unit Six: Passover,* Jewish Education Committee of New York, 1944, pp. 1-9.

[4] Silverman, Althea O., *Habibi and Yow: A Little Boy and His Dog,* Bloch Publishing Co., New York, 1946, pp. 83-92.

[5] Steinberg, Judah, *The Breakfast of the Birds and Other Stories,* trans.

from the Hebrew by Emily Solis-Cohen, Jr., Jewish Publication Society of America, Philadelphia, 1917, pp. 13-19.

[6] Peretz, Isaac Loeb, "It is Good," *World Over*, XV, no. 12 (April 2, 1954).

[7] Belth, Norton, ed., *The World Over Story Book*, Bloch Publishing Co., New York, 1952, pp. 227-232. Copyright by Jewish Education Committee of New York.

[8] Peretz, I. L., *In This World and the Next: Selected Writings*, trans. from the Yiddish by Moshe Spiegel, Thomas Yoseloff, New York, 1958, pp. 226-230.

Chapter XVIII

POEMS FOR PASSOVER

[1] Levy, Sara G., *Mother Goose Rhymes for Jewish Children*, Bloch Publish-Co., New York, 1945, p. 40.

[2] Aronin, Ben, *Jolly Jingles for the Jewish Child*, Behrman House, New York, 1947.

[3] Levinger, Elma Ehrlich, *Jewish Festivals in the Religious School*, Union of American Hebrew Congregations, Cincinnati, 1923, p. 188.

[4] *Ibid.*, p. 187.

[5] Sampter, Jessie E., *Around the Year in Rhymes for the Jewish Child*, Bloch Publishing Co., New York, 1920, p. 54.

[6] Sampter, Jessie E., *Brand Plucked from the Fire*, Jewish Publication Society of America, Philadelphia, 1937, p. 200.

[7] Raskin, Philip M., *Songs of a Wanderer*, Jewish Publication Society of America, Philadelphia, 1917, pp. 161-164.

[8] *Gems of Hebrew Verse: Poems for Young People*, trans. by Harry H. Fein, Bruce Humphries, Boston, 1940, p. 18.

Chapter XIX

PASSOVER CURIOSITIES

[1] Zeitlin, Solomon, "The Liturgy of the First Night of Passover," *Jewish Quarterly Review*, N.S., XXXVIII, no. 4 (April, 1948), p. 456.

[2] *Philo*, with an English translation by F. H. Colson, Harvard University Press, Cambridge, 1937, VII, p. 394.

[3] Lubelsky, Mordecai, "At a Seder in Casablanca," *The Day-Jewish Journal*, April 20, 1958, p. 4.

[4] Pesahim 64b.

[5] *Ibid.* Heinrich Graetz in his *History of the Jews* (Philadelphia, Jewish Publication Society of America, 1893), II, p. 251, gives the account of Agrippa and the High Priest that is in the Talmud but he uses the name "Passover of the Crushing."

[6] *Shulhan Arukh, Orah Hayyim*, 428.3.

[7] Levinsky, Yom-Tob, *Dvar*, Iyar 4, 5710; Davidson, Efraim, *Sehok Pinu*, Matmonim, Tel Aviv, 1951, p. 511.

Notes

[8] Berakot 19a; Roth, Cecil, *The History of the Jews of Italy,* Jewish Publication Society of America, Philadelphia, 1946, p. 16.

[9] Zimmels, H. J., *Ashkenazim and Sephardim,* Oxford University Press, London, 1958, p. 71.

[10] Pesahim 119b.

[11] Greenburg, William H., *The Haggadah according to the Rite of Yemen . . .,* London, 1896, p. 16.

[12] *Orah Hayyim* 477: *Beer Heteb* 4.

[13] Trachtenberg, Joshua, *Jewish Magic and Superstition,* Behrman House, New York, 1939, p. 133.

[14] Breuer, A., *Yehudei Kurdistan,* Jerusalem, 5708, p. 241; Ben-Ezra, A., "Minhagei Ha-Sedarim," *Hadoar,* Nisan 14, 5711, p. 490.

[15] Lubelsky, *supra,* p. 4.

[16] Kaufman, Reuben, "Amulets," *Universal Jewish Encyclopedia,* I, 291.

[17] Abida, Yehudah, *Koso Shel Eliyahu ha-Nabi,* Jewish Agency, Jerusalem, 5718.

[18] Roth, Cecil, "The Day of Shutting In," *American Hebrew,* CXXXIV, no. 21 (April 6, 1934), p. 429.

[19] Roth, Cecil, "A Passover Deliverance," *The Jewish Chronicle,* London, April 15, 1938.

[20] Slouschz, Nahum, *Travels in North Africa,* Jewish Publication Society of America, Philadelphia, 1927, pp. 345-346.

[21] Kehimkar, Haeem Samuel, *The History of the Bene Israel of India,* Tel Aviv, 1937, pp. 16-22.

[22] Scheiber, Alexander, "Ikvot Dramatizatzia be-Tekese ha-Pesah be-Hungaria," *Yeda-Am,* no. 7-8 (May, 1951), p. 6.

[23] Zimmels, *supra,* p. 261.

[24] Davidson, Israel, *Parody in Jewish Literature,* Columbia University Press, New York, 1907, pp. xvii, 16-17, 41-44, 153-172.

[25] Zimlin, Levi Reuben, *Seder Haggadah le-Melamdim,* Odessa, 1885, pp. 15-40; Davidson, *supra,* p. 460.

[26] Katsh, Abraham I., "Hebraic Foundations of American Democracy," *The Hebrew Impact on Western Civilization,* ed. by Dagobert D. Runes, Philosophical Library, New York.

[27] National Archives and Records Service, Washington, D. C., Record group II: Papers of the Continental Congress, no. 23, p. 143; *Journals of the Continental Congress,* Washington, Government Printing Office, 1906, V, 689-690; Lossing, Benson J., "The Great Seal of the United States," *Harper's New Monthly Magazine,* XIII, no. 74 (July, 1856), p. 180; Straus, Oscar S., *The Origin of the Republican Form of Government in the United States of America,* New York, 1885, pp. 139-140.

[28] *Catalogue: Exhibition: Vilna,* Yivo Institute for Jewish Research, New York, 1960, p. 21.

[29] Letter dated June 13, 1959, to P. Goodman from Zvi Shener, Ghetto Fighters' House in Memory of Yitzhak Katznelson, Israel, where a copy of the original handwritten prayer is preserved.

[30] Rosenthal, Jacob, "Seder Ha-Tzamin B'Yerushalayim," *Hadoar,* Nisan 14, 5711, p. 473; Syrkin, Marie, *Blessed is the Match: The Story of Jewish Resistance,* Jewish Publication Society of America, Philadelphia, 1947, p. 322.

490

Chapter XX

PASSOVER FOLKLORE

[1] Goodman, Philip, *Rejoice in Thy Festival: A Treasury of Wisdom, Wit and Humor for the Sabbath and Jewish Holidays,* Bloch Publishing Co., New York, 1956, pp. 177-221.

Chapter XXI

PASSOVER PROGRAMS AND PROJECTS

[1] Pesahim 6a.
[2] Freehof, Solomon B., *Reform Responsa,* Jewish Publication Society of America, Philadelphia, 1960, pp. 55-59.
[3] Pesahim 109a.

Chapter XXII

DANCES FOR PASSOVER

[1] Lapson, Dvora, *Jewish Dances The Year Round,* Jewish Education Committee of New York, 1957, pp. 54, 62-65.

Chapter XXIV

THE OBSERVANCE OF PASSOVER

[1] *Sofrim* 21.2-3. See also Megillat Taanit 1.
[2] *Orah Hayyim* 429.2.
[3] *Tosefot,* Shabbat 87b.
[4] Zeitlin, Solomon, "The Liturgy of the First Night of Passover," *Jewish Quarterly Review,* XXXVIII, no. 4 (April, 1948), pp. 457-459.
[5] Pesahim 6a.
[6] Rashi, Berahot 6b.
[7] *Rama, Orah Hayyim* 430.1.
[8] *Ibid.,* 429.1.
[9] Exodus 12.15,19-20,13.7.
[10] Rashi, Exodus 12.15.
[11] Numbers 31.23.
[12] Pesahim 1.1.
[13] *Rama, Orah Hayyim* 432.
[14] Pesahim 7a.

Notes

[15] *Mishneh Torah: Hilkot Hametz u-Matzah* 2.1-3; 3.6-7; *Orah Hayyim* 434.2.

[16] Pesahim 1.4; *Hilkot Hametz u-Matzah* 1.10; *Orah Hayyim* 443.

[17] *Orah Hayyim* 451.1.

[18] *Hilkot Hametz u-Matzah* 4.5-7; *Orah Hayyim* 448.3; *Kitzur Shulhan Aruk* 114.

[19] Jerusalem Pesahim 10.1.

[20] *Hilkot Hametz u-Matzah* 6.12.

[21] Pesahim 120a.

[22] Rashi, Exodus 12.17.

[23] *Orah Hayyim* 453.2.

[24] *Ibid.*, 470.1.

[25] *Ibid.*, 472.1,2.

[26] *Ibid.*, 473.4.

[27] Shabbat 117b.

[28] Pesahim 10.

[29] Jerusalem Pesahim 10.1, where there are also given other reasons.

[30] *Baer Heteb, Orah Hayyim* 480. Abida, Yehudah, *Koso Shel Eliyahu ha-Nabi,* Jewish Agency, Jerusalem, 5718.

[31] *Rama, Orah Hayyim* 480.

[32] Rosh Hashanah 11b.

[33] Shabbat 114a.

[34] Jerusalem *Rosh ha-Shanah* 1.3.

[35] *Orah Hayyim* 472.2.

[36] Bertinoro, Pesahim 10.1; *Hilkot Hametz u-Matzah* 7.7-8.

[37] Pesahim 10.4.

[38] *Orah Hayyim* 473.2.

[39] Pesahim 115a.

[40] *Orah Hayyim* 158.4.

[41] Pesahim 114b.

[42] Sforno, Exodus, 2.23.

[43] *Orah Hayyim* 473.6.

[44] Pesahim 115a.

[45] Pesahim 10.3; Pesahim 116a.

[46] Pesahim 2.6.

[47] Pesahim 115a.

[48] *Orah Hayyim* 476.

[49] *Ibid.*, 552.

[50] *Ibid.*, 477.1.

[51] Pesahim 109a.

[52] Pesahim 10.7.

[53] Pesahim 118a.

[54] Pesahim 5.7.

[55] Erekin 10a.

[56] Megillah 10b.

[57] Taanit 1.2.

[58] II Maccabees 12.43-45.

[59] Rashi, Ezekiel 37.1.

[60] The first day of Passover. Menahot 65b.

[61] Maimonides, Moses, *Guide for the Perplexed,* trans. by M. Friedlander, London, 1881, p. 352.

Acknowledgments

The editor herewith expresses his sincere appreciation to the following publishers and authors who have kindly granted permission to use the material indicated:

ABELARD-SCHUMAN LTD., New York: "The Samaritan Passover," reprinted by permission of the publishers Abelard-Schuman Limited from *Passover: Its History and Traditions,* by Theodor Herzl Gaster. Copyright 1949.

ALFRED A. KNOPF, INCORPORATED, New York: "Homesickness of the 'Renegade' Jew," from *Prince of the Ghetto,* by Maurice Samuel, copyright 1948 by Maurice Samuel; "Elijah the Prophet," from *Jewish Children,* by Sholom Aleichem, translated by Hannah Berman, copyright 1922, 1926 by Alfred A. Knopf, Incorporated.

The American Zionist, New York, successor to *The New Palestine:* "The Dead of the Wilderness," from *Selected Poems of Hayyim Nahman Bialik,* translated by Maurice Samuel, 1926.

AMERICAN ZIONIST YOUTH COMMISSION, New York: "A Voice Unto Pharaoh," by Arthur Guiterman, from *Poems for Young Judaeans,* 1925.

BEHRMAN HOUSE, New York: excerpt from *A World Passed By,* by Marvin Lowenthal, 1938; "Our Seder," from *Jolly Jingles for the Jewish Child,* by Ben Aronin, 1947.

BLOCH PUBLISHING CO., New York: "Passover in the Caucasus," by Zvi Kasdai, from *The Story of Passover and Its Celebration,* by Hyman E. Goldin, 1930; "The Penitent," from *Old-New Land,* by Theodor Herzl, translated by Lotta Levensohn, 1960; excerpts from *Pirke de-Rabbi Eliezer,* translated by Gerald Friedlander, 1916; "The Train That Knew About Pesach," from *What Danny Did: Stories for the Wee Jewish Child,* by Sadie Rose Weilerstein, 1944; "Habibi and Yow Go to Grandfather's for Seder," from *Habibi and Yow: A Little Boy and His Dog,* by Althea O. Silverman, 1946; "A Song of Seder," from *Mother Goose Rhymes for Jewish Children,* by Sara G. Levy, 1945; "The Questions," from *Around the Year in Rhymes for the Jewish Child,* by Jessie E. Sampter, 1920; "Passover Folklore," from *Rejoice in Thy Festival: A Treasury of Wisdom, Wit and Humor for the Sabbath and Jewish Holidays,* by Philip Goodman, 1956.

BRUCE HUMPHRIES, INC., Boston: "Passover," by Levin Kipnis, from *Gems of Hebrew Verse: Poems for Young People,* translated by Harry H. Fein, copyright 1940 by Bruce Humphries, Inc.

CHARLES SCRIBNER'S SONS, New York: "The Impregnable Rock of Holy Scripture," reprinted with the permission of Charles Scribner's Sons from *Amid These Storms,* by Winston S. Churchill, copyright 1932 Charles Scribner's Sons; renewal copyright 1960.

THE CLARENDON PRESS, Oxford: "Hananiah to Jedoniah, Head of the Jewish Community of Elephantine," from *Aramaic Papyri of the Fifth Century B.C.,* ed. by A. Cowley, 1923; selections from *The Mishnah,* translated by Herbert Danby, 1933.

493

Acknowledgments

CORNELL UNIVERSITY PRESS, Ithaca, N.Y.: "The Origins of Passover," from *Ancient Israel,* by Harry M. Orlinsky, 1954.

COWARD-McCANN, INC., New York: "Moses the Artist," by Heinrich Heine, from *Sun and Shield,* by Gustav Gottheil, 1896.

EAST AND WEST LIBRARY, London: "The Redemption of Israel," from *The Book of Doctrines and Beliefs,* by Saadya Gaon, translated by Alexander Altmann, 1946; "The Master of the Prophets," from *Ahad Ha-Am: Essays, Letters, Memoirs,* translated and edited by Leon Simon, 1946.

EMBASSY OF THE POLISH PEOPLE'S REPUBLIC, Washington, D.C., and WLADYSLAW B. PAWLAK, Warsaw: "The Last Passover in the Warsaw Ghetto," from *Poland Today,* New York.

FARRAR, STRAUS & CUDAHY, INC., New York: "Matzah Baking in an East European Town," from *The Third Pillar,* by Soma Morgenstern, translated by Ludwig Lewisohn, copyright 1955 by Farrar, Straus & Cudahy, Inc. Used by permission of the publishers, Farrar, Straus & Cudahy, Inc.

EDGAR J. GOODSPEED, Los Angeles: "The Plague of Darkness," from *The Apocrypha: An American Translation,* by Edgar J. Goodspeed, University of Chicago Press, Chicago, 1938.

GEORGE ALLEN & UNWIN LTD., London: "Let My People Go," from *God's Trombones: Some Negro Sermons in Verse,* by James Weldon Johnson, 1928.

HABONIM, New York: excerpt from *Revolutionary Constructivism,* by Berl Katzenelson, Young Poale Zion Alliance, New York, 1937.

ALBERT HALPER, New York: "Warm Matzot," from *The Golden Watch,* by Albert Halper, Henry Holt & Co., New York, 1953.

HARPER & BROTHERS, New York: "The Exodus: A Historical Mission," from *Moses and the Vocation of the Jewish People,* by André Neher, translated by Irene Marinoff, 1959 (Men of Wisdom series).

HARVARD UNIVERSITY PRESS, Cambridge: excerpts from *Philo,* translated by F. H. Colson; *Philo,* Supplement II, translated by Ralph Marcus; and *Josephus,* translated by H. St. J. Thackeray, from the Loeb Classical Library. Reprinted by permission of the publishers.

HEBREW PUBLISHING COMPANY, New York: excerpts from *The Code of Jewish Law,* vol. 3, by Solomon Ganzfried, translated by Hyman E. Goldin, 1927.

ISRAEL TODAY, New York: "Festival of Spring in an Israeli Kibbutz," by Sybil Rogow Langer, from *Israel Speaks,* IX, no. 7 (1955).

JEWISH CURRENTS, INC., New York, successor to *Jewish Life:* "Pesach Has Come to the Ghetto Again," by Binem Heller, translated from the Yiddish by Max Rosenfeld, from *"Jewish Life" Anthology, 1946-1956,* 1956.

JEWISH EDUCATION COMMITTEE OF NEW YORK: "It is Good," by Isaac Loeb Peretz, from *World Over;* "The Story of Passover," by Deborah Pessin, from *Jewish Life and Customs: Unit Six: Passover,* edited by Ben M. Edidin, 1944; "Passover Dances," from *Jewish Dances the Year*

Acknowledgments

Round, by Dvora Lapson, 1957; "A Passover in Spain," by Curtis Lubinski, from *The World Over Story Book*, edited by Norton Belth, 1952.

THE JEWISH PUBLICATION SOCIETY OF AMERICA, Philadelphia: "The Falashas," by Jacques Faitlovitch, from *American Jewish Year Book*, 5681, XXII (1920); excerpts from *The Holy Scriptures*, 1917; excerpts from *The Legends of the Jews*, by Louis Ginzberg, 1909-1913; excerpts from *Mekilta de-Rabbi Ishmael*, translated by Jacob Z. Lauterbach, 1932; "The Ethical Significance of the Passover," from *The Ethics of Judaism*, part 1, by Moritz Lazarus, 1900; "Elijah's Goblet," from *Ghetto Comedies*, by Israel Zangwill, 1938; "A Seder That Went Wrong," from *For The Sake of Heaven*, by Martin Buber, translated by Ludwig Lewisohn, 1946; "Passover Psalm," by Solomon ibn Gabirol, from *Selected Religious Poems*, translated by Israel Zangwill, 1923; "The Breakfast of the Birds," from *The Breakfast of the Birds and Other Stories*, by Judah Steinberg, translated by Emily Solis-Cohen, Jr., 1917; "Passover Song," from *Brand Plucked from the Fire*, by Jessie E. Sampter, 1937; "The Seder," from *Songs of a Wanderer*, by Philip M. Raskin, 1917.

The Jewish Quarterly Review, Philadelphia: "Passover and the Last Supper," from "The Liturgy of the First Night of Passover," by Solomon Zeitlin, *The Jewish Quarterly Review*, XXXVIII, no. 4 (April, 1948), pp. 444-449.

LILI KOHLER, New York, "The Season of Joy," from *Jewish Theology*, by Kaufman Kohler, Macmillan Co., New York, 1918.

FANIA KRUGER, Austin, Texas: "Passover Eve," from *The Tenth Jew*, by Fania Kruger, Kaleidograph Press, Dallas, 1949; originally published in *Contemporary Poetry*, Baltimore, Winter, 1946.

LABOR ZIONIST ORGANIZATION OF AMERICA, New York: "Passover Letters from the Desert," from *Letters from the Desert*, by Moshe Mosenson, Sharon Books, New York, 1945.

PETER T. LUCAS, Oklahoma City: "A Passover in Spain," by Curtis Lubinski, from *The World Over Story Book*, edited by Norton Belth, 1952.

RUTH FINER MINTZ, Los Angeles, and *Poetry*, Chicago: "Passover in Jerusalem," by Avigdor Hameiri, translated by Ruth Finer Mintz; first published in *Poetry*.

CANTOR MOSHE NATHANSON, New York: Melody for "L'Shanah ha-Ba'ah."

NATIONAL JEWISH WELFARE BOARD, New York: "G.I. Passover in World War II," from *G.I. Holy Days*, 1944.

NATIONAL WOMEN'S LEAGUE OF THE UNITED SYNAGOGUE OF AMERICA, New York: "The Story of K'tonton, A Mouse and a Bit of Leaven," from *The Adventures of K'tonton: A Little Jewish Tom Thumb*, by Sadie Rose Weilerstein, 1935.

ODHAMS PRESS, LTD., London: "The Impregnable Rock of Holy Scripture," from *Thoughts and Adventures*, by Winston S. Churchill, Thornton Butterworth, London, 1932.

BERNARD G. RICHARDS, New York: excerpts from *Kitab al Khazari*, by Judah Halevi, translated by Hartwig Hirschfeld, Bernard G. Richards Co., New York, 1927.

495

Acknowledgments

ROUTLEDGE & KEGAN PAUL LTD., London: "The Modern Significance of Passover," from *Judaism as Creed and Life*, by Morris Joseph, 1903.

SCHOCKEN BOOKS INC., New York: "The Feast of Deliverance," reprinted from *Franz Rosenzweig: His Life and Thought*, presented by Nahum N. Glatzer, by permission of Schocken Books Inc., New York. Copyright 1953 by Schocken Books Inc., New York; "The Rabbi of Bacharach," reprinted from *Rabbi of Bacharach*, by Heinrich Heine, by permission of Schocken Books Inc., New York. Copyright 1947 by Schocken Books Inc., New York.

LEO W. SCHWARZ, New York: "Haggadah," by Abraham M. Klein, from *A Golden Treasury of Jewish Literature*, edited by Leo W. Schwarz, Farrar & Rinehart, Inc., New York, 1937.

SHULSINGER BROTHERS, New York: excerpts from "Tosefta," from *Introductory Notes and Supplement ... to the Haggadah*, compiled by Sidney B. Hoenig, 1949.

THE SONCINO PRESS LIMITED, London: excerpts from "Shir Ha-Shirim" and "Exodus" from *Midrash Rabbah*, translated under the editorship of H. Freedman and Maurice Simon, 1939; excerpts from "Megillah," "Berakot," "Sotah" and "Pesahim" from *The Babylonian Talmud*, translated under the editorship of I. Epstein, 1935-1950; excerpts from *Zohar*, translated by Harry Sperling and Maurice Simon, 1931-1934.

ST MARTIN'S PRESS, INC., New York: "By the Red Sea," by Judah Halevi, from *The Jewish Year*, translated by Alice Lucas, Macmillan & Company Ltd., New York, 1898.

THOMAS YOSELOFF, INC., New York: "The Magician," from *In This World and the Next: Selected Writings*, by I. L. Peretz, translated by Moshe Spiegel, 1958.

TRUSTEES OF THE LATE DR. J. H. HERTZ and THE SONCINO PRESS LIMITED, London: "Israel in Egypt: The Historical Problems," from *The Pentateuch and Haftorahs*, edited by Joseph H. Hertz, The Soncino Press Limited, London, 1960. Copyright 1960 by The Trustees of the late Dr. J. H. Hertz.

UNION OF AMERICAN HEBREW CONGREGATIONS, New York: "The Marranos Observe Passover," from *The Jewish Festivals*, by Hayyim Schauss, 1938; "Seder Night," by Samuel S. Grossman, and "Why Myer Likes Pesach," by Elma Ehrlich Levinger, from *Jewish Festivals in the Religious School*, by Elma Ehrlich Levinger, 1923.

VIKING PRESS, New York: "Let my People Go," from *God's Trombones: Some Negro Sermons in Verse*, by James Weldon Johnson. Copyright 1927 by the Viking Press, Inc., 1955 by Grace Nail Johnson. Reprinted by permission of the Viking Press, Inc.

YALE UNIVERSITY PRESS, New Haven: excerpts from *The Midrash on Psalms*, II, translated by William G. Braude, 1959; excerpt from *Karaite Anthology*, translated by Leon Nemoy, 1952.

496

Make books your companion
Let your bookshelf be your garden—
Judah Ibn Tibbon

to become a member –
to present a gift –

call 1 (800) 234-3151
or write:
The Jewish Publication Society
1930 Chestnut Street
Philadelphia, Pennsylvania 19103

A Jewish Tradition